FIX-IT and ENJOY-IT!®

HEALTHY
COOKBOOK

400 Great Stove-Top and Oven Recipes

FIX-IT and ENJOY-IT!®

HEALTHY COOKBOOK

400 Great Stove-Top and Oven Recipes

By *The New York Times* bestselling author

PHYLLIS PELLMAN GOOD

With nutritional expertise from

MAYO CLINIC

Good Books®

Intercourse, PA 17534
800/762-7171
www.GoodBooks.com

Although the analysts and editor have attempted full accuracy in the nutritional data and analyses included in this cookbook, many variables (including variations related to particular brands, to the refinement of products, and to the exact amounts of ingredients) could result in the analyses being approximate.

Because many factors influence your health, please check with your healthcare expert before making substantial changes in what you eat.

MAYO, MAYO CLINIC, MAYO CLINIC HEALTH SOLUTIONS and the Mayo triple-shield logo are marks of Mayo Foundation for Medical Education and Research.

Cover illustration and illustrations throughout the book by Cheryl Benner
Design by Cliff Snyder
Photograph on back cover by Jason Varney

FIX-IT AND ENJOY-IT!® HEALTHY COOKBOOK
Copyright © 2008 by Good Books, Intercourse, PA 17534

International Standard Book Number: 978-1-56148-641-0 (paperback edition)
International Standard Book Number: 978-1-56148-643-4 (hardcover gift edition)
International Standard Book Number: 978-1-56148-642-7 (comb-bound paperback edition)
Library of Congress Catalog Card Number: 2008045050

Library of Congress Cataloging-in-Publication Data
Good, Phyllis Pellman,
  Fix-it and enjoy-it healthy cookbook : 400 great stove-top and oven recipes / Phyllis Pellman Good ; with nutritional expertise from Mayo Clinic.
    p. cm.
  Includes index.
  ISBN 978-1-56148-641-0 (pbk. : alk. paper) -- ISBN 978-1-56148-642-7 (comb-bound : alk. paper) -- ISBN 978-1-56148-643-4 (hardcover : alk. paper) 1. Cookery. 2. Nutrition. I. Title.
  TX714.G653 2009
  641.5--dc22   2008045050

Table of Contents

Recipes

How–and Why–Did This Cookbook Come to Be?

Here's my dilemma. I ought to eat more vegetables. In fact, I'd *like* to eat more vegetables. And fruit. And even grains. But where do I find good recipes that take me beyond my practice of steaming a pack of frozen broccoli as a side dish? How do I learn to think *first* about vegetables when I'm planning dinner?

And a bigger step yet–how can I develop a habit of making vegetables, or whole grains or fruit, the *heart* of our main meal each day? It's this simple–where can I find tempting main-dish vegetable, fruit, or whole-grain recipes that will taste good and satisfy?

A Small Confession

I'm not a big violator. I always prepare vegetables or a salad or both for our dinner. And I always have an apple or banana for breakfast. And often some greens for lunch. But they're the colorful edges and not the main game.

The educators have done their part. I have been convinced that I should re-configure our diet so that fruits, whole grains, and vegetables are the main planks and not just the decorative trim. So where are the tasty recipes that will help me do that?

A Few Non-Negotiables

But I've got to be realistic, too. I have a few requirements. I need recipes that don't call for fancy ingredients or ones that need a lot of special handling. I don't have time to track down exotic grains. Nor do I have extra hours to extract juice from whole grapes or reconstitute dried beans or even cook red beets, no matter the charm of their plumy tops and finely shaped root ends. Those are pleasures for free time—and I'm woefully short of that.

And there's something else. I want the people who eat at my table to be satisfied when they finish a meal. I don't want them off scrounging for snacks an hour or two after they've eaten my properly put-together spread of vegetable and fruit dishes. Those of us who anticipate meat or pasta as the center of a meal need a little assistance and patience as we scale those dishes back  in favor of whole grains and sturdy vegetables. So I need recipes that satisfy hearty eaters with substantial yet healthy food.

And I've got to mention this. It can be expensive to furnish your pantry with fresh berries and spinach and salmon and 95%-lean beef. Although, when you fill up the shelves with these items instead of slabs of ribs and steaks and prepared pizzas and pastas and gravies, you'll likely find that you're spending less to feed your household. But cost is an ever-present concern for many of us.

A Little Back Story

Every October, my husband, Merle, and I attend the International Book Fair in Frankfurt, Germany. A couple of years ago, our Good Books exhibit was next to Mayo Clinic's exhibit. During some downtime, we and Mary Rysavy from Mayo admired each other's books. Mayo Clinic had authoritative volumes about health and diet and exercise. Our exhibit was full of cookbooks and children's picture books, histories, books about quiltmaking, justice and peacebuilding, and memoirs.

"We ought to work together on a project," Mary said one day. "Mayo has published some cookbooks, but they really aren't for everyday use. Your cookbooks are put to daily use. I wonder if we could bring Mayo's strength in health together with your strength in finding and presenting make-it-again recipes?"

Merle and I were intrigued. Could we gather a collection of recipes that would solidly reflect Mayo's commitment to healthy eating, expressed so clearly and convincingly in their Mayo Clinic Healthy Weight Pyramid diagram (see page 21)? And could we find, and then agree on, recipes that meet my criteria—recipes that are tasty, quick and easy to prepare, and that come from good home cooks who are scattered all across the country?

Could This Idea Work?

I worried a little, I admit, that we may not find enough *appealing* recipes. Could we discover vegetable main dishes with readily available ingredients—that would work for people with very little time, and with almost no confidence in their cooking skills?

What about whole-grain main-dish recipes that would meet the pickiest kids' standards? And could we move fruit from garnish status to the heart and soul of a meal?

Mayo would insist on healthy recipes. I was dedicated to the idea,

because I knew how much I wanted such a collection of recipes for myself.

And so we set out to try. Merle was no less an ardent believer in the possibility of this project, and he threw his insistent encouragement into it every day.

Bless those resourceful home cooks who have already upped the proportion of vegetables, fruits, and whole grains in their daily cooking! Thank you for sharing your tastiest specialties in this cookbook! Tony Gehman, Esther Becker, Melissa Horst, and Kate Good, all from the Good Books team, also helped me immensely by organizing the recipes, preparing them for testing, and keeping track of their data. Cliff Snyder made the cookbook pages friendly and usable.

Mayo Clinic offered extraordinary expertise to this cookbook. Jennifer Nelson, Associate Professor of Nutrition at Mayo Clinic's College of Medicine, and Director of Clinical Dietetics, Mayo Clinic Rochester, and her team did the Per Serving and Pyramid Serving analyses for each recipe, and advised me about how to adapt certain recipes so that they could meet Mayo's "healthy" criteria. Dr. Donald Hensrud, Chair of Mayo's Division of Preventive,

Occupational, and Aerospace Medicine, and Associate Professor of Preventive Medicine and Nutrition at the College of Medicine, kept watch over the book so that it would fulfill Mayo Clinic's commitment to offer reliable tools for healthier lives. And Chris Frye, Editor-in-Chief of Books and Newsletters for Mayo Clinic Health Solutions, never permitted our joint effort to collapse, even when we weren't sure we could uphold our individual standards in this one book.

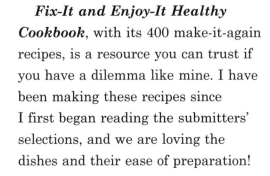

Fix-It and Enjoy-It Healthy Cookbook, with its 400 make-it-again recipes, is a resource you can trust if you have a dilemma like mine. I have been making these recipes since I first began reading the submitters' selections, and we are loving the dishes and their ease of preparation!

One More Thing

To my friends who are wary of anything with "healthy" in their titles, I dare you to try Chicken Greek Salad (page 25), Lasagna Mexicana (page 55), Thai Shrimp and Rice (page 78), Tuscan Bean Salad (page 94), and Berry Breakfast Parfait (page 189). You won't be sorry—and you certainly won't be sacrificing any tasty pleasures!

Phyllis Pellman Good

Greetings from Mayo Clinic – and Best Wishes for Healthy Eating

Healthy food *can* be tasty *and* easy to prepare. The recipes in this cookbook demonstrate that. We are pleased to be a part of this book and hope it will bring you and your family enjoyment and health.

The recipes collected here meet the standards of the Mayo Clinic Healthy Weight Pyramid, both in quantity – with an emphasis on vegetables, fruits, and whole grains – and in the nutritional content of each recipe. The Pyramid represents a philosophy of eating that takes into consideration the influence of diet on both health and weight.

Big Point

There's a great deal of scientific information which suggests that a healthy diet revolves around, among other things, eating plenty of vegetables and fruits. These foods are loaded with vitamins, minerals, antioxidants, fiber, and a host of phytochemicals (plant chemicals) that collectively promote health and prevent disease. For these reasons, they are the foundation of the Mayo Clinic Healthy Weight Pyramid (see page 21). *There's no limit on the daily servings of fresh or frozen vegetables and fruits you can eat when you're eating to the Pyramid.*

Not Impossible to Manage

In the other food groups of the Pyramid, the focus is on making healthy choices within each group. For example, for carbohydrates, whole-grains are preferred over those that are refined. Choose whole-grain breads, cereals and pastas, and brown rice.

For the protein and dairy group, choose lean sources of protein, including beans, fish, and low-fat dairy products. You can obtain all the protein your body needs without the saturated fat and cholesterol that are associated with less-healthy protein and dairy sources.

For fats, the Pyramid emphasizes olive oil, canola and other vegetable oils, and nuts. These contain heart-healthy unsaturated fats. All fats contain the same number of calories, but some can better promote health.

Sweets and treats, such as candies, cookies, cakes, and other desserts contain a relatively large number of calories and few nutrients. So we recommend limiting these foods to an average of 75 calories daily and focusing on healthier alternatives.

Feeling Satisfied

The Mayo Clinic Healthy Weight Pyramid is also based on the concept of energy density. Some foods, such as refined carbohydrates and fat, contain a large number of calories in a small volume. Other foods, including vegetables and fruits, contain a lot of volume and bulk but relatively few calories. (One *cup* of carrots has as many calories as 1½ *teaspoons* of butter. One apple has about as many calories as 1½ tablespoons of jam. And there is the same number of calories in 10 to 11 heads of lettuce, or 35 cups of green beans, as there are in 1⅓ sticks of butter!)

By following the Mayo Clinic Healthy Weight Pyramid and focusing on eating more foods at its base, you will be able to consume fewer calories while eating enough volume of food to feel satisfied. This will help you control your weight.

All of these principles are incorporated into the recipes in this book, which makes this pattern of eating practical, sustainable, and very importantly—enjoyable!

12 Tips for Helping Children Eat Healthy

Helping kids eat a healthy diet doesn't have to be difficult. Here are 12 tips:

1 Make it fun. Serve broccoli and other veggies with a favorite fat-free dip or sauce. Cut foods into various shapes with cookie cutters.

2 Recruit your child's help. At the grocery store, ask your child to help you select fruits, vegetables, and other healthy foods. Don't buy anything that you don't want your child to eat. At home, let your child help choose what to eat, and also help you rinse veggies, stir batter, or set the table.

3 Be cunning. Add chopped broccoli or green peppers to spaghetti sauce, top cereal with fruit slices, and mix grated zucchini and carrots into casseroles and soups. Serve veggies first at mealtime, when children are hungriest.

4 Don't offer dessert as a reward. Withholding dessert sends the message that dessert is the best food, which may only increase your child's desire for sweets. You might select one or two nights a week as dessert nights, and skip dessert the rest of the week. Or redefine dessert as fruit, yogurt, or other healthy choices.

5 Designate a snacking zone. Restrict snacking to the kitchen. You'll save your children countless calories from mindless munching in front of the TV.

6 Make it quick. If your children need to snack on the go, think beyond a bag of potato chips. Offer string cheese, fresh fruit, cereal bars, or other drip-free items.

7 Go for the grain. Whole-grain snacks—such as whole-grain pretzels or tortillas and low-sugar, whole-grain cereals—can give your children energy with some staying power.

8 Pull out the blender. Use skim milk, fat-free yogurt, and fresh fruit to make your own smoothies (see pages 235–237).

9 Promote independence. Make it easy for older children to help themselves. Keep a selection of ready-to-eat veggies in the refrigerator. Leave fresh fruit in a bowl on the counter. Store low-sugar, whole-grain cereal in an easily accessible cabinet. Stock fruit, either canned or packaged in its own juice, in your pantry.

10 Use some imagination. Offer something new, such as fresh pineapple, cranberries, red or yellow peppers, or roasted soy nuts. Slice a whole-wheat pita and serve with hummus (see page 239–241).

11 Mix and match. Serve baby carrots or other raw veggies with fat-free ranch dressing. Dip graham crackers or fresh fruit in fat-free yogurt. Top celery, apples, or bananas with peanut butter.

12 Set a good example. Let your children catch you munching raw vegetables or snacking on a bowl of grapes. If you eat a variety of healthy foods, your child is more likely to follow suit.

Small Practical Steps in the Right Direction

A few simple changes can make a big difference in how well you eat. Here are 10 easy steps to healthier eating.

1 Have at least one serving of fruit at each meal, and another as snacks during the day.

2 Switch from low-fiber breakfast cereal to lower-sugar, higher-fiber alternatives.

3 Lighten your milk by moving down one step in fat content — from whole to 2%, for instance, or from 1% to fat-free.

4 Cook with olive, canola, or other vegetable oil instead of butter or margarine whenever you can.

5 Choose coarse whole-grain breads. Switch to brown rice. Experiment with whole wheat flour when baking.

6 Include at least two servings of vegetables for lunch.

7 Have at least two servings of vegetables for dinner.

8 Have fish as a main course at least twice a week.

9 Serve fresh fruit for dessert.

10 Replace high-calorie sweetened beverages with water, iced tea, or unsweetened fruit juices.

Are You Eating Well?
A Quick Way to Measure

To see how your current food choices match up with healthy eating and cooking, answer the 10 questions below and note your responses. Instead of an exact rating or score, you'll receive a broad view of the way you cook and eat — a view that can guide you toward making some basic choices for better health.

1 How many servings of vegetables do you eat in a typical day? (A serving is 2 cups of leafy greens, 1 cup solid or cut up vegetables.)

   A. Four or more

   B. Two or three

   C. One or none

2 How many servings of fruit do you eat in a typical day? (A serving is usually one medium piece.)

   A. Three or more

   B. Two

   C. One

3 How often does fish appear on your weekly menu?

   A. Two or more times

   B. Once

   C. Rarely or never

4 When you shop for bread, pasta, and rice, how often do you buy whole-grain varieties?

   A. Always

   B. Sometimes

   C. Rarely or never

5 Which of the following are you most likely to use?

  A. Canola or olive oil
  B. Corn oil
  C. Butter or margarine

6 How often during a typical week do you eat out and order hamburgers, cheese-rich pizzas, or sandwiches layered with meat and cheese?

  A. Not more than once
  B. Two or three times
  C. Four or more times

7 A dinner of 2 cups (12 ozs/375 g) of cooked pasta in a tomato sauce is how many servings of carbohydrate?

  A. Four
  B. Not sure
  C. One

8 What kind of milk do you usually drink?

  A. Fat-free milk or soy milk
  B. 1 or 2%
  C. Whole milk or none

9 What are you most likely to reach for when you're thirsty?

  A. Water
  B. Fruit juice
  C. Regular sweetened soda

10 What's your usual snack?

  A. Nuts, fruit, or carrot or celery sticks
  B. Energy bars or other "healthy" sweets
  C. Potato chips, pretzels, or cookies

If you count mostly **A**'s among your answers, congratulations. You're well on your way to healthy eating.

If you count mostly **B**'s and **C**'s, your menu could use a tune-up. You'll find plenty of tips and great-tasting recipes in the following pages.

If you answered with mostly **C**'s and few **A**'s, it's time for some fresh ideas about good food.

Tips for Healthier Eating for Stuck-in-Their-Ways Adults

Are you stuck in a food rut and having a hard time changing to healthier eating habits? If you want to make lasting changes to the way you eat, you need a plan. Follow these steps for changing an unhealthy behavior into a healthy one:

1 List your behaviors that you think are unhealthy. For example, maybe you eat too fast, or snack throughout the day instead of eating regular meals, or eat whenever you're under stress.

2 Choose *one* behavior that you would like to change. (Trying to change everything on your list at once can feel overwhelming.)

3 As you think about strategies for changing, try to figure out how you developed the behavior. For example, do you tend to snack all day because you're under constant stress?

4 Brainstorm about ways to change your behavior. Think of five to seven possible solutions. Then pick one strategy that you think is practical and doable. For example, choose a healthy habit that you can substitute for an unhealthy one.

5 Figure out a way to make your new behavior easy to do. For example, how can you eat more fruit? Maybe you can make sure that a well-stocked bowl is always on your kitchen counter.

6 Identify obstacles that might get in your way. What conflicts might interfere with your strategy? What plans can you make to work around those possible hindrances?

7 Set a date for when you want to achieve your goal of changing your behavior and routine. Establish a comfortable pace for making the change.

8 When you reach the goal date, evaluate your success. What worked and what didn't? What would you do differently?

9 Consider what you need to do to maintain your new approach to food. Think about what you need to do to make your healthy behavior a permanent one.

10 When you're ready, select another behavior you'd like to change and restart the process.

Daily Calories for Maintaining Weight

On average, these are daily calorie goals for people seeking to maintain their weight:

Calories

1,600	Children ages 2 to 6, most women, and some older adults
2,000	Average adult
2,200	Older children, teenage girls, active women, and most men
2,400	Teenage boys and active men

Daily Serving Recommendations for Calorie Levels

Food group	Starting calorie goals				
	1,200	1,400	1,600	1,800	2,000
Vegetables	4 or more	4 or more	5 or more	5 or more	5 or more
Fruits	3 or more	4 or more	5 or more	5 or more	5 or more
Carbohydrates	4	5	6	7	8
Protein/Dairy	3	4	5	6	7
Fats	3	3	3	4	5

For calories levels higher than 2,000, simply follow the principles of eating to the Healthy Weight Pyramid by focusing on unlimited servings of vegetables and fruits, and moderate amounts of whole-grain carbohydrates, lean protein, and heart-healthy fats.

Average Serving Sizes

Below are the average serving sizes for food groups in the Mayo Clinic Healthy Weight Pyramid.

Food group	Average serving size	Calories per serving
Vegetables	2 cups leafy or 1 cup solid	25
Fruits	½ cup sliced or one medium piece	60
Carbohydrates	½ cup grain or 1 slice of bread	70
Protein/Dairy	½ cup beans, 3 ozs. fish, 1 cup skim milk, 2–2½ ozs. meat or hard cheese	110
Fats	1 tsp. oil or 2 tbsp. nuts	45

Substituting Fresh Ingredients

Use the following approximate values to help you substitute fresh items in place of canned or frozen. But fresh is best.

ALL EQUAL ONE POUND UNLESS OTHERWISE STATED

Item	Canned	Frozen	Fresh
Beans, Green or Wax	2 cups	3.3 cups	3 cups
Beans, Black (Turtle), Kidney, or Navy	2 cups		1 cup dry = 2 cups cooked (1 pound dry yields 6 cups cooked)
Beans, Chickpeas (Garbanzo)	2 cups		1 cup dry = 2 cups cooked (1 pound dry yields 5 cups cooked)
Beans, Great Northern	2 cups		2/3 cup dry = 2 cups cooked (1 pound dry yields 6 cups cooked)
Beans, Pinto	2 cups		2/3 cup dry = 2 cups cooked (1 pound dry yields 9 cups cooked)
Beets	3.3 cups		3.3 cups = 6 whole beets, 2" in diameter
Broccoli (chopped)		3 cups	5 cups
Carrots	2 cups	3 cups sliced	3 cups sliced or 5 to 7 medium whole carrots

Item	Canned	Frozen	Fresh
Corn	3 cups	3 cups	3 cups kernels = 7 ears
Mushrooms	3 cups sliced (4-oz can ~ ¾ cups)		7 cups sliced
Potato	2½ cups		2 medium (3" in diameter) or 2½ small (2–2½" in diameter)
Spinach	2 cups	3 cups frozen	15 cups leaves (2½ cups cooked)
Sweet Potato (pieces)	2 cups		3½ cups
Tomatoes › crushed, diced, › puree, sauce, stewed › paste › cherry › whole	2 cups 2 cups (6-oz can=10 Tbsp)		3 cups (26 items) 4 medium (2½" in diameter)

Sources:
Nutrition Facts from multiple food manufacturers
USDA Nutrient Database — http://www.nal.usda.gov/fnic/foodcomp/search/

Item	Dry	Cooked
Pasta—most shapes	2 ounces	8 cups
Brown Rice	2.5 cups	7.5 cups
Wild Rice	2.5 cups	10 cups

Sources:
Nutrition Facts from multiple food manufacturers
Pasta (From National Pasta Association) — http://www.ilovepasta.org/faqs.html#Q10

The Pyramid Servings Diagram

Next to every recipe in this cookbook, you will see a Pyramid Servings graphic with several rows of shaded and unshaded circles. These circles show how the dish stacks up against the Daily Servings Goals of the Mayo Clinic Health Weight Pyramid.

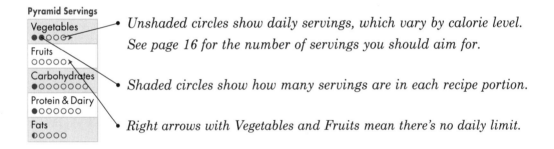

Unshaded circles show daily servings, which vary by calorie level. See page 16 for the number of servings you should aim for.

Shaded circles show how many servings are in each recipe portion.

Right arrows with Vegetables and Fruits mean there's no daily limit.

You won't find daily servings *goals* for sweets, even though they're at the Pyramid's peak. (In a few of the recipes in this book, you will find a Sweets servings line, which simply indicates the presence of sweets in that particular recipe.) That's because candies, cakes, and other goodies made with refined sugar or honey, and usually lots of fat, are high-calorie foods that are low in nutrients. In other words, they are empty calories. They are not off-limits. Satisfy your sweet tooth in moderation—up to an average of 75 calories a day. As an alternative, enjoy fresh fruit sometimes instead of prepared sweets or desserts.

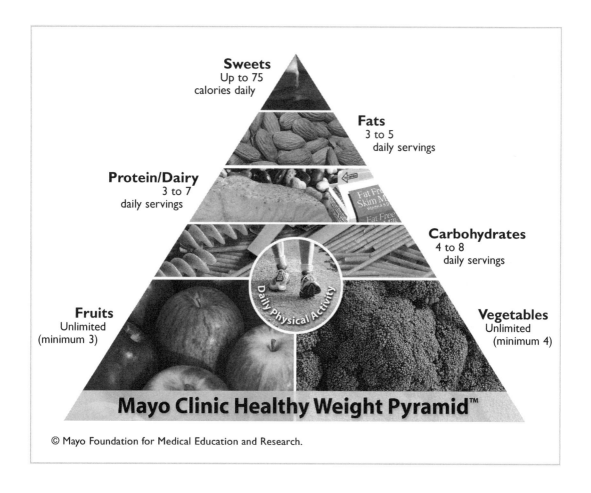

Sweets
Up to 75 calories daily

Fats
3 to 5 daily servings

Protein/Dairy
3 to 7 daily servings

Carbohydrates
4 to 8 daily servings

Daily Physical Activity

Fruits
Unlimited (minimum 3)

Vegetables
Unlimited (minimum 4)

Mayo Clinic Healthy Weight Pyramid™

© Mayo Foundation for Medical Education and Research.

Main Dishes

Main Dishes—Salads

Curried Chicken Salad

Bonita Stutzman, Harrisonburg, VA

Makes 10 main-dish servings

Prep. Time: 20 minutes

1 cup fat-free mayonnaise
¾ cup plain non-fat yogurt
2 Tbsp. honey
1 Tbsp. lemon juice
1½ Tbsp. curry powder
6 cups chopped cooked
  chicken, cooled
3 cups halved red grapes
¾ cup toasted slivered almonds
¾ cup diced celery
Romaine lettuce

Pyramid Servings	
Vegetables	○○○○○➤
Fruits	●○○○○➤
Carbohydrates	○○○○○○○
Protein & Dairy	●○○○○○○○
Fats	●●○○○

1. Mix together first five ingredients in a medium bowl.

2. In a large bowl, toss together chicken, grapes, almonds, and celery.

3. Pour dressing over chicken mixture and toss.

4. Refrigerate until serving time.

5. Serve on a bed of Romaine lettuce.

Per Serving
Calories 252, Kilojoules 1054, Protein 24 g,
Carbohydrates 17 g, Total Fat 10 g, Saturated Fat 2 g,
Monounsaturated Fat 5 g, Polyunsaturated Fat 3 g,
Cholesterol 65 mg, Sodium 200 mg, Fiber 2 g

Fruited Chicken Salad

Dottie Schmidt
Kansas City, MO

Makes 6 main-dish servings

Prep. Time: 20 minutes
Cooking Time: 20 minutes
Chilling Time: 2 hours

Pyramid Servings

Vegetables	○○○○○➤
Fruits	●○○○○➤
Carbohydrates	●●○○○○○○
Protein & Dairy	●○○○○○○
Fats	●○○○○

cooked meat from 2 large
    skinless chicken breast
    halves (about 12 ounces
    total), *or* 13-oz. can
    premium chunk chicken
    breast in water, drained
6-oz. pkg. Uncle Ben's Long Grain and
    Wild Rice Original Recipe
1½ cups water
1 cup fat-free mayonnaise
⅓ cup orange juice
1 cup sliced celery
½ cup chopped pecans
11-oz. can mandarin oranges, drained
½ lb. (about 2½ cups) seedless green
    grapes, washed and halved
Romaine lettuce

1. Cut cooked meat into bite-size pieces.
Chill.
2. Cook rice and seasoning according to
package directions, *except* use 1½ cups water.
Chill cooked rice.
3. When chicken and rice are thoroughly
chilled, combine with remaining ingredients in
a large bowl, tossing very gently. Keep chilled
until ready to serve.
4. Serve on a bed of lettuce.

Per Serving

Calories 344, Kilojoules 1439, Protein 22 g,
Carbohydrates 42 g, Total Fat 10 g, Saturated Fat 1.5 g,
Monounsaturated Fat 5.5 g, Polyunsaturated Fat 3 g,
Cholesterol 52 mg, Sodium 731 mg, Fiber 3 g

Grilled Fiesta Chicken Salad

Liz Clapper
Lancaster, PA

Makes 4 main-dish servings

Prep. Time: 25 minutes
Cooking Time: 10 minutes

Pyramid Servings

Vegetables	●●○○○➤
Fruits	○○○○○➤
Carbohydrates	●○○○○○○○
Protein & Dairy	●●○○○○○
Fats	○○○○○

1 head Bibb lettuce
1 head red leaf lettuce
1 cup shredded carrots
1 medium tomato, diced
2 green onions, chopped
1 lb. boneless, skinless
    chicken breasts
1 tsp. chili powder
1 sweet red pepper
1 Tbsp. olive oil
1 cup thawed frozen corn
½ cup shredded low-fat cheddar cheese
8 Tbsp. fat-free Ranch dressing
2 whole wheat pita breads, 4" diameter

1. Tear up heads of lettuce and toss together
in a large bowl. Top with shredded carrots,
diced tomato, and chopped green onions.
2. Season chicken with chili powder. Grill
chicken 3–4 minutes on each side.
3. Meanwhile, dice red pepper. Toss with
olive oil and cook in a medium skillet over
medium heat for 2 minutes.
4. Add corn and cook for 1 more minute.
5. When chicken has cooled to room temperature, dice chicken.
6. Top salad with diced chicken.
7. Spoon corn and pepper over top.
8. Sprinkle with cheese. Drizzle each salad
with 2 Tbsp. dressing.
9. Grill whole wheat pitas for 2–3 minutes
each side. Cut into fourths. Serve 2 wedges
with each individual salad.

Per Serving
Calories 337, Kilojoules 1410, Protein 36g,
Carbohydrates 33g, Total Fat 8g, Saturated Fat 2g,
Monounsaturated Fat 4g, Polyunsaturated Fat 2g,
Cholesterol 71mg, Sodium 512mg, Fiber 6g

Tip: You can bake pitas at 375° in oven for 10 minutes instead of grilling.

Dietitian's tip: When grilling watch the item closely. To keep it moist, baste with wine, fruit juice, vegetable juice, fat-free dressings, or broth, instead of oil or drippings.

A Tip —

Buy fruits and vegetables when they are in season. They will be cheaper, and their quality will be greater than those that are out of season and have been shipped long distances.

Chicken Greek Salad

Gretchen Lang, Lockport, NY

Makes 4 main-dish servings

Prep. Time: 30 minutes
Cooking Time: 15 minutes

Pyramid Servings

Vegetables
●●○○○➤
Fruits
○○○○○➤
Carbohydrates
○○○○○○○○
Protein & Dairy
●●○○○○○
Fats
●●○○○

6-oz. pkg. (about 6 cups) baby spinach, torn
6 cups Romaine lettuce, torn
1 cucumber, chopped
1 red onion, chopped
3 tomatoes, chopped
half a red sweet pepper, chopped
1 carrot, shredded
1 rib celery, chopped
pepper to taste
2 ozs. (about ½ cup) fat-free feta cheese, crumbled
1 whole skinless chicken breast (8-oz.), grilled and sliced
⅓ cup extra-virgin olive oil
⅓ cup rice vinegar

1. In a large bowl, toss all vegetables and pepper together.
2. Sprinkle cheese on top.
3. Place grilled and sliced chicken pieces on top of salad.
4. Mix oil and vinegar together in a small jar. Pour over all.

Per Serving
Calories 303, Kilojoules 1268, Protein 20g,
Carbohydrates 15g, Total Fat 18g, Saturated Fat 3g,
Monounsaturated Fat 12g, Polyunsaturated Fat 3g,
Cholesterol 35mg, Sodium 395mg, Fiber 6g

Dietitian's tip: Goat cheese, such as feta (Greek) or Montrachet (French), has a soft, creamy texture and a slightly tangy flavor. A little adds lots of taste with few calories and fat.

Rice and Beans Salad

Esther Kraybill
Lancaster, PA

Makes 10 main-dish servings

Prep. Time: 20 minutes
Cooking Time: 45–50 minutes
Chilling Time: 2 hours or more

Pyramid Servings

Vegetables	●○○○○➤
Fruits	○○○○○➤
Carbohydrates	●○○○○○○○
Protein & Dairy	●○○○○○○
Fats	●○○○○

1½ cups uncooked brown rice
3 cups water
½ cup fresh parsley, cut up
2 shallots or several spring
   onions cut up (½ cup)
15-oz. can garbanzo beans, rinsed and
   drained
15-oz. can dark kidney beans, rinsed and
   drained
¼ cup olive oil
⅓–½ cup rice vinegar, according to your
   taste preferences

1. Place rice and water in a stockpot. Cover and cook over medium heat until rice is tender, about 45–50 minutes.
2. Cool to room temperature.
3. Stir in the remaining ingredients.
4. Chill 2 hours or longer.

Per Serving

Calories 250, Kilojoules 1046, Protein 7 g,
Carbohydrates 39 g, Total Fat 7 g, Saturated Fat 1 g,
Monounsaturated Fat 4 g, Polyunsaturated Fat 2 g,
Cholesterol 0 mg, Sodium 206 mg, Fiber 5 g

Fruity Couscous Salad

Esther Nafziger
Bluffton, OH

Makes 10 main-dish servings

Prep. Time: 15 minutes
Cooking/Standing Time: 10 minutes

Pyramid Servings

Vegetables	○○○○○➤
Fruits	●●○○○➤
Carbohydrates	●●○○○○○○
Protein & Dairy	○○○○○○○
Fats	●●○○○

2 cups reduced sodium
   chicken broth
1 tsp. olive oil
1¼ cups raw couscous
¾ cup pecans, chopped and
   lightly toasted
½ cup currants
1 Tbsp. freshly grated orange zest
½ cup chopped fresh parsley
2 11-oz. cans mandarin oranges, drained
pepper to taste
⅓ cup orange juice
3 Tbsp. lemon juice
¼ cup extra-virgin olive oil

1. In saucepan bring broth and oil to boil. Stir in couscous.
2. Remove pan from heat and let stand, covered, for 5 minutes.
3. Fluff couscous gently with a fork.
4. In a large bowl, stir together couscous, pecans, currants, zest, parsley, oranges, and pepper.
5. Mix together in a separate bowl orange juice, lemon juice, and oil.
6. Pour over salad and toss gently. Chill if you wish before serving.

Per Serving

Calories 340, Kilojoules 1423, Protein 8 g,
Carbohydrates 50 g, Total Fat 12 g, Saturated Fat 1.5 g,
Monounsaturated Fat 8 g, Polyunsaturated Fat 2.5 g,
Cholesterol 1 mg, Sodium 40 mg, Fiber 4 g

Bulgur Salad with Fruits and Nuts

Kathy Hertzler
Lancaster, PA

Makes 8 main-dish servings

Prep. Time: 30 minutes
Cooking/Standing Time: 35 minutes

1 cup raw bulgur
2 cups boiling water
⅔ cup coarsely chopped
  walnuts
½ cup raisins, *or* currants
1 large rib celery, finely diced
¼ cup toasted sunflower seeds
2 Tbsp. minced chives
1 medium apple, unpeeled and finely
  diced
juice of half a lemon
¼ cup olive oil
2 Tbsp. honey
½ tsp. cumin
¼ tsp. cinnamon
dash of nutmeg

Pyramid Servings

Vegetables	○○○○○➤
Fruits	●○○○○➤
Carbohydrates	●○○○○○○○
Protein & Dairy	○○○○○○○
Fats	●●●○○

1. Place the bulgur in a heat-proof mixing bowl and pour 2 cups boiling water over it. Cover the bowl and let it stand for 30 minutes, or until the water is absorbed.

2. Fluff with a fork.

3. In a serving bowl, combine the walnuts, raisins, celery, sunflower seeds, and chives.

4. Core (but don't peel) the apple and dice it finely. Toss it with the lemon juice in a small bowl.

5. Add apple, along with the rest of the ingredients, to the nut/raisin mixture. Stir well.

6. Stir in the bulgur.

7. Serve at once, or chill until needed.

Per Serving

Calories 246, Kilojoules 1029, Protein 5 g,
Carbohydrates 26 g, Total Fat 14 g, Saturated Fat 2 g,
Monounsaturated Fat 7 g, Polyunsaturated Fat 5 g,
Cholesterol 0 mg, Sodium 9 mg, Fiber 5 g

Tip: It's better if it stands awhile, chilled, so the flavors can mix.

Dietitian's tip: All walnuts are high in phosphorus, zinc, copper, iron, potassium, and vitamin E and low in saturated fat. But English walnuts have twice as many omega-3 fatty acids as black walnuts do.

A Tip —

Warm a lemon to room temperature before squeezing it in order to get more juice from it.

Tabbouleh with Blueberries and Mint

Pat Bechtel
Dillsburg, PA

Makes 4 main-dish servings

Prep. Time: 20–25 minutes
Marinating Time: 2 hours

Pyramid Servings	
Vegetables	●●○○○▶
Fruits	●○○○○▶
Carbohydrates	●○○○○○○○
Protein & Dairy	○○○○○○○
Fats	●●●○○

2 cups water
1 cup uncooked bulgur wheat, medium grind
½ lb. (about 2) fresh tomatoes, peeled and diced
half a cucumber, diced
4 green onions, white and green parts, minced
2 cups fresh blueberries
5 Tbsp. fresh lemon juice
¼ cup olive oil
½ cup shredded fresh mint leaves
1 Tbsp. chopped fresh parsley
¼ tsp. ground cumin
¼ tsp. salt
¼ tsp. freshly ground black pepper

1. Bring 2 cups water to a boil. Add bulgur and allow to stand 5 minutes.
2. Turn soaked bulgur onto a cloth. Pick up cloth with bulgur inside and squeeze out excess moisture.
3. Combine all ingredients in a large bowl, tossing gently.
4. Cover and refrigerate. Allow to marinate 2 hours before serving.
5. Serve at room temperature.

Per Serving	
Calories 311, Kilojoules 1301, Protein 6g,	
Carbohydrates 41g, Total Fat 14g, Saturated Fat 2g,	
Monounsaturated Fat 10g, Polyunsaturated Fat 2g,	
Cholesterol 0mg, Sodium 162mg, Fiber 10g	

Tip: Get the bulgur as dry as possible after soaking.

Italian Pasta Salad

Monica Kehr
Portland, MI

Makes 8 main-dish servings

Prep. Time: 20 minutes
Cooking Time: 15 minutes

Pyramid Servings	
Vegetables	●○○○○▶
Fruits	○○○○○▶
Carbohydrates	●●●○○○○○
Protein & Dairy	○○○○○○○
Fats	●●○○○

14½-oz. box whole wheat rotini
4 medium-size tomatoes, diced
1 medium red bell sweet pepper, diced
1 medium yellow bell sweet pepper, diced
1 medium cucumber, diced
half a red onion, sliced thin
2 cups fresh broccoli florets, chopped
⅓ cup sliced black olives
1 tsp. salt-free Italian seasoning
¼ cup olive oil
½ cup red wine vinegar
8 tsp. grated Parmesan cheese

1. Cook pasta according to directions. Rinse with cool water.
2. Mix all ingredients, except seasoning, olive oil, vinegar, and cheese, in a large bowl.
3. Combine seasoning, oil, and vinegar in another bowl, or a jar with a tight-fitting lid.
4. Serve pasta, with each individual serving topped with 1½ Tbsp. dressing and 1 tsp. grated cheese.

Per Serving	
Calories 312, Kilojoules 1305, Protein 9g,	
Carbohydrates 47g, Total Fat 10g, Saturated Fat 1.5g,	
Monounsaturated Fat 6g, Polyunsaturated Fat 2.5g,	
Cholesterol 1mg, Sodium 133mg, Fiber 8g	

Tip: Since the dressing and cheese aren't mixed in with everything else, the pasta salad keeps longer so leftovers are good.

Winter Salad

Virginia Graybill
Hershey, PA

Makes 4 main-dish servings

Prep. Time: 30 minutes

1 head (about 4 cups) red
  leaf lettuce
1 head (about 4 cups)
  Romaine lettuce
1 Granny Smith apple, cored
  but unpeeled, and cut up
½ cup raisins, *or* craisins
1 small red onion, thinly sliced
1 brown pear, cored but unpeeled, and
  cut up

Poppy Seed Dressing:
2 Tbsp. honey
¼ cup canola oil
¼ cup lemon juice
1 Tbsp. poppy seeds
1 tsp. Dijon mustard

1. Tear red leaf lettuce and Romaine lettuce into bite-size pieces. Place in large bowl.
2. Add apple, raisins or craisins, onion slices, and pear. Toss gently.
3. Mix dressing ingredients in a separate bowl or a jar with a tight-fitting lid.
4. Pour over salad just before serving.

Pyramid Servings

Vegetables
●●○○○➤

Fruits
●●○○○➤

Carbohydrates
○○○○○○○○

Protein & Dairy
○○○○○○○

Fats
●●○○○

Per Serving
Calories 284, Kilojoules 1188, Protein 2 g,
Carbohydrates 38 g, Total Fat 14 g, Saturated Fat 1 g,
Monounsaturated Fat 9 g, Polyunsaturated Fat 4 g,
Cholesterol 0 mg, Sodium 56 mg, Fiber 4 g

White Rabbit Salad

Esther Nafziger
Bluffton, OH

Makes 6 main-dish servings

Prep. Time: 20 minutes

2 small apples, unpeeled and
  chopped
½ cup raisins
½ cup walnuts, chopped and
  toasted
¼ cup sunflower seeds,
  toasted
2 Tbsp. poppy seeds
1½ cups low-fat (1%) cottage cheese
2 Tbsp. honey
juice of half lemon
lettuce leaves

1. Mix apples, raisins, walnuts, and sunflower and poppy seeds together in a mixing bowl.
2. In a separate bowl, mix together cottage cheese, honey, and lemon juice.
3. Gently mix fruit and nut mixture with cottage cheese mixture.
4. Serve very cold on lettuce greens.

Optional fruits, to be cut and added, or substituted, for apples:
- *fresh firm pears*
- *peaches*
- *green grapes*
- *orange sections*
- *cantaloupe cubes*

Pyramid Servings

Vegetables
○○○○○➤

Fruits
●◑○○○➤

Carbohydrates
○○○○○○○○

Protein & Dairy
◑○○○○○○

Fats
●●○○○

Per Serving
Calories 236, Kilojoules 987, Protein 12 g,
Carbohydrates 22 g, Total Fat 11 g, Saturated Fat 1 g,
Monounsaturated Fat 4 g, Polyunsaturated Fat 6 g,
Cholesterol 2 mg, Sodium 200 mg, Fiber 3 g

Main Dishes– Vegetables

Eggplant Parmesan

Mary Ann Bowman
East Earl, PA

Makes 6 main-dish servings

Prep. Time: 15 minutes
Broiling/Baking Time: 40–45
*   minutes*

Pyramid Servings

Vegetables
●●○○○▶

Fruits
○○○○○▶

Carbohydrates
○○○○○○○○

Protein & Dairy
●●○○○○○

Fats
●○○○○

1 medium eggplant, unpeeled
2 Tbsp. olive oil, *divided*
1 cup bread crumbs
½ tsp. dried basil
½ cup grated Parmesan
    cheese
2 Tbsp. chopped parsley
⅛ tsp. pepper
1 tsp. dried oregano
6 tomatoes, chopped
2 green bell sweet peppers, chopped
2 onions, chopped
1 clove garlic, chopped
2 Tbsp. tomato paste
1 cup grated Swiss cheese
¼ cup additional Parmesan cheese

1. Preheat oven to broil.
2. Cut eggplant into 6 slices, each ½" thick.
3. Place slices on cookie sheet. Brush with half the olive oil.
4. Broil 5 minutes, or until golden.
5. Turn slices. Brush other sides with remaining oil.
6. Return to broiler and brown second sides.
7. Place browned eggplant in lightly greased 9 × 13 baking pan, sprayed generously with non-stick cooking spray.

8. Mix together next 6 ingredients in a small bowl. Sprinkle over eggplant.
9. Combine in saucepan tomatoes, peppers, onions, garlic, and tomato paste. Simmer uncovered about 20 minutes.
10. Then spread on top of crumb mixture.
11. Top with Swiss cheese and additional Parmesan cheese.
12. Bake uncovered at 375° for 10–15 minutes.

Per Serving

Calories 309, Kilojoules 1293, Protein 15 g,
Carbohydrates 30 g, Total Fat 15 g, Saturated Fat 6 g,
Monounsaturated Fat 6 g, Polyunsaturated Fat 3 g,
Cholesterol 29 mg, Sodium 343 mg, Fiber 7 g

Tip: *You can make this ahead and refrigerate it until you're ready to heat and serve it.*

A Tip —

    Keep a ziplock bag in the freezer to collect the unused ends of bread loaves. When the bag is full, whirl in food processor. Return to bag and freeze—you'll always have fresh bread crumbs at your fingertips.

Delectable Eggplant
Thelma Good
Harrisonburg, VA

Makes 3 main-dish servings

Prep. Time: 15–20 minutes
Cooking/Baking Time: 30 minutes

1 slice bacon, fried, drained,
  and crumbled
2 tsp. olive oil
½ cup chopped onion
½ cup chopped green bell
  sweet pepper
½ cup chopped celery
1 medium (about 3 cups) eggplant, peeled
  and chopped
¼ cup brown sugar
1½ tsp. dried basil
¼ tsp. garlic salt
2 8-oz. cans tomato sauce, no salt added
1 cup low-fat mozzarella cheese, shredded

Pyramid Servings	
Vegetables	●●○○○➤
Fruits	○○○○○➤
Carbohydrates	○○○○○○○○
Protein & Dairy	●○○○○○○
Fats	●●○○○

1. In a large skillet, sauté onion, pepper,
celery, and eggplant in olive oil until tender.
2. Stir in brown sugar, basil, garlic salt, and
tomato sauce.
3. Place half of mixture into a 1½–2-quart
baking dish, generously sprayed with non-stick
cooking spray.
4. Sprinkle with half the cheese.
5. Repeat layers.
6. Garnish with bacon.
7. Bake, uncovered, at 325° for 20 minutes.

Per Serving

Calories 276, Kilojoules 1154, Protein 10 g,
Carbohydrates 36 g, Total Fat 10 g, Saturated Fat 3 g,
Monounsaturated Fat 4 g, Polyunsaturated Fat 3 g,
Cholesterol 22 mg, Sodium 340 mg, Fiber 9 g

Moroccan Spiced
Sweet Potato Medley
Pat Bishop
Bedminster, PA

Makes 6 main-dish servings

Prep. Time: 20 minutes
Cooking Time: 35–40 minutes

2 tsp. olive oil
1 medium onion, sliced
2 garlic cloves, crushed
1½ tsp. ground coriander
1½ tsp. ground cumin
¼ tsp. ground red pepper
2 medium (about 1½ lbs.) sweet potatoes,
  peeled and cut into ½" thick slices
14-oz. can stewed tomatoes, undrained, no
  salt added
¾ cup uncooked bulgur
2¼ cups water
15-oz. can garbanzo beans, rinsed and
  drained
½ cup dark raisins
1 cup loosely packed fresh cilantro leaves,
  chopped

Pyramid Servings	
Vegetables	○○○○○➤
Fruits	●○○○○➤
Carbohydrates	●●○○○○○○
Protein & Dairy	●○○○○○○
Fats	○○○○○

1. In a large stockpot, sauté onion in oil
until tender and golden.
2. Add garlic, coriander, cumin, and red
pepper. Cook 1 minute.
3. Add sweet potato slices, tomatoes, bulgur,
and water. Heat to boiling.
4. Reduce heat, cover, and simmer 20
minutes, or until potatoes are fork-tender.
5. Stir in beans, raisins, and cilantro. Heat
through.

Per Serving

Calories 296, Kilojoules 1238, Protein 8 g,
Carbohydrates 60 g, Total Fat 3 g, Saturated Fat 0.4 g,
Monounsaturated Fat 2 g, Polyunsaturated Fat 0.6 g,
Cholesterol 0 mg, Sodium 328 mg, Fiber 10 g

Spicy Mexican Bean Burgers

Lois Hess
Lancaster, PA

Makes 4 burgers

Prep. Time: 30 minutes
Baking Time: 15–20 minutes

16-oz. can red kidney beans,
  rinsed, drained, and
  mashed
½ cup onion, chopped
half a green bell sweet
  pepper, chopped
1 carrot, steamed and mashed
⅛ cup salsa, your choice of flavors
1 cup whole wheat bread crumbs
½ cup whole wheat flour
½ tsp. black pepper, *optional*
dash of chili powder

1. Heat oven to 400°.
2. Combine all ingredients in a good-sized bowl. Add more flour to create a firmer mixture or more salsa if mixture is too stiff.
3. Form into 4 balls and then flatten into patties.
4. Place on a baking sheet, lightly sprayed with cooking spray.
5. Bake 15–20 minutes, or until firm and brown.
6. Serve on a whole wheat bun with lettuce, tomato, and salsa. (These ingredients are not included in the nutritional analyses.)

Pyramid Servings

Vegetables
●○○○○➤

Fruits
○○○○○➤

Carbohydrates
●○○○○○○○

Protein & Dairy
●◐○○○○○

Fats
○○○○○

Per Serving

Calories 123, Kilojoules 515, Protein 5 g,
Carbohydrates 23 g, Total Fat 1 g, Saturated Fat 0.2 g,
Monounsaturated Fat 0.6 g, Polyunsaturated Fat 0.2 g,
Cholesterol *trace*, Sodium 200 mg, Fiber 5 g

Dietitian's tip: Beans are a good way to add fiber to your diet, especially soluble fiber. Generally, ½ cup of cooked beans provides 4 to 6 grams of fiber. The soluble fiber can help lower blood cholesterol. Beans are also high in protein, complex carbohydrates, and iron.

A Tip —
  Keep peeled onions covered in a jar when refrigerated.

Chickpeas with Peppers and Tomatoes

Rika Allen
New Holland, PA

Makes 2 main-dish servings

Prep. Time: 15 minutes
Cooking Time: 25–30 minutes

½ cup onion, chopped
2 tsp. garlic, minced
2 cups (1 large) diced bell
  sweet pepper, your choice
  of colors
1 cup (1 medium) diced
  tomatoes
1 Tbsp. olive oil
1 tsp. ground turmeric
1 tsp. ground cumin
1 tsp. ground coriander
15½-oz. can chickpeas, rinsed and drained
2 Tbsp. water
dash of pepper

Pyramid Servings	
Vegetables	●●●●○❯
Fruits	○○○○○❯
Carbohydrates	○○○○○○○○
Protein & Dairy	●●○○○○○
Fats	●○○○○

1. Chop and dice onion, garlic, bell pepper, and tomatoes before beginning to cook, keeping each vegetable separate.
2. In a good-sized skillet or saucepan, heat olive oil and sauté onion and garlic until translucent.
3. Stir in turmeric, cumin, and coriander.
4. Add peppers and tomatoes and sauté.
5. Then add chickpeas.
6. Stir in water. Cover. Reduce heat and cook for about 15 minutes, or until vegetables are cooked to your liking.
7. Add pepper and cook another minute.
8. Serve as is, or over cooked rice (not included in analysis).

Per Serving
Calories 382, Kilojoules 1598, Protein 13 g,
Carbohydrates 64 g, Total Fat 10 g, Saturated Fat 2 g,
Monounsaturated Fat 6 g, Polyunsaturated Fat 2 g,
Cholesterol 0 mg, Sodium 667 mg, Fiber 14 g

Baked Beans

Esther Lehman
Croghan, NY

Makes 8 main-dish servings

Prep. Time:10–15 minutes
Soaking Time: 8 hours, or
  overnight
Cooking/Baking Time: 8–10 hours

1 lb. dry beans
⅓ cup minced onion
½ cup maple syrup
1 tsp. dry mustard
¼ tsp. salt
2 slices lean bacon, cut into
  1" squares

Pyramid Servings	
Vegetables	○○○○○❯
Fruits	○○○○○❯
Carbohydrates	○○○○○○○○
Protein & Dairy	●●○○○○○
Fats	○○○○○
Sweets	◑

1. Sort and wash beans. Place in a large stockpot. Cover with cold water and soak overnight.
2. In the morning, bring beans to a boil in their soaking water.
3. Cook until beans are tender, about 1½ hours.
4. Stir in other ingredients.
5. Place mixture in baking pan. Cover and bake at 250° for 3–4 hours. Add more water if the mixture becomes too dry.
6. Uncover baking pan and continue baking 3–4 more hours. Stir up from the bottom and along the sides occasionally to prevent sticking.

Per Serving
Calories 257, Kilojoules 1075, Protein 13 g,
Carbohydrates 47 g, Total Fat 2 g, Saturated Fat 0.3 g,
Monounsaturated Fat 0.7 g, Polyunsaturated Fat 1 g,
Cholesterol 0.3 mg, Sodium 124 mg, Fiber 14 g

Dietitian's Tip: While they soak, dried beans will expand to about twice their size. So be sure to use plenty of cold water and a large pot. Soaking beans tenderizes them so they won't take as long to cook, and it helps them to be more digestible and less gas-forming.

Cajun Skillet Beans

Jenny Kennedy, Driggs, ID

Makes 6 main-dish servings

Prep. Time: 20 minutes
Cooking Time: 20 minutes

Pyramid Servings	
Vegetables	●●●○○➤
Fruits	○○○○○➤
Carbohydrates	○○○○○○○○
Protein & Dairy	●○○○○○○
Fats	●○○○○

1 onion, chopped
3 cloves garlic, minced
1 Tbsp. olive oil
3 celery ribs, chopped
2 green, *or* red, bell peppers, chopped
½ tsp. dried thyme
1 Tbsp. dried basil
1 tsp. dried oregano
¼–½ tsp. freshly ground pepper, according to your taste preference
pinch of cayenne pepper
2 cups chopped fresh tomatoes
1 Tbsp. honey, *or* molasses
3 Tbsp. Dijon mustard, *or* less, according to your taste preference
4 cups prepared black-eyed peas, butter beans, red beans, *or* black beans, drained and rinsed
Optional toppings (not included in analyses): 1 cup corn, chopped scallions, grated low-sodium, low-fat cheddar cheese

1. Sauté onion and garlic in olive oil in large skillet.
2. Add celery and peppers. Cook 5 minutes.
3. Add spices and cook another 5 minutes.
4. Add tomatoes, honey, and mustard. Cook 5 more minutes.
5. Add peas or beans, and corn if you wish. Cook until heated through.
6. Top with scallions and grated cheese if you wish, just before serving.

Per Serving
Calories 232, Kilojoules 971, Protein 11 g,
Carbohydrates 38 g, Total Fat 4 g, Saturated Fat 0.5 g,
Monounsaturated Fat 2.5 g, Polyunsaturated Fat 1 g,
Cholesterol 0 mg, Sodium 203 mg, Fiber 12 g

Vegetable Pizza

Deborah Heatwole
Waynesboro, GA

Makes 6 main-dish servings;
1 piece/serving

Prep. Time: 20 minutes
Rising Time: 20–30 minutes
Baking Time: 15–20 minutes

Pyramid Servings	
Vegetables	●●○○○➤
Fruits	○○○○○➤
Carbohydrates	●●○○○○○○
Protein & Dairy	●○○○○○○
Fats	○○○○○

¾ cup warm water
1 Tbsp. yeast
1 tsp. sugar
1 Tbsp. oil
1 tsp. salt
1½ cups whole wheat flour
1½ cups all-purpose flour
1 large tomato, peeled and thinly sliced
1 tsp. olive oil
½ tsp. Italian herb seasoning, no salt added
pepper, according to your taste preference
1 large onion, sliced
1 large green bell sweet pepper, sliced
¼ cup black olives, sliced
1½ cups sliced fresh mushrooms
¾ cup grated low-sodium, low-fat mozzarella cheese
½ tsp. Italian herb seasoning, no salt added

1. In a large bowl, dissolve yeast and sugar in water.

2. Stir in oil, salt, and whole wheat flour.

3. Add white flour gradually until dough is soft but not too sticky.

4. Knead on a lightly floured board for 5 minutes.

5. Cover with a towel. Let rise in a warm place 20–30 minutes.

6. Pat dough out onto a 12–15" pizza stone or pizza pan.

7. Bake at 400° for 5 minutes. Remove from oven.

8. Layer with thinly sliced tomatoes.

9. Brush with oil. Sprinkle with ½ tsp. Italian seasoning and pepper.

10. Layer with remaining vegetables.

11. Top with cheese.

12. Sprinkle with ½ tsp. Italian seasoning.

13. Bake at 400° for 10–15 minutes, or until crust is done and vegetables are tender.

14. Cut pizza into 6 pieces. Serve 1 piece to each person.

Per Serving

Calories 299, Kilojoules 1251, Protein 12 g,
Carbohydrates 52 g, Total Fat 6 g, Saturated Fat 2 g,
Monounsaturated Fat 3 g, Polyunsaturated Fat 1 g,
Cholesterol 8 mg, Sodium 526 mg, Fiber 6 g

Dietitian's tip: To increase the amount of nutrients in your diet—including vitamins, minerals and fiber—try adding three times as many vegetables as meat on pizzas or in casseroles, soups and stews. Better yet, go meatless!

A Tip —

A sharp knife is a safe knife. Keep your knives sharp!

Garden Vegetable Quiche
Susan Kasting, Jenks, OK

Makes 9 servings

Prep. Time: 20 minutes
Cooking/Baking Time: 40–45 minutes
Standing Time: 10 minutes

Pyramid Servings

Vegetables	●○○○○▸
Fruits	○○○○○▸
Carbohydrates	●○○○○
Protein & Dairy	●○○○○○○
Fats	○○○○○

1½ cups egg substitute
3 large eggs
⅓ cup skim milk
½ cup whole wheat pastry flour
8 ozs. low-sodium fat-free cottage cheese
4 cups sliced zucchini
2 cups diced raw potatoes
3 Tbsp. diced onion
1 cup finely chopped green bell sweet pepper
½ lb. fresh mushrooms, sliced
½ cup chopped parsley
2 tomatoes, thinly sliced
1 cup low-fat cheese of your choice, shredded, *divided*

1. Preheat oven to 400°.

2. In a large bowl, beat egg substitute and eggs until fluffy.

3. Stir in milk, flour, and cottage cheese.

4. Sauté zucchini, potatoes, onions, peppers, and mushrooms in pan coated with cooking spray for 5 minutes.

5. Stir sautéed vegetable mixture and parsley into egg mixture.

6. When well combined, pour into a 3-quart baking dish, lightly coated with cooking spray.

7. Top with tomato slices and cheese.

8. Bake 35–40 minutes, or until knife inserted in center comes out clean.

9. Allow to stand 10 minutes before slicing.

Per Serving

Calories 195, Kilojoules 816, Protein 17 g,
Carbohydrates 24 g, Total Fat 3 g, Saturated Fat 1.2 g,
Monounsaturated Fat 1 g, Polyunsaturated 0.8 g,
Cholesterol 75 mg, Sodium 210 mg, Fiber 3 g

Vegetable Quiche Cups to Go

Mary Ann Lefever
Lancaster, PA

Makes 3 main-dish servings, 4 cups per serving

Prep. Time: 15 minutes
Cooking/Baking Time: 20–25 minutes

Pyramid Servings	
Vegetables ●●○○○▸	
Fruits ○○○○○▸	
Carbohydrates ○○○○○○○○	
Protein & Dairy ●○○○○○○	
Fats ○○○○○	

16-oz. pkg. frozen chopped spinach
¾ cup (8-oz. carton) liquid egg substitute
¾ cup shredded reduced-fat mozzarella cheese
¼ cup diced green bell sweet peppers, *or* finely chopped broccoli florets
¼ cup diced onions
3 drops hot-pepper sauce, *optional*

1. Place spinach in microwave-safe bowl. Mic for 2½ minutes on high. Drain off excess liquid. Squeeze dry.
2. Line a 12-cup muffin pan with foil baking cups. Spray cups with cooking spray.
3. Combine thawed spinach, egg substitute, cheese, peppers, onions, and hot pepper sauce if you wish, in a bowl. Mix well.
4. Divide evenly among muffin cups.
5. Bake at 350° for 20 minutes, or until knife inserted in centers comes out clean.

Per Serving

Calories 126, Kilojoules 528, Protein 14 g, Carbohydrates 8 g, Total Fat 4 g, Saturated Fat 2.6 g, Monounsaturated Fat 0.6 g, Polyunsaturated Fat 0.8 g, Cholesterol 16 mg, Sodium 350 mg, Fiber 4 g

Tips:
You can freeze the quiche cups and then reheat them in the microwave when you're ready to use them.
Use any combination of fresh vegetables that you like.

Spinach Pie

Mary Ellen Musser
Reinholds, PA

Makes 4 main-dish servings

Prep. Time: 15 minutes
Baking Time: 40 minutes
Standing Time: 10 minutes

Pyramid Servings	
Vegetables ●○○○○▸	
Fruits ○○○○○▸	
Carbohydrates ○○○○○○○○	
Protein & Dairy ●◐○○○○○	
Fats ○○○○○	

2 cups low-sodium fat-free cottage cheese
10-oz. pkg. frozen chopped spinach, thawed, and squeezed dry
1 cup reduced-fat mozzarella cheese, shredded
egg substitute equivalent to 4 eggs, *or* 8 egg whites, beaten
⅓ cup (1½ ozs.) low-fat Parmesan cheese, grated
1 tsp. dried oregano leaves

1. Mix all ingredients together in a good-sized bowl.
2. Spoon into lightly greased 9" pie plate.
3. Bake at 350° for 40 minutes, or until knife inserted in center comes out clean.
4. Allow to stand for 10 minutes before cutting.

Per Serving

Calories 204, Kilojoules 854, Protein 29 g, Carbohydrates 8 g, Total Fat 6 g, Saturated Fat 4 g, Monounsaturated Fat 1 g, Polyunsaturated Fat 1 g, Cholesterol 24 mg, Sodium 800 mg, Fiber 2 g

Spinach-Stuffed Tomatoes
Charlotte Hagner
Montague, MI

Bonita's Squash Pie
Natalia Showalter
Mt. Solon, VA

Makes 4 main-dish servings

Prep. Time: 15–20 minutes
Cooking/Baking Time: 35 minutes

8 medium tomatoes
10-oz. pkg. frozen spinach
2 Tbsp. finely chopped onion
½ cup fat-free half-and-half
2 egg whites, *or* egg substitute
   equivalent to 1 egg

Pyramid Servings	
Vegetables	●●●●○▶
Fruits	○○○○○▶
Carbohydrates	○○○○○○○○
Protein & Dairy	○○○○○○○
Fats	○○○○○

1. Slice off top of each tomato. Remove pulp and seeds.
2. Place spinach and onion in saucepan with a small amount of water. Cook over medium heat until onions are softened.
3. In a small bowl, combine half-and-half and egg whites or egg substitute.
4. Stir into spinach and onions. Cook 1 minute.
5. Spoon mixture into tomatoes.
6. Place filled tomatoes in lightly greased baking dish.
7. Bake, uncovered, at 350° for 25 minutes.

Per Serving

Calories 92, Kilojoules 384, Protein 6 g,
Carbohydrates 16 g, Total Fat 1.1 g, Saturated Fat 0.4 g,
Monounsaturated Fat 0.2 g, Polyunsaturated Fat 0.5 g,
Cholesterol 2 mg, Sodium 136 mg, Fiber 6 g

Dietitian's tip: Tomatoes are a good source of lycopene, an antioxidant that may help protect against cancer and cardiovascular disease. Lycopene is most plentiful in red tomatoes and is best absorbed when the tomatoes have been cooked.

Makes 4 main-dish servings

Prep. Time: 20 minutes
Baking Time: 30–40 minutes
Standing Time: 10 minutes

3 cups shredded summer
   squash
½ cup chopped onion
½ cup shredded carrots
2 tsp. olive oil
2 egg whites, *or* egg substitute equivalent
   to 1 egg
½ cup fat-free sour cream
¾ cup shredded low-sodium, low-fat
   mozzarella cheese
2 Tbsp. fresh minced parsley
¼ tsp. pepper
¼ tsp. dried oregano
¼ tsp. garlic powder
½ cup cracker crumbs, from about 5 whole
   crackers with unsalted tops, crushed

Pyramid Servings	
Vegetables	●●○○○▶
Fruits	○○○○○▶
Carbohydrates	○○○○○○○○
Protein & Dairy	●○○○○○○
Fats	●●○○○

1. Place shredded squash into a clean cloth kitchen towel. Fold towel over zucchini and twist or press the towel to remove moisture.
2. In a saucepan or large skillet, lightly sauté squash, onion, and carrot in olive oil.
3. Mix in egg whites or egg substitute, sour cream, cheese, parsley, and seasonings.
4. Pour into 9" pie plate.
5. Garnish top with cracker crumbs.
6. Bake at 375° for 20–30 minutes, or until knife inserted in center comes out clean.
7. Allow to stand 10 minutes before cutting.

Per Serving

Calories 204, Kilojoules 854, Protein 12 g,
Carbohydrates 20 g, Total Fat 8 g, Saturated Fat 4 g,
Monounsaturated Fat 3 g, Polyunsaturated Fat 1 g,
Cholesterol 22 mg, Sodium 320 mg, Fiber 4 g

Zucchini Cakes

Jan McDowell, New Holland, PA
Mary Ann Lefever, Lancaster, PA

Makes 2 main-dish servings

Prep. Time: 15 minutes
Cooking Time: 10 minutes

Pyramid Servings	
Vegetables	●●○○○▸
Fruits	○○○○○▸
Carbohydrates	●○○○○○○○
Protein & Dairy	●○○○○○○
Fats	○○○○○

2 cups zucchini, grated and
 drained
2 eggs, beaten, *or* 4 egg
 whites, *or* egg substitute
 equivalent to 2 eggs, *or* ½
 cup soft tofu, blended
¾ cup plain bread crumbs, *divided*
1 Tbsp. light mayonnaise
¼ tsp. Old Bay seasoning
2 Tbsp. minced onion
lemon juice, *optional*, not included in
 analysis
tartar, *or* cocktail, sauce, *optional*, **not
 included in analysis**

1. In a good-sized bowl, mix zucchini, eggs,
egg whites, egg substitute, or tofu, ½ cup
bread crumbs, Old Bay, and onion. Combine
thoroughly.
2. Form into golf-ball-sized balls. Flatten and
roll lightly in remaining ¼ cup bread crumbs.
3. Lightly brown on both sides in non-stick
pan sprayed with oil.
4. Serve sprinkled with lemon juice, or with
tartar or cocktail sauce, if you wish.

Per Serving

Calories 238, Kilojoules 996, Protein 16 g,
Carbohydrates 38 g, Total Fat 3 g, Saturated Fat 0.5 g,
Monounsaturated Fat 0.5 g, Polyunsaturated Fat 2 g,
Cholesterol 1 mg, Sodium 568 mg, Fiber 4 g

Spicy Zucchini Boats

Mary Ann Lefever
Lancaster, PA

Makes 2 main-dish servings

Prep. Time: 20 minutes
Cooking/Baking Time:
 12–15 minutes

Pyramid Servings	
Vegetables	●●○○○▸
Fruits	○○○○○▸
Carbohydrates	○○○○○○○○
Protein & Dairy	●○○○○○○
Fats	○○○○○

4 medium-sized zucchini

Stuffing:
half an 8-oz. pkg. fat-free
 cream cheese, softened
⅓ cup shredded Parmesan cheese
¼ tsp. cayenne pepper
1 tsp. dried chives

1. Preheat oven to 350°.
2. Slice zucchini in half lengthwise to make
boats. Blanche in boiling salted water 2–3
minutes. Drain thoroughly. Blot excess liquid
with paper towels.
3. Using a knife or small spoon, carefully
hollow out center of zucchini by removing
some of the pulp. (Leave ¼" wall.) Save for
filling.
4. Combine cheeses, cayenne pepper, chives,
and removed pulp in bowl.
5. Stuff zucchini with mix. Place in lightly
greased baking dish.
6. Bake until cheese is melted, about 8–10
minutes.
7. If you wish, sprinkle with additional
chives and/or cayenne pepper just before
serving.

Per Serving

Calories 178, Kilojoules 744, Protein 18 g,
Carbohydrates 14 g, Total Fat 6 g, Saturated Fat 3 g,
Monounsaturated Fat 2 g, Polyunsaturated Fat 1 g,
Cholesterol 16 mg, Sodium 568 mg, Fiber 4 g

Tofu Tortilla Casserole with Chile Tomato Sauce

Diann Dunham
State College, PA

Makes 4 main-dish servings

Prep. Time: 15–20 minutes
Cooking/Baking Time: 25–30
minutes

1 Tbsp. olive oil
1 large onion, chopped
1 large green bell sweet
 pepper, chopped
1 lb. light, firm tofu, drained
1½ tsp. chili powder
½ tsp. ground cumin
¼ tsp. coriander
4-oz. can chopped black olives, drained
12-oz. can whole-kernel corn, no salt
 added, drained

Chile Tomato Sauce:
2 cups tomato puree, no salt added
2 Tbsp. white, *or* apple cider, vinegar
1½ tsp. chili powder
½ tsp. ground cumin
½ tsp. coriander
a few drops hot pepper sauce, *optional*

6 corn tortillas, each approximately 6" in
 diameter
½ cup grated low-fat cheddar cheese for
 topping

1. Preheat oven to 350°.
2. In a large skillet heat oil. Sauté onion and pepper until beginning to soften.
3. Mash tofu and add to skillet.
4. Stir in spices and olives.
5. Cook, stirring continually, until tofu is dry. Set aside until needed.
6. Combine all sauce ingredients in saucepan. Simmer a few minutes.

Pyramid Servings

Vegetables
●●●○○▸
Fruits
○○○○○▸
Carbohydrates
●●○○○○○○
Protein & Dairy
●○○○○○○○
Fats
●○○○○

7. Steam tortillas if you wish.
8. In 9 × 13 baking pan, place 2 tortillas side by side.
9. Top with ⅓ of tofu mixture. Top that with ⅓ of corn. Top that with ⅓ of tomato sauce.
10. Repeat layering 2 more times, ending with sauce.
11. Sprinkle with cheese.
12. Bake 15–20 minutes, or until heated through.

Per Serving
Calories 361, Kilojoules 1510, Protein 18 g,
Carbohydrates 51 g, Total Fat 10 g, Saturated Fat 2 g,
Monounsaturated Fat 6 g, Polyunsaturated Fat 2 g,
Cholesterol 3 mg, Sodium 519 mg, Fiber 10 g

Tip: You could add kidney beans or black beans to Step 3 if you wish. (The beans are not included in the nutritional analyses.)

Dietitian's tip: The traditional unleavened bread wrappers of Mexico, tortillas are a versatile way to add grains to your day. Tortillas divide into two basic categories: corn and wheat. Wheat tortillas, made from white flour, are often labeled "flour tortillas." Whole-wheat tortillas are made from whole-grain flour.

Soy Sauce Tofu

Rika Allen
New Holland, PA

Makes 2 main-dish servings

Prep. Time: 7–10 minutes
Standing Time, if needed: 20
  minutes
Cooking Time: 12–15 minutes

Pyramid Servings

Vegetables
○○○○○➤

Fruits
○○○○○➤

Carbohydrates
○○○○○○○○

Protein & Dairy
●○○○○○○○

Fats
●○○○○

1 pkg. firm, light tofu
  (drained weight of 14 ozs.)
2 tsp. minced garlic
1 Tbsp. olive oil
1 Tbsp. reduced-sodium soy sauce

1. Place tofu on a microwave-safe plate lined with paper towel. Mic tofu, uncovered, for 4 minutes.

   If microwave oven is not available, place block of tofu on a paper towel on a cutting board. Cover with a paper towel and put a few cans of food as weight on top. Allow to stand 20 minutes.

   Discard water and pat tofu with paper towel.

2. Slice tofu into ⅓"-thick slices, or about 10 slices.

3. In a large nonstick skillet over medium heat, sauté garlic in olive oil.

4. Place tofu in skillet and brown over medium-high heat.

5. Flip with a metal spatula and brown the other side.

6. Drizzle soy sauce evenly over tofu. Cook 1–2 minutes.

7. Flip one more time and cook 1 more minute.

Per Serving

Calories 141, Kilojoules 590, Protein 12 g,
Carbohydrates 6 g, Total Fat 8 g, Saturated Fat 1 g,
Monounsaturated Fat 5 g, Polyunsaturated Fat 2 g,
Cholesterol 0 mg, Sodium 419 mg, Fiber *trace*

Tips:

  Browning tofu is the key to the flavor of this recipe, and a non-stick pan makes this an easy recipe. Slightly burnt dark edges are particularly tasty.

  Red chili paste/powder (small amount) may be added to Step 4, or may be served on the side for those who like spicy food.

Dietitian's tip: To limit the sodium content of this Asian dish, use low-sodium soy sauce, which has about 50% less sodium but all of the taste of its full-sodium counterpart.

A Tip —

  To preserve garlic longer, separate garlic cloves from the bud. Place in plastic containers and freeze. Take out what you need when you need it.

Main Dishes– Whole Grains and Pastas

Mushroom Microwave Risotto

Carolyn Spohn
Shawnee, KS

Makes 4 main-dish servings

Prep. Time: 15 minutes
Cooking Time: 20–25 minutes
Standing Time: 5 minutes

Pyramid Servings

Vegetables	●●○○○➤
Fruits	○○○○○➤
Carbohydrates	●●○○○○○○
Protein & Dairy	○○○○○○○
Fats	●○○○○

1 Tbsp. extra-virgin olive oil
½ cup finely chopped onion
1 cup chopped mushrooms
1 clove garlic minced
1 cup uncooked Arborio (or similar variety) rice
3¼ cups <u>hot</u> low-fat, low-salt chicken broth, *divided*
¼ cup freshly grated Parmesan cheese
freshly ground black pepper, *optional*

1. Put olive oil in microwave-safe 2-quart dish. Add chopped onion, mushrooms, and garlic and stir to coat with olive oil.
2. Cook uncovered on high, about 2 minutes, until mushrooms and onion begin to soften.
3. Add uncooked rice and stir to coat grains well.
4. Cook on high 1 minute, or until grains appear translucent.
5. Pour in 3 cups <u>hot</u> broth and cook uncovered on high 9 minutes.

6. Stir well and continue to cook on high 9 more minutes, or until rice is cooked through but still a bit chewy.
7. Remove dish from microwave and let stand, covered, 5 minutes, stirring frequently.
8. Uncover and add Parmesan cheese and remaining ¼ cup broth if needed.
9. Taste for seasoning; add pepper if you wish.

Per Serving

Calories 232, Kilojoules 971, Protein 6 g,
Carbohydrates 40 g, Total Fat 5 g, Saturated Fat 2 g,
Monounsaturated Fat 2.5 g, Polyunsaturated Fat 0.5 g,
Cholesterol 5 mg, Sodium 116 mg, Fiber 1 g

Tip: To make plain risotto, omit the mushrooms. Or for a different flavor, substitute ½ cup dry wine for an equal amount of chicken broth. Although this microwave method for making risotto takes about as much time as the traditional stove-top method, it is much less labor-intensive.

Pumpkin Risotto

Marilyn Mowry
Irving, TX

Makes 4 main-dish servings, or 8 side-dish servings

Prep. Time: 10 minutes
Cooking Time: 30 minutes

3½ cups low-sodium chicken broth
4 tsp. olive oil
2 onions, chopped
1 garlic clove, minced
1 cup raw Arborio rice
1 cup dry white wine
1 cup canned pumpkin puree
¼ cup grated Parmesan cheese
pepper to taste
⅛ tsp. ground nutmeg

Pyramid Servings
(As 4 main-dish servings)

Vegetables
●●○○○➤

Fruits
○○○○○➤

Carbohydrates
●●●○○○○○

Protein & Dairy
●○○○○○○

Fats
●○○○○

Pyramid Servings
(As 8 side-dish servings)

Vegetables
●○○○○➤

Fruits
○○○○○➤

Carbohydrates
●●○○○○○○

Protein & Dairy
○○○○○○○

Fats
○○○○○

1. Bring broth to a boil in a saucepan. Reduce heat and keep at a simmer.
2. Heat oil in another saucepan. Add onions and garlic. Sauté until soft.
3. Add rice to onions and garlic and cook, stirring until outer shell of rice is translucent, about 1 minute.
4. Add wine to rice, stirring until completely absorbed.
5. Begin adding simmering broth, ½ cup at a time, stirring continually until it is fully absorbed before adding more.
6. Continue stirring in simmering broth until rice is tender. The cooking time should be about 20 minutes from the first addition of broth.
7. Stir in pumpkin, cheese, and pepper.
8. Heat to serving temperature. Sprinkle with nutmeg. Serve at once.

Per Serving *(As 4 main-dish servings)*

Calories 336, Kilojoules 1406, Protein 10 g,
Carbohydrates 49 g, Total Fat 6 g, Saturated Fat 2 g,
Monounsaturated Fat 3.6 g, Polyunsaturated Fat 0.4 g,
Cholesterol 8 mg, Sodium 208 mg, Fiber 4 g

Per Serving *(As 8 side-dish servings)*

Calories 168, Kilojoules 703, Protein 6 g,
Carbohydrates 26 g, Total Fat 3 g, Saturated Fat 1 g,
Monounsaturated Fat 1.8 g, Polyunsaturated Fat 0.2 g,
Cholesterol 4 mg, Sodium 104 mg, Fiber 2 g

Rice and Beans

Jamie Schwankl
Ephrata, PA

Makes 4 main-dish servings

Prep. Time: 5 minutes
Cooking Time: 50–60 minutes

2 cups raw brown rice
¾ cup cooked, *or* canned, black beans, rinsed and drained
½ cup salsa

Pyramid Servings

Vegetables
●●○○○➤

Fruits
○○○○○➤

Carbohydrates
●●●○○○○○

Protein & Dairy
●○○○○○○

Fats
○○○○○

1. Prepare rice according to package directions.
2. When fully cooked, immediately stir in beans and salsa.
3. Cook covered on medium to low heat for another 10 minutes.

Per Serving

Calories 377, Kilojoules 1577, Protein 10 g,
Carbohydrates 78 g, Total Fat 3 g, Saturated Fat 0.5 g,
Monounsaturated Fat 1.5 g, Polyunsaturated Fat 1 g,
Cholesterol 0 mg, Sodium 288 mg, Fiber 6 g

Dietitian's tip: Only the hull is removed during the processing of brown rice, so it has more vitamins and minerals than white rice does. The bran coating on brown rice is high in soluble fiber and, like oat bran, helps lower cholesterol. Brown rice has a nut-like flavor and is also chewier than white rice.

Barley Risotto with Grilled Peppers

Jean Turner
Williams Lake, BC

Makes 4 main-dish servings

Prep. Time: 20 minutes
Cooking/Baking Time: 60 minutes

1 sweet red bell pepper
1 yellow bell pepper
4 cups low-sodium, low-fat
   chicken stock, *divided*
1 cup raw pearl barley
1 cup chopped onions
2 tsp. garlic, minced
3 Tbsp. grated low-fat Parmesan cheese
¼ tsp. ground black pepper

Pyramid Servings

Vegetables
●●○○○➤

Fruits
○○○○○➤

Carbohydrates
●●●○○○○○

Protein & Dairy
○○○○○○○○

Fats
○○○○○

1. Cut red and yellow peppers in half and remove seeds. Place on baking sheet, cut sides down. Cook under preheated broiler, turning occasionally, for 20 minutes, or until charred on all sides.

2. Remove from oven. When peppers are cool enough to handle, peel, stem, and core them. Cut into chunks. Set aside.

3. Meanwhile, in a saucepan over medium-high heat, combine 2 cups stock with barley. Cover and bring to a boil.

4. Reduce heat to low. Cook, stirring occasionally, for 30 minutes, or until tender but firm. Set aside.

5. While the barley cooks, in a large non-stick skillet, sprayed with non-stick cooking spray, cook onions and garlic over medium-high heat for 4 minutes, or until softened.

6. Add 1½ cups remaining stock to skillet. Bring to a boil.

7. Add cooked barley and roasted peppers. Bring to a boil, stirring often.

8. Cover. Reduce heat to medium-low and cook, stirring often, for 10 minutes, or until barley is creamy.

9. Add extra stock as needed. Stir in Parmesan cheese and pepper. Serve immediately.

Per Serving
Calories 256, Kilojoules 1071, Protein 12 g,
Carbohydrates 49 g, Total Fat 2 g, Saturated Fat 1.3 g,
Monounsaturated Fat 0.5 g, Polyunsaturated Fat 0.2 g,
Cholesterol 8 mg, Sodium 205 mg, Fiber 10 g

Sweet Pepper Burritos

Anita King
Bellefontaine, OH

Makes 6 main-dish servings

Prep. Time: 20 minutes
Cooking/Baking Time: 50–55
minutes, including cooking the
rice or barley
Standing Time: 5 minutes

Pyramid Servings	
Vegetables ●●○○○➤	
Fruits ○○○○○➤	
Carbohydrates ●●○○○○○○	
Protein & Dairy ◐○○○○○○	
Fats ●○○○○	

1 medium onion, chopped
1 Tbsp. canola oil
2 medium sweet red bell
   peppers, diced
1 medium sweet yellow bell pepper, diced
1 medium green bell pepper, diced
2 tsp. ground cumin
2 cups cooked brown rice, *or* barley
1½ cups low-fat cheddar cheese, shredded
3-oz. pkg. fat-free cream cheese, cubed
½ tsp. pepper
6 whole wheat tortillas, about 6" diameter

1. In a large saucepan, sauté onion in oil for 2 minutes.
2. Add peppers and sauté another 5 minutes.
3. Sprinkle with cumin and sauté 1 minute longer.
4. Stir in rice or barley, cheeses, and pepper. Mix well.
5. Spoon ⅔ cup of vegetable mixture off center on each tortilla. Fold and roll up.
6. Place each roll seam-side down in greased 9 × 13 baking pan.
7. Cover and bake at 425° for 10–15 minutes.
8. Let stand 5 minutes. Serve with salsa (not included in analysis) if you wish.

Per Serving

Calories 300, Kilojoules 1255, Protein 15 g,
Carbohydrates 39 g, Total Fat 9 g, Saturated Fat 2 g,
Monounsaturated Fat 3 g, Polyunsaturated Fat 4 g,
Cholesterol 8 mg, Sodium 398 mg, Fiber 5 g

Tip: We also enjoy this mixture as a main dish without rolling it inside tortillas. I add tomato juice (approximately ½ cup) in Step 4 to moisten the mixture. I serve it alongside refried beans. I place salsa, non-fat plain yogurt, and fresh chopped cilantro on the table to use as toppings.

Quinoa and Spinach

Karen Ceneviva, New Haven, CT

Makes 4 main-dish servings, or 8 side-dish servings

Prep. Time: 20 minutes
Soaking Time: 1 hour
CookingTime: 20–25 minutes

Pyramid Servings (As 4 main-dish servings)	
Vegetables ●●●○○➤	
Fruits ○○○○○➤	
Carbohydrates ●●○○○○○○	
Protein & Dairy ○○○○○○○	
Fats ●●○○○	

1½ cups raw quinoa
3 cups water
3 Tbsp. freshly squeezed
   lemon juice
2 Tbsp. extra-virgin olive oil
¼ tsp. sea salt
pepper to taste, *optional*
2 cups fresh spinach leaves,
   well washed, dried, and
   chopped
3 large scallions, thinly sliced
3 Tbsp. fresh dill

Pyramid Servings (As 8 side-dish servings)	
Vegetables ●●○○○➤	
Fruits ○○○○○➤	
Carbohydrates ●○○○○○○○	
Protein & Dairy ○○○○○○○	
Fats ●○○○○	

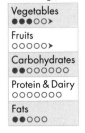

1. Put quinoa in bowl. Cover with water and soak for 1 hour.
2. Drain, discarding soaking water. Rinse quinoa thoroughly.
3. In a good-sized saucepan, bring 3 cups water to boil over medium-high heat. Stir in quinoa.
4. Reduce heat to medium-low, cover, and simmer 15 minutes, or until all liquid has been absorbed.
5. Stir in lemon juice, olive oil, sea salt, and pepper if you wish.

6. Stir in spinach, scallions, and chopped dill.

7. Serve warm, or at room temperature.

Per Serving *(As 4 main-dish servings)*

Calories 304, Kilojoules 1272, Protein 10 g, Carbohydrates 43 g, Total Fat 10 g, Saturated Fat 1.4 g, Monounsaturated Fat 6 g, Polyunsaturated Fat 0.6 g, Cholesterol 0 mg, Sodium 176 mg, Fiber 5 g

Per Serving *(As 8 side-dish servings)*

Calories 152, Kilojoules 636, Protein 5 g, Carbohydrates 22 g, Total Fat 5 g, Saturated Fat 0.7 g, Monounsaturated Fat 3 g, Polyunsaturated Fat 0.3 g, Cholesterol 0 mg, Sodium 88 mg, Fiber 2.5 g

Baked Lentils with Cheese

Kay Nussbaum, Salem, OR
Laura R. Showalter, Dayton, VA
Natalia Showalter, Mt. Solon, VA

Makes 4 main-dish servings, or 8 side-dish servings

Prep. Time: 25–30 minutes
Baking Time: 75–90 minutes

1¾ cups raw lentils, rinsed
2 cups water
1 whole bay leaf
½ tsp. salt
¼ tsp. pepper
⅛ tsp. dried marjoram
⅛ tsp. dried sage
⅛ tsp. dried thyme
2 large onions, chopped
2 cloves garlic, minced
2 cups low-sodium canned tomatoes
2 large carrots, sliced ⅛" thick
½ cup thinly sliced celery
1 bell sweet pepper, chopped, *optional* (not included in analysis)

Pyramid Servings
(As 4 main-dish servings)

Vegetables
●●○○○➤

Fruits
○○○○○➤

Carbohydrates
○○○○○○○○

Protein & Dairy
●●●○○○○

Fats
○○○○○

Pyramid Servings
(As 8 side-dish servings)

Vegetables
●○○○○➤

Fruits
○○○○○➤

Carbohydrates
○○○○○○○○

Protein & Dairy
●◐○○○○

Fats
○○○○○

2 Tbsp. dried parsley flakes
1 cup (4 ozs.) low-fat, low-sodium cheddar cheese, grated

1. Preheat oven to 375°.

2. Mix first 11 ingredients in 9 × 13 baking dish. Cover tightly and bake 30 minutes.

3. Stir in carrots and celery.

4. Bake, covered, 40–50 minutes, or until vegetables are tender.

5. Stir in chopped pepper if you wish, and parsley flakes.

6. Sprinkle shredded cheddar cheese over top. Bake uncovered 5–10 minutes more, until cheese melts.

Per Serving *(As 4 main-dish servings)*

Calories 382, Kilojoules 1598, Protein 26 g, Carbohydrates 66 g, Total Fat 2 g, Saturated Fat 0.8 g, Monounsaturated Fat 0.2 g, Polyunsaturated Fat 1 g, Cholesterol 5 mg, Sodium 400 mg, Fiber 30 g

Per Serving *(As 8 side-dish servings)*

Calories 191, Kilojoules 799, Protein 13 g, Carbohydrates 33 g, Total Fat 1 g, Saturated Fat 0.4 g, Monounsaturated Fat 0.1 g, Polyunsaturated Fat 0.5 g, Cholesterol 2.5 mg, Sodium 200 mg, Fiber 15 g

Asian Rice and Lentil Burgers

Rhoda Atzeff
Lancaster, PA

Makes 4 main-dish servings

Prep. Time: 15–20 minutes
Cooking Time: 60–75 minutes

Pyramid Servings

Vegetables
●●●○○➤
Fruits
○○○○○➤
Carbohydrates
●○○○○○○○
Protein & Dairy
◐○○○○○○
Fats
●○○○○

Burgers:
½ cup raw brown rice
¼ cup raw lentils, rinsed and stones removed
1½ cups water
¼ cup finely chopped cashews
2 Tbsp. unseasoned bread crumbs
2 Tbsp. low-sodium stir-fry sauce
4 medium green onions, finely chopped
egg substitute equivalent to 1 egg, beaten, *or 2 egg whites, beaten*

Vegetable sauce:
1 cup frozen mixed vegetables
½ cup water
2 Tbsp. low-sodium stir-fry sauce

1. Place rice, lentils, and water in 2-quart saucepan. Cover and heat to boiling.
2. Reduce heat to low. Cover and simmer 30–40 minutes, stirring occasionally, until lentils are tender and water is absorbed.
3. Remove lid and cool mixture slightly.
4. In saucepan, mash rice mixture slightly with fork. Stir in remaining burger ingredients.
5. Shape mixture into 4 burgers, each about ½" thick.
6. Spray 10" skillet with cooking spray. Cook burgers in skillet about 10 minutes, turning once halfway through, until golden brown.
7. Remove burgers from skillet. Keep warm.
8. In same skillet, mix sauce ingredients. Cover and heat to boiling.
9. Reduce heat to medium. Add burgers.
10. Cover and cook 5–8 minutes, or until burgers are hot and vegetables are crisp-tender.
11. Serve sauce and burgers over rice. (Note that analysis does not include this additional rice.)

Per Serving

Calories 250, Kilojoules 1046, Protein 10g,
Carbohydrates 38g, Total Fat 6g, Saturated Fat 1g,
Monounsaturated Fat 2.4g, Polyunsaturated Fat 2.6g,
Cholesterol 0mg, Sodium 328mg, Fiber 7g

Pasta Primavera

Marcia S. Myer
Manheim, PA

Makes 6 main-dish servings

Prep. Time: 20–30 minutes
Cooking Time: 25 minutes

Pyramid Servings

Vegetables
●●○○○➤
Fruits
○○○○○➤
Carbohydrates
●●○○○○○○
Protein & Dairy
●○○○○○○
Fats
○○○○○

3 cups broccoli florets, cut bite-size
½ lb. fresh mushrooms, quartered
2 small zucchini, sliced into ¼"-thick rounds
1 Tbsp. olive oil
1–3 cloves garlic, minced, according to your taste preference
1 pint cherry tomatoes, halved
8-oz. pkg. whole-grain fettuccine
black pepper to taste
3 Tbsp. grated reduced-fat Parmesan cheese

Sauce:
¾ cup skim milk
1 Tbsp. olive oil
⅔ cup part-skim ricotta cheese
¼ cup grated reduced-fat Parmesan cheese
2 Tbsp. chopped fresh basil, *or* 1 Tbsp. dried basil
2 tsp. dry sherry

1. In large microwave-safe bowl, layer in broccoli, mushrooms, and zucchini. Cover bowl and microwave on high for 2 minutes.

2. Stir. Cover and cook another 2 minutes on high, or until tender-crisp.

3. In non-stick skillet, heat olive oil. Add garlic and sauté for 1 minute. Add tomatoes and sauté for 2 minutes, or until tomatoes are slightly cooked but not wilted.

4. Cook fettuccine as directed with no salt. Drain. Keep warm.

5. Prepare sauce by combining milk, oil, ricotta cheese, Parmesan cheese, basil, and sherry in a blender.

6. Process until smooth. Heat sauce until warm, on stove or in microwave.

7. In large serving bowl, toss drained pasta, vegetables, and sauce.

8. Garnish with black pepper.

Per Serving

Calories 283, Kilojoules 1184, Protein 13 g,
Carbohydrates 40 g, Total Fat 8 g, Saturated Fat 2 g,
Monounsaturated Fat 4 g, Polyunsaturated Fat 2 g,
Cholesterol 12 mg, Sodium 159 mg, Fiber 7 g

A Tip —

Cook enough for two meals—and you can have a break from meal preparation.

Pasta with Broccoli Rabe

Shirley Hedman
Schenectady, NY

Makes 6 main-dish servings

Prep. Time: 20 minutes
Cooking Time: 20 minutes

Pyramid Servings

| Vegetables |
| ●●○○○▸ |
| Fruits |
| ○○○○○▸ |
| Carbohydrates |
| ●●○○○○○○ |
| Protein & Dairy |
| ○○○○○○○ |
| Fats |
| ●○○○○ |

1 Tbsp. olive oil
3 cloves garlic, minced
dash of red pepper flakes
1 bunch (about 2 cups) broccoli rabe, washed and chopped
1½ cups diced tomatoes
¾ lb. whole-grain uncooked pasta, shells *or* penne
¼ cup reduced-fat grated Parmesan, *or* Romano, cheese

1. Heat oil, garlic, and pepper flakes in large skillet for about 3 minutes.

2. Add chopped broccoli rabe and cook about 5 minutes, until wilted.

3. Add tomatoes and cook about 10 minutes.

4. Meanwhile, in a separate saucepan, cook pasta in plenty of boiling water.

5. Drain. Add to skillet with cooked vegetables. Stir to blend.

6. Place pasta and vegetables in serving bowl. Sprinkle with cheese.

Per Serving

Calories 252, Kilojoules 1054, Protein 9 g,
Carbohydrates 45 g, Total Fat 4 g, Saturated Fat 1 g,
Monounsaturated Fat 2 g, Polyunsaturated Fat 1 g,
Cholesterol 3 mg, Sodium 62 mg, Fiber 3 g

Dietitian's tip: The type of fiber in whole-wheat pasta is insoluble — meaning it doesn't dissolve during digestion. Instead, it maintains its bulk, holds on to water, and, as a result, helps prevent constipation.

Vegetable Spaghetti Sauce

Natalia Showalter
Mt. Solon, VA
Deborah Heatwole
Waynesboro, GA

Makes 14 cups; 1 cup per serving

Prep. Time: 20–30 minutes
Cooking Time: 1–2 hours

Pyramid Servings

Vegetables
●●●○○➤

Fruits
○○○○○➤

Carbohydrates
○○○○○○○○

Protein & Dairy
○○○○○○○

Fats
●○○○○

⅓ cup olive oil
4 medium onions, chopped
4 large bell sweet peppers, chopped
3–6 garlic cloves, minced, according to your taste preference
½ lb. fresh mushrooms, sliced
1 quart low-sodium tomato juice
2 quarts low-sodium chunked tomatoes, drained
6 bay leaves
1 tsp. dried thyme
1 tsp. dried oregano
1 tsp. dried basil
1 tsp. black pepper
1 tsp. chili powder
½ tsp. cumin
½ tsp. cayenne
⅛ cup parsley flakes, dried
¼ cup sugar, *optional* (not included in analysis)
2 Tbsp. honey, *optional* (not included in analysis)

1. Sauté onions, peppers, garlic cloves, and mushrooms in olive oil in a large stockpot over medium heat until onions are tender.
2. Add all remaining ingredients.
3. Cover and simmer 1–2 hours. Remove bay leaves.
4. Serve over cooked spaghetti (not included in analysis).

Per Serving

Calories 114, Kilojoules 477, Protein 3 g,
Carbohydrates 15 g, Total Fat 5 g, Saturated Fat 1 g,
Monounsaturated Fat 3.5 g, Polyunsaturated Fat 0.5 g,
Cholesterol 0 mg, Sodium 110 mg, Fiber 4 g

Variations (not included in analysis):
1. Add ½ tsp. rosemary and 2 Tbsp. red wine vinegar to Step 2 if you wish.
2. Substitute 1 lb. 90% lean ground beef in place of the sliced mushrooms. Or add it as an extra ingredient and keep the mushrooms.
—Deborah Heatwole, Waynesboro, GA

Light Seafood, *or* Poultry, Pasta

Cheryl Householter, Eureka, IL

Makes 6 main-dish servings

Prep. Time: 15 minutes
Cooking Time: 25–30 minutes

Pyramid Servings

Vegetables
●○○○○➤

Fruits
○○○○○➤

Carbohydrates
●●○○○○○○

Protein & Dairy
●○○○○○○

Fats
◐○○○○

8 ozs. whole-wheat linguini, *or* angel hair pasta
3 Tbsp. extra-virgin olive oil, *divided*
1 lb. uncooked rock shrimp, *or* uncooked chicken breast, thinly sliced
3 cloves garlic, minced
3 tomatoes, cut-up, *or* 8 cherry tomatoes, halved
12 fresh basil leaves, thinly sliced
⅛ tsp. pepper

1. Cook pasta as directed on package.
2. Meanwhile, in a large skillet, heat 2 Tbsp. olive oil. Add shrimp or chicken. Cook 2–3 minutes on high heat.
3. Add garlic. Cook 1–2 minutes more.

4. Add tomatoes and basil. Cook 5 minutes longer, or until meat is done. Remove from heat.

5. Toss pasta with remaining 1 Tbsp. oil and with pepper.

6. Toss tomato-meat mixture and pasta together. Serve immediately.

Per Serving

Calories 295, Kilojoules 1234, Protein 21 g,
Carbohydrates 34 g, Total Fat 8 g, Saturated Fat 1 g,
Monounsaturated Fat 5 g, Polyunsaturated Fat 2 g,
Cholesterol 114 mg, Sodium 122 mg, Fiber 5 g

Black Bean Lasagna Rolls

Janelle Reitz, Lancaster, PA

Makes 8 main-dish servings

Prep. Time: 15 minutes
Cooking/Baking Time: 40 minutes

1 cup shredded reduced-fat
  Monterey Jack cheese
1 cup low-fat cottage cheese
4½-oz. can chopped green
  chilies, rinsed and drained
½ tsp. chili powder
8 whole-grain lasagna noodles, uncooked
2 cups cooked black beans, rinsed and
  drained
15½-oz. jar salsa

Pyramid Servings

Vegetables	●○○○○➤
Fruits	○○○○○➤
Carbohydrates	●○○○○○○○
Protein & Dairy	●○○○○○○
Fats	○○○○○

1. Combine first 4 ingredients in a bowl, stirring well.

2. Cook lasagna noodles according to package directions, omitting salt and fat. Drain well. Rinse to keep noodles from sticking together.

3. Spread a portion of cheese mixture over each noodle. Spoon black beans evenly over cheese mixture.

4. Lightly grease a 7 × 11 baking dish. Roll up noodles, jelly-roll fashion, beginning at narrow end. Place lasagna rolls, seam-side down, in baking dish.

5. Pour salsa over rolls.

6. Cover and bake at 350° for 25 minutes, or until thoroughly heated.

Per Serving

Calories 214, Kilojoules 895, Protein 13 g,
Carbohydrates 33 g, Total Fat 4 g, Saturated Fat 2 g,
Monounsaturated Fat 1 g, Polyunsaturated Fat 1 g,
Cholesterol 11 mg, Sodium 786 mg, Fiber 5 g

Variation: Add ½ cup chopped steamed spinach to the cheese mixture in Step 1.
—**Sylvia Martin**, Brownstown, PA

Dietitian's tip: To reduce the amount of sodium in this recipe, use homemade salsa instead of store-bought salsa. See the following recipes: Fresh Chunky Cherry Tomato Salsa (page 244), Fresh Salsa (page 244).

Easy Spinach Lasagna
LaRee Eby
Portland, OR

Makes 12 main-dish servings

Prep. Time: 30 minutes
Chilling Time: 8 hours, or more
Cooking/Baking Time: 1 hour
Standing Time: 10 minutes

Pyramid Servings

Vegetables
●●○○○➤

Fruits
○○○○○➤

Carbohydrates
●○○○○○○○

Protein & Dairy
●○○○○○○

Fats
○○○○○

28-oz. jar low-sodium, low-fat spaghetti sauce
8-oz. can low-sodium tomato sauce
¼ cup water
1 tsp. dried basil
1 tsp. dried oregano
¾ lb. fresh spinach, chopped, *or* 10-oz. box frozen chopped spinach, thawed and squeezed dry
16-oz. container low-fat cottage cheese
egg substitute equivalent to 1 egg, slightly beaten, *or* 2 egg whites, beaten
¼ tsp. black pepper
8-oz. box whole-grain lasagna noodles
2 cups (8 ozs.) grated low-fat mozzarella cheese, *divided*
½ cup reduced-fat Parmesan cheese

1. Mix first 6 ingredients in large bowl.
2. Mix cottage cheese, egg substitute, and black pepper in another bowl.
3. Barely cover bottom of lightly greased 9 × 13 baking dish with spaghetti sauce mixture.
4. Cover that with 3 or 4 uncooked lasagna noodles.
5. Spread some cottage cheese mixture over noodles.
6. Sprinkle with mozzarella.
7. Repeat layers until dish is full.
8. Finish by scattering remaining mozzarella and Parmesan cheeses over top.
9. Cover and refrigerate for 8 hours, or overnight.

10. Uncover. Bake at 350° for 1 hour.
11. Let stand for 10 minutes before serving.

Per Serving

Calories 229, Kilojoules 958, Protein 14 g,
Carbohydrates 28 g, Total Fat 7 g, Saturated Fat 3 g,
Monounsaturated Fat 2 g, Polyunsaturated Fat 2 g,
Cholesterol 17 mg, Sodium 394 mg, Fiber 4.5 g

Chickpea-Stuffed Shells
Karen Burkholder
Narvon, PA

Makes 8 main-dish servings, 2 shells per person

Prep. Time: 30–40 minutes
Cooking/Baking Time: 55–60 minutes

Pyramid Servings

Vegetables
●●○○○➤

Fruits
○○○○○➤

Carbohydrates
●○○○○○○○

Protein & Dairy
●●○○○○○

Fats
○○○○○

16 uncooked jumbo pasta shells
15-oz. can chickpeas, rinsed and drained
2 egg whites
12-oz. carton low-fat cottage cheese
½ cup minced fresh parsley
⅓ cup grated reduced-fat Parmesan cheese
1 small onion, quartered
1 garlic clove, minced
28-oz. jar meatless spaghetti sauce, *divided*
1 cup (4 ozs.) shredded part-skim mozzarella cheese

1. Cook pasta shells according to package directions.
2. Meanwhile, place chickpeas and egg whites in a food processor or blender. Cover and process until smooth.
3. In a bowl, mix chickpeas with cottage cheese, parsley, Parmesan, onion, and garlic. Mix until well blended.
4. Pour 1¼ cups spaghetti sauce into an ungreased 9 × 13 baking dish. Set aside.

5. Stuff drained pasta shells with chickpea-cheese mixture.

6. Place filled shells over sauce. Drizzle with remaining sauce.

7. Bake uncovered at 350° for 30 minutes.

8. Sprinkle with mozzarella cheese.

9. Bake 5–10 minutes longer, or until cheese is melted and sauce is bubbly.

Per Serving

Calories 357, Kilojoules 1494, Protein 20 g,
Carbohydrates 55 g, Total Fat 6 g, Saturated Fat 2 g,
Monounsaturated Fat 2 g, Polyunsaturated Fat 2 g,
Cholesterol 9 mg, Sodium 690 mg, Fiber 5 g

Main Dishes – Beef

Herb Marinated Steak

Linda E. Wilcox
Blythewood, SC

Makes 4 servings

Prep. Time: 10 minutes
Marinating Time: 6–8 hours
Cooking/Baking Time: 12–18 minutes
Standing Time: 10 minutes

¼ cup chopped onion
2 Tbsp. fresh parsley
2 Tbsp. balsamic vinegar
1 Tbsp. olive oil
2 tsp. Dijon-style mustard
1 clove garlic minced
1 lb. London broil, *or* chuck steak

Pyramid Servings

Vegetables ○○○○○➤
Fruits ○○○○○➤
Carbohydrates ○○○○○○○○
Protein & Dairy ●●○○○○○○
Fats ○○○○○

1. Combine onion, parsley, vinegar, oil, mustard, and garlic in a bowl.

2. Place London broil or chuck steak in a sturdy plastic bag. Add onion mixture, spreading it on both sides of the meat. Close bag securely.

3. Place filled bag in a long dish in case of any leaks. Marinate in refrigerator 6–8 hours, or overnight. Turn it over at least once while marinating.

4. Pour off marinade. Place steak on rack in broiler pan so meat is about 5" from heat source. Broil about 6–8 minutes on each side for rare; 9 minutes on each side for medium.

5. When finished broiling, allow meat to stand for 10 minutes.

6. Then carve diagonally across the grain into thin slices.

Per Serving

Calories 210, Kilojoules 879, Protein 23 g,
Carbohydrates 4 g, Total Fat 10 g, Saturated Fat 3 g,
Monounsaturated Fat 6 g, Polyunsaturated Fat 1 g,
Cholesterol 64 mg, Sodium 132 mg, Fiber *trace*

Tip: You can grill the steak, rather than broiling it.

Dietitian's tip: *Marinating meat before grilling not only adds flavor but also reduces the chance that cancer-causing substances will form on the meat during grilling. Marinating also helps keep meat from burning and charring.*

Braised Beef with Cranberries

Audrey L. Kneer, Williamsfield, IL

Makes 8 servings

Prep. Time: 20 minutes
Cooking/Baking Time: 1¾–2¼
hours

2 lbs. sliced, well trimmed
    top round beef
½ tsp. red pepper
1 Tbsp. olive oil
½ cup peeled and diced
    turnip
1 medium onion, chopped
1 green bell sweet pepper, chopped
1 medium carrot, chopped
1 rib celery, cut fine
1 Tbsp. garlic powder
1 cup apple juice
1 cup fresh, *or* frozen (thawed), cranberries
1 Tbsp. cooking sherry
1 sprig parsley
1 bay leaf

Pyramid Servings

Vegetables
●○○○○➤

Fruits
◐○○○○➤

Carbohydrates
○○○○○○○○

Protein & Dairy
●○○○○○○

Fats
●○○○○

1. Rub beef with red pepper. Set aside.
2. Preheat oven to 350°.
3. Heat oil in heavy skillet until hot. Stir in next 6 ingredients.
4. Sauté over medium heat until softened, about 10 minutes.
5. Put half of vegetable mixture in baking dish.
6. Lay beef over vegetables.
7. Spread remaining vegetable mixture over meat.
8. Add apple juice, cranberries, sherry, parsley, and bay leaf to baking dish.
9. Cover and bake 45 minutes.
10. Turn meat over. Cover and continue baking another 45–75 minutes, or until beef is tender but not dried out.

Per Serving

Calories 196, Kilojoules 820, Protein 27 g,
Carbohydrates 10 g, Total Fat 5 g, Saturated Fat 1 g,
Monounsaturated Fat 2.5 g, Polyunsaturated Fat 1.5 g,
Cholesterol 58 mg, Sodium 97 mg, Fiber 2 g

Tip: Bake some potatoes in the oven at the same time as the meat dish.

A Tip —

Always use a portable oven thermometer inside your oven. Most ovens vary at least 25 degrees from their supposed degree settings which can alter baking times significantly.

Veggie and Beef Stir-Fry

Margaret H. Moffitt
Middleton, TN

Makes 4 servings

Prep. Time: 15–20 minutes
Cooking Time: 30–35 minutes

¼ lb. beef tenderloin
2 tsp. olive oil
1 onion, chopped coarsely
1 small zucchini, chopped
    coarsely
3 cups coarsely chopped
    broccoli florets
half a small yellow squash, chopped
    coarsely
½ cup uncooked brown rice
1 cup water
1 tsp. low-sodium teriyaki sauce

1. Cut beef into ¼" wide strips.
2. In a good-sized skillet, stir-fry beef in 2 tsp. olive oil just until no longer pink, about 2 minutes.
3. Add onion and other vegetables. Stir-fry until tender-crisp, about 5–7 minutes.
4. To cook rice, place rice and water in a saucepan. Cover, and bring to a boil. Adjust heat so that mixture simmers, covered. Cook rice until tender, about 20–25 minutes.
5. Just before serving over rice, add teriyaki sauce to beef and vegetables.

Pyramid Servings

Vegetables	●○○○○➤
Fruits	○○○○○➤
Carbohydrates	●○○○○○○○
Protein & Dairy	●○○○○○○
Fats	○○○○○

Per Serving

Calories 206, Kilojoules 862, Protein 11 g,
Carbohydrates 30 g, Total Fat 5 g, Saturated Fat 1 g,
Monounsaturated Fat 2.6 g, Polyunsaturated Fat 1.4 g,
Cholesterol 15 mg, Sodium 80 mg, Fiber 4 g

Beef and Zucchini Casserole

Judi Manos, West Islip, NY

Makes 6 servings

Prep. Time: 15 minutes
Cooking/Baking Time: 50–65
    minutes

2 tsp. canola oil
½ cup finely chopped onions
1 lb. (3 small) zucchini, cut
    into ¼"-thick slices
¼ lb. fresh mushrooms, sliced
1 lb. 95%-lean ground beef
14½-oz. can sliced tomatoes, undrained,
    no salt added
½ tsp. garlic powder
½ tsp. dried oregano
¼ cup grated Parmesan cheese

1. Preheat oven to 350°.
2. Heat oil in large skillet. Add onions and stir until tender and light golden in color.
3. Add zucchini and mushrooms to skillet. Cook over medium heat 3–4 minutes, stirring lightly.
4. Put zucchini mixture into lightly greased 2-quart baking dish.
5. Place ground beef in skillet. Cook over medium heat until no longer pink, stirring frequently. Drain off drippings.
6. Add tomatoes, garlic powder, and oregano to meat in skillet. Mix well.
7. Spoon meat mixture over zucchini in baking dish.
8. Sprinkle cheese on top.
9. Bake, uncovered, 35–45 minutes, or until cheese is lightly browned and dish is heated through.

Pyramid Servings

Vegetables	●●○○○➤
Fruits	○○○○○➤
Carbohydrates	○○○○○○○○
Protein & Dairy	●○○○○○○
Fats	○○○○○

Per Serving

Calories 164, Kilojoules 686, Protein 20 g,
Carbohydrates 6 g, Total Fat 7 g, Saturated Fat 2.5 g,
Monounsaturated Fat 3 g, Polyunsaturated Fat 1.5 g,
Cholesterol 50 mg, Sodium 117 mg, Fiber 2 g

Bob's Zesty Meaty Pasta

Carol Collins
Holly Springs, NC

Makes 8 servings

Prep. Time: 10 minutes
Cooking Time: 1¾–2¼ hours

Pyramid Servings

| Vegetables |
| ●●○○○○➤ |
| Fruits |
| ○○○○○➤ |
| Carbohydrates |
| ●●●○○○○○ |
| Protein & Dairy |
| ●○○○○○○○ |
| Fats |
| ○○○○○ |

½ Tbsp. olive oil
1½ cups chopped onion
1 lb. 95%-lean ground sirloin,
  or bison
3 garlic cloves, minced
2 tsp. black pepper
1 tsp. dried oregano
28-oz. can tomato puree, no salt added
15-oz. can tomato sauce, no salt added
½ tsp. sugar, *optional* (not included in
  analysis)
1 lb. uncooked whole wheat pasta

1. Heat olive oil in large stockpot over medium heat. Add onions and sauté until golden. Remove onions with slotted spoon and reserve.

2. Add ground meat and garlic to stockpot. Cook until meat is browned and no longer pink inside.

3. Add reserved onions, black pepper, oregano, tomato puree, and tomato sauce. Cook over low heat, partially covered, for 1½ hours.

4. Stir occasionally. Add water by ¼ cupfuls if sauce appears too thick.

5. Adjust taste with sugar if you wish.

6. Cook pasta according to package directions. Drain and top with pasta sauce.

Per Serving

Calories 381, Kilojoules 1594, Protein 22 g,
Carbohydrates 62 g, Total Fat 5 g, Saturated Fat 1.5 g,
Monounsaturated Fat 2 g, Polyunsaturated Fat 1 g,
Cholesterol 35 mg, Sodium 90 mg, Fiber 10 g

Tips:
  1. If preparing this recipe for young children, reduce black pepper to 1 tsp.
  2. Serve this sauce over hearty pasta like thick spaghetti or cavatappi (spiral hollow noodles).
  3. Use leftover sauce as a topping for pizza.

Lasagna Mexicana

Barbara Walker, Sturgis, SD

Makes 9 servings

Prep. Time: 20 minutes
Cooking/Baking Time: 80–90
minutes

1 lb. 95%-lean ground beef
16-oz. can fat-free refried
  beans
2 tsp. dried oregano
1 tsp. ground cumin
¾ tsp. garlic powder
9 uncooked lasagna noodles, *divided*
1 cup salsa (or make your own Fresh
  Salsa, page 244)
1 cup water
2 cups reduced-fat sour cream
2¼-oz. can sliced ripe olives, drained
1 cup shredded reduced-fat Mexican-blend
  cheese
½ cup sliced green onions

Pyramid Servings	
Vegetables	●●○○○➤
Fruits	○○○○○➤
Carbohydrates	●○○○○○○○
Protein & Dairy	●●○○○○○
Fats	●○○○○

1. Brown beef in stockpot over medium heat until no longer pink. Drain off drippings.
2. Stir in beans and seasonings. Heat through.
3. Place three uncooked noodles in a lightly greased 9 × 13 baking dish lightly coated with non-stick cooking spray.
4. Cover with half of meat mixture.
5. Repeat layers of noodles and meat.
6. Top with remaining noodles.
7. Combine salsa and water in a bowl. Pour over noodles.
8. Cover. Bake at 350° for 60–70 minutes, or until noodles are tender.
9. Spread with sour cream.
10. Sprinkle with olives, cheese, and onions.

Per Serving

Calories 335, Kilojoules 1402, Protein 22 g,
Carbohydrates 32 g, Total Fat 13 g, Saturated Fat 7 g,
Monounsaturated Fat 3 g, Polyunsaturated Fat 3 g,
Cholesterol 67 mg, Sodium 423 mg, Fiber 6 g

Zucchini Lasagna

Carolyn Snader, Ephrata, PA

Makes 6 servings

Prep. Time: 15–20 minutes
Cooking/Baking Time: 30–35
minutes

6 cups sliced, unpeeled,
  zucchini
1 lb. 95%-lean ground beef
½ tsp. dried basil
½ tsp. dried oregano
⅛ tsp. garlic powder
6-oz. can tomato paste, no salt added
1 cup low-fat cottage cheese
egg substitute equivalent to 1 egg, *or* 2 egg
  whites
2 cups shredded low-fat mozzarella cheese,
  divided

Pyramid Servings	
Vegetables	●●○○○➤
Fruits	○○○○○➤
Carbohydrates	○○○○○○○○
Protein & Dairy	●●○○○○○
Fats	○○○○○

1. Cook sliced zucchini 7–10 minutes on High in microwave, if you wish.
2. Brown ground beef in a skillet.
3. Add basil, oregano, and garlic powder to the beef.
4. Add tomato paste to meat and stir together.
5. In a bowl, mix cottage cheese, egg, and 1 cup mozzarella cheese together.
6. In a lightly greased 9 × 13 baking dish, layer in half the zucchini, half the meat with seasonings, and half the cottage cheese mixture.
7. Repeat layers.
8. Top with remaining cup of mozzarella cheese.
9. Bake, uncovered, at 350° for 30–35 minutes.

Per Serving

Calories 274, Kilojoules 1146, Protein 32 g,
Carbohydrates 12 g, Total Fat 11 g, Saturated Fat 6 g,
Monounsaturated Fat 4 g, Polyunsaturated Fat 1 g,
Cholesterol 71 mg, Sodium 368 mg, Fiber 2.5 g

Cabbage Lasagna

Sylvia Eberly
Reinholds, PA

Makes 8 servings

Prep. Time: 15 minutes
Cooking/Baking Time: 45–50 minutes

Pyramid Servings		
Vegetables		
●●○○○➤		
Fruits		
○○○○○➤		
Carbohydrates		
○○○○○○○○		
Protein & Dairy		
●●○○○○○		
Fats		
○○○○○		

1 medium to large head
    of cabbage, about 6" in
    diameter
1 Tbsp. olive oil
2 garlic cloves, minced or
    pressed
1 medium onion, chopped
1 green bell sweet pepper
¾ lb. 95%-lean ground beef
6-oz. can tomato paste, no salt added
8-oz. can tomato sauce, no salt added
1–3 tsp. dried oregano, according to your
    taste preference
2 tsp. dried basil, *optional*
1 tsp. black pepper
1 cup grated reduced-fat mozzarella
    cheese, *divided*
½ cup low-fat ricotta, *or* low-fat cottage
    cheese, *divided*
½ cup freshly grated Parmesan cheese

1. Preheat oven to 350°.
2. Wash cabbage and remove tough outer leaves. Cut head in half and slice.
3. Arrange finely sliced cabbage in a steamer basket and steam about 3–5 minutes. (You may need to do this in 2 batches.)
4. Drain cabbage well. Set aside.
5. Sauté garlic, onion, and green pepper in olive oil in large skillet over medium heat.
6. Add ground beef to skillet and brown thoroughly. Drain off any drippings.
7. Add tomato paste, tomato sauce, and seasonings to beef mixture. Combine well.
8. Lightly grease a 9 × 13 baking pan. Drain cabbage again. Make layers starting with half the cabbage leaves, half the meat mixture, one-third of the mozzarella, and half the ricotta cheese.
9. Add another layer with remaining cabbage, then the meat mixture, half the mozzarella, and all the remaining ricotta cheese.
10. Top with remaining mozzarella.
11. Finish by scattering Parmesan on top.
12. Bake, covered, for 20 minutes.
13. Uncover and bake 5–10 minutes more, or until lightly browned.

Per Serving
Calories 230, Kilojoules 962, Protein 20 g,
Carbohydrates 18 g, Total Fat 9 g, Saturated Fat 5 g,
Monounsaturated Fat 3 g, Polyunsaturated Fat 1 g,
Cholesterol 49 mg, Sodium 330 mg, Fiber 5 g

Stuffed Cabbage

Becky Gehman
Bergton, VA

Makes 6 servings

Prep. Time: 15–20 minutes
Cooking Time: 1 hour, 40 minutes

Pyramid Servings		
Vegetables		
●○○○○➤		
Fruits		
○○○○○➤		
Carbohydrates		
◑○○○○○○○		
Protein & Dairy		
●○○○○○○		
Fats		
○○○○○		

6–7 large cabbage leaves
1 lb. 95%-fat-free hamburger,
    or extra-lean turkey burger
1 tsp. diced fine onion
¼ tsp. salt
½ tsp. pepper
3 Tbsp. brown rice, uncooked
1 can low-sodium tomato soup
1 soup can water
1 tsp. Italian seasoning without salt, such
    as Mrs. Dash™, *optional*
1 Tbsp. vinegar

1. Place cabbage leaves in large stockpot. Cover with water. Cover pot and cook cabbage

until just tender. Remove leaves from water and drain.

2. Mix hamburger or turkey burger, onion, salt, pepper, and rice together in a bowl.

3. Divide this mixture among the 6 or 7 cooked cabbage leaves. Place in the middle of each leaf.

4. Wrap cabbage leaves around meat mixture to make 6 bundles. Secure each with 2 tooth-picks to keep them from unwrapping.

5. Heat tomato soup, water, and Italian seasoning if you wish, in a large saucepan.

6. Carefully lay cabbage bundles in tomato soup mixture.

7. Allow to simmer, covered, 1½ hours.

8. Stir in vinegar 10 minutes before end of cooking time.

Per Serving

Calories 172, Kilojoules 720, Protein 18 g,
Carbohydrates 13 g, Total Fat 5 g, Saturated Fat 2 g,
Monounsaturated Fat 1.5 g, Polyunsaturated Fat 1.5 g,
Cholesterol 47 mg, Sodium 174 mg, Fiber 2 g

Dietitian's tip: Substituting ground turkey breast for regular ground beef sheds about 200 calories, 7 grams of fat, and 4 grams of saturated fat.

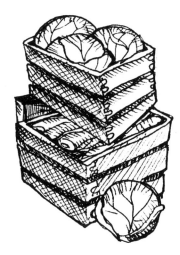

Main Dishes–Pork

Ginger Pork Chops
Mary Fisher
Leola, PA

Makes 2 servings

Prep. Time: 10 minutes
Cooking/Broiling Time: 15 minutes

2 6-oz. (4 ozs. meat) bone-in
   pork chops
1 tsp. cornstarch
2 Tbsp. low-sodium soy sauce
¼ cup honey
1 garlic clove, minced
dash of ground ginger
1 Tbsp. sliced green onion

Pyramid Servings	
Vegetables	○○○○○➤
Fruits	○○○○○➤
Carbohydrates	○○○○○○○○
Protein & Dairy	●●●○○○○
Fats	○○○○○
Sweets	◖

1. Broil pork chops 3–4" from heat for 5–6 minutes on each side.

2. In small saucepan, combine cornstarch and soy sauce until smooth.

3. Stir in honey, garlic, and ginger.

4. Bring to a boil. Cook and stir for 1 minute, or until thickened.

5. Drizzle over cooked chops.

6. Sprinkle with green onion just before serving.

Per Serving

Calories 351, Kilojoules 1469, Protein 32 g,
Carbohydrates 38 g, Total Fat 8 g, Saturated Fat 2.5 g,
Monounsaturated Fat 3.5 g, Polyunsaturated Fat 2 g,
Cholesterol 95 mg, Sodium 665 mg, Fiber *trace*

Baked Pork Chops

Sharon Easter
Yuba City, CA

Makes 4 servings

Prep. Time: 15–20 minutes
Cooking/Baking Time: 2 hours

Pyramid Servings
Vegetables ●○○○○➤
Fruits ○○○○○➤
Carbohydrates ◐○○○○○○○○
Protein & Dairy ●◐○○○○○
Fats ○○○○○

⅛ tsp. pepper
1 tsp. paprika
4 pork chops (about 1 lb. total)
1 onion, sliced
half a green bell sweet
    pepper, sliced in rings
1½ cups canned stewed tomatoes,
    undrained, no salt added
⅓ cup raw brown rice
1½ cups water

1. Mix pepper and paprika in a flat dish. Dredge chops in seasoning mixture.
2. Brown chops on both sides in hot non-stick skillet.
3. Place browned chops side-by-side in baking dish. Place 1 slice onion and 1 ring of green pepper on top of each chop.
4. Spoon tomatoes over top.
5. Brown rice in same skillet as you used for browning chops.
6. Stir water into rice, stirring up any drippings.
7. Spoon rice and water over chops.
8. Cover and bake at 350° for 1–1½ hours, or until rice and chops are tender but not dry.

Per Serving

Calories 242, Kilojoules 1013, Protein 27 g,
Carbohydrates 22 g, Total Fat 5 g, Saturated Fat 1 g,
Monounsaturated Fat 2.5 g, Polyunsaturated Fat 1.5 g,
Cholesterol 73 mg, Sodium 109 mg, Fiber 3 g

Pork Kabobs in Pita Bread

Susan Kasting
Jenks, OK

Makes 8 servings

Prep. Time: 20 minutes
Marinating Time: 8 hours or
    overnight
Grilling Time: 8–10 minutes

Pyramid Servings
Vegetables ○○○○○➤
Fruits ○○○○○➤
Carbohydrates ●◐○○○○○○○
Protein & Dairy ●●○○○○○
Fats ○○○○○

Marinade:
2 lbs. boneless pork loin, cut
    into 1" cubes
¼ cup vegetable oil
¼ cup chopped onion
3 Tbsp. lemon juice
1 Tbsp. chopped parsley
1 clove garlic, minced
½ tsp. dried marjoram
⅛ tsp. pepper

Sauce:
1 cup plain fat-free yogurt
½ cup chopped cucumber
1 Tbsp. chopped onion
1 Tbsp. chopped parsley
1 clove garlic, minced
1 tsp. lemon juice

8 whole wheat pita bread rounds

1. Mix marinade and pork in a re-sealable plastic bag.
2. Place bag with meat and marinade in a bowl (in case of leaks). Refrigerate overnight.
3. Mix sauce ingredients in a bowl.
4. Drain pork. Place on skewers or on a grill pan.
5. Grill 8–10 minutes, turning over at least once.
6. Serve pork in pita bread topped with sauce.

Per Serving

Calories 301, Kilojoules 1259, Protein 33 g,
Carbohydrates 33 g, Total Fat 5 g, Saturated Fat 1 g,
Monounsaturated Fat 1.5 g, Polyunsaturated Fat 2.5 g,
Cholesterol 74 mg, Sodium 428 mg, Fiber 6 g

Tip: Heat pitas to make them pliable.

Dietitian's tip: Healthy cooking techniques—such as braising, broiling, grilling, and steaming—can capture the flavor and nutrients of your food without adding excessive amounts of fat, oil, or sodium. If your recipe calls for frying the ingredients in oil or butter, try baking, broiling, or poaching the food instead.

A Tip —

Wrap cut-up onions or peppers in a paper towel before placing them in a ziplock bag and refrigerating. The paper towel absorbs moisture and delays spoiling.

Healthy Joes
Gladys M. High
Ephrata, PA

Makes 4 servings

Prep. Time: 20 minutes
Cooking Time: 20 minutes

¾ lb. 90%-lean ground pork loin
1 cup chopped onion
1 medium bell sweet pepper, chopped
1½ cups diced tomatoes, no salt added, undrained
1 medium zucchini, shredded, *optional*
1 Tbsp. chili powder
1 tsp. paprika
½ tsp. minced garlic
pepper to taste
3 Tbsp. tomato paste
4 whole wheat hamburger buns

Pyramid Servings

Vegetables ●●○○○▶
Fruits ○○○○○▶
Carbohydrates ●●○○○○○○
Protein & Dairy ●◐○○○○○
Fats ○○○○○

1. In large skillet, cook ground pork, onion, and bell pepper until meat is brown and onion is tender. Drain off drippings.
2. Stir in diced tomatoes, zucchini if you wish, chili powder, paprika, garlic, and pepper. Cover and bring to a boil. Reduce heat.
3. Add tomato paste to thicken. Simmer, uncovered, for 5 minutes.
4. Spoon mixture into buns and enjoy.

Per Serving

Calories 343, Kilojoules 1435, Protein 27 g,
Carbohydrates 44 g, Total Fat 7 g, Saturated Fat 2 g,
Monounsaturated Fat 3.5 g, Polyunsaturated Fat 1.5 g,
Cholesterol 53 mg, Sodium 273 mg, Fiber 7 g

Dietitian's tip: Substituting ground turkey breast for regular ground beef sheds about 200 calories, 7 grams of fat and 4 grams of saturated fat.

Beans with Pork

Lauren Eberhard
Seneca, IL

Makes 6 servings

Prep. Time: 10 minutes
Cooking Time: 10 minutes

Pyramid Servings	
Vegetables	⚬⚬⚬⚬⚬▸
Fruits	⚬⚬⚬⚬⚬▸
Carbohydrates	⚬⚬⚬⚬⚬⚬⚬⚬
Protein & Dairy	●●⚬⚬⚬⚬⚬
Fats	⚬⚬⚬⚬⚬

2 15-oz. cans white beans,
  rinsed and drained
1 smoked pork chop (about
  4 ozs. lean meat), cut into
  small pieces
½ cup fresh mushrooms
  chopped
½ cup frozen peas
¼ cup low-fat, low-sodium chicken stock
  (use more if needed)
½ tsp. dried basil

1. Put all ingredients in skillet and mix well.
2. Cover and warm through over medium heat.

Per Serving

Calories 217, Kilojoules 908, Protein 16 g,
Carbohydrates 34 g, Total Fat 2 g, Saturated Fat 0.5 g,
Monounsaturated Fat 0.9 g, Polyunsaturated Fat 0.6 g,
Cholesterol 11 mg, Sodium 294 mg, Fiber 8 g

Dietitian's tip: White beans get their name from their light color. You can use any variety in this recipe, including marrow beans, Great Northern beans or navy beans. White beans are a good source of many nutrients, including iron, folate, magnesium, phosphorus and potassium.

Vegetable Pork Fried Rice with Cabbage

Elizabeth L. Richards
Rapid City, SD

Makes 4 servings

Prep. Time: 15–20 minutes
Cooking Time: 30 minutes

Pyramid Servings	
Vegetables	●●⚬⚬⚬▸
Fruits	⚬⚬⚬⚬⚬▸
Carbohydrates	●●⚬⚬⚬⚬⚬⚬
Protein & Dairy	●●⚬⚬⚬⚬⚬
Fats	⚬⚬⚬⚬⚬

1 cup uncooked brown rice
1 medium onion, chopped
1–2 cloves garlic, diced fine
1 cup sliced celery
1 lb. 90%-lean ground pork
  loin
1½ cups mixed frozen vegetables
1½ cups cabbage, coarsely chopped
¼–½ tsp. pepper, according to your taste
  preference
egg substitute equivalent to 1 egg, *or* 2 egg
  whites, well beaten
2 tsp. low-sodium soy sauce

1. Steam or cook rice according to package directions while making the rest of the recipe.
2. Sweat onion, garlic and celery until just tender in a large non-stick skillet. Remove from skillet to a bowl.
3. Cook pork in skillet until no longer pink.
4. Add mixed vegetables and chopped cabbage. Stir until tender-crisp.
5. Return lightly cooked onions, garlic, and celery to skillet.
6. Stir in pepper.
7. Pour beaten egg over ingredients in skillet and stir until egg is just-cooked.
8. Stir cooked rice into meat and vegetables.
9. Stir in low-sodium soy sauce.

Per Serving
Calories 411, Kilojoules 1720, Protein 34 g,
Carbohydrates 51 g, Total Fat 7 g, Saturated Fat 3 g,
Monounsaturated Fat 3 g, Polyunsaturated Fat 1 g,
Cholesterol 70 mg, Sodium 285 mg, Fiber 6 g

Dietitian's tip: Rice that has been cooked and refrigerated overnight (up to 3 days ahead of time) makes better fried rice because the rice tends to clump together. Before using, break up the large clumps with a spoon.

Tomato Ham Pasta
Anna Stoltzfus
Honey Brook, PA

Makes 8 servings

Prep. Time: 15 minutes
Cooking Time: 20 minutes

3 cups uncooked whole wheat
    penne pasta
2 garlic cloves, minced
1 Tbsp. olive oil
4 medium tomatoes, peeled,
    seeded, and chopped
1 cup fully cooked and diced low-sodium
    lean ham
½ tsp. salt-free Italian seasoning
¼ tsp. pepper

Pyramid Servings

| Vegetables |
| ●○○○○➤ |
| Fruits |
| ○○○○○➤ |
| Carbohydrates |
| ●●○○○○○○ |
| Protein & Dairy |
| ◐○○○○○○ |
| Fats |
| ○○○○○ |

1. Cook pasta according to package directions.
2. Meanwhile, in a large skillet sauté garlic in oil until tender.
3. Add tomatoes. Cover and simmer 5 minutes.
4. Stir in ham and seasonings. Cook 8 minutes.
5. Drain pasta and add to ham mixture.

Per Serving
Calories 220, Kilojoules 920, Protein 11 g,
Carbohydrates 35 g, Total Fat 4 g, Saturated Fat 1 g,
Monounsaturated Fat 2 g, Polyunsaturated Fat 1 g,
Cholesterol 15 mg, Sodium 283 mg, Fiber 5 g

Variations:
    1. Add 1–2 cups thinly sliced zucchini or yellow squash to skillet in Step 2. Sauté along with garlic.
    2. Serve with a dusting of Parmesan cheese (not included in analyses).
    —**Linda E. Wilcox**, Blythewood, S.C.

Dietitian's tip: Though this recipe calls for penne — a diagonally cut tube pasta with ridges — you can substitute any type of pasta, including mostaccioli or ziti (smooth tubes), rotelle (spiral twists), or farfalle (bow tie).

A Tip —

Don't be afraid to ask the experienced cooks in your church and community for their recipes. At age 64, I still do.

Main Dishes– Poultry

Sesame Ginger Chicken
Joanne E. Martin
Stevens, PA

Makes 4 servings

Prep. Time: 10–15 minutes
Grilling/Broiling Time: 8–10 minutes

2 Tbsp. light soy sauce
2 Tbsp. honey
1 Tbsp. sesame seeds, toasted
½ tsp. ground ginger
4 (1 lb. total) boneless skinless chicken breast halves
2 green onions with tops, cut into thin strips

Pyramid Servings	
Vegetables	○○○○○➤
Fruits	○○○○○➤
Carbohydrates	○○○○○○○○
Protein & Dairy	●○○○○○○○
Fats	○○○○○
Sweets	●

1. In a small bowl, combine the first four ingredients. Set aside.
2. Flatten each chicken breast to ¼" thickness.
3. Grill over medium-hot heat, turning and basting frequently with soy sauce mixture for 8 minutes, or until juices run clear. Or broil instead of grilling, following the same procedure.
4. Garnish with onions just before serving.

Per Serving	
Calories 180, Kilojoules 753, Protein 27 g,	
Carbohydrates 12 g, Total Fat 2.5 g, Saturated Fat 0.5 g,	
Monounsaturated Fat 1 g, Polyunsaturated Fat 1 g,	
Cholesterol 66 mg, Sodium 339 mg, Fiber 0.5 g	

Dietitian's tip: To see if the chicken is cooked through to its center, cut into the thickest part. Any juices should run clear, and the meat should show no signs of uncooked or pink flesh. Using a food thermometer, check to make sure it registers 165°F.

Oven Chicken Fingers
Barb Harvey
Quarryville, PA

Makes 6 servings

Prep. Time: 20 minutes
Cooking/Baking Time: 20 minutes

1 cup Italian bread crumbs
2 Tbsp. grated Parmesan cheese
1 garlic clove, minced
2 Tbsp. vegetable oil
6 (about 2 lbs. total) boneless skinless chicken breast halves

Pyramid Servings	
Vegetables	○○○○○➤
Fruits	○○○○○➤
Carbohydrates	●○○○○○○○
Protein & Dairy	●●○○○○○
Fats	●○○○○
Sweets	◐

Honey Mustard Sauce:
2 Tbsp. cornstarch
1 cup water, *divided*
½ cup honey
¼ cup prepared mustard

1. In plastic bag, mix bread crumbs and cheese.
2. In a small bowl, combine garlic and oil.
3. Flatten chicken to ½" thickness. Cut into 1"-wide strips.
4. Dip each strip in garlic oil.
5. Coat each with crumb mixture. Place on a greased baking sheet without letting the strips touch each other.
6. Bake at 350° for 20 minutes, or until golden brown.

7. To make sauce, dissolve cornstarch in 1 Tbsp. water in a saucepan.

8. Stir in honey, mustard, and remaining water.

9. Bring to a boil over medium heat, stirring constantly.

10. Serve as a dipping sauce for the chicken fingers.

Per Serving

Calories 382, Kilojoules 1598, Protein 36 g,
Carbohydrates 41 g, Total Fat 8 g, Saturated Fat 1.5 g,
Monounsaturated Fat 3 g, Polyunsaturated Fat 3.5 g,
Cholesterol 84 mg, Sodium 585 mg, Fiber 1.5 g

Dietitian's tip: By using boneless skinless chicken breast instead of chicken wings, you cut fat and saturated fat by half and save more than 100 calories.

A Tip —

To clear honey out of your measuring cup easily, first spray the measuring cup with cooking spray.

Chicken Cutlets

Dorothy VanDeest
Memphis, TN

Makes 6 servings

Prep. Time: 20 minutes
Baking Time: 20–25 minutes

6 (about 1½ lbs. total) boneless skinless chicken breast halves
1¼ cups dry bread crumbs
½ cup reduced-fat Parmesan cheese topping
2 Tbsp. dry wheat germ
1 tsp. dried basil
½ tsp. garlic powder
1 cup low-fat plain yogurt

Pyramid Servings

Vegetables
○○○○○➤

Fruits
○○○○○➤

Carbohydrates
●○○○○○○○

Protein & Dairy
●●○○○○○

Fats
○○○○○

1. Flatten each chicken breast half to ½"-thickness.

2. In a shallow dish, combine bread crumbs, Parmesan topping, wheat germ, basil, and garlic powder.

3. Place the yogurt in another shallow dish.

4. Dip chicken in yogurt, then coat with crumb mixture.

5. Place in a 10 × 15 baking pan coated with non-stick cooking spray.

6. Bake, uncovered, at 350° for 20–25 minutes, or until juices run clear.

Per Serving

Calories 279, Kilojoules 1167, Protein 33 g,
Carbohydrates 24 g, Total Fat 5 g, Saturated Fat 2 g,
Monounsaturated Fat 2 g, Polyunsaturated Fat 1 g,
Cholesterol 74 mg, Sodium 399 mg, Fiber 1.5 g

Basil Chicken Strips

Mary Fisher
Leola, PA

Makes 4 servings

Prep. Time: 10 minutes
Cooking Time: 10–12 minutes

Pyramid Servings

Vegetables	○○○○○▸
Fruits	○○○○○▸
Carbohydrates	●○○○○○○○
Protein & Dairy	●○○○○○○
Fats	●○○○○

1 lb. boneless skinless
  chicken strips
4 Tbsp. flour
4 Tbsp. tub-style margarine,
  non-hydrogenated
1 clove garlic, minced,
  optional
4 Tbsp. red wine vinegar
1 tsp. dried basil
¼ cup fresh parsley, *optional*
¼ cup fresh cilantro, chopped, *optional*

1. In a large re-sealable bag, shake chicken strips in flour until coated.
2. In a large skillet over medium-high heat, melt margarine.
3. Add chicken, and garlic if you wish, and sauté 5 minutes.
4. Stir in vinegar, basil, and parsley, and cilantro, if you wish. Cook until chicken juices run clear.
5. Serve over brown or wild rice (not included in analyses).

Per Serving

Calories 257, Kilojoules 1075, Protein 27 g,
Carbohydrates 7 g, Total Fat 13 g, Saturated Fat 2 g,
Monounsaturated Fat 8 g, Polyunsaturated Fat 3 g,
Cholesterol 66 mg, Sodium 230 mg, Fiber *trace*

Tomato-Topped Chicken

Carol Sherwood
Batavia, NY

Makes 2 servings

Prep. Time: 15–20 minutes
Marinating Time: 2 hours
Baking Time: 30–35 minutes

Pyramid Servings

Vegetables	●○○○○▸
Fruits	○○○○○▸
Carbohydrates	●○○○○○○○
Protein & Dairy	●○○○○○○
Fats	○○○○○

2 boneless skinless chicken
  breast halves, about 5 ozs.
  each
½ cup fat-free Italian salad
  dressing, *divided*
4 tomato slices, each ¼" thick
4 tsp. seasoned bread crumbs
1 tsp. minced fresh basil, *or* ¼ tsp. dried
  basil
1 tsp. grated Parmesan cheese

1. Place chicken in a shallow bowl. Pour ¼ cup dressing over chicken. Cover and refrigerate for 2 hours.
2. Transfer chicken to a shallow baking dish. Discard marinade. Drizzle with remaining dressing.
3. Cover and bake at 400° for 10 minutes.
4. Top each chicken with tomato slice, crumbs, basil, and cheese.
5. Cover and bake 10 minutes more.
6. Uncover and bake 10–15 minutes longer, or until chicken juices run clear.

Per Serving

Calories 213, Kilojoules 891, Protein 27 g,
Carbohydrates 20 g, Total Fat 2 g, Saturated Fat 0.5 g,
Monounsaturated Fat 0.8 g, Polyunsaturated Fat 0.7 g,
Cholesterol 66 mg, Sodium 490 mg, Fiber *trace*

Skinny Chicken Stroganoff

Carol Sherwood
Batavia, NY

Makes 6 servings

Prep. Time: 10–15 minutes
Cooking Time: 20–25 minutes

4 slices turkey bacon, cooked and broken
6 ozs. uncooked whole wheat noodles
¾ cup reduced-fat sour cream
¼ cup all-purpose flour
14½-oz. can low-fat low-sodium chicken broth
⅛ tsp. black pepper
1 lb. boneless skinless chicken breasts, cut into ¼" strips
8 ozs. sliced fresh mushrooms
1 cup chopped onion
1 clove garlic, pressed
2 Tbsp. snipped fresh parsley

Pyramid Servings

Vegetables
●○○○○➤

Fruits
○○○○○➤

Carbohydrates
●○○○○○○○

Protein & Dairy
●◑○○○○○

Fats
○○○○○

1. Cook bacon until crisp in a large skillet. Remove from pan, break, and set aside.
2. Cook noodles according to package instructions. Drain and keep warm.
3. Meanwhile, in a good-sized bowl, whisk together sour cream and flour until smooth.
4. Gradually whisk in chicken broth until smooth. Stir in pepper. Set aside.
5. Heat skillet that you used for bacon over high heat until hot. Add chicken. Cook, stirring continually for 3 minutes, or until meat is no longer pink. Remove from pan and set aside. Keep warm.
6. Reduce heat to medium. Add mushrooms, onion, and garlic. Cook and stir 3 minutes.
7. Stir in chicken and bacon.
8. Stir in sour cream mixture. Bring to a boil.
9. Reduce heat. Simmer 2 minutes, stirring constantly.
10. Remove from heat. Stir in parsley.
11. Serve over prepared noodles (not included in analyses).

Per Serving

Calories 278, Kilojoules 1163, Protein 26 g, Carbohydrates 36 g, Total Fat 3 g, Saturated Fat 1 g, Monounsaturated Fat 1 g, Polyunsaturated Fat 1 g, Cholesterol 53 mg, Sodium 256 mg, Fiber 4 g

A Tip —

Use freshly ground black pepper and freshly picked herbs to add an extra pop of flavor.

Chicken Asparagus Bake

Jean Butzer
Batavia, NY

Makes 4 servings

Prep. Time: 15–20 minutes
Chilling Time: 8–24 hours
Cooking/Baking Time: 1¼ hours

Pyramid Servings

Vegetables
●○○○○➤
Fruits
○○○○○➤
Carbohydrates
●○○○○○○○
Protein & Dairy
●●○○○○○
Fats
●○○○○

1 lb. boneless, skinless chicken breasts, cooked
¾ lb. fresh asparagus spears, *or* 10-oz. pkg. frozen asparagus spears
2 Tbsp. trans-fat-free buttery spread
5 Tbsp. flour
1 cup skim milk
1 cup low-fat low-sodium chicken broth
½ lb. fresh mushrooms, sliced, *or* 6-oz. can sliced mushrooms, drained
⅛ tsp. nutmeg
dash of pepper
¼ cup bread crumbs
2 Tbsp. snipped parsley
2 Tbsp. slivered almonds
2 Tbsp. trans-fat-free buttery spread

1. Slice breasts into ¼"-thick slices and set aside.
2. Cook asparagus lightly in microwave or in a saucepan on the stovetop. Drain.
3. In a skillet or saucepan, melt 2 Tbsp. buttery spread. Blend in flour.
4. Whisk in milk and chicken broth. Cook, stirring constantly, until mixture is thickened and bubbly.
5. Stir in mushrooms, nutmeg, and pepper.
6. Arrange chicken slices in bottom of lightly greased 6 × 10 baking pan.
7. Spoon half of mushroom sauce over chicken.
8. Arrange asparagus over sauce.
9. Pour remaining sauce over asparagus spears.
10. Cover and refrigerate up to 24 hours.

11. In a bowl, toss bread crumbs, parsley, almonds, and 2 Tbsp. buttery spread together. Set aside.
12. Bake casserole, covered, for 30 minutes at 375°.
13. Remove cover. Sprinkle crumbs on top.
14. Bake, uncovered, until heated through, about 15 minutes longer.

Per Serving

Calories 365, Kilojoules 1527, Protein 36 g,
Carbohydrates 22 g, Total Fat 15 g, Saturated Fat 2.5 g,
Monounsaturated Fat 6.4 g, Polyunsaturated Fat 6.1 g,
Cholesterol 68 mg, Sodium 193 mg, Fiber 3.5 g

Dietitian's tip: This casserole is a great option for serving up leftovers after a large turkey or chicken dinner. To make it a meal, serve with a tossed salad or steamed peas and carrots and fresh fruit for dessert.

Confetti Chicken

Liz Clapper
Lancaster, PA

Makes 6 servings

Prep. Time: 15 minutes
Cooking/Baking Time: 35–40 minutes

Pyramid Servings

Vegetables
●○○○○➤
Fruits
○○○○○➤
Carbohydrates
◐○○○○○○○
Protein & Dairy
●○○○○○○
Fats
○○○○○

1 lb. chicken cutlets
1 Tbsp. chili powder
hot sauce
10¾-oz. can cream of chicken soup, Healthy variety
½ cup skim milk
1 red bell sweet pepper, diced
1 green bell sweet pepper, diced
1 cup frozen corn
1 green onion, chopped

1. Preheat oven to 375°.

2. Spread chicken pieces in lightly greased 9 × 13 baking dish.

3. Sprinkle each cutlet chicken with chili powder and a dash of hot sauce.

4. In a bowl, whisk cream of chicken soup and milk together.

5. Spoon soup mixture over chicken. Top with diced peppers, corn, and green onion.

6. Bake, uncovered, at 375° for 35 minutes, or until hot and bubbly.

Per Serving

Calories 156, Kilojoules 653, Protein 20 g,
Carbohydrates 14 g, Total Fat 2.5 g, Saturated Fat 1 g,
Monounsaturated Fat 1 g, Polyunsaturated Fat 0.5 g,
Cholesterol 48 mg, Sodium 391 mg, Fiber 2 g

Tip: Serve over brown rice, and sprinkle with low-fat shredded cheddar cheese (not included in analyses).

Chicken Dinner in a Packet
Bonnie Whaling
Clearfield, PA

Makes 4 servings

Prep. Time: 25 minutes
Baking Time: 30–35 minutes

4 5-oz. boneless skinless
   chicken breast halves
2 cups sliced fresh mushrooms
2 medium carrots, cut in thin
   strips, about 1 cup
1 medium zucchini, unpeeled
   and sliced, about 1½ cups
2 Tbsp. olive, *or* canola, oil
2 Tbsp. lemon juice
4 tsp. fresh basil, *or* 1 tsp. dry basil
¼ tsp. salt
¼ tsp. black pepper

Pyramid Servings

Vegetables
●○○○○➤

Fruits
○○○○○➤

Carbohydrates
○○○○○○○○

Protein & Dairy
●◑○○○○○

Fats
●○○○○

1. Preheat oven to 375°.

2. Fold four 12" × 28" pieces of foil in half to make four 12" × 14" rectangles. Place one chicken breast half on each piece of foil.

3. Top with mushrooms, carrots, and zucchini, dividing vegetables equally among chicken bundles.

4. In a small bowl, stir together oil, lemon juice, basil, salt, and pepper.

5. Drizzle oil mixture over vegetables and chicken.

6. Pull up two opposite edges of foil. Seal with a double fold. Then fold in remaining edges, leaving enough space for steam to build.

7. Place bundles side-by-side in a shallow baking pan.

8. Bake 30–35 minutes, or until chicken reaches 170° on an instant-read thermometer.

9. Serve dinners in foil packets, or transfer to serving plate.

Per Serving

Calories 250, Kilojoules 1046, Protein 34 g,
Carbohydrates 7 g, Total Fat 9 g, Saturated Fat 1.5 g,
Monounsaturated Fat 6 g, Polyunsaturated Fat 1.5 g,
Cholesterol 82 mg, Sodium 263 mg, Fiber 2 g

Dietitian's tip: To increase the amount of nutrients in your diet—including vitamins, minerals, and fiber—try adding three times as many vegetables as meat on pizzas or in casseroles, soups, and stews. Better yet, go meatless!

A Tip —

   Use a meat thermometer to determine if a meat is done. Avoid over- or under-cooking meat.

Chicken Honey Stir-Fry

Anya Kauffman
Sheldon, WI

Makes 6 servings

Prep. Time: 15 minutes
Cooking Time: 10 minutes

Pyramid Servings

Vegetables	●○○○○➤
Fruits	●○○○○➤
Carbohydrates	○○○○○○○○
Protein & Dairy	●○○○○○○
Fats	●○○○○
Sweets	●

1 lb. boneless skinless
  chicken breast
2 Tbsp. canola oil, *divided*
4 cups sliced raw vegetables
  (your choice of a
  combination of cabbage,
  onion, celery, carrots,
  broccoli, cauliflower,
  sweet peppers)

Sauce:
1½ cups orange juice
⅔ cup honey
1 Tbsp. low-sodium soy sauce
2 Tbsp. cornstarch
½ tsp. ground ginger

1. Slice chicken breast into thin strips. Set aside.
2. Combine sauce ingredients in a bowl.
3. In a large skillet, stir-fry meat in 1 Tbsp. oil until no longer pink. Remove from skillet and set aside.
4. In remaining oil and in same skillet, stir-fry vegetables on high heat until crisp-tender.
5. Stir in meat and sauce until sauce is somewhat thickened.
6. Serve over hot brown rice (not included in analyses).

Per Serving

Calories 292, Kilojoules 1222, Protein 20 g,
Carbohydrates 40 g, Total Fat 6 g, Saturated Fat 0.5 g,
Monounsaturated Fat 3 g, Polyunsaturated Fat 2.5 g,
Cholesterol 44 mg, Sodium 168 mg, Fiber 2 g

Chicken in Tomato Vegetable Sauce

Irene Klaeger
Inverness, FL

Makes 6 servings

Prep. Time: 15 minutes
Cooking Time: 25–30 minutes

Pyramid Servings

Vegetables	●●○○○➤
Fruits	○○○○○➤
Carbohydrates	●○○○○○○○
Protein & Dairy	●○○○○○○
Fats	●○○○○

1 Tbsp. olive oil
1 cup sliced leeks
2 cloves garlic, minced
1 lb. boneless skinless
  chicken breast, cut into
  thin strips
1 tsp. dried basil
1 tsp. dried oregano
14½-oz. can tomatoes, no salt added,
  undrained and chopped
1 medium zucchini, unpeeled and sliced
½ cup low-sodium chicken broth
¼ cup Chablis, *or other dry white wine*
¼ tsp. salt
¼ cup tomato paste, no salt added
3 cups cooked brown rice
2 Tbsp. grated Parmesan cheese
fresh basil sprigs, *optional*

1. Heat oil in large skillet over medium heat until hot. Add leeks and garlic. Sauté 3 minutes, or until tender.
2. Add chicken. Sauté 7 minutes, or until done.
3. Stir in basil and oregano.
4. Remove chicken and seasonings. Set aside and keep warm.
5. Add next 6 ingredients to skillet. Stir well.
6. Cover skillet. Reduce heat and simmer 10 minutes.
7. Add chicken and cook until thoroughly heated.

8. Serve over cooked rice. Sprinkle with Parmesan cheese. Garnish with basil sprigs if you wish.

Per Serving

Calories 269, Kilojoules 1125, Protein 22 g,
Carbohydrates 33 g, Total Fat 5 g, Saturated Fat 1 g,
Monounsaturated Fat 2.5 g, Polyunsaturated Fat 1.5 g,
Cholesterol 46 mg, Sodium 227 mg, Fiber 4 g

Chicken Rice Bake

Nanci Keatley, Salem, OR

Makes 6 servings

Prep. Time: 20 minutes
Baking Time: 1½ hours
Standing Time: 10 minutes

Pyramid Servings

Vegetables	●●●○○➤
Fruits	○○○○○➤
Carbohydrates	●○○○○○○○
Protein & Dairy	●●○○○○○
Fats	○○○○○

2 lbs. boneless skinless chicken breasts, cut into bite-sized pieces
3½ cups low-sodium chicken broth
1½ cups uncooked brown rice
1 cup chopped celery
1 cup chopped carrots
1 cup finely diced onions
2 cups sliced fresh mushrooms
1½ tsp. salt
1 tsp. pepper
1 tsp. dill weed
1 tsp. garlic, chopped

1. Spray a 2-quart baking dish with nonstick cooking spray.
2. Combine all ingredients in large mixing bowl.
3. Spoon into baking dish. Bake at 350° for 1½ hours.
4. Allow to stand 10 minutes before serving.

Per Serving

Calories 390, Kilojoules 1632, Protein 43 g,
Carbohydrates 45 g, Total Fat 4 g, Saturated Fat 1 g,
Monounsaturated Fat 2 g, Polyunsaturated Fat 1 g,
Cholesterol 88 mg, Sodium 755 mg, Fiber 3.3 g

A Tip —

Always rinse rice before cooking it to remove the excess starch that makes cooked rice gummy.

Chicken Bulgur Skillet

Alice Rush
Quakertown, PA

Makes 6 servings

Prep. Time: 15–20 minutes
Cooking Time: 27–30 minutes

Pyramid Servings	
Vegetables	●○○○○▸
Fruits	○○○○○▸
Carbohydrates	●●○○○○○○
Protein & Dairy	●○○○○○○
Fats	○○○○○

1 lb. boneless skinless
   chicken breast, cut into 1"
   cubes
2 tsp. olive oil
2 medium carrots, chopped
⅔ cup chopped onion
3 Tbsp. chopped walnuts
½ tsp. caraway seeds
¼ tsp. ground cumin
1½ cups uncooked bulgur
2 cups low-sodium chicken broth
2 Tbsp. raisins, *or* dried cranberries
¼ tsp. salt
⅛ tsp. ground cinnamon

1. In large non-stick skillet, cook chicken in oil over medium-high heat until no longer pink. Remove chicken from skillet and keep warm.
2. In same skillet, stir-fry carrots, onion, nuts, caraway seeds, and cumin for 3–4 minutes, or until onion starts to brown.
3. Stir in bulgur. Gradually add broth.
4. Bring to a boil over medium-high heat. Reduce heat.
5. Add raisins or dried cranberries, salt, cinnamon, and chicken.
6. Cover and simmer 12–15 minutes, or until bulgur is tender.

Per Serving

Calories 274, Kilojoules 1146, Protein 25 g,
Carbohydrates 33 g, Total Fat 5 g, Saturated Fat 1 g,
Monounsaturated Fat 2 g, Polyunsaturated Fat 2 g,
Cholesterol 45 mg, Sodium 213 mg, Fiber 8 g

Sassy Lentils, Rice, and Chicken

Janelle Reitz
Lancaster, PA

Makes 6 servings

Prep. Time: 10–15 minutes
Cooking Time: 1 hour

Pyramid Servings	
Vegetables	●○○○○▸
Fruits	●○○○○▸
Carbohydrates	●●○○○○○○
Protein & Dairy	●○○○○○○
Fats	●○○○○

1 Tbsp. olive oil
3" cinnamon stick
¾ tsp. ground cumin
6 cloves garlic, minced
1 onion, sliced
¾ lb. boneless skinless
   chicken breast, cubed
1 cup uncooked brown rice
3 cups low-sodium, fat-free chicken broth
½ cup uncooked lentils
1 tsp. ground cardamom
½ cup raisins
2 Tbsp. chopped fresh cilantro
½ cup toasted almonds, *optional*

1. Heat oil in a large saucepan. Sauté cinnamon stick, cumin, and garlic for 2 minutes over low heat.
2. Add onion and sauté until tender.
3. Add chicken and cook 10 minutes.
4. With a slotted spoon, remove chicken and keep warm.
5. Stir rice into saucepan. Sauté 5 minutes.
6. Increase heat and add broth, lentils, and cardamom.
7. Bring to a boil. Cover and simmer at reduced heat 40 minutes.
8. Remove cinnamon stick. Add raisins, cilantro, and almonds if you wish.

Per Serving

Calories 361, Kilojoules 1510, Protein 24 g,
Carbohydrates 47 g, Total Fat 9 g, Saturated Fat 1.3 g,
Monounsaturated Fat 5 g, Polyunsaturated Fat 2.7 g,
Cholesterol 35 mg, Sodium 112 mg, Fiber 8 g

Sweet Potatoes and Chicken a la King

Bernita Boyts
Shawnee Mission, KS

Makes 4 servings

Prep. Time: 10–15 minutes
Cooking/Baking Time: 45 minutes

3 medium sweet potatoes
3 cups low-fat, low-sodium chicken broth
½ cup whole wheat pastry flour
1 cup water
pepper
¼ tsp. garlic powder, *or* poultry seasoning
2 cups leftover cooked poultry, cut into small pieces
10-oz. package frozen peas

Pyramid Servings

Vegetables	○○○○○▸
Fruits	○○○○○▸
Carbohydrates	●●○○○○○○
Protein & Dairy	●◐○○○○○
Fats	○○○○○

1. Wash and prick sweet potatoes. Bake about 45 minutes at 375°, or until potatoes are soft when squeezed.
2. While potatoes are baking, heat broth in saucepan to boiling.
3. Combine flour and water in a jar with tight-fitting lid. Shake until smooth.
4. Pour flour-water paste slowly into boiling broth. Stir constantly until smooth and thick.
5. Stir in pepper and other seasoning.
6. Add cooked poultry to gravy along with peas. Cook on low until heated through.
7. Slice sweet potatoes diagonally and serve topped with gravy.

Per Serving

Calories 297, Kilojoules 1243, Protein 30 g,
Carbohydrates 41 g, Total Fat 2 g, Saturated Fat 0.6 g,
Monounsaturated Fat 1.2 g, Polyunsaturated Fat 0.2 g,
Cholesterol 53 mg, Sodium 267 mg, Fiber 8 g

Italian Chicken and Broccoli

Liz Clapper, Lancaster, PA

Makes 6 servings

Prep. Time: 15–20 minutes
Cooking Time: 15–20 minutes

2 cups uncooked whole grain macaroni
1 lb. chicken tenderloins
1 Tbsp. olive oil
4 medium carrots, sliced thin
2 cloves garlic, finely chopped
1 head broccoli, chopped into florets (about 4 cups)
½ cup low-fat, low-sodium chicken broth
1½ Tbsp. Italian seasoning, unsalted, like Mrs. Dash™
¼ cup Parmesan shredded cheese

Pyramid Servings

Vegetables	●●○○○▸
Fruits	○○○○○▸
Carbohydrates	●●○○○○○○
Protein & Dairy	●○○○○○○○
Fats	●○○○○

1. Cook pasta according to package directions until al dente.
2. Meanwhile, in a large skillet or saucepan, cook chicken in olive oil about 7 minutes, or until cooked through.
3. Remove chicken from pan and keep warm.
4. Add sliced carrots to same pan. Sauté 2 minutes.
5. Add garlic and broccoli to carrots. Sauté 2 minutes.
6. Add broth and Italian seasoning. Heat until broth simmers.
7. Cut chicken into bite-sized pieces. Stir into skillet with vegetables and cook 3 more minutes.
8. Toss with cooked pasta. Sprinkle with Parmesan and serve immediately.

Per Serving

Calories 279, Kilojoules 1167, Protein 26 g,
Carbohydrates 33 g, Total Fat 5 g, Saturated Fat 1 g,
Monounsaturated Fat 2.5 g, Polyunsaturated Fat 1.5 g,
Cholesterol 46 mg, Sodium 168 mg, Fiber 6 g

Chicken Fajitas

Becky Frey, Lebanon, PA

Makes 12 servings

Prep. Time: 20–30 minutes
Marinating Time: 15 minutes
Cooking Time: 6–8 minutes

Pyramid Servings	
Vegetables	●○○○○▸
Fruits	○○○○○▸
Carbohydrates	●○○○○○○
Protein & Dairy	●○○○○○○
Fats	●○○○○

¼ cup lime juice
1–2 garlic cloves minced
1 tsp. chili powder
½ tsp. ground cumin
3 lbs. boneless skinless
   chicken breasts, cut into ¼" slices
1 large onion sliced
half a green bell sweet pepper, slivered
half a red bell sweet pepper, slivered
12 whole wheat tortillas, 8" in diameter
½ cup salsa
½ cup non-fat sour cream
½ cup your favorite low-fat shredded cheese

1. Combine first four ingredients in a large bowl.
2. Add chicken slices. Stir until chicken is well coated.
3. Marinate for 15 minutes.
4. Cook chicken mixture in large hot non-stick skillet for 3 minutes, or until no longer pink.
5. Stir in onions and peppers. Cook 3–5 minutes, or until done to your liking.
6. Divide mixture evenly among tortillas.
7. Top each with 2 tsp. salsa, 2 tsp. sour cream and 2 tsp. shredded cheese.
8. Roll up and serve.

Per Serving

Calories 334, Kilojoules 1397, Protein 34 g,
Carbohydrates 30 g, Total Fat 9 g, Saturated Fat 2 g,
Monounsaturated Fat 6 g, Polyunsaturated Fat 1 g,
Cholesterol 68 mg, Sodium 689 mg, Fiber 6 g

Tips: Partially frozen chicken slices much more easily than completely thawed chicken. If you like a higher heat index, add your favorite hot pepper along with the sweet peppers.

Tasty Home-Style Chicken

Elaine Good
Lititz, PA

Makes 10 servings

Prep. Time: 15 minutes
Cooking/Baking Time: 1¼–1¾
  hours

Pyramid Servings	
Vegetables	●○○○○▸
Fruits	○○○○○▸
Carbohydrates	◐○○○○○○
Protein & Dairy	●●○○○○○
Fats	○○○○○

4 lbs. chicken pieces, washed,
   dried, and skinned
1 cup chopped onion
1 cup chopped celery
water
¾ cup sliced fresh mushrooms
½ cup, plus 1 Tbsp., whole wheat pastry
   flour
¾ tsp. salt
dash of pepper
2½ cups water
parsley flakes, *or* paprika, *optional*

1. Arrange chicken pieces in a 9 × 13 baking pan that's been lightly sprayed with non-stick cooking spray.
2. In a saucepan, sauté onion and celery in a few spoonfuls of water until somewhat tender.
3. Add mushrooms. Continue to cook until mushrooms give off a bit of liquid.
4. Add flour, salt, and pepper, stirring until well mixed.
5. Gradually add 2½ cups water, cooking and stirring continually until thickened and smooth.
6. Remove from heat. Pour sauce over chicken in baking pan.
7. If you wish, sprinkle chicken with parsley or paprika.
8. Bake, covered, at 350° for 45 minutes.
9. Uncover, and continue baking 30–45 more minutes, or until chicken is tender.
10. Remove chicken to a warm platter and serve.

Per Serving

Calories 253, Kilojoules 1059, Protein 40 g,
Carbohydrates 9 g, Total Fat 6 g, Saturated Fat 1.5 g,
Monounsaturated Fat 2 g, Polyunsaturated Fat 2.5 g,
Cholesterol 126 mg, Sodium 386 mg, Fiber 2 g

Baked Crumb-Covered Chicken

Linda Thomas
Sayner, WI

Makes 4 servings

Prep. Time: 10–15 minutes
Baking Time: 35–40 minutes

Pyramid Servings

Vegetables
○○○○○➤
Fruits
○○○○○➤
Carbohydrates
○○○○○○○○
Protein & Dairy
●●○○○○○○
Fats
○○○○○

3 Tbsp. grated Parmesan
  cheese
½ cup dry bread crumbs
½ tsp. rosemary
½ tsp. dried thyme
¼ tsp. garlic powder
¼ tsp. onion powder
¼ tsp. black pepper
¾ cup low-fat buttermilk
1 lb. skinned chicken pieces

1. Cover a baking sheet with aluminum foil. Spray lightly with non-stick cooking spray.
2. In a shallow dish combine all ingredients except chicken and buttermilk.
3. In a separate shallow bowl, dip chicken in buttermilk.
4. Then roll chicken pieces in dry mixture.
5. Place chicken pieces on baking sheet.
6. Bake at 400° for 35–40 minutes, or until golden brown.

Per Serving

Calories 213, Kilojoules 891, Protein 31 g,
Carbohydrates 13 g, Total Fat 4 g, Saturated Fat 1.5 g,
Monounsaturated Fat 2 g, Polyunsaturated Fat 0.5 g,
Cholesterol 71 mg, Sodium 277 mg, Fiber 1 g

Honey Baked Chicken

Rhoda Nissley
Parkesburg, PA

Makes 10 servings

Prep. Time: 5–10 minutes
Baking Time: 1–1¼ hours

Pyramid Servings

Vegetables
○○○○○➤
Fruits
○○○○○➤
Carbohydrates
○○○○○○○○
Protein & Dairy
●○○○○○○○
Fats
●●○○○
Sweets
◐

3 lbs. chicken pieces, skinned
1 Tbsp. butter, melted
1 Tbsp. olive oil
2 Tbsp. prepared mustard
1 tsp. curry powder
⅓ cup honey
⅓ cup water

1. Preheat oven to 350°.
2. Arrange chicken in a single layer in a shallow, lightly greased baking dish.
3. Combine all other ingredients in a bowl. Pour over chicken.
4. Place in oven, uncovered. Baste chicken with sauce every 15 minutes.
5. Bake until nicely browned and tender, about 1–1¼ hours.

Per Serving

Calories 232, Kilojoules 971, Protein 29 g,
Carbohydrates 10 g, Total Fat 8 g, Saturated Fat 2 g,
Monounsaturated Fat 4 g, Polyunsaturated Fat 2 g,
Cholesterol 98 mg, Sodium 147 mg, Fiber *trace*

Barbecued Chicken Thighs

Ida H. Goering
Dayton, VA

Makes 6 servings

Prep. Time: 10 minutes
Marinating Time: 2–4 hours
Grilling Time: 15–22 minutes

Pyramid Servings

Vegetables
○○○○○➤

Fruits
○○○○○➤

Carbohydrates
○○○○○○○○

Protein & Dairy
●●○○○○○○

Fats
●○○○○

6 Tbsp. apple cider vinegar
3 Tbsp. canola oil
3 Tbsp. ketchup
¼ tsp. black pepper
¼ tsp. poultry seasoning
12 boneless skinless chicken thighs

1. Combine all ingredients except chicken thighs in a large bowl.
2. Submerge thighs in sauce in bowl.
3. Marinate 2–4 hours, stirring several times to be sure meat is well covered.
4. Grill over medium heat, turning after 10–15 minutes.
5. Grill another 5–7 minutes. Watch carefully so meat doesn't dry out. Remove from grill earlier if finished.

Per Serving

| Calories 273, Kilojoules 1142, Protein 35 g, |
| Carbohydrates 2 g, Total Fat 13 g, Saturated Fat 2 g, |
| Monounsaturated Fat 7 g, Polyunsaturated Fat 4 g, |
| Cholesterol 141 mg, Sodium 242 mg, Fiber *trace* |

Dietitian's tip: Healthy cooking techniques — such as braising, broiling, grilling, and steaming — can capture the flavor and nutrients of your food without adding excessive amounts of fat, oil, or sodium. If your recipe calls for frying the ingredients in oil or butter, try baking, broiling, or poaching the food instead.

Turkey Meat Loaf

Delores A. Gnagey
Saginaw, MI

Makes 10 servings

Prep. Time: 20 minutes
Baking Time: 90 minutes
Standing Time: 10 minutes

Pyramid Servings

Vegetables
○○○○○➤

Fruits
○○○○○➤

Carbohydrates
○○○○○○○○

Protein & Dairy
●◐○○○○○

Fats
○○○○○

2 lbs. skinless, dark and
    white turkey meat, ground
half a medium onion (½ cup),
    minced
3 Tbsp. minced fresh parsley
2 egg whites, *or* egg substitute equivalent
    to 1 egg
¼ cup skim milk
1 tsp. dry mustard
¼ tsp. salt
¼ tsp. ground white pepper
⅛ tsp. nutmeg
2 slices whole wheat bread, lightly toasted,
    made into coarse crumbs
2 Tbsp. ketchup
2 Tbsp. water

1. Preheat oven to 350°.

2. Mix together ground turkey, onion, and parsley in a large bowl. Set aside.

3. In a medium bowl, whisk egg whites, or egg substitute, until frothy.

4. Add milk, mustard, salt, pepper, and nutmeg to egg. Whisk to blend.

5. Add bread crumbs to egg mixture. Let rest 10 minutes.

6. Add egg mixture to meat mixture and blend well.

7. Shape into loaf. Place in 5 × 9 loaf pan.

8. Blend together ketchup and water in a small bowl. Spread mixture on top of meat.

9. Bake until meat is no longer pink, about 90 minutes.

10. Allow meat to stand 10 minutes before slicing to serve.

Per Serving

Calories 173, Kilojoules 724, Protein 18 g,
Carbohydrates 7 g, Total Fat 8 g, Saturated Fat 2 g,
Monounsaturated Fat 4 g, Polyunsaturated Fat 2 g,
Cholesterol 72 mg, Sodium 223 mg, Fiber 1 g

Meatballs

Christie Detamore-Hunsberger
Harrisonburg, VA

Makes 14 servings

Prep. Time: 30–40 minutes
Baking Time: 15–25 minutes

Pyramid Servings

Vegetables
○○○○○▸
Fruits
○○○○○▸
Carbohydrates
◑○○○○○○○
Protein & Dairy
●○○○○○○○
Fats
○○○○○

1 lb. extra-lean low-fat turkey sausage, *or* use Turkey Sausage recipe on page 190

2 lbs. extra-lean ground turkey

2 egg whites, *or* egg substitute equivalent to 1 egg

1 additional egg white

¼ cup grated Parmesan cheese

2 large garlic cloves, minced

1 medium onion minced

1 cup bread crumbs

1 small can evaporated skim milk

1½ tsp. dried oregano

½ tsp. ground pepper

1. Mix all ingredients together thoroughly.

2. Form into balls.

3. Place on broiler pan. Bake at 400° for 15 minutes.

4. Cut into center of several meatballs to see if they're cooked through. If not, continue baking another 10 minutes or so, until finished.

5. Use immediately, or freeze, for spaghetti and meatballs. Or bake at 350° for 30 minutes in baking dish with low-sodium mushroom or celery soup. Or heat with tomato sauce and make meatball sandwiches.

Per Serving

Calories 152, Kilojoules 636, Protein 24 g,
Carbohydrates 9 g, Total Fat 2 g, Saturated Fat 0.5 g,
Monounsaturated Fat 1.3 g, Polyunsaturated Fat 0.2 g,
Cholesterol 38 mg, Sodium 171 mg, Fiber *trace*

A Tip —

To clean Pyrex and stainless steel containers, take them outside and spray with oven cleaner. Let stand for an hour. Bring them back in and wash in hot soapy water.

Turkey Quesadillas

Tara P. Detweiler
Pennsburg, PA

Dietitian's tip: A quesadilla is a flour tortilla layered with cooked meat, refried beans, cheese, or other ingredients that are grilled or baked. Serve these chicken quesadillas as a main dish or cut them in strips and serve as an appetizer.

Makes 8 servings

Prep. Time: 15 minutes
Cooking/Baking Time: 20 minutes

Pyramid Servings	
Vegetables	●○○○○➤
Fruits	○○○○○➤
Carbohydrates	●○○○○○○○○
Protein & Dairy	●●○○○○○
Fats	●○○○○

1 lb. ground turkey
4 tsp. olive oil
1 large onion, chopped
1 red bell sweet pepper, chopped
4 cloves garlic, chopped
1 tsp. ground cumin
1 tsp. chili powder
1 tsp. dried oregano
15-oz. can tomato sauce, no salt added
15½-oz. can kidney, *or* black, beans, drained and rinsed
8 whole wheat flour tortillas, about 9" in diameter
2 Tbsp. parsley
1 tsp. cilantro
½ cup grated low-fat cheddar cheese for topping

1. Cook ground turkey with olive oil and onion in large skillet until turkey is no longer pink.
2. Add red pepper, garlic, and all spices. Cook gently until vegetables are just tender.
3. Stir in tomato sauce and beans. Heat through.
4. Place tortillas on greased cookie sheets. Spoon turkey mixture evenly onto tortillas (approximately ¼ cup per tortilla).
5. Top each with 1 Tbsp. grated cheese.
6. Bake, uncovered, at 400° for 15 minutes.

Per Serving

Calories 358, Kilojoules 1498, Protein 25 g,	
Carbohydrates 40 g, Total Fat 11 g, Saturated Fat 2 g,	
Monounsaturated Fat 8 g, Polyunsaturated Fat 1 g,	
Cholesterol 24 mg, Sodium 745 mg, Fiber 10 g	

A Tip —

To chop onions painlessly, place your cutting board on a front unheated burner. Turn on the rear burner and chop the onions. The heat from the back burner will pull the "teary" oils away from you.

Spaghetti Pie

Marlene Fonken
Upland, CA

Makes 4 servings

Prep. Time: 15 minutes
Cooking/Baking Time: 45 minutes

4 ozs. uncooked thin
whole wheat spaghetti,
or vermicelli (*or* 2 cups
cooked)
1 Tbsp. olive oil
2 Tbsp. reduced-fat Parmesan
cheese
egg substitute equivalent to 1 egg, *or* 2 egg
whites, beaten
⅔ cup non-fat cottage cheese, *or* ½ cup
non-fat ricotta
1 clove garlic, minced
½ cup diced onion
½ cup diced green *or* red bell sweet pepper
½ lb. lean ground turkey
1 cup canned tomatoes, no salt added,
chopped, undrained
¼ cup tomato paste, no salt added
½ tsp. dried basil
½ tsp. dried oregano
¼ cup low-fat mozzarella cheese, shredded

Pyramid Servings

Vegetables
●○○○○➤

Fruits
○○○○○➤

Carbohydrates
●○○○○○○○○

Protein & Dairy
●●○○○○○

Fats
○○○○○

1. Cook spaghetti according to package
directions. Drain. Return to saucepan.
2. Stir oil, Parmesan cheese, and beaten egg
substitute or white into cooked spaghetti. Mix
well.
3. Spray a glass 8" pie plate or 7 × 9 baking
dish with non-stick cooking spray. Spread
spaghetti mixture over bottom and up sides to
form a crust.
4. Spread cottage cheese over bottom of
crust.
5. In saucepan, cook garlic, onion, pepper,
and turkey together until meat loses its pink
color. (You may need to add a little water to
pan to prevent sticking.)

6. Add tomatoes, tomato paste, basil, and
oregano to pan. Cook until heated through.
7. Spoon turkey-tomato mixture over cottage
cheese.
8. Bake, uncovered, approximately 20
minutes at 350°.
9. Sprinkle mozzarella cheese on top.
10. Continue to bake another 5 minutes, or
until cheese is melted.

Per Serving

Calories 316, Kilojoules 1322, Protein 24 g,
Carbohydrates 35 g, Total Fat 9 g, Saturated Fat 2.5 g,
Monounsaturated Fat 3.5 g, Polyunsaturated Fat 3 g,
Cholesterol 42 mg, Sodium 335 mg, Fiber 5 g

*Dietitian's tip: The type of fiber in whole-wheat
pasta is insoluble — meaning it doesn't dissolve
during digestion. Instead, it maintains its bulk,
holds on to water and, as a result, helps prevent
constipation.*

Main Dishes– Seafood

Shrimp Stir-Fry

Jean Binns Smith
Bellefonte, PA

Makes 4 servings

Prep. Time: 10 minutes
Cooking Time: 8–10 minutes

Pyramid Servings	
Vegetables	●○○○○▸
Fruits	○○○○○▸
Carbohydrates	○○○○○○○○
Protein & Dairy	●○○○○○○
Fats	◑○○○○

1–2 cloves garlic, chopped
⅛ tsp. grated, *or* finely
   chopped, fresh ginger
1 Tbsp. olive oil
2½ cups (about ½ lb.) fresh
   sugar snap peas
½ cup chopped red bell sweet pepper,
   optional
12 ozs. medium-sized raw shrimp, peeled
   and deveined

1. Sauté garlic and ginger in oil in large skillet until fragrant.
2. Stir in sugar peas, and chopped pepper if you wish. Sauté until crisp-tender.
3. Stir in shrimp. Cook over medium heat 3–4 minutes until shrimp are just opaque in centers.
4. Serve with steamed rice (not included in analyses).

Per Serving

Calories 156, Kilojoules 653, Protein 19 g,
Carbohydrates 8 g, Total Fat 5 g, Saturated Fat 0.7 g,
Monounsaturated Fat 2.5 g, Polyunsaturated Fat 1.8 g,
Cholesterol 129 mg, Sodium 136 mg, Fiber 2 g

Thai Shrimp and Rice

Pat Bechtel, Dillsburg, PA

Makes 6 servings

Prep. Time: 10 minutes
Cooking Time: 25–30 minutes

Pyramid Servings	
Vegetables	●●○○○▸
Fruits	○○○○○▸
Carbohydrates	●○○○○○○○
Protein & Dairy	●○○○○○○
Fats	●○○○○

1 tsp. olive oil
½ cup sliced scallions
1 Tbsp. chopped garlic
14-oz. can light coconut milk
water
1½ cups jasmine, *or*
   converted, white rice
1 cup shredded carrots
1 tsp. salt
12 ozs. raw shrimp, peeled and deveined
2½ cups (about ½ lb.) fresh snow peas
2 tsp. lime zest
lime wedges
cilantro for garnish

1. Heat olive oil in a large skillet over medium heat. Sauté scallions and garlic.
2. Pour coconut milk into a quart measure. Add enough water to make 3¼ cups.
3. Add milk mixture to skillet and bring to a boil.
4. Stir in rice, carrots, and salt.
5. Cover. Reduce heat and simmer 12 minutes, or until rice is nearly tender.
6. Stir in shrimp, snow peas, and lime zest. If rice looks dry add ¼ cup water.
7. Cover and bring to a simmer. Cook 3–4 minutes, or until shrimp and peas are crisp-tender.
8. Garnish with lime wedges and chopped cilantro just before serving.

Per Serving

Calories 296, Kilojoules 1238, Protein 17 g,
Carbohydrates 44 g, Total Fat 6 g, Saturated Fat 4 g,
Monounsaturated Fat 1 g, Polyunsaturated Fat 1 g,
Cholesterol 86 mg, Sodium 499 mg, Fiber 4 g

Tip: Cook shrimp only until pink.

Shrimp Curry

Margaret Thorpe, Lancaster, PA

Makes 5 servings

Prep. Time: 10 minutes
Cooking Time: 14 minutes

Pyramid Servings

Vegetables	●●○○○▸
Fruits	○○○○○▸
Carbohydrates	●○○○○○○○
Protein & Dairy	●○○○○○○
Fats	●○○○○

¼ cup olive oil
1 medium green bell sweet
    pepper, cut into ½" squares
½ cup sliced celery
2 Tbsp. sliced green onions
¼ cup cornstarch
2 tsp. curry powder
½ tsp. salt
2 cups low-fat, low-sodium chicken broth
8-oz. can sliced water chestnuts, drained
1½ cups cooked shrimp
2 Tbsp. chopped pimento
2 cups brown rice, cooked

1. Place olive oil, green pepper, celery, and onions in 2-quart baking dish. Cover loosely. Microwave 2 minutes at 100 percent power. Stir. Cover and continue microwaving another 2 minutes at 100 percent power.

2. In a small bowl, blend cornstarch with curry powder and salt. Stir into vegetable mixture.

3. Add chicken broth, drained water chestnuts, and shrimp to vegetables. Mix well.

4. Cover loosely. Microwave 2–3 minutes on 100 percent power. Stir.

5. Microwave, covered, another 2–3 minutes on 100 percent power. Stir.

6. Microwave, covered, yet another 2–3 minutes on 100 percent power, or until sauce thickens.

7. Stir in pimento. Serve over brown rice.

Per Serving

Calories 278, Kilojoules 1163, Protein 14 g,
Carbohydrates 31 g, Total Fat 11 g, Saturated Fat 3 g,
Monounsaturated Fat 5 g, Polyunsaturated Fat 3 g,
Cholesterol 87 mg, Sodium 296 mg, Fiber 5 g

Dietitian's tip: Though shrimp is higher in cholesterol than most meat and poultry, it's lower in fat and saturated fat. And fat, not cholesterol, has the greatest effect on blood cholesterol. Shrimp also has omega-3 fatty acids, a type of fat that's good for your heart.

Easy Tilapia

Karen Ceneviva
New Haven, CT

Makes 4 servings

Prep. Time: 2 minutes
Cooking Time: 6–7 minutes

Pyramid Servings

Vegetables	○○○○○▸
Fruits	○○○○○▸
Carbohydrates	○○○○○○○○
Protein & Dairy	●○○○○○○
Fats	●○○○○

1 Tbsp. olive oil
4 6-oz. tilapia fillets
lemon pepper

1. Heat oil in large skillet.

2. Lay fish in hot skillet, being careful not to splash yourself with hot oil.

3. Sprinkle fish lightly with lemon pepper.

4. Cook 3 minutes.

5. Flip fish carefully. Sprinkle lightly with lemon pepper.

6. Cook another 3 minutes, or just until fish flakes when picked with a fork.

Per Serving

Calories 193, Kilojoules 808, Protein 34 g,
Carbohydrates *trace*, Total Fat 6 g, Saturated Fat 2 g,
Monounsaturated Fat 3.5 g, Polyunsaturated Fat 0.5 g,
Cholesterol 85 mg, Sodium 108 mg, Fiber 0 g

Dietitian's tip: To see if the fish is thoroughly done, use the tip of a small, sharp knife to cut into the flesh. The fish should separate into flakes and be opaque throughout.

Baked Fish

Patricia Howard
Green Valley, AZ

Makes 4 servings

Prep. Time: 5 minutes
Baking Time: 10–15 minutes

Pyramid Servings	
Vegetables	○○○○○➤
Fruits	○○○○○➤
Carbohydrates	○○○○○○○○
Protein & Dairy	●○○○○○○
Fats	○○○○○

4 4-oz. fish fillets (hake, cod,
    or mahi-mahi)
juice from half a lemon
1 tsp. dill weed
1 tsp. dried basil
1 tsp. original Mrs. Dash
1½ tsp. parsley flakes
4 thin slices lemon

1. Preheat oven to 350°.
2. Spray baking dish with nonstick cooking spray. Add fish fillets to dish in one layer.
3. Squeeze lemon juice over fish.
4. Sprinkle fish with dill weed, basil, Mrs. Dash, and parsley.
5. Place lemon slices on top. Cover with foil.
6. Bake 10–15 minutes. Do not over-bake. The thinner the fillet, the faster it cooks, and the less time it takes. Check for flakiness with the tines of a fork after 10 minutes. Continue baking only if needed.

Per Serving

Calories 99, Kilojoules 414, Protein 20 g,
Carbohydrates 2 g, Total Fat 1 g, Saturated Fat 0.2 g,
Monounsaturated Fat 0.5 g, Polyunsaturated Fat 0.3 g,
Cholesterol 49 mg, Sodium 63 mg, Fiber 1 g

Tip: If fish is frozen, adjust cooking time accordingly.

Dietitian's tip: Whether baking, broiling, grilling, or poaching fish, cook for 8 to 10 minutes per 1 inch of thickness measured at the thickest point. Test for doneness at the earliest time given, to prevent the fish from overcooking and losing its moist, tender texture.

Baked Halibut Steaks

Kristi See
Weskan, KS

Makes 4 servings

Prep. Time: 15 minutes
Cooking/Baking Time: 25 minutes

Pyramid Servings	
Vegetables	●●○○○➤
Fruits	○○○○○➤
Carbohydrates	○○○○○○○○
Protein & Dairy	●●○○○○○
Fats	○○○○○

1 tsp. olive oil
1 cup unpeeled diced
    zucchini
½ cup minced onion
1 clove garlic, peeled and
    minced
2 cups diced fresh tomatoes
2 Tbsp. chopped fresh basil
¼ tsp. salt
¼ tsp. pepper
4 6-oz. halibut steaks
⅓ cup crumbled feta cheese

1. Preheat oven to 450°. Lightly grease shallow baking dish.
2. Heat olive oil in a medium saucepan over medium heat. Stir in zucchini, onion, and garlic.
3. Cook for 5 minutes, or until tender. Stir now and then.
4. Remove saucepan from heat. Mix in tomatoes, basil, salt, and pepper.
5. Arrange halibut steaks in a single layer in the prepared baking dish.
6. Spoon equal amounts of zucchini mixture over each steak.
7. Top each steak with feta cheese.
8. Bake 15 minutes in the preheated oven, or until fish is easily flaked with a fork.

Per Serving

Calories 257, Kilojoules 1075, Protein 38 g,
Carbohydrates 7 g, Total Fat 8 g, Saturated Fat 2 g,
Monounsaturated Fat 5 g, Polyunsaturated Fat 1 g,
Cholesterol 64 mg, Sodium 371 mg, Fiber 2 g

Simple Salmon
Evie Hershey, Atglen, PA

Makes 4 servings

Prep. Time: 5 minutes
Cooking/Baking Time: 10-12 minutes

1 tsp. olive oil
1 lb. salmon fillet
½ tsp. fine bread crumbs
½ tsp. Old Bay seasoning, *or*
    rosemary, *or* chives

Pyramid Servings	
Vegetables	○○○○○➤
Fruits	○○○○○➤
Carbohydrates	○○○○○○○○
Protein & Dairy	●●○○○○○
Fats	○○○○○

1. Preheat oven to 450°.
2. Warm olive oil in oven-proof skillet.
3. Place salmon fillet skin-side down in skillet.
4. Cook 5 minutes, sprinkling with bread crumbs and your choice of seasoning.
5. Place skillet in oven. Bake, uncovered, 5–8 minutes depending on thickness of fillets. Check after 5 minutes to see if fish flakes easily with fork. Continue baking only if it doesn't.

Per Serving

Calories 172, Kilojoules 720, Protein 22 g,
Carbohydrates 2 g, Total Fat 8 g, Saturated Fat 1.5 g,
Monounsaturated Fat 3.5 g, Polyunsaturated Fat 3 g,
Cholesterol 62 mg, Sodium 131 mg, Fiber *trace*

Dietitian's tip: Salmon is a good source of omega-3 fatty acids—a type of fat that may be beneficial to your heart.

A Tip —

When purchasing a new skillet make sure it has weight to it. Heavier skillets distribute heat more evenly.

Roasted Salmon
Gloria Julien, Gladstone, MI

Makes 2 servings

Prep. Time: 7-10 minutes
Baking Time: 10-12 minutes

2 5-oz. pieces salmon with skin
2 tsp. extra-virgin olive oil
1 Tbsp. chopped chives
1 Tbsp. fresh tarragon leaves,
    optional

Pyramid Servings	
Vegetables	○○○○○➤
Fruits	○○○○○➤
Carbohydrates	○○○○○○○○
Protein & Dairy	●●○○○○○
Fats	●○○○○

1. Preheat oven to 425°.
2. Line a baking sheet with foil.
3. Rub salmon all over with 2 tsp. oil.
4. Roast skin side down on foil-lined baking sheet until fish is cooked through, about 12 minutes. (Check if fish flakes easily with fork after it bakes 10 minutes. Continue baking only if it doesn't.)
5. Using a metal spatula, lift salmon off skin and place salmon on serving plate. Discard skin.
6. Sprinkle salmon with herbs and serve.

Per Serving

Calories 241, Kilojoules 1008, Protein 28 g,
Carbohydrates *trace*, Total Fat 14 g, Saturated Fat 2 g,
Monounsaturated Fat 7 g, Polyunsaturated Fat 5 g,
Cholesterol 78 mg, Sodium 62 mg, Fiber *trace*

Dietitian's tip: The American Heart Association recommends two servings of fish every week. Salmon is a good source of omega-3 fatty acids, which help keep blood from forming clots and protect against irregular heartbeats that may cause a heart attack.

Salmon in a Skillet

Bernita Boyts
Shawnee Mission, KS

Makes 4 servings

Prep. Time: 10 minutes
Cooking Time: 10–15 minutes

Pyramid Servings	
Vegetables ●○○○○➤	
Fruits ○○○○○➤	
Carbohydrates ○○○○○○○○	
Protein & Dairy ●●○○○○○○	
Fats ●○○○○	

1 lb. wild salmon fillet, cut
  to fit in your skillet
1 tsp. olive oil
dash of pepper
2 Tbsp. butter
1 clove garlic, chopped fine
¼ cup white wine, *or* water
2 Tbsp. capers
2 green onions, finely chopped
1 tsp. fresh, *or* ¼ tsp. dried dill weed
1 medium tomato, chopped
1 Tbsp. lemon juice

1. Rinse salmon in cool water; pat dry.
2. Heat oil in skillet.
3. Pepper fillet and place carefully in skillet, skin side up. Cook over medium heat 3–5 minutes. Allow longer time for a thick fillet.
4. Turn fillet over. Cook another 3–5 minutes, or until fish flakes when prodded with a fork. Don't overcook in skillet; it will finish on serving platter.
5. Remove fish from skillet. Place on platter and cover.
6. Melt butter in skillet. Add garlic. Stir and cook about 30 seconds.
7. Add wine and heat until bubbling, scraping brown bits into liquid.
8. Add capers, onions, and dill. Cook another minute.
9. Stir in chopped tomatoes. Heat through.
10. Sprinkle lemon juice over salmon.
11. Top with sauce and serve.

Per Serving

Calories 245, Kilojoules 1025, Protein 24 g,	
Carbohydrates 5 g, Total Fat 14 g, Saturated Fat 5 g,	
Monounsaturated Fat 5 g, Polyunsaturated Fat 4 g,	
Cholesterol 78 mg, Sodium 221 mg, Fiber 1 g	

Tip: Leftovers are wonderful served cold on top of a green salad.

Grilled Caesar Salmon Fillets

Gloria D. Good, Harrisonburg, VA

Makes 6 servings

Prep. Time: 10 minutes
Marinating Time: 2 hours
Grilling Time: 15–20 minutes

Pyramid Servings	
Vegetables ○○○○○➤	
Fruits ○○○○○➤	
Carbohydrates ○○○○○○○○	
Protein & Dairy ●●○○○○○○	
Fats ○○○○○	

6 4-oz. salmon fillets
½ cup fat-free Caesar salad
  dressing
1½ Tbsp. reduced-sodium soy
  sauce
1 garlic clove, minced

1. Place fillets in plastic bag. Add salad dressing. Seal bag and turn to coat.
2. Refrigerate for at least 2 hours.
3. Drain and discard marinade.
4. Place salmon, skin-side down, on grill rack. Grill, covered, over medium heat for 5 minutes.
5. In shallow bowl combine soy sauce and garlic. Brush over salmon.
6. Grill 10–15 minutes longer, or until fish flakes easily with a fork, basting occasionally.

Per Serving

Calories 170, Kilojoules 711, Protein 23 g,	
Carbohydrates 2 g, Total Fat 7 g, Saturated Fat 1 g,	
Monounsaturated Fat 3 g, Polyunsaturated Fat 3 g,	
Cholesterol 62 mg, Sodium 460 mg, Fiber *trace*	

Dietitian's tip: Salmon works well on the grill. After you've wrapped the fish in aluminum foil, grill until firm and opaque throughout, about 10 minutes on each side. Serve on couscous with steamed green beans on the side.

Maple-Glazed Salmon
Jenelle Miller
Marion, SD

Makes 6 servings

Prep. Time: 10 minutes
Grilling Time: 8–9 minutes

2 tsp. paprika
2 tsp. chili powder
½ tsp. ground cumin
½ tsp. brown sugar
1 tsp. kosher salt, *optional*
    (included in analysis)
6 4-oz. salmon fillets
1 Tbsp. maple syrup

Pyramid Servings		
Vegetables OOOOO➤		
Fruits OOOOO➤		
Carbohydrates OOOOOOOO		
Protein & Dairy ●●OOOOO		
Fats OOOOO		

1. Spray grill rack with cooking spray. Heat grill to medium.
2. Combine first four ingredients in a small bowl.
3. Sprinkle fillets with salt if you wish. Rub with paprika mixture.
4. Place fish on grill rack. Grill 7 minutes.
5. Drizzle fish with maple syrup.
6. Grill 1–2 minutes more, or until fish flakes easily when tested with a fork.

Per Serving

Calories 221, Kilojoules 925, Protein 23 g,
Carbohydrates 3 g, Total Fat 13 g, Saturated Fat 3 g,
Monounsaturated Fat 5 g, Polyunsaturated Fat 5 g,
Cholesterol 66 mg, Sodium 397 mg, Fiber 0.5 g

Salmon with Spaghetti
Scarlett von Bernuth
Canon City, CO

Makes 6 servings

Prep. Time: 15 minutes
Baking Time: 20–30 minutes

6 5-oz. salmon fillets
2 Tbsp. olive oil
15-oz. can chopped tomatoes,
    no salt added, undrained
1 Tbsp. chopped parsley
1 Tbsp. minced onion
1 Tbsp. chopped green bell sweet pepper
dash of black pepper
½ lb. whole wheat spaghetti, cooked
1 Tbsp. parsley
¼ cup bread crumbs

Pyramid Servings		
Vegetables OOOOO➤		
Fruits OOOOO➤		
Carbohydrates ●●OOOOOO		
Protein & Dairy ●●OOOOO		
Fats ●OOOO		

1. Coat baking pan with oil. Lay salmon fillets in pan.
2. In a good-sized bowl, mix together tomatoes, parsley, onion, green pepper, and black pepper.
3. Stir in spaghetti. Mix and spoon over salmon.
4. Bake at 350° for 20–30 minutes.
5. Sprinkle with parsley and bread crumbs.

Per Serving

Calories 416, Kilojoules 1741, Protein 34 g,
Carbohydrates 38 g, Total Fat 14 g, Saturated Fat 2 g,
Monounsaturated Fat 7.5 g, Polyunsaturated Fat 4.5 g,
Cholesterol 78 mg, Sodium 131 mg, Fiber 5 g

Quick Salmon Patties

Dorothy VanDeest
Memphis, TN

Makes 3 servings

Prep. Time: 10 minutes
Cooking Time: 3–4 minutes

2 6-oz. cans salmon, boned,
  skinned, and drained
2 egg whites, *or* egg substitute
  equivalent to 1 egg
½ tsp. Worcestershire sauce
⅛ tsp. pepper
⅓ cup finely chopped onion
5 soda crackers with unsalted tops,
  crushed
2 tsp. olive oil

Pyramid Servings	
Vegetables	OOOOO▸
Fruits	OOOOO▸
Carbohydrates	OOOOOOOO
Protein & Dairy	●OOOOOO
Fats	●OOOO

1. In a good-sized bowl, combine first six
ingredients and mix well.
2. Shape into six patties.
3. In a skillet, cook patties in oil over
medium heat for 1½–2 minutes.
4. Flip patties over. Cook 1½–2 minutes
more, or until heated through.

Per Serving

Calories 220, Kilojoules 920, Protein 29 g,
Carbohydrates 5 g, Total Fat 9 g, Saturated Fat 1.5 g,
Monounsaturated Fat 5 g, Polyunsaturated Fat 2.5 g,
Cholesterol 92 mg, Sodium 537 mg, Fiber 0.5 g

Parsnip Tuna Burgers

Karel Umble
New Holland, PA

Makes 8 servings

Prep. Time: 20 minutes
Cooking Time: 7–9 minutes

2 large parsnips, cooked until
  soft
2 egg whites, lightly beaten
3 tsp. fresh chopped parsley,
  or 1 tsp. dried parsley
  flakes
2 tsp. fresh lemon juice
½ tsp. lemon zest
½ tsp. dried dill weed
¼ tsp. pepper
2 6-oz. cans water-packed tuna, drained
1½ Tbsp. olive oil

Pyramid Servings	
Vegetables	OOOOO▸
Fruits	OOOOO▸
Carbohydrates	OOOOOOOO
Protein & Dairy	●OOOOOO
Fats	OOOOO

1. Mash parsnips.
2. In a bowl, combine all ingredients except
olive oil.
3. Form into 8 burgers.
4. Cook in olive oil over medium heat in a
large skillet until lightly browned on one side,
about 4–5 minutes.
5. Flip burgers. Continue cooking until
browned on the other side, about 3–4 minutes.

Per Serving

Calories 105, Kilojoules 439, Protein 12 g,
Carbohydrates 6 g, Total Fat 4 g, Saturated Fat 1 g,
Monounsaturated Fat 2 g, Polyunsaturated Fat 1 g,
Cholesterol 18 g, Sodium 180 mg, Fiber 1 g

Jamaican Seafood Medley

Mary Ann Lefever
Lancaster, PA

Makes 4 servings

Prep. Time: 15–20 minutes
Marinating Time: 2 hours
Cooking Time: 20 minutes

Pyramid Servings

| Vegetables |
| ○○○○○➤ |
| Fruits |
| ○○○○○➤ |
| Carbohydrates |
| ◑○○○○○○○ |
| Protein & Dairy |
| ●◑○○○○○ |
| Fats |
| ●○○○○ |

2 Tbsp. packed brown sugar
1½ Tbsp. orange juice
1½ Tbsp. lime juice
2 cloves garlic, minced
½ tsp. minced ginger
1 tsp. grated orange peel
1 tsp. grated lime peel
1 tsp. salt
½ tsp. black pepper
⅛ tsp. ground cinnamon
dash ground cloves
½ tsp. Tabasco sauce
½ lb. orange roughy, cut into bite-sized
   pieces
½ lb. sea scallops, cut in half, *or* quarters
   if very large
½ lb. shrimp, shelled and deveined
1 Tbsp. olive oil
¾ cup baby corn ears, snapped in fourths,
   or ¾ cup corn kernels
1 Tbsp. green onions, sliced
half a green bell sweet pepper, julienne-
   sliced

1. Combine sugar, juices, and seasonings in a bowl or jar with a tight-fitting lid.
2. Place seafood in a good-sized bowl. Pour seasoned juices over seafood. Mix well.
3. Cover and refrigerate at least 2 hours.
4. Drain seafood and discard marinade.
5. In a large skillet or saucepan, sauté seafood and vegetables in olive oil over medium heat for 15 minutes, or until fish is just tender and vegetables are crisp-tender.

Per Serving

Calories 226, Kilojoules 946, Protein 20 g,
Carbohydrates 24 g, Total Fat 6 g, Saturated Fat 0.8 g,
Monounsaturated Fat 4 g, Polyunsaturated Fat 1.2 g,
Cholesterol 53 mg, Sodium 290 mg, Fiber 1 g

Dietitian's tip: Though shrimp is higher in cholesterol than most meat and poultry, it's lower in fat and saturated fat. And fat, not cholesterol, has the greatest effect on blood cholesterol. Shrimp also has omega-3 fatty acids, a type of fat that's good for your heart.

A Tip —

When testing new recipes have your family rate them. Write comments, along with the date that you made the recipe, in the page margins next to the recipe.

Mediterranean Fish Stew

Willard Roth
Elkhart, IN

Makes 8 servings

Prep. Time: 15–20 minutes
Cooking Time: 50–60 minutes

4-oz. jar dried tomatoes
2 cups water
1 large onion, chopped
1 green bell sweet pepper,
   chopped
2 Tbsp. olive oil
2 8-oz. bottles clam juice, *divided*
28-oz. can diced tomatoes, no salt added,
   undrained
1 cup dry red wine
4 garlic cloves, crushed
2 Tbsp. fresh herbs, *or* 2 tsp. dried (such
   as thyme, rosemary, basil, marjoram)
2 bay leaves
½ cup Kalamata olives, sliced
2 15-oz. cans navy, *or* pinto, beans, rinsed
   and drained
1 lb. fresh firm fish (such as tuna, tilapia,
   grouper), cut in 2" chunks
2 tsp. fennel seeds, crushed
½ cup freshly grated Parmesan cheese

Pyramid Servings

Vegetables
●●●○○▸

Fruits
○○○○○▸

Carbohydrates
○○○○○○○○

Protein & Dairy
●●○○○○○

Fats
●●○○○

1. Simmer dried tomatoes in 2 cups water
in a saucepan until soft, about 15 minutes.
Discard water.
2. Sauté onion and green pepper in oil in
large cooking pot.
3. In blender or processor, combine softened
dried tomatoes with 1 bottle clam juice until
smooth. Add to cooking pot.
4. Stir in second bottle of juice, diced
tomatoes, wine, garlic, herbs, and olives. Cover
and simmer 20 minutes.
5. Add beans, fish, and fennel seeds. Cover
and simmer about 15 minutes. Remove bay
leaves.

6. Ladle into bowls. Top each serving with
1 Tbsp. cheese.

Per Serving

Calories 392, Kilojoules 1640, Protein 27 g,
Carbohydrates 54 g, Total Fat 7 g, Saturated Fat 2 g,
Monounsaturated Fat 4 g, Polyunsaturated Fat 1 g,
Cholesterol 30 mg, Sodium 730 mg, Fiber 16 g

Baltimore Crab Cakes

Cathy Kruba
Balto, MD

Makes 4 servings

Prep. Time: 10–15 minutes
Baking Time: 25 minutes

1 lb. crabmeat, flaked
4 slices whole wheat bread
   made into crumbs
¼ cup minced fresh parsley
¼ cup light mayonnaise
2 Tbsp. prepared mustard
¼ tsp. salt
⅛ tsp., or a few drops, hot sauce, *optional*

Pyramid Servings

Vegetables
○○○○○▸

Fruits
○○○○○▸

Carbohydrates
●○○○○○○○

Protein & Dairy
●●○○○○○

Fats
●○○○○

1. Combine all ingredients thoroughly in a
large bowl.
2. Divide mixture evenly into 8 portions and
shape into patties.
3. Place on lightly greased baking sheet.
4. Bake at 350° for 15 minutes.
5. Turn crab cakes over. Bake 10 minutes
longer, or until crispy.

Per Serving

Calories 266, Kilojoules 1113, Protein 24 g,
Carbohydrates 24 g, Total Fat 8 g, Saturated Fat 1.5 g,
Monounsaturated Fat 2.5 g, Polyunsaturated Fat 4 g,
Cholesterol 94 mg, Sodium 748 mg, Fiber 3 g

Salads

Strawberry Spinach Salad with Turkey or Chicken

Genelle Taylor
Perrysburg, OH

Makes 4 main-dish servings

Prep. Time: 45–60 minutes

1 lb. asparagus spears
¼ cup poppy seed dressing
1 tsp. grated orange peel
1 Tbsp. orange juice
8 cups torn fresh spinach, *or* assorted greens
2 cups sliced fresh strawberries and/or whole blueberries
¾ lb. cooked turkey *or* grilled chicken, cubed
¼ cup pecan halves

Pyramid Servings	
Vegetables	●●○○○▶
Fruits	◐○○○○▶
Carbohydrates	○○○○○○○○
Protein & Dairy	●○○○○○○○
Fats	●●○○○

1. Snap off and discard woody bases from asparagus. Cut into 1" pieces.

2. In a 1-quart microwaveable covered dish, cook asparagus with 2 tablespoons of water for 5–7 minutes, or until tender-crisp. Drain. Rinse with cold water; drain again.

3. In a medium bowl, stir together poppy seed dressing, orange peel, and orange juice. Set aside.

4. In a salad bowl, combine asparagus, greens, berries, and turkey or chicken. Add dressing mixture and toss.

5. Top with pecans just before serving.

Per Serving

Calories 288, Kilojoules 1205, Protein 29 g,
Carbohydrates 13 g, Total Fat 13 g, Saturated Fat 2 g,
Monounsaturated Fat 8 g, Polyunsaturated Fat 3 g,
Cholesterol 73 mg, Sodium 200 mg, Fiber 5 g

Blueberry Chicken Salad

Mary Fisher
Leola, PA

Makes 4 main-dish servings

Prep. Time: 30 minutes
Chilling Time: 30 minutes or more

Pyramid Servings	
Vegetables	●○○○○➤
Fruits	○●○○○➤
Carbohydrates	○○○○○○○○
Protein & Dairy	●○○○○○○
Fats	○○○○○

2 cups fresh blueberries,
    divided
2 cups cubed cooked chicken
    breast
¾ cup chopped celery
½ cup diced sweet red pepper
½ cup thinly sliced green onions
6-oz. carton low-fat lemon yogurt
    (sweetened with low calorie sweetener)
3 Tbsp. fat-free mayonnaise
½ tsp. salt substitute
Bibb lettuce leaves, *optional*

1. Set aside a few blueberries for garnish.
2. In a large bowl, gently combine the chicken, celery, red pepper, onions, and remaining blueberries.
3. In a separate bowl, combine yogurt, mayonnaise, and salt substitute.
4. Drizzle dressing mixture over chicken mixture and gently toss to coat.
5. Cover and refrigerate at least 30 minutes.
6. Serve over lettuce-lined plates, if you wish.
7. Top each plate with reserved blueberries.

Per Serving

Calories 216, Kilojoules 904, Protein 23 g,
Carbohydrates 20 g, Total Fat 5 g, Saturated Fat 0.5 g,
Monounsaturated Fat 3 g, Polyunsaturated Fat 1.5 g,
Cholesterol 64 mg, Sodium 198 mg, Fiber 3 g

Turkey Mandarin Salad

Linda E. Wilcox
Blythewood, SC

Makes 4 main-dish servings

Prep. Time: 20 minutes

Pyramid Servings	
Vegetables	●○○○○➤
Fruits	○●○○○➤
Carbohydrates	○○○○○○○○
Protein & Dairy	●○○○○○○
Fats	○○○○○

5 cups red leaf, *or* Romaine,
    lettuce
2 cups fresh spinach leaves
½ lb. roasted turkey, cut in
    julienne strips
11-oz. can mandarin oranges,
    drained
¼ cup orange juice
1½ tsp. red wine vinegar
1½ tsp. poppy seeds
2 Tbsp. honey
1½ tsp. olive oil
1 tsp. Dijon mustard
⅛ tsp. black pepper

1. In a large bowl, combine lettuce, spinach, turkey, and oranges.
2. In a small bowl, whisk together orange juice, vinegar, poppy seeds, honey, oil, mustard, and pepper.
3. Pour dressing over turkey mixture. Toss to coat evenly. Serve immediately.

Per Serving

Calories 188, Kilojoules 787, Protein 19 g,
Carbohydrates 19 g, Total Fat 4 g, Saturated Fat 1 g,
Monounsaturated Fat 1.5 g, Polyunsaturated Fat 1.5 g,
Cholesterol 39 mg, Sodium 146 mg, Fiber 2 g

Tip: You can use leftover turkey from another meal for this recipe.

Tossed Chicken Salad

Marci Baum, Manheim, PA

Makes 10 main-dish servings

Prep. Time: 40–50 minutes

Pyramid Servings

Vegetables
●●○○○➤

Fruits
○○○○○➤

Carbohydrates
○○○○○○○

Protein & Dairy
●○○○○○○○

Fats
●○○○○

4 cups coarsely shredded
  cooked chicken
½ cup chopped scallions
½ lb. (about 3½ cups) snow
  peas
1 lb. (about 6 cups) Napa
  cabbage, cut in ⅓" strips
1 lb. (about 8 cups) Romaine lettuce, torn
½ cup chopped fresh cilantro
¼ cup sliced almonds, toasted
2 Tbsp. sesame seeds, toasted

Dressing:
¼ cup reduced-sodium soy sauce
¼ cup lemon juice
2 Tbsp. honey
1 Tbsp. vinegar
½ tsp. black pepper
1 Tbsp. sesame oil
2 Tbsp. canola oil
2 Tbsp. water

1. Prepare Dressing by whisking together first 5 ingredients in a medium bowl.
2. Whisk oils and water in next until thoroughly combined. Set aside.
3. Tear, chop, shred, and toast individual main-salad ingredients.
4. Just before serving, toss chicken, scallions, and half of dressing together in a large bowl.
5. Add remaining ingredients and remaining dressing. Toss to coat.
6. Serve immediately.

Per Serving

Calories 201, Kilojoules 841, Protein 21 g,
Carbohydrates 11 g, Total Fat 9 g, Saturated Fat 1.5 g,
Monounsaturated Fat 4.5 g, Polyunsaturated Fat 3 g,
Cholesterol 47 mg, Sodium 254 mg, Fiber 3 g

Tabbouleh with Garbanzos and Mint

Jenelle Miller
Marion, SD

Makes 6 main-dish servings

Prep. Time: 20 minutes
Standing Time: 3 hours
Chilling Time: 1 hour or more

Pyramid Servings

Vegetables
●●○○○➤

Fruits
○○○○○➤

Carbohydrates
●○○○○○○○

Protein & Dairy
◐○○○○○○

Fats
●○○○○

1¼ cups raw bulgur wheat, *or*
  cracked wheat
4 cups boiling water
1 cup cooked garbanzos,
  rinsed and drained
1¼ cups fresh minced parsley
¾ cup fresh minced mint
¾ cup minced scallions
3 tomatoes, chopped
¾ cup lemon juice
2 Tbsp. olive oil
2 Tbsp. water

1. Place raw bulgur into large stockpot. Pour 4 cups boiling water over bulgur. Let stand 3 hours.
2. Meanwhile, mince and chop other ingredients. Refrigerate until needed.
3. At the end of the 3 hours, drain bulgur well.
4. Add remaining ingredients to bulgur and stir well.
5. Chill at least 1 hour before serving.

Per Serving

Calories 211, Kilojoules 883, Protein 7 g,
Carbohydrates 36 g, Total Fat 6 g, Saturated Fat 3.5 g,
Monounsaturated Fat 1 g, Polyunsaturated Fat 1.5 g,
Cholesterol 1 mg, Sodium 18 mg, Fiber 9 g

Fruit and Rice

Jean Binns Smith
Bellefonte, PA

Makes 8 main-dish servings

Prep. Time: 20 minutes
Cooking Time: 45–50 minutes
Chilling Time: 1 hour or more

Pyramid Servings	
Vegetables	○○○○○➤
Fruits	●●●○○➤
Carbohydrates	●○○○○○○○
Protein & Dairy	○○○○○○○
Fats	●●●○○

1 cup uncooked brown rice
2½ cups water
1½ cups raisins
½ cup dried cranberries
2 Tbsp. fresh mint
2 Tbsp. fresh parsley
2 Tbsp. fresh chives
2 cups chopped, unpeeled apple
1 Tbsp. lemon juice
1½ cups red grapes, halved
⅔ cup pecans

Dressing:
¼ cup extra-virgin olive oil
¾ cup orange juice
3 Tbsp. honey

1. Cook rice in water in a stockpot over low heat, covered. Cook 45–50 minutes, or until rice is tender.

2. Meanwhile, mix dressing in a bowl. Stir in raisins and cranberries, mint, parsley, and chives.

3. Place apples in a separate container. Sprinkle with lemon juice. Refrigerate until needed.

4. Chill cooked rice for 1 hour.

5. When thoroughly chilled, stir in apples, grapes, and nuts.

6. Stir in dressing and serve.

Per Serving
Calories 367, Kilojoules 1536, Protein 4 g,
Carbohydrates 58 g, Total Fat 14 g, Saturated Fat 2 g,
Monounsaturated Fat 9 g, Polyunsaturated Fat 3 g,
Cholesterol 0 mg, Sodium 7 mg, Fiber 4 g

Tip: You can add pineapple or change the fruit to suit your meal.

Refried Bean Salad

Sylvia Beiler
Lowville, NY

Makes 4 main-dish servings

Prep. Time: 15 minutes
Cooking Time: 15 minutes

Pyramid Servings	
Vegetables	●●○○○➤
Fruits	○○○○○➤
Carbohydrates	○○○○○○○○
Protein & Dairy	●○○○○○○
Fats	●○○○○

⅓ cup diced green pepper
1 tsp. diced hot pepper
⅓ cup diced onion
1 Tbsp. canola oil
15-oz. can pinto, kidney, *or* black beans, rinsed and drained (ideally without added salt)
2 tsp. taco seasoning mix
⅛ tsp. pepper
2 tomatoes, diced
2 cups torn lettuce

1. In a medium-sized saucepan, sauté green pepper, hot pepper, and onion in oil until tender.

2. Blend beans and sautéed vegetables in blender until smooth, or mash with potato masher.

3. Return vegetable mixture to saucepan. Add taco seasoning and pepper. Heat until bubbly hot.

4. Serve over lettuce and top with chopped fresh tomatoes.

Per Serving
Calories 146, Kilojoules 611, Protein 7 g,
Carbohydrates 21 g, Total Fat 4 g, Saturated Fat 0.5 g,
Monounsaturated Fat 2.5 g, Polyunsaturated Fat 1 g,
Cholesterol 0 mg, Sodium 280 mg, Fiber 8 g

Asparagus Tossed Salad

Carolyn Baer, Conrath, WI

Makes 8 servings

Prep. Time: 15 minutes
Cooking Time: 5 minutes
Standing Time: 30 minutes

Pyramid Servings		
Vegetables		
●○○○○▸		
Fruits		
○○○○○▸		
Carbohydrates		
○○○○○○○○		
Protein & Dairy		
○○○○○○○		
Fats		
●○○○○		

4 cups water
2 medium carrots, sliced
1 lb. fresh asparagus, cut into
    1" pieces
8 cups torn Bibb lettuce

Orange Ginger Vinaigrette:
¼ cup orange juice
4½ tsp. olive, *or* canola, oil
2 Tbsp. white wine vinegar, rice vinegar,
    or cider vinegar
1 Tbsp. honey
1 tsp. Dijon mustard
¼ tsp. ground ginger
½ tsp. grated orange peel
⅛ tsp. salt

1. In a large saucepan, bring 4 cups water to a boil. Add carrots. Cover and boil 1 minute.
2. Add asparagus. Cover and boil 3 minutes longer.
3. Drain and immediately place vegetables in ice water. Drain and pat dry. Place in large mixing bowl.
4. In a jar with a tight-fitting lid, combine the vinaigrette ingredients. Shake well.
5. Drizzle over vegetables and toss to coat.
6. Let stand 30 minutes to allow dressing flavors to penetrate vegetables.
7. Combine lettuce, carrots, asparagus, and dressing. Serve immediately.

Per Serving

Calories 59, Kilojoules 247, Protein 2 g,
Carbohydrates 7 g, Total Fat 3 g, Saturated Fat 0.5 g,
Monounsaturated Fat 2 g, Polyunsaturated Fat 0.5 g,
Cholesterol 0 mg, Sodium 64 mg, Fiber 2 g

Beet Walnut Salad

Jenny Kennedy
Driggs, ID

Makes 8 servings

Prep. Time: 20 minutes
Cooking Time: 45 minutes

Pyramid Servings		
Vegetables		
●○○○○▸		
Fruits		
◐○○○○▸		
Carbohydrates		
○○○○○○○○		
Protein & Dairy		
○○○○○○○		
Fats		
●○○○○		

1 small bunch beets, *or*
    enough canned beets (no
    salt added) to make 3 cups,
    drained
¼ cup red wine vinegar
¼ cup chopped apple
¼ cup chopped celery
3 Tbsp. balsamic vinegar
1 Tbsp. olive oil
1 Tbsp. water
8 cups fresh salad greens
freshly ground pepper
3 Tbsp. chopped walnuts
¼ cup Gorgonzola cheese, crumbled

1. Steam raw beets in water in saucepan until tender. Slip off skins. Rinse to cool.
2. Slice in ½" rounds. In a medium bowl, toss with red wine vinegar.
3. Add apples and celery. Toss together.
4. In a large bowl, combine balsamic vinegar, olive oil, and water. Add salad greens and toss.
5. Put greens onto individual salad plates. Top with sliced beet mixture.
6. Sprinkle with pepper, walnuts, and cheese. Serve immediately.

Per Serving

Calories 89, Kilojoules 372, Protein 3 g,
Carbohydrates 8 g, Total Fat 5 g, Saturated Fat 1.6 g,
Monounsaturated Fat 2 g, Polyunsaturated Fat 1.4 g,
Cholesterol 5 mg, Sodium 115 mg, Fiber 2.5 g

Edamame/Soybean Salad

Esther Porter
Minneapolis, MN

Makes 4 servings

Prep. Time: 15–20 minutes

16 ozs. fresh, *or* frozen, green
    soybeans (thawed if frozen)
¼ cup seasoned rice vinegar
1 Tbsp. corn oil
⅛ tsp. black pepper
sliced radishes and fresh
    cilantro leaves for
    garnishing

Pyramid Servings	
Vegetables ○○○○○➤	
Fruits ○○○○○➤	
Carbohydrates ○○○○○○○○	
Protein & Dairy ●○○○○○○	
Fats ●○○○○	

1. Mix together rice vinegar, oil, and black
pepper. Pour over soybeans in a large bowl.
2. Garnish with radishes and cilantro.
3. Chill and serve.

Per Serving

Calories 164, Kilojoules 686, Protein 12 g,
Carbohydrates 9 g, Total Fat 9 g, Saturated Fat 0.5 g,
Monounsaturated Fat 5.5 g, Polyunsaturated Fat 3 g,
Cholesterol 0 mg, Sodium 11 mg, Fiber 6 g

Tip: Also good served over low-fat cottage cheese.

A Tip —

    Some really good dishes can be very easy
to make. Learn to enjoy the pleasure of
simple foods.

My Brother's Black Bean Salad

Shirley Hedman
Schenectady, NY

Makes 16 servings

Prep. Time: 20 minutes

3 cups black beans (2 15-oz.
    cans, drained and rinsed)
1½ cups corn, fresh, frozen,
    or canned
1 cup chopped red sweet
    bell pepper
¾ cup chopped red onion
4–6 cloves minced garlic, according to
    your taste preference
½ cup chopped fresh cilantro
1 minced jalapeño, *or* a 4-oz. can chopped
    green chilies
⅓ cup olive oil
½ cup lemon juice
¼ tsp. white pepper

Pyramid Servings	
Vegetables ●○○○○➤	
Fruits ○○○○○➤	
Carbohydrates ○○○○○○○○	
Protein & Dairy ◑○○○○○○	
Fats ●○○○○	

1. Drain and rinse the beans, and the corn
if it's canned. (If you're using fresh or frozen
corn, you don't need to cook it.)
2. Mix all ingredients in a large bowl.
3. Serve immediately, or refrigerate until 2
hours before serving. Remove from fridge and
serve at room temperature.

Per Serving

Calories 116, Kilojoules 485, Protein 4 g,
Carbohydrates 14 g, Total Fat 5 g, Saturated Fat 1 g,
Monounsaturated Fat 3 g, Polyunsaturated Fat 1 g,
Cholesterol 0 mg, Sodium 135 mg, Fiber 3 g

*Dietitian's tip: It's a good idea to wear rubber
or plastic gloves when preparing hot peppers such
as jalapeños because the oils can burn your eyes
and skin. If you don't wear gloves, thoroughly
wash your hands with soap and hot water after
handling the peppers.*

Chickpea Salad

Elaine Gibbel

Lititz, PA

Makes 8 servings

Prep. Time: 20–25 minutes
Chilling Time: 4–24 hours

Pyramid Servings

Vegetables
●●○○○►

Fruits
○○○○○►

Carbohydrates
○○○○○○○○

Protein & Dairy
◐○○○○○○

Fats
●○○○○

3 cups coarsely chopped fresh
   tomatoes (about 4 medium)
15-oz. can chickpeas (aka as
   garbanzo beans), rinsed
   and drained
half a large cucumber, peeled,
   quartered, and sliced (about 1 cup)
1 cup chopped green sweet bell pepper
¼ cup finely chopped onion
½ cup snipped parsley, *or* cilantro
¼ cup olive oil
3 Tbsp. red wine vinegar
1 clove garlic, minced
pinch of sugar (about ⅛ tsp.)
mixed salad greens, *optional*
lemon wedges, *optional*

1. In a large bowl combine vegetables and
parsley or cilantro.
2. To make dressing, combine oil, vinegar,
garlic, and sugar in a jar and shake well.
3. Pour dressing over vegetables and toss.
Cover and chill 4–24 hours.
4. Before serving, let stand at room temperature 15 minutes.
5. Serve alone or with mixed greens. Serve
with lemon wedges to squeeze over salad.

Per Serving

Calories 152, Kilojoules 636, Protein 4 g,
Carbohydrates 17 g, Total Fat 8 g, Saturated Fat 1 g,
Monounsaturated Fat 5 g, Polyunsaturated Fat 2 g,
Cholesterol 0 mg, Sodium 167 mg, Fiber 5 g

Lentil Salad

Sharon Brubaker

Myerstown, PA

Makes 8 servings

Prep. Time: 20 minutes
Cooking Time: 15–25 minutes
Chilling Time: 30 minutes

Pyramid Servings

Vegetables
●○○○○►

Fruits
○○○○○►

Carbohydrates
○○○○○○○○

Protein & Dairy
●○○○○○○

Fats
●●○○○

½ cup dry lentils
1½ cups water
15-oz. can garbanzo beans,
   rinsed and drained
4 green onions, chopped
1 green sweet bell pepper, julienned
1 red sweet bell pepper, julienned
1 yellow sweet bell pepper, julienned
1 Tbsp. lemon juice
⅓ cup olive oil
½ cup vinegar
⅓ cup sugar

1. Place lentils and water in saucepan and
bring to boil. Reduce to simmer, cover, and
cook 15–25 minutes, or until lentils are tender.
2. Drain lentils. Combine with remaining
vegetables in a mixing bowl.
3. Mix dressing ingredients (lemon juice,
olive oil, vinegar, and sugar) until thoroughly
blended.
4. Stir dressing into vegetables.
5. Chill at least 30 minutes. Serve chilled.

Per Serving

Calories 235, Kilojoules 983, Protein 6 g,
Carbohydrates 31 g, Total Fat 10 g, Saturated Fat 1.5 g,
Monounsaturated Fat 7.5 g, Polyunsaturated Fat 1 g,
Cholesterol 0 mg, Sodium 164 mg, Fiber 7 g

Tuscan Bean Salad

Eileen B. Jarvis
St. Augustine, FL

Makes 8 servings

Prep. Time: 20 minutes
Chilling Time: 8 hours

Pyramid Servings	
Vegetables	●○○○○▸
Fruits	○○○○○▸
Carbohydrates	○○○○○○○○
Protein & Dairy	●○○○○○○
Fats	●○○○○

3 Tbsp. fresh lemon juice
2 Tbsp. red wine vinegar
2 Tbsp. olive oil
2 tsp. grated lemon zest
1 tsp. honey
½ tsp. freshly ground pepper
3 garlic cloves, minced
2 anchovy fillets, minced, *optional*
1 cup halved grape tomatoes
¾ cup (about ¼ medium) English
    cucumber, chopped
½ cup chopped celery
½ cup thinly sliced red onion
¼ cup chopped fresh flat leaf parsley
1 Tbsp. chopped fresh sage
15½-oz. can garbanzo beans (chickpeas),
    rinsed and drained
15½-oz. can white beans, rinsed and
    drained

1. Combine first 7 ingredients (plus ancho-
vies if you wish) in a small bowl. Stir well
with a whisk.
2. Combine tomatoes and next 7 ingredients
in a large bowl.
3. Add dressing. Toss gently.
4. Cover and chill at least 8 hours, stirring
occasionally.

Per Serving

Calories 172, Kilojoules 720, Protein 7 g,
Carbohydrates 27 g, Total Fat 4 g, Saturated Fat 0.5 g,
Monounsaturated Fat 2.5 g, Polyunsaturated Fat 1 g,
Cholesterol 1 mg, Sodium 199 mg, Fiber 6 g

Crunchy Cabbage Salad

Natalia Showalter
Mt. Solon, VA

Makes 12 servings

Prep. Time: 30 minutes

Pyramid Servings	
Vegetables	●○○○○▸
Fruits	○○○○○▸
Carbohydrates	○○○○○○○○
Protein & Dairy	○○○○○○○
Fats	●○○○○

¼ cup sliced almonds, *or*
    pecan pieces
2 Tbsp. sunflower seeds
1 Tbsp. sesame seeds
half a large head cabbage
    (about 6 cups)
4 green onions, sliced
half a green sweet bell pepper, sliced in
    quarter rings
half a red, *or* yellow, sweet bell pepper,
    sliced

Dressing:
2 Tbsp. canola oil
2 Tbsp. water
2 Tbsp. honey
1 Tbsp. vinegar
½ tsp. pepper
1 tsp. low-sodium chicken bouillon
    granules
¼ tsp. garlic powder
¼ tsp. onion powder
¼ tsp. celery seed

1. Lightly toast nuts and seeds in a dry
skillet. Stir frequently to prevent burning.
Cool. Set aside.
2. Place cabbage flat side down on a cutting
board. With a very sharp chef's knife, slice
thin long strips of cabbage.
3. Combine sliced cabbage, onions, and
peppers in a good-sized bowl.
4. Combine dressing ingredients in jar with
tight seal and shake well.
5. Pour over vegetables.
6. Add toasted nuts and seeds. Toss well to
coat. Serve immediately.

Calories 67, Kilojoules 280, Protein 1 g,
Carbohydrates 7 g, Total Fat 4 g, Saturated Fat 0.3 g,
Monounsaturated Fat 2.4 g, Polyunsaturated Fat 1.3 g,
Cholesterol *trace*, Sodium 11 mg, Fiber 2 g

Tip: You can prepare the vegetables ahead of time and store them in the fridge. You can toast the nuts ahead of time, also, and keep them in the freezer. Then the salad will go together quickly at the last minute.

Confetti Salad
Beth Guntlisbergen
Green Bay, WI

Makes 6 servings
Prep. Time: 20 minutes

Pyramid Servings
Vegetables
○○○○○▸
Fruits
●○○○○▸
Carbohydrates
○○○○○○○○
Protein & Dairy
①○○○○○○○
Fats
●●○○○

2 cups red cabbage, shredded
15½-oz. can white (cannellini) beans, rinsed and drained
11-oz. can mandarin oranges, drained
⅓ cup walnuts, toasted
2 large scallions with green tops, sliced
3 Tbsp. olive oil
2 Tbsp. balsamic vinegar
2 Tbsp. orange juice
pepper to taste

1. Put first 5 ingredients in a bowl.
2. Place olive oil, vinegar, juice, and pepper in a jar with a tight-fitting lid. Shake until thoroughly mixed.
3. Toss everything together.
4. Serve immediately.

Calories 192, Kilojoules 803, Protein 7 g,
Carbohydrates 18 g, Total Fat 11 g, Saturated Fat 2 g,
Monounsaturated Fat 6 g, Polyunsaturated Fat 3 g,
Cholesterol 0 mg, Sodium 197 mg, Fiber 5 g

Flavorful Cole Slaw
Sara Kinsinger
Stuarts Draft, VA

Makes 10 servings
Prep. Time: 20 minutes

Pyramid Servings
Vegetables
●○○○○▸
Fruits
①○○○○▸
Carbohydrates
○○○○○○○○
Protein & Dairy
○○○○○○○○
Fats
●○○○○

1 head green cabbage, shredded
1 cucumber, peeled and diced
1 cup fresh *or* unsweetened (if canned, drained) pineapple, chopped
1 jalapeño pepper, minced
2 Tbsp. extra-virgin cold-pressed olive oil
2 Tbsp. water
1 avocado, pit removed, peeled, and coarsely chopped
2 Tbsp. pine nuts
1 Tbsp. cider vinegar
2 tsp. celery seed

1. Combine prepared cabbage, cucumber, pineapple, and pepper in a bowl.
2. In a blender, combine olive oil, water, avocado, pine nuts, vinegar, and celery seed.
3. Blend well. Pour over cabbage mixture and mix together thoroughly.

Calories 99, Kilojoules 414, Protein 2 g,
Carbohydrates 11 g, Total Fat 5 g, Saturated Fat 0.5 g,
Monounsaturated Fat 3 g, Polyunsaturated Fat 1.5 g,
Cholesterol 0 mg, Sodium 20 mg, Fiber 3 g

Cranberry Walnut Cole Slaw

Marci Baum
Manheim, PA

Makes 8 servings

Prep. Time: 20 minutes
Chilling Time: 3 hours

Pyramid Servings	
Vegetables	●○○○○►
Fruits	●○○○○►
Carbohydrates	○○○○○○○○
Protein & Dairy	○○○○○○○
Fats	●○○○○

1 cup dried cranberries
2 cups red cabbage, finely
   sliced
2 cups green cabbage, finely
   sliced
¼ cup thinly sliced red onion
6 Tbsp. walnuts, coarsely chopped

Dressing:
3 Tbsp. cider vinegar
1 Tbsp. canola oil
2 Tbsp. water
3 Tbsp. honey
1 tsp. celery seed

1. Mix Dressing ingredients together in jar with a tight-fitting lid. Shake until well mixed.
2. Put all cole slaw ingredients except walnuts into bowl and toss with Dressing.
3. Cover and refrigerate 3 hours before serving.
4. Stir and drain off all liquid before serving.
5. Top each salad with 1 Tbsp. chopped walnuts.

Per Serving

Calories 136, Kilojoules 569, Protein 2 g,
Carbohydrates 22 g, Total Fat 5 g, Saturated Fat 0.3 g,
Monounsaturated Fat 2 g, Polyunsaturated Fat 2.7 g,
Cholesterol 0 mg, Sodium 9 mg, Fiber 2 g

Tip: This keeps for about five days, covered and refrigerated.

Marinated Cucumbers

Clarice Williams
Fairbank, IA

Makes 4 servings

Prep. Time: 15 minutes
Chilling Time: 2–24 hours

Pyramid Servings	
Vegetables	●○○○○►
Fruits	○○○○○►
Carbohydrates	○○○○○○○○
Protein & Dairy	○○○○○○○
Fats	●○○○○
Sweets	◐

¼ cup water
1 Tbsp. sugar
3 Tbsp. vinegar
2 tsp. canola oil
½ tsp. dried basil, crushed
⅛ tsp. pepper
several dashes bottled hot
   pepper sauce
2 medium cucumbers, thinly sliced (about
   3 cups)
1 small onion, thinly sliced
½ cup sliced radishes
4 lettuce leaves, *optional*

1. In a medium mixing bowl, stir together water, sugar, vinegar, oil, basil, pepper, and hot pepper sauce.
2. Add cucumbers and onion. Toss to coat.
3. Cover and refrigerate 2–24 hours.
4. Just before serving, toss radishes with cucumbers and onion.
5. Serve on lettuce-lined plates, if you wish.

Per Serving

Calories 80, Kilojoules 335, Protein 2 g,
Carbohydrates 13 g, Total Fat 2 g, Saturated Fat *trace*
Monounsaturated Fat 1 g, Polyunsaturated Fat 1 g,
Cholesterol 0 mg Sodium 18 mg, Fiber 2 g

Cucumbers in Yogurt

Charlotte Hagner
Montague, MI

Makes 4 servings

Prep. Time: 20 minutes
Chilling Time: 1 hour or more

Pyramid Servings	
Vegetables	●●○○○➤
Fruits	○○○○○➤
Carbohydrates	○○○○○○○○
Protein & Dairy	○○○○○○○
Fats	○○○○○

2 medium cucumbers
1 medium white onion
¼ tsp. salt
⅛ tsp. coarsely ground black pepper
½ cup plain low-fat yogurt
½ tsp. dill weed
4 Romaine lettuce leaves, *optional*
4 grape, *or* cherry, tomatoes, *optional*
4 radishes, sliced thin, *optional*

1. Peel cucumbers and make tracks down their sides with tines of a fork. Slice thin.
2. Peel onion and slice very thin into rings.
3. Spread half the cucumber slices in layers over bottom of serving bowl.
4. Follow with half the onion rings.
5. Sprinkle with half the salt, pepper, yogurt, and dill weed. Repeat layers.
6. Refrigerate for at least 1 hour before serving to allow flavors to blend.
7. Bring full bowl to the table, or make 4 individual side salads, each on a leaf of Romaine lettuce garnished with a grape or cherry tomato and/or radish.

Per Serving

Calories 52, Kilojoules 218, Protein 3 g,
Carbohydrates 9 g, Total Fat 1 g, Saturated Fat 0.4 g,
Monounsaturated Fat 0.3 g, Polyunsaturated Fat 0.3 g,
Cholesterol 2 mg, Sodium 171 mg, Fiber 2 g

Shoe Peg Salad

Charlene Bement
Las Cruces, NM

Makes 8 servings

Prep. Time: 15 minutes
Chilling Time: 24 hours

Pyramid Servings	
Vegetables	●●○○○➤
Fruits	○○○○○➤
Carbohydrates	●○○○○○○○
Protein & Dairy	○○○○○○○
Fats	●○○○○

12-oz. can (about 2¼ cups) shoe peg corn, with no salt added, drained
8½-oz. can tiny peas, with no salt added, drained
8-oz. can (or larger) French green beans, with no salt added, drained
1 cup chopped celery
1 cup chopped green onion
1 medium bell sweet pepper, chopped
2-oz. jar red pimento, drained and chopped

Marinade:
¼ cup olive oil
½ cup vinegar
3 Tbsp. sugar

1. Place vegetables in mixing bowl.
2. Combine Marinade ingredients and stir well.
3. Pour Marinade over vegetables and stir well.
4. Cover and refrigerate 24 hours. Stir salad occasionally while it marinates.

Per Serving

Calories 160, Kilojoules 669, Protein 3 g,
Carbohydrates 21 g, Total Fat 7 g, Saturated Fat 1 g,
Monounsaturated Fat 5 g, Polyunsaturated Fat 1 g,
Cholesterol 0 mg, Sodium 41 mg, Fiber 4 g

Couscous Salad

Joan Terwilliger
Lebanon, PA

Makes 12 servings

Prep. Time: 10 minutes
Cooking Time: 10 minutes

3½ cups low-sodium chicken broth
3 Tbsp. unseasoned rice vinegar
1 Tbsp. honey
1 Tbsp. minced ginger
½ tsp. dry mustard
2 cups uncooked couscous

Pyramid Servings

Vegetables	○○○○○➤
Fruits	○○○○○➤
Carbohydrates	●●●○○○○○
Protein & Dairy	○○○○○○○
Fats	○○○○○

1. Bring chicken broth to a boil over high heat in a 3- or 4-quart pan.
2. Add rice vinegar, honey, ginger, and mustard. Blend.
3. Stir in couscous. Cover and remove from heat.
4. Let stand 5 minutes.
5. Fluff with fork, and then serve.

Per Serving

Calories 200, Kilojoules 837, Protein 8 g,
Carbohydrates 40 g, Total Fat 0.5 g, Saturated Fat 0.2 g,
Monounsaturated Fat 0.1 g, Polyunsaturated Fat 0.2 g,
Cholesterol 1 mg, Sodium 40 mg, Fiber 2.6 g

Cranberry Couscous Salad

Rhoda Atzeff
Lancaster, PA

Makes 6 servings

Prep. Time: 20 minutes
Cooking/Standing Time: 20 minutes

1 cup water
¾ cup raw couscous
¾ cup dried cranberries
½ cup chopped carrots
½ cup chopped seeded cucumber
¼ cup thinly sliced green onions
3 Tbsp. balsamic vinegar
1 Tbsp. olive, *or* canola, oil
2 tsp. Dijon mustard
⅛ tsp. pepper
¼ cup slivered almonds, toasted

Pyramid Servings

Vegetables	●○○○○➤
Fruits	○○○○○➤
Carbohydrates	●●○○○○○○
Protein & Dairy	○○○○○○○
Fats	●○○○○

1. In a saucepan, bring water to a boil. Stir in couscous. Remove from heat. Cover and let stand 5 minutes.
2. Fluff with fork. Cool 10 minutes.
3. In a bowl, combine couscous, cranberries, carrots, cucumber, and green onions.
4. In a small bowl, combine vinegar, oil, mustard, and pepper.
5. Pour over couscous mixture. Mix well. Refrigerate if you wish.
6. Just before serving, stir in almonds.

Per Serving

Calories 280 Kilojoules 1172, Protein 7 g,
Carbohydrates 52 g, Total Fat 5 g, Saturated Fat *trace*,
Monounsaturated Fat 3 g, Polyunsaturated Fat 2 g,
Cholesterol 0 mg, Sodium 55 mg, Fiber 4 g

Barley Salad with Feta and Cranberries

Mary Ann Lefever
Lancaster, PA

Makes 6 main-dish servings

Prep. Time: 30 minutes
Cooking/Standing Time: 20–25 minutes

2 cups water
1 cup raw quick barley
½ cup dried cranberries
¼ cup reduced-fat crumbled feta cheese
15-oz. can chickpeas, drained and rinsed
1 cup (about 5) cherry tomatoes, halved
1 medium cucumber, seeded, and diced (about 2 cups)
¼ cup packed fresh parsley leaves, chopped
3 Tbsp. balsamic vinaigrette
freshly ground black pepper, to taste

Pyramid Servings

Vegetables
●○○○○➤

Fruits
●○○○○➤

Carbohydrates
●○○○○○○○

Protein & Dairy
◐○○○○○○

Fats
○○○○○

1. Bring water to boil in medium saucepan over high heat. Add barley. Cover and reduce heat to simmer.

2. Cook 10–12 minutes, or until barley is tender. Let stand covered another 5 minutes.

3. Transfer barley to a large plate, spreading in an even layer. Set plate in freezer for 5 minutes to cool.

4. While barley cools, in a large bowl combine cranberries, feta cheese, chickpeas, tomatoes, cucumbers, and parsley.

5. When barley is cooled, stir into other ingredients.

6. Drizzle vinaigrette over salad and mix in. Sprinkle with pepper.

Per Serving
Calories 229, Kilojoules 958, Protein 8 g, Carbohydrates 45 g, Total Fat 2 g, Saturated Fat 0.4 g, Monounsaturated Fat 1 g, Polyunsaturated Fat 0.6 g, Cholesterol 1.6 mg, Sodium 247 mg, Fiber 7 g

Dietitian's Tip: Cranberries, also known as "bounceberries" because ripe cranberries bounce, are high in vitamin C. One serving can provide about 40 percent of most people's daily needs for vitamin C. Cranberry juice may help fight urinary tract infections because it contains compounds that help stop certain bacteria from attaching to the walls of the bladder and urinary tract.

A Tip —

Recipes using fresh cranberries can be made all year if you purchase them in season (around the holidays) and freeze them right in the bag or other closed container.

Dilled Barley Salad

Esther Nafziger, Bluffton, OH

Makes 8 main-dish servings

Prep. Time: 20 minutes
Cooking/Standing Time: 60–70 minutes
Chilling Time: 1 hour

3 cups water
⅔ cup raw pearl barley
½ cup non-fat mayonnaise
½ cup sliced fresh mushrooms
1 medium carrot, chopped (about ½ cup)
½ cup red bell sweet pepper strips
⅓ cup sliced celery
2 Tbsp. sliced green onion
2 tsp. fresh lemon juice
2 tsp. fresh dill weed
⅛ tsp. pepper
2 Tbsp. chopped walnuts
1 Tbsp. dried currants, *optional* (not calculated in analyses)
lettuce leaves

Pyramid Servings	
Vegetables	●○○○○➤
Fruits	◐○○○○➤
Carbohydrates	◐○○○○○○○
Protein & Dairy	○○○○○○○
Fats	○○○○○

1. Bring water to boil in a 2-quart saucepan over high heat. Stir in barley. Cover. Reduce heat to low. Simmer 45–50 minutes, or until barley is tender.

2. Let stand 5 minutes. Drain. Cool completely.

3. In a medium salad or mixing bowl, combine barley and remaining ingredients, except walnuts, and currants if you wish. Cover with plastic wrap. Chill.

4. Serve salad on lettuce-lined plates. Garnish evenly with walnuts and currants.

Per Serving
Calories 88, Kilojoules 368, Protein 3 g,
Carbohydrates 15 g, Total Fat 2 g, Saturated Fat 0.2 g,
Monounsaturated Fat 0.8 g, Polyunsaturated Fat 1 g,
Cholesterol 1.4 mg, Sodium 140 mg, Fiber 4 g

Tip: If you wish, use 1 cup quick-cooking barley and simmer for 10–12 minutes.

Broccoli Salad

Mary Seielstad
Sparks, NV

Makes 6 servings

Prep. Time: 15 minutes
Chilling Time: 8 hours, or overnight

Dressing:
½ cup light, *or* reduced-fat, mayonnaise
2 Tbsp. sugar
2 tsp. red wine vinegar

Salad:
1 medium head broccoli , cut into florets (about 3 cups)
1 red bell sweet pepper, chopped
4 green onions, chopped
¼ cup chopped walnuts

Pyramid Servings	
Vegetables	●●○○○➤
Fruits	○○○○○➤
Carbohydrates	○○○○○○○○
Protein & Dairy	○○○○○○○
Fats	●○○○○

1. Combine Dressing ingredients in a jar with a tight-fitting lid. Shake to combine and chill overnight.

2. Combine salad ingredients. Pour Dressing over salad and toss to mix.

Per Serving
Calories 88, Kilojoules 368, Protein 3 g,
Carbohydrates 10 g, Total Fat 4 g, Saturated Fat 0.5 g,
Monounsaturated Fat 1.5 g, Polyunsaturated Fat 2 g,
Cholesterol 0 mg, Sodium 178 mg, Fiber 3 g

Dietitian's tip: All walnuts are high in phosphorus, zinc, copper, iron, potassium, and vitamin E and low in saturated fat. But English walnuts have twice as many omega-3 fatty acids as black walnuts do.

Dressed-Up Broccoli Salad

Elaine Vigoda
Rochester, NY

Makes 8 servings

Prep. Time: 20 minutes
Chilling Time: 1 hour or more

Pyramid Servings	
Vegetables ●○○○○➤	
Fruits ◐○○○○➤	
Carbohydrates ○○○○○○○○	
Protein & Dairy ○○○○○○○	
Fats ●○○○○	

4 cups fresh broccoli florets,
  coarsely chopped
½ cup dried cranberries
  (craisins)
½ cup finely chopped sweet,
  or red, onion
⅓ cup peanuts, dry roasted, unsalted
3 Tbsp. red wine, *or* rice wine, vinegar
2 Tbsp. sugar
1 Tbsp. extra-virgin olive oil
3 Tbsp. water
¼ cup light mayonnaise
1 Tbsp. prepared mustard

  1. Combine broccoli, craisins, onion, and peanuts in a large bowl.
  2. In a separate bowl, combine dressing ingredients—vinegar, sugar, oil, water, mayonnaise, and mustard. Blend well.
  3. Pour dressing over broccoli mix. Toss well.
  4. Cover and chill at least 1 hour before serving.

Per Serving

Calories 115, Kilojoules 481, Protein 3 g,
Carbohydrates 16 g, Total Fat 5 g, Saturated Fat 0.6 g,
Monounsaturated Fat 2.7 g, Polyunsaturated Fat 1.7 g,
Cholesterol 1 mg, Sodium 100 mg, Fiber 2 g

Grape Broccoli Salad

Robin Schrock
Millersburg, OH

Makes 15 servings

Prep. Time: 30 minutes

Pyramid Servings	
Vegetables ●○○○○➤	
Fruits ○○○○○➤	
Carbohydrates ○○○○○○○○	
Protein & Dairy ○○○○○○○	
Fats ●○○○○	

6 cups fresh broccoli florets
6 green onions, sliced
1 cup diced celery
2 cups halved green grapes
1 cup low-fat mayonnaise
⅓ cup sugar
1 Tbsp. cider vinegar
1 cup slivered almonds, toasted

  1. In a large salad bowl, combine broccoli, onions, celery, and grapes.
  2. In another bowl, whisk together mayonnaise, sugar, and vinegar.
  3. Pour dressing over broccoli mixture and toss to coat.
  4. Cover and refrigerate until serving. Stir in almonds just before serving.

Per Serving

Calories 83, Kilojoules 347, Protein 3 g,
Carbohydrates 9 g, Total Fat 4 g, Saturated Fat 0.5 g,
Monounsaturated Fat 2.5 g, Polyunsaturated Fat 1 g,
Cholesterol 2 mg, Sodium 147 mg Fiber 3 g

Apple Broccoli Salad

Melanie Mohler
Ephrata, PA

Makes 6 servings

Prep. Time: 20 minutes

Pyramid Servings

Vegetables	●○○○○➤
Fruits	●○○○○➤
Carbohydrates	○○○○○○○○
Protein & Dairy	○○○○○○○
Fats	●●○○○

2 McIntosh, Empire, *or*
    Cortland apples, unpeeled,
    but cored and chopped
3 cups fresh raw broccoli,
    cut up
¼ cup chopped walnuts
1 Tbsp. chopped red onion
⅓ cup raisins
½ cup fat-free vanilla yogurt, sweetened
    with low-calorie sweetener
lettuce leaves

1. Mix all ingredients, except lettuce,
together in a large bowl.
2. Serve on a bed of lettuce.

Per Serving

Calories 109, Kilojoules 456, Protein 4 g,
Carbohydrates 17 g, Total Fat 3.5 g, Saturated Fat 0.2 g,
Monounsaturated Fat 0.8 g, Polyunsaturated Fat 2.5 g,
Cholesterol 0 mg, Sodium 29 mg, Fiber 3 g

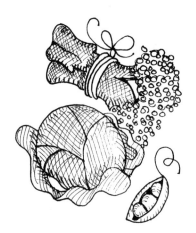

Creamy Lettuce Salad

Janeen L. Zimmerman
Denver, PA

Makes 6 servings

Prep. Time: 20 minutes

Pyramid Servings

Vegetables	●○○○○➤
Fruits	○○○○○➤
Carbohydrates	○○○○○○○○
Protein & Dairy	●○○○○○○
Fats	○○○○○

1 head green leaf lettuce
    (about 4 cups)
1 onion, minced
¼ cup grated Parmesan
    cheese
1 tsp. salt
2½ Tbsp. sugar
1 tsp. prepared mustard
2 Tbsp. fat-free half-and-half
2 Tbsp. vinegar
¼ cup fat-free mayonnaise-type salad
    dressing

1. Wash lettuce and tear coarsely into a
mixing bowl.
2. Add onion and grated cheese.
3. In a separate bowl, mix together salt,
sugar, mustard, and half-and-half.
4. Add vinegar and salad dressing and stir
until smooth.
5. Pour dressing over lettuce and mix
lightly.
6. Serve immediately.

Per Serving

Calories 64, Kilojoules 268, Protein 2 g,
Carbohydrates 10 g, Total Fat 1 g, Saturated Fat 0.6 g,
Monounsaturated Fat 0.3 g, Polyunsaturated Fat 0.1 g,
Cholesterol 3 mg, Sodium 172 mg, Fiber 1 g

Colorful Lettuce Salad

Anna Wise
Seneca Falls, NY

Makes 8 servings
Prep. Time: 20 minutes

Pyramid Servings		
Vegetables ●●○○○➤		
Fruits ○○○○○➤		
Carbohydrates ○○○○○○○○		
Protein & Dairy ○○○○○○○		
Fats ○○○○○		

6 cups red leaf lettuce
1 sweet bell pepper, chopped
   or sliced
½ cup shredded carrots
4 radishes, sliced
1 onion, minced
½ cup shredded low-fat
   cheddar, *or* Colby, cheese
2½ Tbsp. honey
1 tsp. prepared mustard
2 Tbsp. skim milk
2 Tbsp. vinegar
½ cup fat-free mayonnaise

1. Wash lettuce and pull apart coarsely into 2-quart bowl. Add sweet pepper, carrots, radishes, onion, and cheese.
2. In another bowl, whisk together honey, mustard, and milk. Add vinegar and mayonnaise and whisk until smooth.
3. Pour dressing over salad greens and mix lightly. Serve immediately.

Per Serving

Calories 66, Kilojoules 276, Protein 3 g,
Carbohydrates 11 g, Total Fat 1 g, Saturated Fat 0.4 g,
Monounsaturated Fat 0.5 g, Polyunsaturated Fat 0.1 g,
Cholesterol 3 mg, Sodium 198 mg, Fiber 1 g

Dietitian's tip: Vary your salad greens to take advantage of a multitude of flavors and textures. There are four basic types. Head lettuce (iceberg) has a crisp texture and mild flavor. Butterhead (Boston or Bibb) lettuce is delicate in texture and flavor. Loose-leaf lettuce (oak leaf, red leaf, or green leaf) has easily separated leaves that are flavorful and crisp. Romaine (cos) lettuce has a crunchy texture and somewhat bitter taste. Try a different variety each week.

Italian Bean and Potato Salad

Kathy Stoltzfus
Leola, PA

Makes 8 servings
Prep. Time: 20 minutes
Cooking Time: 15 minutes
Marinating time: 45 minutes

Pyramid Servings		
Vegetables ●●○○○➤		
Fruits ○○○○○➤		
Carbohydrates ○○○○○○○○		
Protein & Dairy ●○○○○○○		
Fats ●○○○○		

1 large potato
2 Tbsp. olive oil
2 Tbsp. balsamic vinegar
black pepper
2 15½-oz. cans navy, *or*
   cannellini, beans, rinsed and drained
half a large cucumber, peeled, halved
   lengthwise, and thinly sliced
3 green onions, chopped
1 large sweet bell pepper, chopped
¼ cup fresh basil, chopped
¼ cup fresh parsley, chopped
lettuce leaves
1 large tomato, cut into wedges

1. Cook potato in water 15 minutes. Cool, drain, peel, quarter, and slice thinly.
2. In a large bowl, whisk together oil, vinegar, and black pepper.
3. Add potato, beans, cucumber, and onions. Toss well.
4. Cover and marinate for 30 minutes.
5. Add sweet pepper, basil, and parsley. Marinate an additional 15 minutes, tossing occasionally.
6. Serve on lettuce with tomato wedges.

Per Serving

Calories 217, Kilojoules 908, Protein 10 g,
Carbohydrates 36 g, Total Fat 4 g, Saturated Fat 1 g,
Monounsaturated Fat 2.5 g, Polyunsaturated Fat 0.5 g,
Cholesterol 0 mg, Sodium 187 mg, Fiber 13 g

Dietitian's tip: Cannellini beans are white kidney beans. They're an excellent source of folate and a good source of iron and fiber. Their high-quality protein makes them a great stand-in for meat.

Dutch Potato Salad

Jean Harris Robinson
Cinnaminson, NJ

Makes 8 servings

Prep. Time: 15 minutes
Cooking Time: 15 minutes

2 lbs. small red potatoes
3 qts. cold water
4 slices lean bacon
½ cup thinly sliced red onion
2 Tbsp. olive oil
¼ cup apple cider vinegar
pinch of sugar
dash of black pepper
½ Tbsp. chopped fresh parsley

Pyramid Servings
Vegetables ●○○○○➤
Fruits ○○○○○➤
Carbohydrates ●○○○○○○○
Protein & Dairy ○○○○○○○
Fats ●○○○○

1. Cut cleaned potatoes into bite-size pieces. Place in saucepan and bring to a boil in 3 quarts cold water.

2. Cook about 10 minutes. Drain potatoes, reserving ⅓ cup cooking liquid (important!).

3. Meanwhile, cook bacon until crisp. Drain well on paper towel.

4. Put cooked potatoes into serving bowl. Add sliced onion and stir through.

5. Pour bacon drippings out of pan. Cool pan, and then blot pan with paper towel.

6. Add oil, vinegar, sugar, and reserved potato water to pan. Cook over low heat for one minute, stirring to loosen brown residue left from bacon.

7. Pour dressing over potatoes. Stir and serve warm.

8. Add crumbled bacon just before serving.

Per Serving

Calories 156, Kilojoules 653, Protein 4 g,
Carbohydrates 23 g, Total Fat 5 g, Saturated Fat 1 g,
Monounsaturated Fat 3 g, Polyunsaturated Fat 1 g,
Cholesterol 4 mg, Sodium 105 mg, Fiber 2 g

Tomato Salad

Ruth Fisher
Leicester, NY

Makes 12 servings

Prep. Time: 25 minutes
Chilling Time: 3–4 hours

6 ripe tomatoes, diced
3 sweet bell peppers, sliced
(try a red, a green, and a
yellow for color)
1 red onion, sliced thin
1 cup pitted black olives
⅔ cup olive oil
¼ cup apple cider vinegar
¼ cup fresh parsley
¼ cup chopped green onions
¼ tsp. pepper
2 tsp. sugar
¼ tsp. dried basil

Pyramid Servings
Vegetables ●●○○○➤
Fruits ○○○○○➤
Carbohydrates ○○○○○○○○
Protein & Dairy ○○○○○○○
Fats ●●○○○

1. Combine all vegetables in a large mixing bowl.

2. Mix remaining ingredients together in a separate bowl.

3. Pour dressing over vegetables. Mix thoroughly.

4. Cover and refrigerate 3–4 hours.

Per Serving

Calories 146, Kilojoules 611, Protein 1 g,
Carbohydrates 7 g, Total Fat 13 g, Saturated Fat 2 g,
Monounsaturated Fat 10 g, Polyunsaturated Fat 1 g,
Cholesterol 0 mg, Sodium 103 mg, Fiber 2 g

Summer Squash Salad

Colleen J. Heatwole
Burton, MI

Makes 6 servings

Prep. Time: 15 minutes
Chilling Time: 1 hour

4 medium zucchini, *or*
   summer squash, julienned
3 Tbsp. fresh basil
3 Tbsp. freshly grated
   Parmesan cheese

Dressing:
¼ cup olive oil
2 Tbsp. rice vinegar
2 Tbsp. red wine vinegar
2 tsp. minced garlic
½ tsp. salt
¼ tsp. pepper
¼ tsp. sugar

1. Toss together summer squash, fresh basil, and Parmesan cheese in a large mixing bowl.

2. Combine dressing ingredients in a separate bowl and pour over salad.

3. Mix together well.

4. Cover and chill at least 1 hour before serving. The salad is best if eaten the same day it's made.

Pyramid Servings

Vegetables	●○○○○➤
Fruits	○○○○○➤
Carbohydrates	○○○○○○○○
Protein & Dairy	○○○○○○○
Fats	●●○○○

Per Serving

Calories 115, Kilojoules 481, Protein 3 g,
Carbohydrates 4 g, Total Fat 10 g, Saturated Fat 2 g,
Monounsaturated Fat 7 g, Polyunsaturated Fat 1 g,
Cholesterol 2 mg, Sodium 52 mg, Fiber 1 g

Greek Pasta Salad

Judi Manos
West Islip, NY

Makes 10 servings

Prep. Time: 20 minutes
Cooking Time: 10 minutes
Chilling Time: 1 hour

12-oz. pkg. tri-color rotini
   pasta
⅔ cup unpeeled, seeded,
   diced cucumber
½ cup green onions, thinly
   sliced (reserve the tops!)
1¼ cups frozen baby peas, defrosted
1 cup red bell sweet pepper, diced
¼ cup fat-free mayonnaise
½ cup low-fat cottage cheese
½ cup plain non-fat yogurt
¼ cup green onion tops, sliced
1½ Tbsp. dill weed, finely chopped
¼ tsp. black pepper
2½ ounces (about ⅔ cup) fat-free feta
   cheese, crumbled

1. Cook pasta in boiling water for 7 minutes. Drain and place in a large bowl.

2. Add cucumber, ½ cup green onions, peas, and bell pepper. Set aside.

3. In food processor with metal blade, combine mayonnaise, cottage cheese, yogurt, and ¼ cup green onion tops. Process until completely smooth.

4. Add dill and black pepper and process briefly.

5. Pour over pasta mixture and stir to mix well. Cover and refrigerate until well chilled.

6. Scatter cheese over top just before serving.

Pyramid Servings

Vegetables	●●○○○➤
Fruits	○○○○○➤
Carbohydrates	●○○○○○○○○
Protein & Dairy	◐○○○○○○
Fats	○○○○○

Per Serving

Calories 179, Kilojoules 749, Protein 9 g,
Carbohydrates 31 g, Total Fat 1 g, Saturated Fat 0.1 g,
Monounsaturated Fat 0.4 g, Polyunsaturated Fat 0.5 g,
Cholesterol 1.3 mg, Sodium 200 mg, Fiber 2 g

Berry Good Salad

Barbara Walker
Sturgis, SD

Makes 10 servings
Prep. Time: 20 minutes

Pyramid Servings

Vegetables	●○○○○➤
Fruits	●○○○○➤
Carbohydrates	○○○○○○○○
Protein & Dairy	○○○○○○○
Fats	●○○○○

6 cups torn Romaine lettuce
4 cups spinach leaves
⅓ cup chopped onions
11-oz. can mandarin oranges,
  drained, with juice
  reserved
2 cups cut-up fresh
  strawberries
½ cup craisins
2 cups of your choice of blackberries,
  blueberries, halved grapes, *or* any
  combination of these

Dressing:
3 Tbsp. extra-virgin olive oil
3 Tbsp. honey
½ tsp. pepper
½ tsp. low-sodium beef bouillon granules
¼ tsp. dried basil
3 Tbsp. vinegar
3 Tbsp. reserved mandarin orange juice

1. In a jar with a tight-fitting lid, combine Dressing ingredients. Shake well. Set aside.
2. In a large bowl, combine salad ingredients.
3. Just before serving, shake Dressing again and add to salad. Toss gently.

Per Serving

Calories 120, Kilojoules 502, Protein 1 g,
Carbohydrates 21 g, Total Fat 4.5 g, Saturated Fat 0.5 g,
Monounsaturated Fat 3 g, Polyunsaturated Fat 1 g,
Cholesterol *trace*, Sodium 16 mg, Fiber 3 g

Spinach Berry Salad

Carolyn Baer
Conrath, WI
Gloria Frey
Lebanon, PA

Makes 4 servings
Prep. Time: 20 minutes

Pyramid Servings

Vegetables	●○○○○➤
Fruits	●○○○○➤
Carbohydrates	○○○○○○○○
Protein & Dairy	○○○○○○○
Fats	●○○○○
Sweets	◑

4 packed cups torn fresh
  spinach
1 cup sliced fresh
  strawberries
1 cup fresh, *or* frozen,
  blueberries
1 small sweet onion, sliced
¼ cup chopped pecans,
  toasted

Curry Salad Dressing:
2 Tbsp. white wine vinegar, *or* cider
  vinegar
2 Tbsp. balsamic vinegar
2 Tbsp. honey
2 tsp. Dijon mustard
1 tsp. curry powder (can be eliminated if
  you're serving cautious eaters!)
⅛ tsp. pepper

1. In a large salad bowl, toss together spinach, strawberries, blueberries, onion, and pecans.
2. In a jar with a tight-fitting lid, combine Dressing ingredients. Shake well.
3. Pour over salad and toss to coat. Serve immediately.

Per Serving

Calories 158, Kilojoules 661, Protein 4 g,
Carbohydrates 25 g, Total Fat 5 g, Saturated Fat 0.5 g,
Monounsaturated Fat 3 g, Polyunsaturated Fat 1.5 g,
Cholesterol 0 mg, Sodium 197 mg, Fiber 4 g

Blueberry Spinach Salad
Judi Robb
Manhattan, KS

Makes 8 servings
Prep. Time: 15–20 minutes

Pyramid Servings

Vegetables	●○○○○➤
Fruits	○○○○○➤
Carbohydrates	○○○○○○○○
Protein & Dairy	○○○○○○○
Fats	●●●○○

⅓ cup olive oil
¼ cup raspberry vinegar
2 tsp. Dijon mustard
1 tsp. sugar
10-oz. pkg. fresh spinach, torn
1 cup fresh, or frozen,
  blueberries
¼ cup chopped pecans, toasted
8 Tbsp. blue cheese, crumbled

1. In a jar with a tight-fitting lid, combine first 4 ingredients and shake well.
2. In a large salad bowl, toss spinach, blueberries, and pecans.
3. Add dressing and toss gently.
4. Top each salad with 1 Tbsp. blue cheese. Serve immediately.

Per Serving

Calories 155, Kilojoules 649, Protein 3 g,
Carbohydrates 4 g, Total Fat 14 g, Saturated Fat 3 g,
Monounsaturated Fat 9 g, Polyunsaturated Fat 2 g,
Cholesterol 6 mg, Sodium 197 mg, Fiber 1 g

Spinach and Apple Salad
Elva Bare, Lancaster, PA

Makes 10 servings
Prep. Time: 20–30 minutes

Pyramid Servings

Vegetables	●○○○○➤
Fruits	●○○○○➤
Carbohydrates	○○○○○○
Protein & Dairy	○○○○○○○
Fats	●○○○○

8 cups, or 9-oz. bag, fresh
  baby spinach
⅔ cup dried cherries, *or*
  craisins
2 medium crisp, tart apples,
  unpeeled and diced
½ cup crumbled fat-free feta
  cheese
fresh blueberries, *optional* (and not
  included in analyses)

Poppy Seed Dressing:
2 Tbsp. honey
2 Tbsp. lemon juice
2 Tbsp. chopped onion
3 Tbsp. extra-virgin olive oil
3 Tbsp. water
1½ tsp. poppy seeds

1. Layer spinach, cherries or craisins, apples, feta, and blueberries if you wish, in a large salad bowl.
2. Shake Dressing ingredients in a jar or whip in blender.
3. Pour Dressing over salad just before serving. Toss together gently.

Per Serving

Calories 115, Kilojoules 481, Protein 1 g,
Carbohydrates 18 g, Total Fat 4 g, Saturated Fat 0.6 g,
Monounsaturated Fat 3 g, Polyunsaturated Fat 0.4 g,
Cholesterol 0 mg, Sodium 73 mg, Fiber 2 g

Dietitian's tip: Extra-virgin olive oil is cold-pressed from ripe olives using no chemicals or heat. It's the least processed of the different grades of olive oil. As a result, it retains the highest levels of antioxidants found in the oil. Antioxidants appear to protect the body from age-related changes and certain diseases.

Fruit 'n Veggie Salad

Marcia Kauffman
Waynesboro, VA

Makes 6 servings

Prep. Time: 20 minutes

1½ cups torn fresh spinach
⅔ cup chopped unpeeled
  apple
½ cup broccoli florets
4 Tbsp. raisins
4 dried apricots, chopped
2 tsp. lemon juice
1½ Tbsp. olive, *or* canola, oil
3 Tbsp. water
2 Tbsp. cider vinegar
2 Tbsp. honey
1 Tbsp. sunflower seeds
2 tsp. sesame seeds, toasted

Pyramid Servings		
Vegetables		
◐○○○○▸		
Fruits		
●○○○○▸		
Carbohydrates		
○○○○○○○		
Protein & Dairy		
○○○○○○○		
Fats		
●○○○○		

1. Combine first 5 ingredients in a mixing bowl.

2. In a jar with a tight-fitting lid, combine lemon juice, oil, water, vinegar, and honey. Shake well.

3. Drizzle salad ingredients with dressing just before serving. Toss to coat.

4. Top with sunflower and sesame seeds.

Per Serving
Calories 107, Kilojoules 448, Protein 1 g,
Carbohydrates 16 g, Total Fat 5 g, Saturated Fat 0.5 g,
Monounsaturated Fat 3 g, Polyunsaturated Fat 1.5 g,
Cholesterol 0 mg, Sodium 10 mg, Fiber 2 g

Citrus-Strawberry Spinach Salad

Susan Guarneri
Three Lakes, WI

Makes 12 servings

Prep. Time: 25 minutes

2 navel oranges, peeled and
  sectioned
1 grapefruit, peeled and
  sectioned
1 lb. (about 15 cups) fresh
  spinach, torn into pieces
1 cup strawberries, sliced
¼ cup thinly sliced red onion
2 Tbsp. chopped walnuts, toasted
2 Tbsp. flaxseeds, crushed

Citrus-Balsamic Vinaigrette:
¼ cup extra-virgin olive oil
¼ cup balsamic vinegar
¼ cup reserved orange and grapefruit juices
¼ tsp. pepper

Pyramid Servings		
Vegetables		
●○○○○▸		
Fruits		
◐○○○○▸		
Carbohydrates		
○○○○○○○○		
Protein & Dairy		
○○○○○○○		
Fats		
●○○○○		

1. Over a bowl, peel and section oranges and grapefruit. Reserve juices for dressing.

2. In a large bowl, arrange orange and grapefruit sections, strawberries, and onion slices on bed of spinach.

3. Sprinkle with walnuts and flaxseeds.

4. Whisk together Vinaigrette ingredients in a bowl, or combine in a jar with a tight-fitting lid and shake until well mixed.

5. Drizzle with Citrus-Balsamic Vinaigrette just before serving.

Per Serving
Calories 91, Kilojoules 381, Protein 1 g,
Carbohydrates 9 g, Total Fat 5 g, Saturated Fat 0.5 g,
Monounsaturated Fat 3.5 g, Polyunsaturated Fat 1 g,
Cholesterol 0 mg, Sodium 31 mg, Fiber 2 g

6. Toss dressing with spinach, orange, and beets just before serving.

7. Sprinkle with walnuts if you wish.

Per Serving
Calories 82, Kilojoules 343, Protein 1 g, Carbohydrates 10 g, Total Fat 4 g, Saturated Fat 0.3 g, Monounsaturated Fat 2 g, Polyunsaturated Fat 1.7 g, Cholesterol 0 mg, Sodium 46 mg, Fiber 3 g

Rainbow Spinach Salad

Karen Ceneviva, New Haven, CT

Makes 3 servings

Prep. Time: 20 minutes

3 cups fresh spinach
1 navel orange
half a 14½-oz. can sliced beets, no salt added, drained
½ Tbsp. extra-virgin olive oil
1 Tbsp. red onion, *or shallots,* minced
1½ Tbsp. raspberry, *or red wine,* vinegar
½ tsp. ground black pepper
2 tsp. walnuts, *optional* (not included in analyses)

Pyramid Servings

Vegetables
●○○○○➤

Fruits
○○○○○➤

Carbohydrates
○○○○○○○○

Protein & Dairy
○○○○○○○

Fats
●○○○○

1. Wash spinach and place in bowl.

2. Peel orange over a separate bowl, reserving its juice.

3. Remove orange segments from bowl and cut into slices.

4. Top spinach with beets and orange slices.

5. Combine reserved orange juice, olive oil, onions, vinegar, and pepper.

Apple Crunch Salad

Delores Gnagey, Saginaw, MI

Makes 6 servings

Prep. Time: 20 minutes

1 cup Granny Smith apples, unpeeled and diced
1 cup Golden Delicious apples, unpeeled and diced
½ cup Gala, Fuji, *or* Red Delicious apples, unpeeled and diced
1 cup sectioned oranges
1 medium banana, sliced

Dressing:
¾ cup fat-free sour cream
2 Tbsp. fresh orange juice
2½ tsp. honey
2 tsp. toasted unsweetened coconut

Pyramid Servings

Vegetables
○○○○○➤

Fruits
●◑○○○➤

Carbohydrates
○○○○○○

Protein & Dairy
○○○○○○○

Fats
○○○○○

1. Combine all the fruit in a serving bowl.

2. Mix dressing ingredients together in a small bowl.

3. Toss with fruit mixture and serve.

Per Serving
Calories 93, Kilojoules 389, Protein 2 g, Carbohydrates 22 g, Total Fat *trace*, Saturated Fat *trace*, Monounsaturated Fat *trace*, Polyunsaturated Fat *trace*, Cholesterol 3 mg, Sodium 46 mg, Fiber 2 g

Mom's Apple Salad with Peanut Butter Dressing
Natalia Showalter
Mt. Solon, VA

Makes 8 servings

Prep. Time: 20–25 minutes

2 Golden Delicious apples
2 Red Delicious apples
1 banana, sliced
1½ cups sliced grapes
¼ cup coarsely chopped peanuts

Dressing:
½ cup smooth peanut butter, preferably natural or trans-fat-free
1 Tbsp. brown sugar
1 tsp. lemon juice, *or* vinegar
¼ cup skim milk

1. Wash and chop unpeeled apples into bite-size pieces. Place in mixing bowl.
2. Gently stir in banana and grapes.
3. Combine dressing ingredients in a small bowl.
4. Pour over fruit, tossing to coat.
5. Garnish with chopped peanuts. Serve immediately.

Pyramid Servings	
Vegetables	○○○○○➤
Fruits	●◑○○○➤
Carbohydrates	○○○○○○○○
Protein & Dairy	○○○○○○○
Fats	●●○○○

Per Serving

Calories 192, Kilojoules 803, Protein 6 g,
Carbohydrates 21 g, Total Fat 10 g, Saturated Fat 2 g,
Monounsaturated Fat 5 g, Polyunsaturated Fat 3 g,
Cholesterol *trace*, Sodium 94 mg, Fiber 4 g

Want More Salad
Sherry H. Kauffman
Minot, ND

Makes 4 servings

Prep. Time: 20 minutes

2 Granny Smith apples, unpeeled and cut fine
3 ribs celery, chopped fine
¼ cup raisins
2 Tbsp. sunflower seeds
7-oz. can pineapple chunks in water, drained well, with juice reserved

Dressing:
¼ cup light mayonnaise
¼ cup plain nonfat yogurt
2 Tbsp. orange juice, *or* liquid from canned pineapple
2 tsp. honey

1. Combine first five ingredients in a salad bowl.
2. Combine dressing ingredients in a separate bowl.
3. Pour dressing over fruit. Toss and refrigerate until ready to serve.

Pyramid Servings	
Vegetables	○○○○○➤
Fruits	●◑○○○➤
Carbohydrates	○○○○○○○○
Protein & Dairy	○○○○○○○
Fats	●○○○○

Per Serving

Calories 146, Kilojoules 611, Protein 3 g,
Carbohydrates 28 g, Total Fat 3 g, Saturated Fat 0.3 g,
Monounsaturated Fat 0.7 g, Polyunsaturated Fat 2 g,
Cholesterol 2 mg, Sodium 164 mg, Fiber 4 g

Spiced Fruit Salad

Teresa Koenig
Leola, PA

Makes 8 servings

Prep. Time: 20 minutes

1½ cups fat-free plain yogurt
¼ cup brown sugar
¼ tsp. cinnamon
⅛ tsp. nutmeg
3 medium bananas, sliced
2 medium apples, unpeeled
    and cubed
1 Tbsp. lemon juice
1 lb. seedless grapes, halved

Pyramid Servings

Vegetables
○○○○○➤
Fruits
●○○○○➤
Carbohydrates
○○○○○○○○
Protein & Dairy
◐○○○○○○
Fats
○○○○○

1. In a small bowl, combine yogurt, sugar, and spices.
2. In another bowl, gently toss bananas and apples with lemon juice. Stir in grapes.
3. Drizzle fruit with yogurt topping. Serve immediately.

Per Serving

Calories 116, Kilojoules 485, Protein 3g,
Carbohydrates 26g, Total Fat *trace*, Saturated Fat *trace*,
Monounsaturated Fat *trace*, Polyunsaturated Fat *trace*,
Cholesterol 0mg, Sodium 31mg, Fiber 3g

Fruit Salad

Kelly Amos
Pittsboro, NC

Makes 6 servings

Prep. Time: 20 minutes

20-oz. can unsweetened
    pineapple chunks
1 small pkg. sugar-free
    vanilla instant pudding
    mix
1 firm banana, cut into bite-
    size pieces
1 Tbsp. lemon juice
1½ cups grapes, cut in halves
1 cup blueberries
1 apple, unpeeled and cut into bite-size
    pieces

Pyramid Servings

Vegetables
○○○○○➤
Fruits
●○○○○➤
Carbohydrates
○○○○○○○○
Protein & Dairy
◐○○○○○○
Fats
○○○○○

1. Drain pineapple, reserving juice. Add enough water to juice to make 1 cup.
2. In a mixing bowl, combine 1 cup liquid with dry pudding mix.
3. In another bowl, drizzle banana with lemon juice. Mix in remaining fruit.
4. Fold fruit into pudding dressing.
5. Refrigerate until ready to serve.

Per Serving

Calories 116, Kilojoules 485, Protein 1g,
Carbohydrates 29g, Total Fat *trace*, Saturated Fat *trace*,
Monounsaturated Fat *trace*, Polyunsaturated Fat *trace*,
Cholesterol *trace*, Sodium 200mg, Fiber 3g

Tip: Substitute other fruit such as pears, peaches, or mango.

7-Fruit Salad

Joanna Harrison
Lafayette, CO

Makes 8 servings

Prep. Time: 30 minutes
Chilling Time: 1 hour

⅓ cup lime, *or* lemon, juice
½ cup water
½ cup agave nectar, *or* honey
2 medium nectarines,
    unpeeled and sliced
1 large firm banana, sliced
1 pint blueberries
1 pint fresh strawberries,
    sliced
1½ cups watermelon balls
1 cup green grapes, halved
1 kiwi fruit, peeled and chopped

Pyramid Servings	
Vegetables	○○○○○➤
Fruits	●◑○○○➤
Carbohydrates	○○○○○○○○
Protein & Dairy	○○○○○○○
Fats	○○○○○
Sweets	●

1. Combine lime juice, water, and agave nectar in mixing bowl.
2. Add nectarines and banana to dressing. Toss to coat.
3. In a 2½-quart bowl, combine remaining fruit. Add nectarines, banana, and dressing. Stir gently.
4. Cover and refrigerate 1 hour before serving.

Per Serving

Calories 151, Kilojoules 632, Protein 2 g,
Carbohydrates 36 g, Total Fat *trace*, Saturated Fat *trace*,
Monounsaturated Fat *trace*, Polyunsaturated Fat *trace*,
Cholesterol 0 mg, Sodium 2 mg, Fiber 3 g

Citrus Salad

Sue Williams
Gulfport, MS

Makes 6 servings

Prep. Time: 20 minutes
Chilling Time: 2–8 hours

1 pink grapefruit
2 navel oranges
2 tangerines
1 Tbsp. honey
⅓ cup chopped pecans, *or*
    walnuts

Pyramid Servings	
Vegetables	○○○○○➤
Fruits	●○○○○➤
Carbohydrates	○○○○○○○○
Protein & Dairy	○○○○○○○
Fats	●○○○○

1. Over a large bowl, peel and section grapefruit, oranges, and tangerines. Remove membranes.
2. Stir honey into fruit.
3. Cover and refrigerate 2 hours, or overnight.
4. Sprinkle each individual serving with nuts just before serving.

Per Serving

Calories 101, Kilojoules 423, Protein 1 g,
Carbohydrates 17 g, Total Fat 4 g, Saturated Fat 0.3 g,
Monounsaturated Fat 2.2 g, Polyunsaturated Fat 1.5 g,
Cholesterol 0 mg, Sodium *trace*, Fiber 3 g

Fruit Mediterranean-Style

Jane S. Lippincott, Wynnewood, PA

Makes 2 servings

Prep. Time: 15 minutes
Chilling Time: 1 hour

1 orange, peeled and cut up
6 dates, chopped
half lemon, juiced
1 tsp. ground cinnamon
2 Tbsp. sliced almonds

Pyramid Servings	
Vegetables	○○○○○➤
Fruits	●●○○○➤
Carbohydrates	○○○○○○○○
Protein & Dairy	○○○○○○○
Fats	●○○○○

1. Mix orange sections, dates, lemon juice, and cinnamon in a bowl.
2. Cover and refrigerate until thoroughly chilled.
3. Serve topped with sliced almonds.

Per Serving

Calories 145, Kilojoules 607, Protein 3 g,
Carbohydrates 25 g, Total Fat 4 g, Saturated Fat 1 g,
Monounsaturated Fat 2 g, Polyunsaturated Fat 1 g,
Cholesterol 0 mg, Sodium 1 mg, Fiber 5 g

Blushing Fruit

Linda Miller, Harrisonburg, VA

Makes 6 servings

Prep. Time: 20 minutes
Chilling Time: 1–3 hours

4 cups of a variety of fresh
    fruits, such as blueberries,
    kiwi, strawberries, oranges,
    mango, papaya, etc.

Pyramid Servings	
Vegetables	○○○○○➤
Fruits	●○○○○➤
Carbohydrates	○○○○○○○○
Protein & Dairy	○○○○○○○
Fats	○○○○○

Sauce:
2 Tbsp. frozen unsweetened orange juice
    concentrate, undiluted
¼ cup red wine
¼ tsp. cardamom
¼ tsp. ground ginger

1. Prepare fruit, chunking the larger fruits into bite-size pieces. Place in mixing bowl.
2. Mix sauce ingredients in a small bowl.
3. Pour sauce over chunked fruit.
4. Chill until ready to serve. Serve within 2–3 hours.

Per Serving

Calories 67, Kilojoules 280, Protein 1 g,
Carbohydrates 15 g, Total Fat *trace*, Saturated Fat *trace*,
Monounsaturated Fat *trace*, Polyunsaturated Fat *trace*,
Cholesterol 0 mg, Sodium 3 mg, Fiber 2 g

Mango Tango Salad

Karen Ceneviva, New Haven, CT

Makes 6 servings

Prep. Time: 25 minutes
Standing Time: 10 minutes

3 ripe mangos, pitted and cubed
juice of 1 lime
1 tsp. minced red onion
2 Tbsp. chopped fresh
    cilantro leaves
half of one jalapeño pepper,
    seeded and minced

Pyramid Servings	
Vegetables	○○○○○➤
Fruits	●○○○○➤
Carbohydrates	○○○○○○○○
Protein & Dairy	○○○○○○○
Fats	○○○○○

1. Combine all ingredients in a mixing bowl. Let stand 10 minutes.
2. Toss just before serving.

Per Serving

Calories 75, Kilojoules 314, Protein 1 g,
Carbohydrates 19 g, Total Fat *trace*, Saturated Fat *trace*,
Monounsaturated Fat *trace*, Polyunsaturated Fat *trace*,
Cholesterol 0 mg, Sodium 10 mg, Fiber 2 g

Mango Cashew Salad

Janelle Reitz
Lancaster, PA

Makes 6 servings

Prep. Time: 20 minutes
Chilling Time: 1–2 hours

Pyramid Servings	
Vegetables	○○○○○➤
Fruits	◑○○○○➤
Carbohydrates	○○○○○○○○
Protein & Dairy	○○○○○○○
Fats	●○○○○

1 mango, peeled, seeded, and cubed
1 large apple, peeled, cored, and diced
½ cup unsalted cashews, coarsely chopped
1½ Tbsp. lime juice
¼ tsp. ground cinnamon
¼ tsp. ground ginger

1. Toss all ingredients together in a medium bowl.
2. Cover and refrigerate 1–2 hours before serving to allow flavors to blend.

Per Serving

Calories 84, Kilojoules 351, Protein 2 g,
Carbohydrates 12 g, Total Fat 4 g, Saturated Fat 1 g,
Monounsaturated Fat 2 g, Polyunsaturated Fat 1 g,
Cholesterol 0 mg, Sodium 1 mg, Fiber 2 g

Dietitian's tip: *The skin of a mango is tough and not meant to be eaten. But peeling and pitting the fruit can be a challenge as the flesh clings to both the skin and large, flat seed at its center. For best results, cut downward along one side removing a "cheek." Remove the other cheek the same way. Place the cut portion on the cutting board flesh-side up and cut ¼-inch squares in the flesh. Turn the cheek inside out and remove the fruit from the skin with a knife.*

Cranberry Salad

Sharlene Allgyer
Nt. Vernon, IL

Makes 12 servings

Prep. Time: 40 minutes
Chilling Time: 3–4 hours

Pyramid Servings	
Vegetables	○○○○○➤
Fruits	●○○○○➤
Carbohydrates	○○○○○○○○
Protein & Dairy	○○○○○○○
Fats	○○○○○
Sweets	●

1 lb. cranberries
2 apples, cored and quartered
2 oranges, cut up (a little rind is good)
1 cup strawberries, *optional* (not included in analyses)
20-oz. can unsweetened crushed pineapple
4 Tbsp. plain gelatin
1½ cups cold water
1½ cups hot water
¾ cup honey

1. Blend cranberries, apples, oranges, and strawberries in blender or food processor until coarsely chopped. Place in mixing bowl.
2. Stir undrained crushed pineapple into blended fruit. Set aside.
3. In another bowl, soak gelatin in cold water approximately 5–10 minutes, or until clear when stirred.
4. Pour in hot water and stir until gelatin is completely dissolved.
5. Stir honey into gelatin mixture.
6. Stir honey-gelatin mixture into fruit.
7. Pour fruit into large salad mold, or two smaller molds.
8. Cover and refrigerate for several hours, or until set.

Per Serving

Calories 138, Kilojoules 577, Protein 2 g,
Carbohydrates 33 g, Total Fat *trace*, Saturated Fat *trace*,
Monounsaturated Fat *trace*, Polyunsaturated Fat *trace*,
Cholesterol 0 mg, Sodium 10 mg, Fiber 3 g

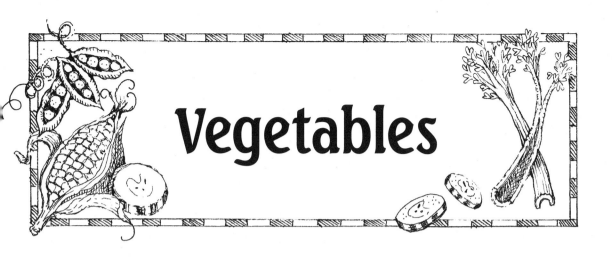

Vegetables

Stir-Fried Asparagus

Sylvia Beiler, Lowville, NY

Makes 6 servings

Prep. Time: 5 minutes
Cooking Time: 2–3 minutes

1 Tbsp. canola oil
3 cups asparagus, sliced
    diagonally
4 scallions, *or* green onions,
    sliced diagonally
1 garlic clove, minced, *optional*
1 tsp. lemon juice

Pyramid Servings

Vegetables	●○○○○➤
Fruits	○○○○○➤
Carbohydrates	○○○○○○○
Protein & Dairy	○○○○○○○
Fats	◐○○○○

1. Heat oil in pan. Add sliced vegetables.
2. Stir-fry until crisp-tender.
3. Sprinkle with lemon juice. Serve immediately.

Per Serving

Calories 38, Kilojoules 159, Protein 2 g,
Carbohydrates 3 g, Total Fat 2.5 g, Saturated Fat 0.2 g,
Monounsaturated Fat 1.5 g, Polyunsaturated Fat 0.8 g,
Cholesterol 0 mg, Sodium 3 mg, Fiber 1 g

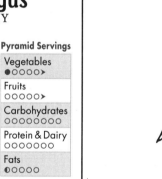

Dietitian's tip: Distinctively rich in flavor, asparagus is a good source of vitamin C, folate, iron, and copper. To prepare asparagus for cooking, hold a piece of asparagus in the middle. Grab the cut end and bend it downward until the cut end snaps off. The asparagus will break in the right spot to remove its woody end.

Roasted Asparagus
Barbara Walker
Sturgis, SD

Makes 6 servings

Prep. Time: 5 minutes
Cooking Time: 12 minutes

Pyramid Servings	
Vegetables	●○○○○➤
Fruits	○○○○○➤
Carbohydrates	○○○○○○○○
Protein & Dairy	○○○○○○○
Fats	●○○○○

1 lb. fresh asparagus spears
2–3 Tbsp. olive oil
⅛ tsp. pepper
2 Tbsp. balsamic vinegar

1. Place asparagus in bowl with olive oil. Toss together to coat asparagus.

2. Place asparagus spears on a baking sheet in a single layer. Sprinkle with pepper.

3. Roast uncovered at 450°. Shake pan once or twice to turn spears after about 6 minutes.

4. Roast another 6 minutes, or until asparagus is tender-crisp.

5. Put on a plate and drizzle with balsamic vinegar. Serve immediately.

Per Serving

Calories 58, Kilojoules 243, Protein 3 g,
Carbohydrates 5 g, Total Fat 3 g, Saturated Fat 0.5 g,
Monounsaturated Fat 2 g, Polyunsaturated Fat 0.5 g,
Cholesterol 0 mg, Sodium 3 mg, Fiber 3 g

Tip: The asparagus spears may need more or less roasting time, depending on their size and thickness.

Grilled Asparagus
Kelly Amos
Pittsboro, NC

Makes 4 servings

Prep. Time: 10 minutes
Marinating Time: 30 minutes
Grilling Time: 5–10 minutes

Pyramid Servings	
Vegetables	●○○○○➤
Fruits	○○○○○➤
Carbohydrates	○○○○○○○○
Protein & Dairy	○○○○○○○
Fats	●○○○○

1 lb. (about 3½ cups) asparagus

Dressing:
3 Tbsp. balsamic vinegar
2 Tbsp. lemon juice
1 Tbsp. olive oil
2 tsp. low-sodium soy sauce
black pepper to taste

1. Snap off rough ends of cleaned asparagus.

2. Combine dressing ingredients together in a good-sized mixing bowl.

3. Add asparagus to dressing. Let marinate for approximately 30 minutes.

4. Brush grill grates with some oil. Turn grill onto low.

5. Cook asparagus on grill 5–10 minutes, turning every few minutes until lightly browned.

Per Serving

Calories 64, Kilojoules 268, Protein 3 g,
Carbohydrates 6 g, Total Fat 3.5 g, Saturated Fat 0.5 g,
Monounsaturated Fat 2.5 g, Polyunsaturated Fat 0.5 g,
Cholesterol 0 mg, Sodium 90 mg, Fiber 2.5 g

Nutrition Tip: Never oil a hot grate on a grill, especially using non-stick spray. It will flare up and may lead to severe burns. Always make sure the grates are cold, then oil them, and turn on the grill when you're finished.

Asparagus with Egg

Kathy Hertzler
Lancaster, PA

Makes 4 servings

Prep. Time: 10 minutes
Cooking Time: 10 minutes

1½ lbs. asparagus, bottoms
  cut off at point where
  spears break easily
1 hard-boiled egg
4 tsp. melted soft-tub
  margarine, non-
  hydrogenated variety
lemon juice, *optional*

Pyramid Servings		
Vegetables ●○○○○➤		
Fruits ○○○○○➤		
Carbohydrates ○○○○○○○○		
Protein & Dairy ○○○○○○○		
Fats ●○○○○		

1. Wash and trim asparagus.
2. Steam asparagus in a bit of water in a saucepan until barely cooked, but not crunchy.
3. Chop hard-boiled egg finely.
4. Melt margarine in microwave or in saucepan on stove.
5. Serve steamed asparagus on warmed plate, with chopped egg sprinkled and melted margarine drizzled on top.
6. Sprinkle with a few drops lemon juice if you wish.

Per Serving

Calories 88, Kilojoules 368, Protein 5 g,
Carbohydrates 6 g, Total Fat 5 g, Saturated Fat 1 g,
Monounsaturated Fat 2.5 g, Polyunsaturated Fat 1.5 g,
Cholesterol 53 mg, Sodium 70 mg, Fiber 4 g

Tip: Save the preparation for this recipe until about 20 minutes before you eat. It is best eaten very hot.

Asparagus Almondine

Jean Turner
Williams Lake, BC

Makes 6 servings

Prep. Time: 10 minutes
Cooking Time: 10–15 minutes

1½ lbs. (about 7 cups)
  asparagus
water
¼ cup sliced blanched almonds
2 tsp. olive oil
2 cloves garlic, finely chopped
2 Tbsp. freshly grated Parmesan cheese
pepper to taste

Pyramid Servings		
Vegetables ●○○○○➤		
Fruits ○○○○○➤		
Carbohydrates ○○○○○○○○		
Protein & Dairy ○○○○○○○		
Fats ●○○○○		

1. Snap off asparagus ends. Cut spears on diagonal into 2" lengths.
2. In large nonstick skillet, bring ½ cup water to boil. Cook asparagus for 2 minutes after water returns to boil, or until asparagus is tender-crisp.
3. Run asparagus under cold water to chill. Drain and set aside.
4. Dry skillet. Place over medium heat. Add almonds and toast, stirring often for 2–3 minutes, or until golden brown. Remove and reserve nuts.
5. Add oil to skillet. Increase heat to medium-high. Cook asparagus and garlic, stirring for 4 minutes, or until asparagus is just tender.
6. Sprinkle with Parmesan cheese. Season with pepper.
7. Transfer to serving bowl. Top with almonds.

Per Serving

Calories 70, Kilojoules 293, Protein 4 g,
Carbohydrates 5 g, Total Fat 4 g, Saturated Fat 1 g,
Monounsaturated Fat 2.5 g, Polyunsaturated Fat 0.5 g,
Cholesterol 1.4 mg, Sodium 28 mg, Fiber 3 g

Tip: Substitute green beans for the asparagus for a tasty alternative. Trim ends off the beans. Cut beans into 1½" lengths. Cook in boiling water for 5 minutes. Continue with Steps 3–7 above.

Green Bean Stir-Fry

Sharon Eshleman
Ephrata, PA

Makes 6 servings

Prep. Time: 10 minutes
Cooking Time: 10 minutes

1 Tbsp. canola oil
¾ lb. green beans, fresh *or* frozen
1 Tbsp. low-sodium soy sauce
2 garlic cloves, minced
1 tsp. sesame seeds, toasted
1 tsp. brown sugar
1 tsp. peanut butter

Pyramid Servings	
Vegetables	●○○○○➤
Fruits	○○○○○➤
Carbohydrates	○○○○○○○○
Protein & Dairy	○○○○○○○
Fats	◐○○○○

1. Stir-fry green beans in oil in large skillet until tender. Remove from heat.
2. Mix together remaining ingredients in small bowl.
3. Stir into green beans until well coated.

Per Serving

Calories 51, Kilojoules 213, Protein 1 g,
Carbohydrates 5 g, Total Fat 3 g, Saturated Fat 0.2 g,
Monounsaturated Fat 1.8 g, Polyunsaturated Fat 1 g,
Cholesterol 0 mg, Sodium 99 mg, Fiber 1.5 g

Dietitian's tip: To limit the sodium content of this oriental dish, use low-sodium soy sauce, which has about 50-percent less sodium but all of the taste of its full-sodium counterpart.

Tangy Green Beans

Mary B. Sensenig
New Holland, PA

Makes 10 servings

Prep. Time: 5 minutes
Cooking Time: 8–10 minutes

1½ lbs. green beans, fresh, frozen, *or* canned
⅓ cup diced sweet red bell peppers
4½ tsp. olive, *or* canola, oil
4½ tsp. water
1½ tsp. vinegar
1½ tsp. prepared mustard
¼ tsp. salt
¼ tsp. pepper
⅛ tsp. garlic powder

Pyramid Servings	
Vegetables	●○○○○➤
Fruits	○○○○○➤
Carbohydrates	○○○○○○○○
Protein & Dairy	○○○○○○○
Fats	◐○○○○

1. Cook beans and red peppers in a steamer basket over water until crisp-tender.
2. Whisk together all remaining ingredients in a small bowl.
3. Transfer beans to a serving bowl. Add dressing and stir to coat.

Per Serving

Calories 39, Kilojoules 163, Protein 1 g,
Carbohydrates 5 g, Total Fat 2 g, Saturated Fat 0.3 g,
Monounsaturated Fat 1.5 g, Polyunsaturated Fat 0.2 g,
Cholesterol 0 mg, Sodium 68 mg, Fiber 2 g

Holiday Green Beans

Joanne Kennedy
Plattsburgh, NY
Jean Ryan
Peru, NY

Makes 10 servings

Prep. Time: 10 minutes
Cooking Time: 20–30 minutes

2 lbs. (about 8 cups) fresh
  green beans
1 large red onion, thinly
  sliced
3 cloves fresh garlic, minced
1 tsp. olive oil
½ cup slivered almonds
pepper to taste

Pyramid Servings	
Vegetables	●○○○○➤
Fruits	○○○○○➤
Carbohydrates	○○○○○○○○
Protein & Dairy	○○○○○○○
Fats	●○○○○

1. Steam beans in saucepan until just slightly crisp.
2. Sauté onion and garlic in olive oil in large skillet for 3 minutes.
3. Add beans to skillet. Sauté 1 minute.
4. Add slivered almonds and pepper to beans. Toss together and then serve.

Per Serving

Calories 73, Kilojoules 305, Protein 3 g,
Carbohydrates 7 g, Total Fat 4 g, Saturated Fat 0.3 g,
Monounsaturated Fat 2.2 g, Polyunsaturated Fat 1.5 g,
Cholesterol 0 mg, Sodium 6 mg, Fiber 4 g

Dietitian's tip: Green beans, also known as string beans or snap beans, are good sources of fiber and vitamin C. Another way to preserve their fresh flavor and texture is to blanch (parboil) the beans: immerse them in boiling water for about 2 minutes, then plunge into ice water to set their color, then sauté briefly.

Green Beans with Tomatoes and Garlic

Shirley Sears
Sarasota, FL

Makes 6 servings

Prep. Time: 15 minutes
Cooking Time: 60–70 minutes

1 Tbsp. olive oil
4 cloves garlic, chopped
1½ lbs. green beans, washed
  and stemmed
2 8-oz. cans crushed
  tomatoes, no salt added
1 tsp. dried oregano

Pyramid Servings	
Vegetables	●●○○○➤
Fruits	○○○○○➤
Carbohydrates	○○○○○○○○
Protein & Dairy	○○○○○○○
Fats	◑○○○○

1. Heat oil in large skillet over medium heat.
2. Add garlic and sauté briefly.
3. Add beans and stir to coat with oil.
4. Add tomatoes.
5. Bring to a boil. Reduce heat to a low simmer.
6. Stir in oregano.
7. Cover and cook 45–60 minutes, or until beans are done to your liking and liquid is nearly absorbed.

Per Serving

Calories 73, Kilojoules 305, Protein 3 g,
Carbohydrates 12 g, Total Fat 2 g, Saturated Fat 0.2 g,
Monounsaturated Fat 1.5 g, Polyunsaturated Fat 0.3 g,
Cholesterol 0 mg, Sodium 37 mg, Fiber 5 g

Simply Beets

Colleen Konetzni
Rio Rancho, NM

Makes 4 servings

Prep. Time: 30 minutes
Cooking Time: 30–45 minutes

Pyramid Servings

Vegetables	●●●○○➤
Fruits	○○○○○➤
Carbohydrates	○○○○○○○○
Protein & Dairy	○○○○○○○
Fats	○○○○○

6 fresh red beets
water
1 tsp. olive oil
dill weed
pepper

1. Wash beets and cut off roots and leafy stems. Place in saucepan and cover with water.
2. Boil until beets are fork-tender.
3. Remove from pan and cool. The beets' peels should slip right off.
4. Slice beets ¼" thick. Place back in pan, along with oil.
5. Heat through over low heat.
6. To serve, sprinkle with dill weed and pepper.

Per Serving

Calories 63, Kilojoules 264, Protein 2 g,
Carbohydrates 11 g, Total Fat 1.5 g, Saturated Fat 0.2 g,
Monounsaturated Fat 0.8 g, Polyunsaturated Fat 0.5 g,
Cholesterol 0 mg, Sodium 96 mg, Fiber 3 g

A Tip —

Cook according to the season. Focus on the vegetables and fruits that are ripe for the month you're in. Visit a local farmers market for inspiration.

Sweet and Sour Beets

Frances L. Kruba
Baltimore, MD

Makes 8 servings

Prep. Time: 15 minutes
Cooking Time: 25 minutes

Pyramid Servings

Vegetables	●●○○○➤
Fruits	○○○○○➤
Carbohydrates	●○○○○○○○
Protein & Dairy	○○○○○○○
Fats	○○○○○

½ cup sugar
1 Tbsp. cornstarch
2 whole cloves
½ cup vinegar
3 15-oz. cans sliced beets, no salt added, drained
3 Tbsp. reduced-in-sugar orange marmalade
2 Tbsp. soft-tub margarine, non-hydrogenated variety

1. Combine sugar, cornstarch, and cloves in a large heavy saucepan. Stir in vinegar.
2. Cook over medium heat, stirring constantly until thickened and bubbly.
3. Add beets to sauce. Cover and cook 15 minutes.
4. Stir in marmalade and margarine until both are melted.

Per Serving

Calories 122, Kilojoules 510, Protein 1 g,
Carbohydrates 26 g, Total Fat 1.5 g, Saturated Fat 0.2 g,
Monounsaturated Fat 1 g, Polyunsaturated Fat 0.3 g,
Cholesterol 0 mg, Sodium 53 mg, Fiber 2 g

Italian-Style Broccoli

Shirley Hedman
Schenectady, NY

Makes 4–6 servings

Prep. Time: 10 minutes
Cooking Time: 10 minutes

4 cups broccoli florets
1 Tbsp. olive oil
2 cloves garlic, minced or
　crushed
¼ tsp. red pepper flakes
1 tsp. grated Parmesan cheese

Pyramid Servings	
Vegetables ●○○○○▸	
Fruits ○○○○○▸	
Carbohydrates ○○○○○○○○	
Protein & Dairy ○○○○○○○	
Fats ◐○○○○	

   1. Steam broccoli for 3 minutes in non-stick pan. Remove from pan and wipe pan dry.
   2. Add olive oil, garlic, and red pepper flakes to pan. Cook slowly, about 3 minutes.
   3. Add broccoli and shake in pan to cook evenly.
   4. Sprinkle with grated cheese and serve warm.

Per Serving

Calories 43, Kilojoules 180, Protein 2 g,
Carbohydrates 4 g, Total Fat 2 g, Saturated Fat 0.3 g,
Monounsaturated Fat 1.5 g, Polyunsaturated Fat 0.2 g,
Cholesterol *trace*, Sodium 25 mg, Fiber 1.5 g

Roasted Broccoli

Andrea Cunningham
Arlington, KS

Makes 4 servings

Prep. Time: 10 minutes
Baking Time: 20 minutes

1 head (about 5 cups)
　broccoli, cut into long
　pieces all the way through
　(you will eat the stems)
1 Tbsp. olive oil
2–3 cloves garlic, sliced thin
pepper
lemon wedges

Pyramid Servings	
Vegetables ●○○○○▸	
Fruits ○○○○○▸	
Carbohydrates ○○○○○○○○	
Protein & Dairy ○○○○○○○	
Fats ●○○○○	

   1. Preheat oven to 400°.
   2. Place broccoli in baking pan with sides. Drizzle with olive oil. Toss to coat.
   3. Sprinkle garlic and pepper over top.
   4. Transfer to oven and roast 15–20 minutes, or until broccoli is crispy on the ends and a little browned.
   5. Sprinkle with lemon juice.

Per Serving

Calories 71, Kilojoules 297, Protein 3 g,
Carbohydrates 6 g, Total Fat 4 g, Saturated Fat 0.5 g,
Monounsaturated Fat 2.5 g, Polyunsaturated Fat 1 g,
Cholesterol 0 mg, Sodium 38 mg, Fiber 3 g

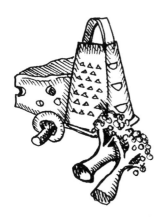

Broccoli Dijon

Jean Butzer
Batavia, NY

Makes 4 servings

Prep. Time: 15 minutes
Cooking Time: 10 minutes

1½ lbs. broccoli
2 Tbsp. olive oil
1 medium onion, finely
   chopped
2 cloves garlic, finely chopped
½ cup fat-free sour cream
1 Tbsp. Dijon mustard
1 Tbsp. lemon juice
pepper to taste

Pyramid Servings		
Vegetables ●○○○○➤		
Fruits ○○○○○➤		
Carbohydrates ○○○○○○○○		
Protein & Dairy ◐○○○○○○○		
Fats ●○○○○		

1. Cut broccoli into florets. Peel and slice the stalks. Steam or boil in water in saucepan until tender, but still firm and bright green. Drain, and keep warm.

2. Meanwhile heat oil in a skillet over moderate heat. Sauté onion and garlic until tender but not brown, about 5 minutes.

3. Add remaining ingredients to skillet and stir over low heat.

4. Place broccoli in serving dish. Spoon sauce over top. Serve immediately.

Per Serving

Calories 124, Kilojoules 519, Protein 6 g,
Carbohydrates 17 g, Total Fat 4 g, Saturated Fat 1 g,
Monounsaturated Fat 2 g, Polyunsaturated Fat 1 g,
Cholesterol 3 mg, Sodium 230 mg, Fiber 5 g

Dietitian's tip: Broccoli is high in vitamins A and C, which are considered antioxidant vitamins. Broccoli also has isothiocyanates, indoles, and flavonoids — phytochemicals that may help prevent cancer.

Sesame Broccoli

Marci Baum
Manheim, PA

Makes 6 servings

Prep. Time: 10 minutes
Cooking Time: 10 minutes

1 head (about 6 cups) broccoli
1 tsp. canola oil
1 Tbsp. sesame seeds
2 Tbsp. water
1 Tbsp. low-sodium soy sauce
¼ tsp. red pepper flakes,
   crushed
½ Tbsp. fresh lemon juice

Pyramid Servings		
Vegetables ●○○○○➤		
Fruits ○○○○○➤		
Carbohydrates ○○○○○○○○		
Protein & Dairy ○○○○○○○○		
Fats ◐○○○○		

1. Cut broccoli into small florets. Peel and dice stem and add to florets.

2. Heat a large skillet over medium-high heat. Pour oil into skillet and swirl to coat bottom. Cook sesame seeds for 1 minute, stirring constantly.

3. Stir in broccoli. Increase heat to high and cook 3 minutes, or until broccoli is bright green, stirring constantly.

4. Stir in remaining ingredients. Reduce heat to medium and cook, covered, 5 minutes, or until broccoli becomes crisp-tender.

Per Serving

Calories 49, Kilojoules 205, Protein 3 g,
Carbohydrates 5 g, Total Fat 2 g, Saturated Fat 0.1 g,
Monounsaturated Fat 0.8 g, Polyunsaturated Fat 1.1 g,
Cholesterol 0 mg, Sodium 114 mg, Fiber 3 g

Broccoli with Cranberries

Yvonne Kauffman Boettger
Harrisonburg, VA

Makes 6 servings

Prep. Time: 5 minutes
Cooking Time: 10 minutes

4–6 cups chopped broccoli
1 Tbsp. olive oil
½ cup dried cranberries
¼ cup slivered almonds

Pyramid Servings		
Vegetables ●○○○○➤		
Fruits ●○○○○➤		
Carbohydrates ○○○○○○○○		
Protein & Dairy ○○○○○○○		
Fats ◐○○○○		

1. Microwave broccoli with a little water until slightly tender.
2. Heat oil in skillet. Add broccoli, cranberries, and almonds.
3. Stir-fry until broccoli reaches the tenderness you like.

Per Serving

Calories 108, Kilojoules 452, Protein 3 g,
Carbohydrates 12 g, Total Fat 5 g, Saturated Fat 0.5 g,
Monounsaturated Fat 3.5 g, Polyunsaturated Fat 1 g,
Cholesterol 0 mg, Sodium 30 mg, Fiber 3 g

Corn and Broccoli Bake

Vera Schmucker
Goshen, IN

Makes 6 servings

Prep. Time: 10 minutes
Baking Time: 45 minutes

16-oz. can cream-style corn, no salt added
16-oz. pkg. frozen chopped broccoli, thawed
¼ cup crushed soda crackers with unsalted tops
1 egg, beaten
1 Tbsp. dried onion, minced
⅛ tsp. pepper
¼ cup crushed soda crackers with unsalted tops
1 Tbsp. soft-tub margarine, non-hydrogenated

Pyramid Servings		
Vegetables ●○○○○➤		
Fruits ○○○○○➤		
Carbohydrates ●○○○○○○○		
Protein & Dairy ○○○○○○○		
Fats ◐○○○○		

1. In a bowl combine first six ingredients. Place in 1½-quart lightly greased baking dish.
2. Combine margarine and ¼ cup soda crackers. Sprinkle on top of filled baking dish.
3. Bake at 350° for 45 minutes.

Per Serving

Calories 117, Kilojoules 490, Protein 5 g,
Carbohydrates 17 g, Total Fat 4 g, Saturated Fat 0.5 g,
Monounsaturated Fat 2 g, Polyunsaturated Fat 1.5 g,
Cholesterol *trace*, Sodium 122 mg, Fiber 4 g

Cabbage on the Grill

Kristi See
Weskan, KS

Makes 8 servings

Prep. Time: 15 minutes
Grilling Time: 40 minutes

1 head cabbage
4 tsp. olive oil
1 tsp. garlic powder
¼ tsp. pepper

Pyramid Servings	
Vegetables	●○○○○▸
Fruits	○○○○○▸
Carbohydrates	○○○○○○○○
Protein & Dairy	○○○○○○○
Fats	◐○○○○

1. Preheat grill for medium heat.
2. Cut cabbage into 8 wedges. Remove core.
3. Place all wedges on a piece of aluminum foil large enough to fully wrap cabbage.
4. Brush wedges with oil.
5. Sprinkle with garlic powder and pepper. Wrap cabbage up securely in foil.
6. Grill 30–40 minutes on preheated grill, or until tender.

Per Serving

Calories 50, Kilojoules 209, Protein 1 g,	
Carbohydrates 7 g, Total Fat 2 g, Saturated Fat 0.2 g,	
Monounsaturated Fat 1.5 g, Polyunsaturated Fat 0.3 g,	
Cholesterol 0 mg, Sodium 21 mg, Fiber 3 g	

Tip: You can add wedged onions and/or baby carrots to the packets (not included in the nutritional analysis).

Sautéed Cabbage

Laverne Nafziger
Goshen, IN

Makes 6 servings

Prep. Time: 15 minutes
Cooking Time: 15–20 minutes

1 Tbsp. canola oil
1 Tbsp. mustard seed
½ cup chopped onion
1 tsp. chopped garlic
1½ tsp. ground cumin
6 cups shredded cabbage
pepper to taste, *optional*

Pyramid Servings	
Vegetables	●○○○○▸
Fruits	○○○○○▸
Carbohydrates	○○○○○○○○
Protein & Dairy	○○○○○○○
Fats	◐○○○○

1. Heat oil in large skillet. Add mustard seeds. Heat until they start to pop.
2. Add onion and garlic. Sauté 2–3 minutes.
3. Add cumin and cabbage. Sauté, stirring every 5 minutes. Cook until cabbage is tender but not too soft.
4. Sprinkle with pepper if you wish before serving.

Per Serving

Calories 44, Kilojoules 184, Protein 1 g,	
Carbohydrates 5 g, Total Fat 2 g, Saturated Fat 0.2 g,	
Monounsaturated Fat 1.4 g, Polyunsaturated Fat 0.3 g,	
Cholesterol 0 mg, Sodium 13 mg, Fiber 2 g	

Red Cabbage with Apples

Jean Butzer
Batavia, NY
Louise Thieszen
North Newton, KS

Makes 8 servings

Prep. Time: 15 minutes
Cooking Time: 40 minutes

1 medium head red cabbage,
  shredded
1 large onion, chopped
2 Tbsp. canola oil
2 medium apples, unpeeled,
  cored and sliced
¼ cup cider vinegar
¼ tsp. pepper
1 Tbsp. caraway seeds, *optional*

Pyramid Servings

Vegetables	●○○○○➤
Fruits	◖○○○○➤
Carbohydrates	○○○○○○○○
Protein & Dairy	○○○○○○○
Fats	●○○○○

1. In a large skillet, sauté cabbage and onion in oil 5–8 minutes, or until crisp-tender.
2. Add apples, vinegar, pepper, and caraway seeds if you wish. Bring to a boil.
3. Reduce heat. Cover and simmer 25 minutes, or until cabbage is tender.

Per Serving

Calories 90, Kilojoules 377, Protein 2g,
Carbohydrates 12g, Total Fat 4g, Saturated Fat 0.5g,
Monounsaturated Fat 2.5g, Polyunsaturated Fat 1g,
Cholesterol 0mg, Sodium 31mg, Fiber 3g

Carrots with Dill

Marilyn Mowry
Irving, TX

Makes 4 servings

Prep. Time: 5 minutes
Cooking Time: 12–15 minutes

4 cups water
2 cups fresh carrots, peeled
  and sliced
1 Tbsp. soft-tub margarine,
  non-hydrogenated
2 Tbsp. honey
¼ tsp. Lowry's lemon pepper
¼ tsp. salt, *optional*
⅛–¼ tsp. dill weed

Pyramid Servings

Vegetables	●○○○○➤
Fruits	○○○○○➤
Carbohydrates	○○○○○○○○
Protein & Dairy	○○○○○○○
Fats	●○○○○

1. Bring 4 cups water to a boil in saucepan. Add carrots. Cover and boil 1 minute.
2. Drain carrots. Add remaining ingredients to carrots in saucepan and mix well. Heat through over low heat.
3. Stir again and spoon into serving dish.

Per Serving

Calories 69, Kilojoules 289, Protein 1g,
Carbohydrates 10g, Total Fat 3g, Saturated Fat 0.5g,
Monounsaturated Fat 1.5g, Polyunsaturated Fat 1g,
Cholesterol 0mg, Sodium 249mg, Fiber 2g

Dietitian's tip: Carrots are an excellent source of beta-carotene, which is converted by the body into vitamin A (retinol). Vitamin A helps maintain vision and promotes the growth of healthy cells and tissues. Carrots also contain lutein, which is thought to protect the retina.

Rosemary Carrots

Orpha Herr
Andover, NY

Makes 6 servings

Prep. Time: 15 minutes
Cooking Time: 15–20 minutes

Pyramid Servings	
Vegetables	●●○○○▸
Fruits	○○○○○▸
Carbohydrates	○○○○○○○
Protein & Dairy	○○○○○○○
Fats	◐○○○○

1½ lbs. carrots, sliced
1 Tbsp. olive oil
½ cup diced green sweet bell peppers
1 tsp. dried rosemary, crushed
¼ tsp. coarsely ground pepper

1. In a skillet cook and stir carrots in oil 10–12 minutes, or until tender-crisp.
2. Add green pepper. Cook and stir 5 minutes, or until carrots and green peppers are tender, but not too soft.
3. Sprinkle with rosemary and pepper. Heat through.

Per Serving

Calories 70, Kilojoules 293, Protein 1 g,
Carbohydrates 11 g, Total Fat 2.5 g, Saturated Fat 0.3 g,
Monounsaturated Fat 1.7 g, Polyunsaturated Fat 0.5 g,
Cholesterol 0 mg, Sodium 80 mg, Fiber 4 g

Dietitian's tip: Rosemary—an herb with a piney flavor—can season a variety of foods including roasted potatoes, mushrooms, stuffing, ripe melon, poultry, and meats. Use the herb with care, however. Too much can be overpowering.

A Tip —
Don't overcook vegetables.

Honey-Glazed Carrots

Janet Oberholtzer
Ephrata, PA

Makes 4 servings

Prep. Time: 5 minutes
Cooking Time: 10–15 minutes

Pyramid Servings	
Vegetables	●●○○○▸
Fruits	○○○○○▸
Carbohydrates	○○○○○○○
Protein & Dairy	○○○○○○○
Fats	◐○○○○

16-oz. pkg. baby carrots
2 tsp. olive oil
1 Tbsp. honey
½ Tbsp. lemon juice

1. Cook carrots in a bit of water in a saucepan until they're as tender as you like.
2. Meanwhile, combine olive oil, honey, and lemon juice in a small microwave-safe dish. Microwave on high 20–30 seconds. Stir.
3. Drain carrots. Pour glaze over top and toss to coat.

Per Serving

Calories 76, Kilojoules 318, Protein 1 g,
Carbohydrates 13 g, Total Fat 2.5 g, Saturated Fat 0.3 g,
Monounsaturated Fat 1.7 g, Polyunsaturated Fat 0.5 g,
Cholesterol 0 mg, Sodium 89 mg, Fiber 3 g

Cauliflower Mashed "Potatoes"

Anne Hummel
Millersburg, OH

Makes 4 servings

Prep. Time: 20 minutes
Cooking Time: 20–30 minutes

1 head cauliflower
1 clove garlic
1 leek, white only, split in 4
   pieces
1 Tbsp. soft-tub margarine,
   non-hydrogenated
pepper to taste

1. Break cauliflower into small pieces.
2. In a good-sized saucepan, steam cauliflower, garlic, and leeks in water until completely tender, about 20–30 minutes.
3. While cauliflower is hot, puree until the vegetables resemble mashed potatoes. (Use a food processor, or if you prefer a smoother texture, use a blender. Process only a small portion at a time, holding the blender lid on firmly with a tea towel.)
4. Add a little hot water if vegetables seem dry.
5. Stir in margarine and pepper to taste.

Per Serving

Calories 67, Kilojoules 280, Protein 2 g,
Carbohydrates 9 g, Total Fat 3 g, Saturated Fat 0.5 g,
Monounsaturated Fat 1.5 g, Polyunsaturated Fat 1 g,
Cholesterol 0 mg, Sodium 75 mg, Fiber 3 g

Baked Corn

Samuel Stoltzfus
Bird-in-Hand, PA

Makes 8 servings

Prep. Time: 15 minutes
Baking Time: 35–50 minutes

2 cups corn, fresh *or* frozen
   (and thawed if frozen)
egg substitute equivalent to
   2 eggs, slightly beaten, *or* 4
   egg whites, slightly beaten
1 tsp. sugar
1 Tbsp. soft-tub margarine, non-
   hydrogenated, melted
2 Tbsp. flour
1 cup skim milk
¼ tsp. salt

1. Mix all ingredients together in a large bowl.
2. Pour into a greased 2-quart baking dish.
3. Bake at 350° for 35–50 minutes, or until corn is firm in the middle and browned around the edges.

Per Serving

Calories 73, Kilojoules 305, Protein 4 g,
Carbohydrates 11 g, Total Fat 2 g, Saturated Fat 0.4 g,
Monounsaturated Fat 0.8 g, Polyunsaturated Fat 0.8 g,
Cholesterol 0.5 mg, Sodium 127 mg, Fiber 1 g

Corn Extraordinary

Judy Newman
St. Mary's, ON

Makes 6 servings

Prep. Time: 5–7 minutes
Cooking Time: 4–6 minutes

2 garlic cloves
¼ cup chives
2 tsp. olive oil
4 cups corn (best if cut
straight off the cob; if you
use canned, it should be
without added salt)
pinch of pepper

Pyramid Servings	
Vegetables	○○○○○➤
Fruits	○○○○○➤
Carbohydrates	●○○○○○○○
Protein & Dairy	○○○○○○○
Fats	●○○○○

1. Chop garlic and chives.
2. Heat oil in large skillet over medium heat. Gently sauté garlic. (Reserve chives.)
3. Add corn. Sauté 3–5 minutes.
4. Season to taste with pepper and chives.

Per Serving

Calories 118, Kilojoules 494, Protein 3 g,
Carbohydrates 21 g, Total Fat 3 g, Saturated Fat 0.5 g,
Monounsaturated Fat 2 g, Polyunsaturated Fat 0.5 g,
Cholesterol 0 mg, Sodium 3 mg, Fiber 3 g

Quick Stir-Fried Vegetables

Judith Govotsos
Frederick, MD

Makes 5 servings

Prep. Time: 20 minutes
Cooking Time: 7–10 minutes

4 cloves garlic, sliced thin
4 carrots, sliced thin on angle
1 small yellow squash, sliced
thin on angle
1 small green zucchini
squash, sliced thin on angle
1 large onion, sliced thin
1 Tbsp. olive oil
¼ tsp. salt
⅛ tsp. pepper

Pyramid Servings	
Vegetables	●●○○○➤
Fruits	○○○○○➤
Carbohydrates	○○○○○○○○
Protein & Dairy	○○○○○○○
Fats	●○○○○

1. Prepare all vegetables. Do not mix together.
2. Place olive oil in large non-stick skillet.
3. Add garlic and carrot. Stir-fry 2–3 minutes.
4. Add remainder of vegetables. Cook and stir until just lightly cooked, about 5–7 more minutes.
5. Stir in seasonings and serve.

Per Serving

Calories 98, Kilojoules 410, Protein 2 g,
Carbohydrates 16 g, Total Fat 3 g, Saturated Fat 0.4 g,
Monounsaturated Fat 2 g, Polyunsaturated Fat 0.6 g,
Cholesterol 0 mg, Sodium 194 mg, Fiber 4 g

Roasted Summer Vegetables

Moreen Weaver,
Bath, NY

Makes 6 servings

Prep. Time: 20–30 minutes
Baking Time: 20 minutes

8–10 cups fresh vegetables:
   your choice of any summer
   squash, onions, potatoes,
   tomatoes, green beans,
   broccoli, cauliflower,
   carrots, green or red bell
   sweet peppers, mild chili peppers,
   eggplant, mushrooms, or fennel

Pyramid Servings

Vegetables	●●●○○➤
Fruits	○○○○○➤
Carbohydrates	○○○○○○○○
Protein & Dairy	○○○○○○○
Fats	◑○○○○

Seasoning 1:
3 Tbsp. fresh basil, chopped
2 Tbsp. fresh cilantro, chopped
1½ Tbsp. fresh thyme, chopped
1 Tbsp. olive oil
½ tsp. pepper
3 cloves garlic, minced

Seasoning 2:
4 cloves garlic, minced
1 Tbsp. olive oil
2 Tbsp. fresh thyme
2 Tbsp. fresh oregano
2 Tbsp. fresh basil, chopped
2 Tbsp. balsamic vinegar
1 Tbsp. Dijon mustard
¼ tsp. pepper

1. Cut vegetables into bite-size pieces for even cooking. For example, slice potatoes thinly, but chop summer squash in chunks. Place prepared vegetables in large mixing bowl as you go.

2. Toss vegetables with one of the seasoning options.

3. Spread seasoned vegetables in a thin layer on a lightly greased baking sheet with sides.

4. Bake in preheated oven at 425° for 20 minutes. Stir occasionally.

Per Serving

Calories 99, Kilojoules 414, Protein 3 g,
Carbohydrates 17 g, Total Fat 2.6 g, Saturated Fat 0.3 g,
Monounsaturated Fat 1.7 g, Polyunsaturated Fat 0.6 g,
Cholesterol 0 mg, Sodium 95 mg, Fiber 4 g

For a main dish: *Serve over cooked penne pasta, wild rice, or couscous. Top with freshly grated Parmesan cheese (not included in nutritional analyses).*

For a salad: *Cool vegetables and add 2 cups diced tomatoes, 3 ounces crumbled feta cheese, and an additional amount of Seasoning 2 to serve as dressing (not included in nutritional analyses).*

A Tip —

   Beginner cooks should always measure carefully. With more experience you learn to adjust recipes.

Oven-Roasted Root Vegetables

Bonnie Whaling
Clearfield, PA

Makes 8 servings

Prep. Time: 20 minutes
Baking Time: 40–50 minutes

Pyramid Servings	
Vegetables ●○○○○➤	
Fruits ○○○○○➤	
Carbohydrates ●○○○○○○○	
Protein & Dairy ○○○○○○○	
Fats ○○○○○	

2 medium (about 3 cups)
    parsnips, peeled,
    quartered, and cut into ½"
    slices
half a medium (about 3 cups)
    rutabaga, peeled and cut
    into ½" cubes
1 cup baby carrots
1 cup pearl onions, peeled, *or* 1 red onion,
    cut into wedges
½ Tbsp. olive oil
black pepper

1. Preheat oven to 350°.
2. In a 9 × 9 baking pan, combine all vegetables.
3. Drizzle with olive oil.
4. Lightly season with pepper. Toss to coat.
5. Bake covered for 20 minutes. Uncover and stir vegetables.
6. Bake uncovered 20 minutes more, or until vegetables are starting to brown, stirring occasionally.

Per Serving

Calories 82, Kilojoules 343, Protein 2 g,
Carbohydrates 17 g, Total Fat 1 g, Saturated Fat *trace*,
Monounsaturated Fat 0.6 g, Polyunsaturated Fat 0.4 g,
Cholesterol 0 mg, Sodium 37 mg, Fiber 5 g

Italian Veggie Bake

Orpha Herr
Andover, NY

Makes 8 servings

Prep. Time: 20 minutes
Cooking/Baking Time: 45–50 minutes

Pyramid Servings	
Vegetables ●●○○○➤	
Fruits ○○○○○➤	
Carbohydrates ○○○○○○○○	
Protein & Dairy ○○○○○○○	
Fats ●○○○○	

⅓ cup reduced-fat Italian
    dressing
1 large onion, chopped
1 small unpeeled eggplant,
    cubed
2 medium zucchini, sliced thin
1 large red sweet bell pepper, chopped
6-oz. pkg. fresh mushrooms, sliced
2 cups freshly diced tomatoes
⅓ cup shredded Parmesan cheese
1 Tbsp. chopped fresh parsley

1. Heat dressing in large skillet over medium-high heat.
2. Add onion and steam or stir-fry 5 minutes, or until just tender.
3. Add eggplant and steam or stir-fry 5 minutes.
4. Add zucchini, pepper, and mushrooms. Steam or stir-fry 5 minutes more.
5. Add tomatoes and bring to a boil.
6. Pour mixture into lightly greased baking dish. Sprinkle with cheese.
7. Bake uncovered at 350° for 25–30 minutes, or until bubbly.
8. Sprinkle with parsley just before serving.

Per Serving

Calories 70, Kilojoules 293, Protein 4 g,
Carbohydrates 11 g, Total Fat 1.5 g, Saturated Fat 0.5 g,
Monounsaturated Fat 0.8 g, Polyunsaturated Fat 0.2 g,
Cholesterol 3 mg, Sodium 202 mg, Fiber 5 g

Tip: You can prepare this a day before you need it and then refrigerate it. Cover and heat through in the oven, or microwave, just before serving.

Roasted Onions
Elaine Gibbel
Lititz, PA

Makes 4 servings

Prep. Time: 10 minutes
Baking Time: 1 hour

Pyramid Servings

Vegetables
●○○○○➤

Fruits
○○○○○➤

Carbohydrates
○○○○○○○○

Protein & Dairy
○○○○○○○

Fats
●○○○○

Sweets
●

2 large Vidalias, *or sweet,*
    onions
1 Tbsp. water
3 Tbsp. honey
1 Tbsp. soft-tub margarine,
    non-hydrogenated, melted
1 tsp. paprika
½ tsp. salt
½ tsp. curry powder
⅛–¼ tsp. ground red pepper, according to
    your taste preference

1. Preheat oven to 350°.
2. Peel onions and cut in half crosswise.
Place onions, cut sides down, in 8" square
baking dish.
3. Sprinkle with water. Cover with foil.
4. Bake at 350° for 30 minutes.
5. Meanwhile, combine remaining ingredients in small bowl.
6. Turn onions over and brush with half of
honey mixture.
7. Bake 30 minutes more, uncovered, until
tender, basting with remaining honey mixture
after 15 minutes.

Per Serving

Calories 129, Kilojoules 540, Protein 1 g,
Carbohydrates 25 g, Total Fat 3 g, Saturated Fat 0.5 g,
Monounsaturated Fat 1.5 g, Polyunsaturated Fat 1 g,
Cholesterol 0 mg, Sodium 52 mg, Fiber 2 g

Orange-Glazed Parsnips
Sandra Haverstraw
Hummelstown, PA

Makes 6 servings

Prep. Time: 15 minutes
Cooking Time:15 minutes

Pyramid Servings

Vegetables
○○○○○➤

Fruits
○○○○○➤

Carbohydrates
●○○○○○○○

Protein & Dairy
○○○○○○○

Fats
●○○○○

Sweets
◐

4½ cups parsnips, cut
    diagonally in ½" slices
¾–1 cup water
2 Tbsp. soft-tub margarine,
    non-hydrogenated
1 Tbsp. honey
¼ cup orange juice
1 Tbsp. grated orange peel
¼ tsp. nutmeg

1. Cook parsnips in water in saucepan,
about 10 minutes, or until softened.
2. Drain and remove parsnips from pan.
3. Combine remaining ingredients in pan.
Heat until margarine and honey are melted
and ingredients are heated through.
4. Stir sauce into parsnips.
5. Serve hot.

Per Serving

Calories 134, Kilojoules 561, Protein 1 g,
Carbohydrates 24 g, Total Fat 4 g, Saturated Fat 1 g,
Monounsaturated Fat 1 g, Polyunsaturated Fat 2 g,
Cholesterol 0 g, Sodium 63 mg, Fiber 5 g

*Tip: These parsnips are especially good with
turkey or pork. You can also use the orange
glaze over cooked, cubed winter squash or sweet
potatoes.*

Easy Spicy Oven French Fries

Trudy Kutter
Corfu, NY

Makes 8 servings

Prep. Time: 15 minutes
Baking Time: 25–30 minutes

1¼ lbs. potatoes, scrubbed,
    but unpeeled
2 tsp. chili powder
2 tsp. minced garlic
¼ tsp. salt

Pyramid Servings	
Vegetables ○○○○○➤	
Fruits ○○○○○➤	
Carbohydrates ●○○○○○○○	
Protein & Dairy ○○○○○○○	
Fats ○○○○○	

   1. Heat oven to 450°. Spray jelly-roll baking pan with non-stick cooking spray.
   2. Cut potatoes into about ½"-thick sticks. Put in mixing bowl.
   3. Toss julienned potatoes with chili powder, garlic, and salt.
   4. Spread in prepared baking pan.
   5. Bake until crisp, browned, and tender, about 25–30 minutes.

Per Serving

Calories 70, Kilojoules 293, Protein 2 g,
Carbohydrates 15 g, Total Fat *trace*, Saturated Fat *trace*,
Monounsaturated Fat *trace*, Polyunsaturated Fat *trace*,
Cholesterol 0 mg, Sodium 84 mg, Fiber 2 g

Tip: If your family does not care for garlic or chili powder, try a bit of paprika, or use herbs such as oregano or thyme.

Baked Basil Fries

Sharon Brubaker, Myerstown, PA

Makes 6 servings

Prep. Time: 15 minutes
Baking Time: 30 minutes

2 Tbsp. Parmesan cheese
2 tsp. olive oil
1 Tbsp. dried basil
¼ tsp. garlic powder
4 medium red potatoes

Pyramid Servings	
Vegetables ○○○○○➤	
Fruits ○○○○○➤	
Carbohydrates ●○○○○○○○	
Protein & Dairy ○○○○○○○	
Fats ●○○○○	

   1. Combine first 4 ingredients in a good-sized bowl.
   2. Cut potatoes into ¼"-thick matchsticks. Toss with cheese mixture in bowl.
   3. Place in jelly-roll baking pan, lightly coated with non-stick cooking spray.
   4. Bake at 425° for 15 minutes.
   5. Turn potatoes with a metal spatula. Bake an additional 15 minutes, or until potatoes are crisp-tender.

Per Serving

Calories 109, Kilojoules 456, Protein 3 g,
Carbohydrates 19 g, Total Fat 2 g, Saturated Fat 0.5 g,
Monounsaturated Fat 1 g, Polyunsaturated Fat 0.5 g,
Cholesterol 1 mg, Sodium 38 mg, Fiber 2 g

Oven Fries

Sherry H. Kauffman
Minot, ND

Makes 6 servings

Prep. Time: 15 minutes
Baking Time: 25 minutes

3 medium unpeeled baking
   potatoes (1½ lbs.)
2 large carrots, peeled
2 tsp. vegetable, *or* canola, oil
¼ tsp. salt
¼ tsp. pepper
nonfat cooking spray

Pyramid Servings

Vegetables	●○○○○➤
Fruits	○○○○○➤
Carbohydrates	●○○○○○○○
Protein & Dairy	○○○○○○○
Fats	◐○○○○

  1. Scrub potatoes. Cut potatoes and carrots into 3½" × ½" strips. Pat dry with paper towel.
  2. Combine oil, salt, and pepper in large bowl. Add potatoes and carrots. Toss to coat.
  3. Arrange in a single layer on a baking sheet coated with nonfat cooking spray.
  4. Bake at 475° for 25 minutes, or until tender and brown, turning after 15 minutes.

Per Serving

Calories 111, Kilojoules 464, Protein 3 g,
Carbohydrates 21 g, Total Fat 2 g, Saturated Fat 0.5 g,
Monounsaturated Fat 1 g, Polyunsaturated Fat 0.5 g,
Cholesterol 0 mg, Sodium 117 mg, Fiber 2 g

Dietitian's tips:
  1. If salt is omitted, each serving may be reduced by another 100 milligrams of sodium.
  2. Potatoes are a good source of vitamin C, vitamin B-6, and potassium. If you eat them with their skins, you nearly double the amount of fiber.

Guilt-Free Golden Mashed Potatoes

Sharon Wantland
Menomonee Falls, WI

Makes 8 servings

Prep. Time: 30 minutes
Cooking/Baking Time: 40–45 minutes

2 lbs. Yukon Gold potatoes
2 reduced-sodium chicken
   bouillon cubes
¼ cup skim milk
half an 8-oz. pkg. fat-free
   cream cheese, softened
¼ cup fat-free sour cream
½ cup low-fat shredded sharp cheddar
   cheese
¼ tsp. white pepper
2 tsp. chopped fresh parsley

Pyramid Servings

Vegetables	○○○○○➤
Fruits	○○○○○➤
Carbohydrates	●○○○○○○○
Protein & Dairy	◐○○○○○○
Fats	○○○○○

  1. Peel and cut potatoes into small cubes. Place in 4-quart saucepan with bouillon and water to cover.
  2. Cover pan. Bring to a boil and cook until very tender, about 30 minutes.
  3. Drain and return potatoes to pan.
  4. Preheat oven to 425°.
  5. Mash potatoes with electric mixer or hand-held ricer.
  6. Add all remaining ingredients to potatoes except parsley. Mix well.
  7. Place 6 oval-shaped mounds of potatoes on cookie sheet, lightly covered with vegetable spray coating.
  8. Bake in preheated oven 10–15 minutes, or until golden brown.
  9. Garnish with parsley just before serving.

Per Serving

Calories 118, Kilojoules 494, Protein 6 g,
Carbohydrates 22 g, Total Fat 0.5 g, Saturated Fat 0.3 g,
Monounsaturated Fat 0.1 g, Polyunsaturated Fat 0.1 g,
Cholesterol 3 mg, Sodium 200 mg, Fiber 2 g

Potato-Vegetable Medley

Kathryn K. Good
Dayton, VA

Makes 8 servings

Prep. Time: 25 minutes
Baking Time: 40 minutes

2 large white potatoes
2 medium sweet potatoes
2 medium carrots
2 cups cubed butternut squash
2 onions
¼ cup olive oil
¼ tsp. pepper
½ tsp. garlic powder
2 tsp. dill weed

Pyramid Servings	
Vegetables	●○○○○▸
Fruits	○○○○○▸
Carbohydrates	●○○○○○○○
Protein & Dairy	○○○○○○○
Fats	●○○○○

1. Peel and cut vegetables into bite-sized pieces.
2. Place in large mixing bowl. Toss with oil and seasonings.
3. Spread onto large baking sheet with sides, which you've sprayed with non-stick cooking spray.
4. Bake at 375°, covered, for 15 minutes.
5. Uncover and stir.
6. Bake, uncovered, for 25 minutes more.

Per Serving

Calories 132, Kilojoules 552, Protein 2 g,
Carbohydrates 22 g, Total Fat 4 g, Saturated Fat 0.5 g,
Monounsaturated Fat 2.5 g, Polyunsaturated Fat 1 g,
Cholesterol 0 mg, Sodium 179 mg, Fiber 4 g

Sweet Potatoes

Elaine Good
Lititz, PA

Makes 10 servings

Cooking Time: 25–35 minutes

2 lbs. fresh sweet potatoes, scrubbed and trimmed

Pyramid Servings	
Vegetables	○○○○○▸
Fruits	○○○○○▸
Carbohydrates	●○○○○○○○
Protein & Dairy	○○○○○○○
Fats	○○○○○
Sweets	●

1. Place sweet potatoes in a saucepan and add water to a depth of about 2".
2. Cover and bring to a boil. Reduce heat and simmer until potatoes are soft, about 20–30 minutes. Drain.

Now you have several options:
• Serve immediately. The cooked potatoes can be mashed on individual plates and sprinkled with a bit of pepper or cinnamon. Eat everything, including skins, for good fiber!
• Allow to cool. Pull off peels and, depending on size of potato, cut lengthwise or crosswise. Store in refrigerator or freezer. To serve, simply warm in the microwave or oven.
• Use in other recipes such as this one:

¾ cup water
⅓ cup sugar-free orange-flavored gelatin (3-oz. pkg.)
½ cup brown sugar
2 Tbsp. soft-tub margarine, non-hydrogenated
¼ cup water
1 Tbsp. cornstarch
2 lbs. cooked sweet potatoes, peeled and cut in circles or lengthwise
¼ tsp. allspice, *optional*

1. In a skillet, heat ¾ cup water to boiling. Stir in gelatin until dissolved.
2. Add sugar and margarine. Mix in thoroughly.

3. In a small bowl, combine ¼ cup water and cornstarch. Stir into skillet, cooking and stirring until thickened and clear.

4. Add cooked sweet potato slices, spooning sauce over them.

5. Simmer until thoroughly heated. Sprinkle with allspice.

Per Serving

Calories 130, Kilojoules 544, Protein 1 g,
Carbohydrates 26 g, Total Fat 2 g, Saturated Fat 0.3 g,
Monounsaturated Fat 1 g, Polyunsaturated Fat 0.7 g,
Cholesterol 0 mg, Sodium 88 mg, Fiber 3 g

Variation: Prepare the sauce in a saucepan (Steps 1–3). Place potato pieces in a lightly greased oven-proof pan or dish. Pour sauce over potatoes. Sprinkle with allspice. Bake uncovered at 350° for 30 minutes, or until heated through.

Other options (not included in nutritional analyses):

1. Replace water and orange gelatin with ¾ cup orange juice.

2. Replace margarine with an additional ¼ cup orange juice.

3. Skip the sugar. The potatoes will touch the palate a bit differently, but still be good.

Healthy Sweet Potato Fries

Gladys M. High
Ephrata, PA

Makes 4 servings

Prep. Time: 15 minutes
Baking Time: 30 minutes

olive oil cooking spray
2 large sweet potatoes, peeled and cut into wedges
¼ tsp. salt
¼ tsp. black pepper
oregano, thyme, rosemary, garlic powder, *optional*

Pyramid Servings

Vegetables
○○○○○▸
Fruits
○○○○○▸
Carbohydrates
●○○○○○○○○
Protein & Dairy
○○○○○○○
Fats
○○○○○

1. Preheat oven to 400°.

2. Coat baking sheet with organic olive oil cooking spray.

3. Arrange potato wedges on baking sheet in a single layer. Coat with cooking spray.

4. Sprinkle potatoes with salt, pepper, and any additional optional seasoning of your choice.

5. Roast 30 minutes, or until tender and golden brown.

Per Serving

Calories 56, Kilojoules 234, Protein 1 g,
Carbohydrates 13 g, Total Fat *trace*, Saturated Fat *trace*,
Monounsaturated Fat *trace*, Polyunsaturated Fat *trace*,
Cholesterol 0 mg, Sodium 181 mg, Fiber 2 g

Sweet Potato Casserole

Joyce Shackelford
Green Bay, WI

Makes 6 servings

Prep. Time: 20 minutes
Cooking/Baking Time: 1 hour

Pyramid Servings	
Vegetables	ooooo➤
Fruits	ooooo➤
Carbohydrates	●ooooooo
Protein & Dairy	ooooooo
Fats	●oooo

4 medium sweet potatoes
1 Tbsp. olive oil
¼ cup orange juice,
   unsweetened
2 Tbsp. chopped walnuts,
   plus 2 tsp. for garnish
¼ tsp. nutmeg

1. Cook whole sweet potatoes in boiling water in a covered saucepan 25–30 minutes, or until tender. Drain.

2. Allow potatoes to cool enough to hold. Then peel and mash in a mixer or with a hand-held ricer.

3. Add olive oil, orange juice, 2 Tbsp. chopped walnuts, and nutmeg. Mix thoroughly.

4. Place in lightly greased 1-quart baking dish. Garnish with 2 tsp. chopped walnuts.

5. Bake uncovered at 375° for 25 minutes.

Per Serving

Calories 120, Kilojoules 502, Protein 2 g,
Carbohydrates 18 g, Total Fat 4 g, Saturated Fat 0.5 g,
Monounsaturated Fat 2 g, Polyunsaturated Fat 1.5 g,
Cholesterol 0 mg, Sodium 48 mg, Fiber 3 g

Sweety Potato Custard

Patricia Alger
Mt. Crawford, VA

Makes 6 servings

Prep. Time: 25–30 minutes
Cooking/Baking Time: 40–45
   minutes

Pyramid Servings	
Vegetables	ooooo➤
Fruits	●oooo➤
Carbohydrates	●ooooooo
Protein & Dairy	●oooooo
Fats	ooooo

1 cup sweet potato, cooked
½ cup (about 2) small
   bananas
1 cup evaporated skim milk
2 Tbsp. (packed) brown sugar
½ cup egg substitute, beaten
¼ tsp. salt
¼ cup raisins
1 Tbsp. honey
1 tsp. ground cinnamon

1. In medium bowl, mash together sweet potato and banana.

2. Add milk, blending well.

3. Add brown sugar, egg substitute, and salt, mixing thoroughly.

4. Spray 1-quart baking dish with non-stick cooking spray. Transfer sweet potato mixture to baking dish.

5. Combine raisins, honey, and cinnamon in a small bowl. Sprinkle over top of sweet potato mixture.

6. Bake in oven uncovered at 325° for 40–45 minutes, or until knife inserted near center comes out clean.

Per Serving

Calories 113, Kilojoules 473, Protein 5 g,
Carbohydrates 23 g, Total Fat *trace*, Saturated Fat *trace*,
Monounsaturated Fat *trace*, Polyunsaturated Fat *trace*,
Cholesterol 2 mg, Sodium 185 mg, Fiber 1.2 g

Dietitian's tip: To save time, poke several holes in the sweet potatoes and microwave on high power for about 3 minutes. Turn and cook another 3 minutes or until tender. Set aside to cool and use as directed.

Sweet Potato and Apple Casserole

Penny Blosser
Beavercreek, OH

Makes 8 servings

Prep. Time: 20 minutes
Cooking/Baking Time: 30 minutes

1 tsp. olive oil
¼ cup chopped onion
2 tsp. dried sage
40-oz. can sweet potatoes,
    drained and sliced, *divided*
4 cups peeled and sliced
    apples, *divided*

Pyramid Servings

Vegetables	○○○○○►
Fruits	●○○○○►
Carbohydrates	●●○○○○○○
Protein & Dairy	○○○○○○○
Fats	○○○○○

1. In small saucepan, cook onions in olive oil until tender. Stir in sage.
2. Place layer of sweet potatoes in 3-quart baking dish, using about one-third of the sweet potatoes.
3. Add half the onion mixture and half the apples.
4. Add second layer of sweet potatoes to baking dish, using about half of what remains.
5. Top with remaining onions and apples.
6. Top with remaining sweet potatoes.
7. Bake, covered, for 30 minutes at 350°, or until tender.

Per Serving

Calories 165, Kilojoules 690, Protein 3 g,
Carbohydrates 36 g, Total Fat *trace*, Saturated Fat *trace*,
Monounsaturated Fat *trace*, Polyunsaturated Fat *trace*,
Cholesterol 0 mg, Sodium 76 mg, Fiber 4 g

Snow Peas with Sesame Seeds

Sylvia Beiler
Lowville, NY

Makes 6 servings

Prep. Time: 15 minutes
Cooking/Baking Time: 10 minutes

3 cups trimmed fresh snow
    peas
2 Tbsp. diced onions
1 Tbsp. canola oil
3 Tbsp. sesame seeds
¼ tsp. freshly ground pepper

Pyramid Servings

Vegetables	●○○○○►
Fruits	○○○○○►
Carbohydrates	○○○○○○○○
Protein & Dairy	○○○○○○○
Fats	●○○○○

1. Slice each snow pea diagonally into 2–3 pieces.
2. Sauté onions and peas in oil in large skillet until tender.
3. Meanwhile, place sesame seeds in baking pan. Toast in 350° oven for 8 minutes, or until lightly browned.
4. Add sesame seeds to onions and peas. Sauté 1 minute until peas are coated with seeds.
5. Sprinkle with freshly ground pepper.

Per Serving

Calories 60, Kilojoules 251, Protein 2 g,
Carbohydrates 3 g, Total Fat 4.5 g, Saturated Fat 0.5 g,
Monounsaturated Fat 2.5 g, Polyunsaturated Fat 1.5 g,
Cholesterol 0 mg, Sodium 90 mg, Fiber 1 g

Spinach with Parmesan Cheese

Clarice Williams
Fairbank, IA

Makes 4 servings

Prep. Time: 10 minutes
Cooking Time: 7½–10 minutes

Pyramid Servings	
Vegetables ●○○○○▸	
Fruits ○○○○○▸	
Carbohydrates ○○○○○○○○	
Protein & Dairy ○○○○○○○	
Fats ○○○○○	

2 green onions, sliced
1 clove garlic, minced
2 Tbsp. water
1 lb. (about 12 cups) fresh
  spinach leaves, washed and
  trimmed*
1 Tbsp. grated Parmesan cheese
1 tsp. lemon juice

1. In 3-quart microwave-safe bowl, combine onions, garlic, and water. Cook in microwave on 100 percent power (High) for 30–60 seconds, or until onions are tender.

2. Add spinach. Cook, covered, on High for 7–9 minutes, or until spinach is tender, stirring once. Drain well.

3. Sprinkle with Parmesan cheese and lemon juice.

Per Serving

Calories 35, Kilojoules 146, Protein 1 g,
Carbohydrates 5 g, Total Fat 1 g, Saturated Fat 0.2 g,
Monounsaturated Fat 0.7 g, Polyunsaturated Fat 0.1 g,
Cholesterol 1 mg, Sodium 110 mg, Fiber 3 g

* Note: If you wish, you can substitute one 10-oz. pkg. frozen spinach, chopped, for fresh spinach. Use a 1½-quart microwave-safe dish. Decrease second cooking time to 6–8 minutes.

Walnut Spinach

Rika Allen
New Holland, PA

Makes 8 servings

Prep. Time: 5 minutes
Cooking Time: 5 minutes

Pyramid Servings	
Vegetables ●○○○○▸	
Fruits ○○○○○▸	
Carbohydrates ○○○○○○○○	
Protein & Dairy ○○○○○○○	
Fats ●○○○○	

1 lb. (about 12 cups) fresh
  spinach, washed and
  trimmed
½ cup walnuts, coarsely
  ground
2 Tbsp. reduced sodium soy
  sauce

1. Cook spinach with small amount of water in large saucepan with lid, just until it wilts.

2. Drain well. Squeeze out water as much as possible.

3. Add walnuts and soy sauce to spinach. Mix well.

Per Serving

Calories 65, Kilojoules 272, Protein 2 g,
Carbohydrates 2 g, Total Fat 5 g, Saturated Fat 0.3 g,
Monounsaturated Fat 2 g, Polyunsaturated Fat 2.7 g,
Cholesterol 0 mg, Sodium 171 mg, Fiber 2 g

Tip: This dish is also good using toasted and coarsely ground sesame seeds instead of walnuts.

A Tip —

To bake potatoes quickly, place them in boiling water for 10-15 minutes. Pierce skins with a fork and then bake them in a pre-heated oven.

Spinach Surprise

Leona Yoder
Hartville, OH

Makes 6 servings

Prep. Time: 10 minutes
Cooking Time:12–15 minutes

Pyramid Servings	
Vegetables	●○○○○➤
Fruits	◐○○○○➤
Carbohydrates	○○○○○○○
Protein & Dairy	○○○○○○○
Fats	◐○○○○

2 boxes frozen, chopped
  spinach, thawed
½ cup raisins
½ cup slivered almonds

1. Cook spinach according to
package directions. Drain thoroughly.
2. Just before serving, stir in raisins and
almonds.
3. Return to heat just long enough to warm
added ingredients.

Per Serving

Calories 89, Kilojoules 372, Protein 5 g,
Carbohydrates 11 g, Total Fat 3 g, Saturated Fat 0.2 g,
Monounsaturated Fat 1.8 g, Polyunsaturated Fat 1 g,
Cholesterol 0 mg, Sodium 71 mg, Fiber 4 g

Creamed Spinach

Mary Ann Lefever
Lancaster, PA

Makes 6 servings

Prep. Time: 15 minutes
Cooking/Baking Time: 30–40
  minutes

Pyramid Servings	
Vegetables	●○○○○➤
Fruits	○○○○○➤
Carbohydrates	○○○○○○○
Protein & Dairy	◐○○○○○○
Fats	●○○○○

16-oz. bag frozen chopped
  baby spinach
half onion, minced (about ¾
  cup)
2 Tbsp. olive oil
¼ tsp. black pepper
½ tsp. garlic powder, *or* 1 clove garlic,
  chopped
3 Tbsp. flour
1½ cups skim milk
⅓ cup fat-free half-and-half
¼ cup grated Parmesan cheese

1. Cook spinach in microwave or on
stovetop, according to package directions.
2. Drain very well, squeezing out excess
water. Set aside.
3. Cook onion in large saucepan or skillet in
olive oil until tender.
4. Add pepper, garlic powder, and flour.
Cook until beginning to brown.
5. Stir in milk and half-and-half. Cook over
low heat, stirring continually, until thickened.
6. Stir in cooked spinach and Parmesan
cheese.
7. Coat a 9" glass pie plate with non-fat
cooking spray. Spread spinach mixture in pie
plate.
8. Bake uncovered at 300° for 20 minutes.

Per Serving

Calories 120, Kilojoules 502, Protein 6 g,
Carbohydrates 12 g, Total Fat 5 g, Saturated Fat 1.3 g,
Monounsaturated Fat 3.5 g, Polyunsaturated Fat 0.2 g,
Cholesterol 5 mg, Sodium 186 mg, Fiber 2 g

Succotash

Esther Nafziger
Bluffton, OH

Makes 6 servings

Prep. Time: 20 minutes
Cooking Time: 10–12 minutes

Pyramid Servings	
Vegetables	○○○○○➤
Fruits	○○○○○➤
Carbohydrates	◑○○○○○○○
Protein & Dairy	◑○○○○○○
Fats	●○○○○

2 cups frozen shelled
  soybeans
2 slices lean bacon, cut into
  ¼" pieces
1 medium onion, chopped
1 rib celery, cut into ¼" pieces
2 cups fresh, canned (no salt added), *or*
  frozen corn (thawed)
¼ cup low-fat, low-sodium chicken broth,
  or water
⅛ tsp. pepper

1. Rinse beans under hot water to begin to
thaw. Drain.
2. In 12" skillet, cook bacon over medium
heat until browned. With slotted spoon,
transfer bacon to paper towels to drain.
3. Carefully blot out bacon fat from pan
with paper towels. Add onion and celery
to skillet. Cook over medium-high heat 5
minutes, or until vegetables are tender and
golden, stirring frequently.
4. Stir in beans, corn, broth, and pepper.
5. Reduce heat to low. Cover and simmer
2 minutes, or until heated through.

Per Serving

Calories 134, Kilojoules 561, Protein 9 g,
Carbohydrates 17 g, Total Fat 4 g, Saturated Fat 1 g,
Monounsaturated Fat 1.5 g, Polyunsaturated Fat 1.5 g,
Cholesterol 0.5 mg, Sodium 80 mg, Fiber 4 g

Scalloped Cheesy Tomatoes

Scarlett Von Bernuth
Canon City, CO

Makes 6 servings

Prep. Time: 15 minutes
Baking Time: 35 minutes

Pyramid Servings	
Vegetables	●●○○○➤
Fruits	○○○○○➤
Carbohydrates	◑○○○○○○○
Protein & Dairy	○○○○○○○
Fats	●○○○○

4 fresh tomatoes, sliced,
  divided
1 cup soft bread cubes,
  divided
1 Tbsp. fresh parsley, *divided*
2 Tbsp. olive oil, *divided*
½ cup cracker crumbs (made from
  crackers with unsalted tops)
¼ cup low-sodium, low-fat grated cheese
pepper

1. Fill a lightly greased baking dish with
alternate layers of tomatoes and bread cubes.
2. Sprinkle parsley and olive oil over each
layer.
3. Cover top with cracker crumbs. Sprinkle
with cheese.
4. Bake uncovered in 350°–375° oven for
35 minutes.

Per Serving

Calories 126, Kilojoules 527, Protein 4 g,
Carbohydrates 18 g, Total Fat 4 g, Saturated Fat 1 g,
Monounsaturated Fat 2 g, Polyunsaturated Fat 1 g,
Cholesterol 3 mg, Sodium 200 mg, Fiber 2 g

A Tip —

To easily and cleanly crush crackers,
put them in a plastic bag. Then crush them
with a rolling pin.

Stewed Tomatoes

Colleen J. Heatwole
Burton, MI

Makes 8 servings

Prep. Time: 15 minutes
Cooking Time: 15 minutes

½ cup finely chopped onion
½ cup diced green, *or* red,
   bell sweet pepper
½ cup diced celery
1 Tbsp. olive, *or* canola, oil
2 14½-oz. cans low-sodium
   tomatoes, *or* 1 quart canned tomatoes
   (no salt added)
1 tsp. sugar
¾ tsp. dry basil

1. In large skillet or saucepan, sauté onion, bell pepper, and celery in 1 Tbsp. oil until tender, about 5 minutes.
2. Add rest of ingredients and heat to boiling.
3. Reduce heat, cover, and simmer 5 minutes.

Pyramid Servings	
Vegetables	●○○○○➤
Fruits	○○○○○➤
Carbohydrates	○○○○○○○○
Protein & Dairy	○○○○○○○
Fats	●○○○○

Per Serving
Calories 44, Kilojoules 184, Protein 1 g,
Carbohydrates 6 g, Total Fat 2 g, Saturated Fat 0.2 g,
Monounsaturated Fat 1 g, Polyunsaturated Fat 0.8 g,
Cholesterol 0 mg, Sodium 46 mg, Fiber 2 g

Tip: In the summer-time use fresh tomatoes and fresh basil.

Grilled Zucchini

Joan Terwilliger
Lebanon, PA

Makes 1 serving

Prep. Time: 10 minutes
Marinating time: 1 hour
Grilling Time: 14 minutes

1 medium zucchini per
   serving, unpeel
2 tsp. low-fat Italian dressing
1 Tbsp. Parmesan cheese,
   grated or shredded

1. Slice zucchini lengthwise into ¼"-thick slices.
2. Put in plastic zip-top bag with Italian dressing. Squeeze bag gently to distribute dressing over zucchini slices.
3. Marinate for about one hour.
4. Remove zucchini from marinade. Place on non-stick release aluminum foil.
5. Grill on high heat in covered grill about 14 minutes, turning once halfway through.
6. Sprinkle with Parmesan cheese after turning.

Pyramid Servings	
Vegetables	●●○○○➤
Fruits	○○○○○➤
Carbohydrates	○○○○○○○○
Protein & Dairy	○○○○○○○
Fats	○○○○○

Per Serving
Calories 57, Kilojoules 238, Protein 4 g,
Carbohydrates 6 g, Total Fat 2 g, Saturated Fat 1 g,
Monounsaturated Fat 0.6 g, Polyunsaturated Fat 0.4 g,
Cholesterol 5 mg, Sodium 200 mg, Fiber 2 g

Cheesy Zucchini Caterpillar

Delores Gnagey
Saginaw, MI

Makes 2 servings

Prep. Time: 10 minutes
Baking Time: 35–37 minutes

1 medium zucchini (about 6"
   long)
1 tsp. olive oil
⅛ tsp. garlic powder
⅛ tsp. onion powder
2 Tbsp. grated Parmesan
   cheese

Pyramid Servings	
Vegetables	●○○○○▸
Fruits	○○○○○▸
Carbohydrates	○○○○○○○○
Protein & Dairy	○○○○○○○
Fats	●○○○○

1. Preheat oven to 375°.
2. Trim ends off zucchini and discard. At ½" intervals, slice ¾ of the way through the zucchini, being careful not to cut all the way through (the slices should be connected).
3. Gently dry zucchini with paper towel.
4. Place zucchini on piece of aluminum foil large enough to wrap completely around zucchini.
5. Drizzle top of zucchini with olive oil.
6. Sprinkle with garlic and onion powders.
7. Wrap zucchini in foil and pinch closed. Lay on baking sheet.
8. Bake 30–35 minutes, or until zucchini is tender when poked with fork.
9. Remove from oven, open foil, and sprinkle cheese over zucchini.
10. With foil open, return zucchini to oven for 1–2 minutes. Or turn oven to Broil and lightly brown "caterpillar."

Per Serving

Calories 57, Kilojoules 238, Protein 3 g,	
Carbohydrates 3 g, Total Fat 4 g, Saturated Fat 1.2 g,	
Monounsaturated Fat 2.5 g, Polyunsaturated Fat 0.3 g,	
Cholesterol 4 mg, Sodium 86 mg, Fiber 1 g	

Zucchini Ribbons

Delores Gnagey
Saginaw, MI

Makes 4 servings

Prep. Time: 15 minutes
Cooking Time: 9 minutes

1 large zucchini, unpeeled,
   ends trimmed
1 Tbsp. olive oil
3 garlic cloves, minced
1 cup cherry tomato halves
½ tsp. dried basil
pepper to taste

Pyramid Servings	
Vegetables	●○○○○▸
Fruits	○○○○○▸
Carbohydrates	○○○○○○○○
Protein & Dairy	○○○○○○○
Fats	●○○○○

1. With vegetable peeler, slice zucchini into long, lengthwise strips, thick enough not to bend. (If strips are too thin, they'll get mushy while sautéing.)
2. Heat oil in large skillet over medium heat. Add zucchini ribbons. Sauté 4 minutes.
3. Add garlic and sauté 2 more minutes.
4. Add cherry tomatoes and sauté 2 additional minutes.
5. Sprinkle with basil and pepper to taste. Cook 1 minute.

Per Serving

Calories 58, Kilojoules 243, Protein 1 g,	
Carbohydrates 5 g, Total Fat 4 g, Saturated Fat 0.5 g,	
Monounsaturated Fat 2.5 g, Polyunsaturated Fat 1 g,	
Cholesterol 0 mg, Sodium 13 mg, Fiber 2 g	

Zucchini Souffle

Sharon Eshleman
Ephrata, PA

Makes 4 servings

Prep. Time: 15 minutes
Baking Time: 20 minutes

2 cups shredded raw zucchini
½ cup low-fat milk
egg substitute equivalent to 1
    egg, beaten, *or* 2 egg whites,
    beaten
1 tsp. chopped onion
½ cup grated low-fat sharp cheddar cheese
¾ cup fine bread crumbs, *or* cracker
    crumbs (made from crackers without
    salted tops), *divided*

Pyramid Servings	
Vegetables	●○○○○➤
Fruits	○○○○○➤
Carbohydrates	○○○○○○○○
Protein & Dairy	●○○○○○○
Fats	○○○○○

1. Squeeze moisture out of shredded
zucchini by pressing with paper towels.
2. In a bowl, mix together all ingredients,
except cheese and ½ cup bread or cracker
crumbs.
3. Place mixture into greased 2-quart baking
dish.
4. Sprinkle with cheese and remaining
crumbs.
5. Bake uncovered at 400° for 20 minutes.

Per Serving

Calories 136, Kilojoules 569, Protein 10 g,
Carbohydrates 18 g, Total Fat 2 g, Saturated Fat 1 g,
Monounsaturated Fat 0.5 g, Polyunsaturated Fat 0.5 g,
Cholesterol 4 mg, Sodium 295 mg, Fiber 2 g

*Tip: You can substitute 1 cup shredded carrots
for 1 cup shredded zucchini.*

Squash Apple Bake

Lavina Hochstedler
Grand Blanc, MI

Makes 6 main-dish servings

Prep. Time: 30 minutes
Baking Time: 45–50 minutes

4 cups cubed butternut
    squash, *divided*
3 Tbsp. honey, *or* brown
    sugar
⅓ cup orange, *or* apple, juice
2 tsp. cornstarch
2–3 apples, cut in short thick slices, *divided*
¼ cup raisins, *divided*
cinnamon
1 Tbsp. soft-tub margarine, non-
    hydrogenated

Pyramid Servings	
Vegetables	○○○○○➤
Fruits	●○○○○➤
Carbohydrates	●○○○○○○○
Protein & Dairy	○○○○○○○
Fats	●○○○○

1. Slice butternut squash into ¾" rounds.
Peel and cut into cubes.
2. Combine honey, juice, and cornstarch in a
small bowl.
3. In greased 2- or 3-quart baking dish, layer
in half the squash, followed by a layer of half
the apples, and then a layer of half the raisins.
4. Repeat layers.
5. Sprinkle generously with cinnamon.
6. Pour juice mixture over all.
7. Dot with margarine.
8. Cover and bake at 350° for 45–50
minutes, or until tender. Serve warm as a
vegetable.

Per Serving

Calories 150, Kilojoules 628, Protein 1 g,
Carbohydrates 33 g, Total Fat 2 g, Saturated Fat 0.2 g,
Monounsaturated Fat 0.8 g, Polyunsaturated Fat 1 g,
Cholesterol 0 mg, Sodium 31 mg, Fiber 4 g

Baked Butternut Squash and Cranberries

Anne Hummel
Millersburg, OH

Makes 6 servings

Prep. Time: 20–30 minutes
Baking Time: 75–80 minutes

Pyramid Servings

Vegetables
○○○○○➤

Fruits
◐○○○○➤

Carbohydrates
●○○○○○○○

Protein & Dairy
○○○○○○○

Fats
◐○○○○

1 medium butternut squash
　(about 4 lbs. before peeling
　and removing seeds),
　peeled and cubed
half onion, sliced
1 Tbsp. olive oil
pinch of sage
pinch of dried thyme
pinch of cinnamon
½ cup dried cranberries
¼ cup white, *or* red, cranberry juice,
　without added sugar

1. In large bowl, toss cubed squash and onion with olive oil.

2. Stir in herbs and cranberries.

3. Spread in lightly greased 3- or 4-quart baking dish.

4. Preheat oven to 350°.

5. Cover dish and bake 1 hour.

6. Pour juice over squash. Return to oven, and continue baking 15–20 minutes, uncovered.

7. Serve warm or cold.

Per Serving

Calories 130, Kilojoules 544, Protein 2 g,
Carbohydrates 26 g, Total Fat 2.5 g, Saturated Fat 0.3 g,
Monounsaturated Fat 1.7 g, Polyunsaturated Fat 0.5 g,
Cholesterol 0 mg, Sodium 6 mg, Fiber 4 g

A Tip —

　We eat with our "eyes" as well as our mouths. Vary the colors and textures of food you serve at a meal.

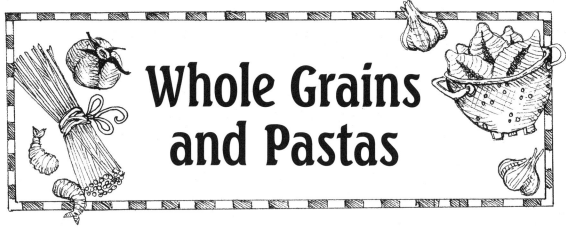

Whole Grains and Pastas

Apple-Cranberry Wild Rice

Heather Horst
Lebanon, PA

Makes 4 servings

Prep. Time: 10 minutes
Baking Time: 1½–2 hours

1½ cups water
⅓ cup raw brown rice
⅓ cup raw wild rice
1 tsp. dried savory
1 small leek (white portion
  only), coarsely chopped, *or*
  3 Tbsp. chopped onion
1 tsp. olive oil
⅓ cup dried cranberries
¼ cup chopped dried apples
⅓ tsp. low-sodium chicken bouillon
  granules
½ tsp. onion powder
½ tsp. lemon-pepper seasoning

Pyramid Servings

| Vegetables |
| ○○○○○► |
| Fruits |
| ●◐○○○► |
| Carbohydrates |
| ●○○○○○○○○ |
| Protein & Dairy |
| ○○○○○○○ |
| Fats |
| ○○○○○ |

1. Lightly grease a 1½-quart baking dish.
2. Measure all ingredients into prepared baking dish. Stir thoroughly to mix well.
3. Cover tightly and bake at 350° for 1½–2 hours.

Per Serving

Calories 170, Kilojoules 711, Protein 3 g,
Carbohydrates 36 g, Total Fat 2 g, Saturated Fat 0.3 g,
Monounsaturated Fat 1 g, Polyunsaturated Fat 0.7 g,
Cholesterol 0 mg, Sodium 158 mg, Fiber 3 g

Wild Rice with Walnuts and Dates

Patricia Andreas
Wausau, WI

Makes 8 servings

Prep. Time: 15–20 minutes
Cooking Time: 60–70 minutes

1 small onion, chopped
2 cups celery, chopped
1 tsp. extra-virgin olive oil
1 cup uncooked wild rice, rinsed and drained
14-oz. can low-sodium, low-fat broth (chicken, beef, *or* vegetable)
1 cup water
⅓ cup pitted dates
½ cup walnuts, chopped and toasted

Pyramid Servings

Vegetables
●○○○○➤

Fruits
◐○○○○➤

Carbohydrates
◐○○○○○○○

Protein & Dairy
○○○○○○○

Fats
●○○○○

1. In a 10" skillet, cook onion and celery in olive oil until tender. Remove vegetables and keep warm.
2. Add rice and sauté 3 minutes.
3. Add broth and water. Bring to boil and then reduce heat.
4. Cover and simmer 50–60 minutes, or until rice is tender.
5. Meanwhile, toast walnuts in dry small skillet over medium heat. Stir constantly.
6. Stir dates, walnuts, and reserved vegetables into rice. Cook uncovered 3–4 minutes.

Per Serving

Calories 149, Kilojoules 623, Protein 6 g,
Carbohydrates 20 g, Total Fat 5 g, Saturated Fat 0.5 g,
Monounsaturated Fat 1.5 g, Polyunsaturated Fat 3 g,
Cholesterol 1 mg, Sodium 46 mg, Fiber 3 g

Salsa Rice

Lois Stoltzfus
Honey Brook, PA

Makes 6 servings

Prep. Time: 5–10 minutes
Cooking Time: 35–45 minutes

1 Tbsp. extra-virgin olive oil
½ cup low-sodium tomato juice
1½ cups water
½ cup salsa
¼–½ tsp. cumin
¼ tsp. chili powder
½ tsp. garlic powder
½ tsp. minced onion
1 Tbsp., *or less*, brown sugar
1 cup raw long-grain rice

Pyramid Servings

Vegetables
●○○○○➤

Fruits
○○○○○➤

Carbohydrates
●○○○○○○○

Protein & Dairy
○○○○○○○

Fats
●○○○○

1. Combine all ingredients except rice in a large saucepan.
2. Cover and bring to a boil.
3. Stir well. Add rice. Stir again.
4. Cover and cook on low 20–30 minutes, or until liquids are absorbed. Do not stir again until ready to serve.

Per Serving

Calories 153, Kilojoules 640, Protein 3 g,
Carbohydrates 28 g, Total Fat 3 g, Saturated Fat 0.5 g,
Monounsaturated Fat 2 g, Polyunsaturated Fat 0.5 g,
Cholesterol 0 mg, Sodium 146 mg, Fiber 2 g

Dietitian's tip: To reduce the amount of sodium in this recipe, use homemade salsa instead of store-bought salsa. See the following recipes: Fresh Chunky Cherry Tomato Salsa (page 244), Fresh Salsa (page 244).

Rice Medley
Doyle Rounds
Bridgewater, VA

Makes 10 servings

Prep. Time: 5 minutes
Cooking Time: 20–25 minutes

1 cup raw brown rice
2¼ cups water
2 cups frozen peas, thawed
1 carrot, shredded
1½ tsp. salt-free herb
  seasoning
1 tsp. low-sodium chicken bouillon
  granules
1 tsp. lemon juice

Pyramid Servings	
Vegetables	○○○○○▸
Fruits	○○○○○▸
Carbohydrates	◑○○○○○○○
Protein & Dairy	◑○○○○○○
Fats	○○○○○

1. In a large saucepan, combine first six ingredients.
2. Cover and bring to a boil.
3. Reduce heat and simmer 15 minutes, or until rice is tender.
4. Remove from heat and add lemon juice. Fluff with a fork.

Per Serving

Calories 97, Kilojoules 406, Protein 3 g,
Carbohydrates 19 g, Total Fat 0.6 g, Saturated Fat 0.1 g,
Monounsaturated Fat 0.2 g, Polyunsaturated Fat 0.3 g,
Cholesterol *trace*, Sodium 33 mg, Fiber 3 g

Dietitian's tip: Use any variety of herbs in this recipe: cilantro (Mexican), nutmeg (Middle Eastern), oregano (Italian), or rosemary (French). Also try different vegetables, such as green onions, thinly sliced tomatoes, eggplant, hearts of palm, sliced mushrooms, or asparagus tips. For variety, try roasting the vegetables first.

Lemon Curry Rice Mix
Susan Kasting
Jenks, OK

Makes 16 servings

Prep. Time: 10 minutes
Drying Time for lemon rind: 1 hour
Cooking Time: 30–40 minutes

2 Tbsp. grated lemon rind
4 cups raw brown rice
1 cup golden raisins
1 cup slivered almonds
1 Tbsp. curry powder
1 tsp. ground white pepper
½ tsp. cumin
½ tsp. crushed red pepper

Pyramid Servings	
Vegetables	○○○○○▸
Fruits	●○○○○▸
Carbohydrates	●●○○○○○○
Protein & Dairy	○○○○○○○
Fats	●○○○○

1. Dry lemon rind by spreading evenly on a plate for 1 hour.
2. Combine rind and remaining ingredients in a large zip-lock bag and mix until blended.
3. To use, mix 1 cup raw rice mixture with 2 cups water in a saucepan.
4. Cover and bring to a boil.
5. Reduce heat to very low. Cook, covered, 30–40 minutes, or until water is absorbed and rice is tender.

Per Serving

Calories 239, Kilojoules 1000, Protein 5 g,
Carbohydrates 44 g, Total Fat 5 g, Saturated Fat 0.5 g,
Monounsaturated Fat 2.6 g, Polyunsaturated Fat 1.9 g,
Cholesterol 0 mg, Sodium 225 mg, Fiber 3 g

Artichokes and Brown Rice

Betty K. Drescher
Quakertown, PA

Makes 6 servings

Prep. Time: 5–10 minutes
Cooking Time: 40–50 minutes

1 cup raw brown rice
1 Tbsp. extra-virgin olive oil
14½-oz. can artichokes,
    drained and cut into
    chunks

Pyramid Servings

Vegetables
●○○○○➤

Fruits
○○○○○➤

Carbohydrates
●○○○○○○○

Protein & Dairy
○○○○○○○

Fats
●○○○○

1. Cook rice according to package directions, using olive oil instead of butter or margarine.
2. When finished cooking, stir in artichokes.

Per Serving

Calories 150, Kilojoules 628, Protein 3 g,
Carbohydrates 27 g, Total Fat 3 g, Saturated Fat 0.5 g,
Monounsaturated Fat 1.9 g, Polyunsaturated Fat 0.6 g,
Cholesterol 0 mg, Sodium 200 mg, Fiber 2 g

Herbed Rice Pilaf

Betty K. Drescher
Quakertown, PA

Makes 8 servings

Prep. Time: 15–20 minutes
Cooking/Baking Time: 50 minutes

2 cups raw brown rice
1 cup chopped celery
½ cup chopped onion
1 Tbsp. olive oil
4 cups low-sodium, fat-free
    chicken broth
1 tsp. Worcestershire sauce
1 tsp. low-sodium soy sauce
1 tsp. dried oregano
1 tsp. dried thyme

Pyramid Servings

Vegetables
●○○○○➤

Fruits
○○○○○➤

Carbohydrates
●●○○○○○○

Protein & Dairy
○○○○○○○

Fats
●○○○○

1. Sauté rice, celery, and onion in olive oil in skillet until rice is lightly browned and vegetables are tender.
2. Pour into lightly greased 2-quart baking dish.
3. Combine all remaining ingredients in a bowl. Pour over rice mixture.
4. Cover and bake at 325° for 50 minutes, or until rice is done.

Per Serving

Calories 206, Kilojoules 862, Protein 6 g,
Carbohydrates 38 g, Total Fat 3 g, Saturated Fat 1 g,
Monounsaturated Fat 1.7 g, Polyunsaturated Fat 0.3 g,
Cholesterol 2 mg, Sodium 108 mg, Fiber 2 g

Variations (not included in analyses):
1. Add ½ cup grated carrot to Step 1.
2. Add ½ cup chopped red bell pepper and 1 Tbsp. dried parsley to Step 3.
—**Jean Turner**, Williams Lake, B.C.

Dietitian's tip: If you want to use fresh herbs in place of dried, double or triple the amount. Fresh herbs are less intense in flavor compared to dried.

Crunchy Brown Rice

Lizzie Ann Yoder
Hartville, OH

Makes 6 servings

Prep. Time: 10–15 minutes
Cooking Time: 40 minutes

2½ cups low-sodium, fat-free chicken, *or* vegetable, stock
4 green onions (include green part), sliced
1 cup raw brown rice
¼ cup fresh, *or* frozen, corn
¼ cup instant non-fat dry milk
1 cup chopped tomato
¼ cup fresh basil, *or* 2 tsp. dried basil
¼ cup water chestnuts, drained and chopped coarsely

1. Combine stock and onion in large saucepan. Bring to a boil.
2. Stir in rice. Reduce heat. Cover and simmer 30 minutes.
3. Add corn, dry milk, tomato, basil, and water chestnuts.
4. Simmer about 10 more minutes, or until rice is tender.

Pyramid Servings	
Vegetables	●○○○○➤
Fruits	○○○○○➤
Carbohydrates	●○○○○○○○
Protein & Dairy	○○○○○○○
Fats	○○○○○

Per Serving

Calories 150, Kilojoules 628, Protein 6 g,
Carbohydrates 30 g, Total Fat 1 g, Saturated Fat 0.5 g,
Monounsaturated Fat 0.3 g, Polyunsaturated Fat 0.2 g,
Cholesterol 2 mg, Sodium 80 mg, Fiber 2 g

Dietitian's tip: Only the hull is removed during the processing of brown rice, so it has more vitamins and minerals than white rice does. The bran coating on brown rice is high in soluble fiber and, like oat bran, helps lower cholesterol. Brown rice has a nut-like flavor and is also chewier than white rice.

Curried Barley Side Dish

Diann J. Dunham
State College, PA

Makes 6 servings

Prep. Time: 15 minutes
Cooking Time: 25–30 minutes

2 cups water
⅔ cup raw, quick-cooking barley
½ cup chopped carrots
½ cup chopped onion
½ cup chopped celery
1½ tsp. low-sodium instant chicken bouillon granules, *or* 2 cups low-sodium, fat-free chicken, *or* vegetable, broth (omit 2 cups water if using broth)
1 tsp. curry powder
a few golden raisins, *optional* (not included in analyses)
1 Tbsp. toasted sliced almonds
1 Tbsp. snipped fresh parsley

1. In medium-sized saucepan stir together water, barley, carrots, onion, celery, chicken bouillon granules, and curry powder. Add raisins if you wish.
2. Cover and bring to a boil. Reduce heat. Simmer, covered, about 15 minutes, or until barley is nearly tender.
3. Uncover and cook 3 to 5 minutes more, or until barley reaches desired consistency.
4. Stir in almonds and parsley just before serving.

Pyramid Servings	
Vegetables	●○○○○➤
Fruits	○○○○○➤
Carbohydrates	●○○○○○○○
Protein & Dairy	○○○○○○○
Fats	○○○○○

Per Serving

Calories 104, Kilojoules 435, Protein 4 g,
Carbohydrates 20 g, Total Fat 1 g, Saturated Fat 0.4 g,
Monounsaturated Fat 0.6 g, Polyunsaturated Fat 1 g,
Cholesterol 2.5 mg, Sodium 98 mg, Fiber 6 g

Millet Casserole

Lizzie Ann Yoder
Hartville, OH

Makes 6 main-dish servings, or 12 side-dish servings

Prep. Time: 20 minutes
Baking Time: 45 minutes

4 fresh tomatoes
1 cup salsa of your choice
2 cloves garlic
1 green bell sweet pepper, cut up
4 cups cooked millet*

1. Cut up tomatoes.
2. Combine in a bowl with salsa, garlic, and green peppers.
3. Place mixture in blender container and blend 20–30 seconds.
4. Combine with millet and place in oven-proof dish.
5. Bake uncovered in 350° oven for 45 minutes.

Pyramid Servings
(As 6 main-dish servings)

Vegetables
●●●○○➤
Fruits
○○○○○➤
Carbohydrates
●●○○○○○○
Protein & Dairy
○○○○○○○
Fats
○○○○○

Pyramid Servings
(As 12 side-dish servings)

Vegetables
●●○○○➤
Fruits
○○○○○➤
Carbohydrates
●○○○○○○○
Protein & Dairy
○○○○○○○
Fats
○○○○○

Per Serving *(As 6 main-dish servings)*

Calories 223, Kilojoules 933, Protein 6 g,
Carbohydrates 45 g, Total Fat 2 g, Saturated Fat 0.3 g,
Monounsaturated Fat 0.3 g, Polyunsaturated Fat 1.4 g,
Cholesterol 0 mg, Sodium 234 mg, Fiber 4 g

Per Serving *(As 12 side-dish servings)*

Calories 111, Kilojoules 464, Protein 3 g,
Carbohydrates 22 g, Total Fat 1 g, Saturated Fat 0.2 g,
Monounsaturated Fat 0.2 g, Polyunsaturated Fat 0.6 g,
Cholesterol 0 mg, Sodium 117 mg, Fiber 2 g

*** Note:** To prepare millet, bring 3¼ cups water to a boil in a saucepan. Stir in 1½ cups raw millet. Cover pan. Turn to low and simmer 25 minutes. Do not stir or lift lid during cooking time.*

Golden Millet

Carolyn Spohn
Shawnee, KS

Makes 4 servings

Prep. Time: 15 minutes
Cooking Time: 30–35 minutes
Standing Time: 5 minutes

½ cup hulled, raw millet
1 Tbsp. extra-virgin olive oil
1 small onion, finely minced
1 clove garlic, minced
4 medium carrots, peeled and shredded
1 cup low-fat low-sodium chicken broth
½ cup skim milk
¼ tsp. black pepper

Pyramid Servings

Vegetables
●○○○○➤
Fruits
○○○○○➤
Carbohydrates
●○○○○○○○
Protein & Dairy
○○○○○○○
Fats
●○○○○

1. Roast raw millet in heavy dry skillet over medium-high heat until millet begins to turn golden brown. Stir frequently. Remove from heat.
2. Heat olive oil in medium saucepan over medium-low heat. Add minced onion and cook about 3 minutes until soft.
3. Add minced garlic and cook about 2 more minutes.
4. Add toasted millet. Stir to coat with onion/oil mixture.
5. Add shredded carrots, chicken stock, milk, and pepper.
6. Bring mixture to boil. Reduce heat, cover, and cook on medium-low heat until millet is tender and liquid is absorbed, about 20 minutes.
7. Remove from heat and let stand about 5 minutes in covered pan.

Per Serving

Calories 175, Kilojoules 732, Protein 6 g,
Carbohydrates 27 g, Total Fat 5 g, Saturated Fat 1 g,
Monounsaturated Fat 3 g, Polyunsaturated Fat 1 g,
Cholesterol 2 mg, Sodium 92 mg, Fiber 4 g

Bulgur Casserole with Vegetables

Lizzie Ann Yoder
Hartville, OH

*Makes 4 main-dish servings, or
8 side-dish servings*

Prep. Time: 10–15 minutes
Cooking Time: 20–25 minutes

1 cup chopped onion
2 cloves garlic, minced
½ lb. fresh mushrooms,
 sliced
1½ cups low-sodium, low-fat
 chicken, *or* vegetable, stock,
 divided
1 cup raw bulgur wheat
14-oz. can tomatoes with
 juice, no salt added
1 chopped zucchini
½ tsp. dried oregano
1 or 2 leaves fresh basil, torn,
 or 1 tsp. dried basil
½ tsp. dried thyme
freshly ground pepper
plain low-fat yogurt, *optional*
 (not included in analyses)

Pyramid Servings
(As 4 main-dish servings)

Vegetables	●●○○○▸
Fruits	○○○○○▸
Carbohydrates	●●○○○○○○
Protein & Dairy	○○○○○○○
Fats	○○○○○

Pyramid Servings
(As 8 side-dish servings)

Vegetables	●○○○○▸
Fruits	○○○○○▸
Carbohydrates	●○○○○○○○
Protein & Dairy	○○○○○○○
Fats	○○○○○

1. In good-sized saucepan, sauté onions, garlic, and mushrooms in ½ cup stock until vegetables are tender.

2. Add bulgur, tomatoes and juice, zucchini, all seasonings, and remaining stock. Mix well.

3. Cover, bring to a boil, and simmer 15–20 minutes, or until all liquid is absorbed.

4. Serve warm. Garnish individual servings with yogurt, if you wish.

Per Serving *(As 4 main-dish servings)*

Calories 186, Kilojoules 778, Protein 9 g,
Carbohydrates 36 g, Total Fat 1 g, Saturated Fat 0.3 g,
Monounsaturated Fat 0.3 g, Polyunsaturated Fat 0.4 g,
Cholesterol 2 mg, Sodium 78 mg, Fiber 9 g

Per Serving *(As 8 side-dish servings)*

Calories 93, Kilojoules 389, Protein 5 g,
Carbohydrates 18 g, Total Fat *trace*, Saturated Fat *trace*,
Monounsaturated Fat *trace*, Polyunsaturated Fat *trace*,
Cholesterol 1 mg, Sodium 39 mg, Fiber 4.5 g

Bulgur Pilaf

Mary Kathryn Yoder
Harrisonville, MO

Makes 8 servings

Prep. Time: 15 minutes
Cooking/Baking Time: 30–40 minutes

1 medium onion chopped
½ cup chopped celery
1 Tbsp. olive oil
1 cup raw bulgur
2 cups low-sodium, fat-free chicken broth
½ tsp. poultry seasoning
¼ cup chopped nuts

Pyramid Servings	
Vegetables	○○○○○➤
Fruits	○○○○○➤
Carbohydrates	●○○○○○○○
Protein & Dairy	○○○○○○○
Fats	●○○○○

1. In a saucepan, sauté onion and celery in olive oil, 5–8 minutes.
2. Add bulgur and sauté 3 more minutes.
3. Stir in broth and seasoning.
4. Cover and simmer 30 minutes, or bake 20 minutes at 350°.
5. Just before serving stir in chopped nuts.

Per Serving

Calories 113, Kilojoules 473, Protein 4 g,
Carbohydrates 15 g, Total Fat 4 g, Saturated Fat 0.5 g,
Monounsaturated Fat 2 g, Polyunsaturated Fat 1.5 g,
Cholesterol 1 mg, Sodium 44 mg, Fiber 4 g

Barbecued Lentils

Sherri Grindle
Goshen, IN

Makes 4 main-dish servings, or 8 side-dish servings

Prep. Time: 10 minutes
Cooking Time: 35–40 minutes

1 Tbsp. extra-virgin olive oil
1 cup chopped red onion
1 Tbsp. minced garlic
2 tsp. chili powder
1 tsp. dry mustard
2 cups low-fat, low-sodium chicken, *or* vegetable, broth
¾ cup low-sodium tomato sauce
3 Tbsp. balsamic vinegar
1 Tbsp. Dijon mustard
2 Tbsp. honey
1½ cups raw brown lentils, rinsed
pepper to taste

Pyramid Servings	
(As 4 main-dish servings)	
Vegetables	○○○○○➤
Fruits	○○○○○➤
Carbohydrates	○○○○○○○○
Protein & Dairy	●●○○○○○
Fats	●○○○○
Sweets	●

Pyramid Servings	
(As 8 side-dish servings)	
Vegetables	○○○○○➤
Fruits	○○○○○➤
Carbohydrates	○○○○○○○○
Protein & Dairy	●○○○○○○
Fats	◐○○○○
Sweets	◐

1. Heat oil in 2-quart saucepan over medium heat. Add onion and sauté until soft and translucent, about 3 minutes.
2. Add garlic, chili powder, and dry mustard. Sauté until fragrant, about 1 minute. Do not brown garlic.
3. Add broth, tomato sauce, vinegar, mustard, honey, and lentils.
4. Stir well. Cover and bring to a boil.
5. Reduce heat to low. Cover and simmer until lentils are tender but intact, about 30 minutes.
6. If lentils are not tender, add ¼ cup water and simmer 5 minutes longer.
7. Season with pepper.

Per Serving *(As 4 main-dish servings)*

Calories 376, Kilojoules 1573, Protein 21 g,
Carbohydrates 61 g, Total Fat 5 g, Saturated Fat 1 g,
Monounsaturated Fat 3 g, Polyunsaturated Fat 1 g,
Cholesterol 2 mg, Sodium 214 mg, Fiber 24 g

Per Serving *(As 8 side-dish servings)*

Calories 188, Kilojoules 787, Protein 11 g,
Carbohydrates 30 g, Total Fat 2.5 g, Saturated Fat 0.5 g,
Monounsaturated Fat 1.5 g, Polyunsaturated Fat 0.5 g,
Cholesterol 1 mg, Sodium 107 mg, Fiber 12 g

Asparagus and Red Peppers with Orzo

Alice Rush
Quakertown, PA

Makes 4 main-dish servings, or
8 side-dish servings

Prep. Time: 20 minutes
CookingTime: 20–25 minutes

6 cups water
¾ cup raw orzo
1 lb. fresh asparagus,
   trimmed and cut into 1"
   pieces, *or* 9-oz. pkg. frozen
   cut-up asparagus
half a medium red bell sweet
   pepper, cut into strips
1 medium (1 Tbsp.) shallot,
   thinly sliced
¼ cup water
½ Tbsp. honey, *or* maple
   syrup
1 tsp. dried oregano,
   crumbled
1 tsp. white wine vinegar
¼ tsp. crushed red pepper
   flakes

Pyramid Servings
(As 4 main-dish servings)

Vegetables
●●○○○➤

Fruits
○○○○○➤

Carbohydrates
●○○○○○○○

Protein & Dairy
○○○○○○○

Fats
○○○○○

Pyramid Servings
(As 8 side-dish servings)

Vegetables
●○○○○➤

Fruits
○○○○○➤

Carbohydrates
●○○○○○○○

Protein & Dairy
○○○○○○○

Fats
○○○○○

1 tsp. olive oil
⅛ tsp. salt
⅛ tsp. pepper

1. In medium saucepan, bring 6 cups water to a boil. Stir in orzo. Cover and cook 8 minutes, or until tender. Drain well.

2. Meanwhile, place asparagus, bell pepper, shallot, ¼ cup water, honey, oregano, vinegar, and red pepper flakes in a large skillet. Bring to a simmer over medium-high heat.

3. Simmer uncovered 5 minutes, or until asparagus is crisp-tender.

4. Add cooked orzo, stirring gently until well mixed.

Per Serving *(As 4 main-dish servings)*

Calories 140, Kilojoules 586, Protein 4 g,
Carbohydrates 28 g, Total Fat 2 g, Saturated Fat 0.4 g,
Monounsaturated Fat 1 g, Polyunsaturated Fat 0.6 g,
Cholesterol 0 mg, Sodium 88 mg, Fiber 2 g

Per Serving *(As 8 side-dish servings)*

Calories 70, Kilojoules 293, Protein 2 g,
Carbohydrates 14 g, Total Fat 1 g, Saturated Fat 0.2 g,
Monounsaturated Fat 0.5 g, Polyunsaturated Fat 0.3 g,
Cholesterol 0 mg, Sodium 44 mg, Fiber 1 g

Chili and Pasta

Darla Sathre
Baxter, MN

Makes 10 main-dish servings

Prep. Time: 15 minutes
Cooking Time: 35 minutes

1 lb. whole-wheat penne
   pasta
2 tsp. olive oil
1 cup chopped onion
2 cloves minced garlic
1 Tbsp. chili powder
½ tsp. cumin
¼ tsp. garlic pepper, *or* more
15-oz. can diced tomatoes, no salt added
15-oz. can kidney beans, rinsed and
   drained
15-oz. can sliced carrots, no salt added,
   drained
¼ cup grated Parmesan cheese

Pyramid Servings
Vegetables ●●○○○▶
Fruits ○○○○○▶
Carbohydrates ●●○○○○○○
Protein & Dairy ◑○○○○○○
Fats ○○○○○

1. Prepare pasta according to package directions.
2. Meanwhile, in saucepan, sauté onion, garlic, and seasonings in olive oil until tender.
3. Add tomatoes, beans, and carrots.
4. Cover and simmer until heated thoroughly.
5. Serve over pasta.
6. Sprinkle each serving with about 1 tsp. grated cheese, and with additional garlic pepper, if you wish.

Per Serving

Calories 250, Kilojoules 1046, Protein 10 g,
Carbohydrates 48 g, Total Fat 2 g, Saturated Fat 0.5 g,
Monounsaturated Fat 1 g, Polyunsaturated Fat 0.5 g,
Cholesterol 2 mg, Sodium 199 mg, Fiber 9 g

A Tip —

Fresh ingredients are always the best. If you substitute less expensive ingredients, test the dish before serving it to guests.

Soups

Oven-Baked Bean Soup

Esther H. Becker
Gordonville, PA

Makes 8 servings

Soaking Time: 8 hours or overnight
Prep. Time: 30 minutes
Cooking/Baking Time: 2–2¼ hours

8 ozs. (about 1¼ cups) dried
    white beans
water to cover
3 cups low-fat, low-sodium
    chicken broth
1 onion, diced
2 cups raw sweet potatoes
    (about 2 medium potatoes), diced
1 cup green bell sweet pepper, diced
¼ tsp. ground cloves
¼ tsp. black pepper
½ tsp. dried thyme
½ cup ketchup
¼ cup molasses

Pyramid Servings		
Vegetables ●○○○○➤		
Fruits ○○○○○➤		
Carbohydrates ●○○○○○○○		
Protein & Dairy ◐○○○○○○		
Fats ○○○○○		
Sweets ●		

1. Soak beans in water overnight. Drain and rinse.

2. Place drained beans in large stockpot. Cover with water. Cover pot. Cook on top of stove for 30 minutes. Drain.

3. Preheat oven to 375°.

4. Place beans in ovenproof Dutch oven, or small roasting pan, along with all but the ketchup and molasses.

5. Cover and bake until beans and sweet potatoes are tender, about 1½ hours.

6. Stir in ketchup, molasses, and more water if necessary.

7. Bake until heated through.

Per Serving
Calories 185, Kilojoules 774, Protein 9 g,
Carbohydrates 37 g, Total Fat *trace*, Saturated Fat *trace*,
Monounsaturated Fat *trace*, Polyunsaturated Fat *trace*,
Cholesterol 2 mg, Sodium 250 mg, Fiber 6 g

Dietitian's Tip: If you don't have time to soak beans overnight, use this quick method: Rinse beans well and cover with water (1 cup beans needs 5 cups water). Bring water to a boil and cook for 3 minutes. Remove from heat and let stand in the water for at least 1 hour (preferably up to 4 hours). Drain them and use as directed by the recipe.

Escarole and Bean Soup

Karen Ceneviva
New Haven, CT

Makes 8 servings

Prep. Time: 10 minutes
Cooking Time: 1½ hours

Pyramid Servings

Vegetables	●○○○○➤
Fruits	○○○○○➤
Carbohydrates	○○○○○○○○
Protein & Dairy	●○○○○○○
Fats	●○○○○

2 14½-oz cans low-sodium, fat-free chicken broth
2 heads escarole, well washed and cut medium-fine (about 8 cups)
4 garlic cloves, sliced very thin
2 Tbsp. extra-virgin olive oil
2 15-oz. cans cannelloni beans, rinsed and drained
½ cup water
3 basil leaves chopped fine, *or* 1 Tbsp. dried basil

1. Place broth and escarole in large stockpot. Bring to a boil. Cover and simmer 30 minutes.
2. In another saucepan, gently sauté garlic in olive oil until transparent, but not browned.
3. Add beans, with half-cup water, to garlic. Cover and simmer until mixture thickens.
4. Gently stir bean mixture into greens. Cover and let simmer 15 minutes. Stir occasionally with wooden spoon.
5. The soup should be soupy. If it's not, add more water.

Per Serving

Calories 172, Kilojoules 720, Protein 10 g,
Carbohydrates 25 g, Total Fat 4 g, Saturated Fat 1 g,
Monounsaturated Fat 2.5 g, Polyunsaturated Fat 0.5 g,
Cholesterol 2 mg, Sodium 76 mg, Fiber 7 g

Black Bean Soup with Onion, Cilantro, and Lime Salsa

Melanie Mohler
Ephrata, PA

Makes 6 servings

Prep. Time: 15 minutes
Cooking Time: 15 minutes

Pyramid Servings

Vegetables	●○○○○➤
Fruits	○○○○○➤
Carbohydrates	○○○○○○○○
Protein & Dairy	●○○○○○○
Fats	○○○○○

4 cups canned black beans, rinsed and drained
1 Tbsp. minced fresh garlic
1½ cups low-sodium, fat-free chicken broth, *divided*
¼–½ tsp. dried thyme, according to your taste preference
3 Tbsp. fat-free sour cream

Salsa Ingredients:
⅓ cup fresh cilantro, washed and stemmed
half an onion, coarsely chopped
juice of half a lime, *or* 1 Tbsp. bottled lime juice

1. Puree black beans and garlic in blender or food processor, adding chicken broth as needed to help with blending.
2. Pour puree into saucepan. Add remaining chicken broth and thyme.
3. Cover and simmer over low heat, about 15 minutes.
4. While soup is simmering, puree cilantro, onion, and lime juice in processor until smooth. Place in small bowl.
5. Place sour cream in another small bowl.
6. Serve salsa and sour cream with soup, to be spooned on top of each serving.

Calories 164, Kilojoules 686, Protein 11 g, Carbohydrates 28 g, Total Fat 1 g, Saturated Fat 0.4 g, Monounsaturated Fat 0.1 g, Polyunsaturated Fat 0.5 g, Cholesterol 2 mg, Sodium 465 mg, Fiber 11 g	

Dietitian's tip: For convenience, canned black beans instead of the dried variety are used in this recipe. Although canned beans typically contain more sodium than home-cooked beans, you can rinse and drain them before use to help lessen the amount of sodium by about 40 percent.

Lentil Soup
Marcia S. Myer
Manheim, PA

Makes 6 servings

Prep. Time: 15 minutes
Cooking Time: 1 hour

Pyramid Servings

Vegetables
●●○○○▸

Fruits
○○○○○▸

Carbohydrates
○○○○○○○○

Protein & Dairy
●○○○○○○○

Fats
○○○○○

2 large onions, chopped
1 carrot, chopped
½ tsp. dried thyme
½ tsp. dried marjoram
3 cups low-sodium, fat-free chicken, *or vegetable*, broth
1 cup uncooked lentils
¼ cup chopped fresh parsley
1 lb. canned tomatoes, no salt added, undrained
¼ cup sherry, *optional* (not included in analyses)
⅔ cup grated low-fat cheese, *optional* (not included in analyses)

1. Spray bottom of large stockpot with nonstick cooking spray. Sauté onions and carrot 3–5 minutes.
2. Add thyme and marjoram.
3. Add broth, lentils, parsley, and tomatoes.
4. Cover and simmer about 45 minutes, or until lentils are tender.
5. Stir in sherry, if you wish.
6. Top each individual serving of soup with 1½ Tbsp. grated cheese, if you wish.

Calories 160, Kilojoules 669, Protein 11 g, Carbohydrates 27 g, Total Fat 1 g, Saturated Fat 0.3 g, Monounsaturated Fat 0.5 g, Polyunsaturated Fat 0.2 g, Cholesterol 3 mg, Sodium 111 mg, Fiber 12 g	

Dietitian's tip: If you want to use fresh herbs in place of dried, double or triple the amount. Fresh herbs are less intense in flavor compared to dried.

A Tip —

Freeze extra onions and celery rather than letting them spoil in the refrigerator. You can use them later in chili, soups, or barbecue.

Hearty Lentil and Barley Soup

Sherri Grindle
Goshen, IN

Makes 10 servings

Prep. Time: 15 minutes
Cooking Time: 65 minutes

2 ribs celery, thinly sliced
1 medium onion, chopped
1 clove garlic, minced
2 Tbsp. olive oil
6 cups water
28-oz. can diced tomatoes, no
   salt added, undrained
¾ cup uncooked lentils, rinsed
¾ cup uncooked pearl barley
2 Tbsp. (or 3 cubes) low-sodium chicken
   bouillon granules
½ tsp. dried oregano
½ tsp. dried rosemary, crushed
¼ tsp. pepper
1 cup thinly sliced carrots
1 cup (4 ozs.) shredded low-fat Swiss cheese,
   optional, not included in analyses

Pyramid Servings	
Vegetables	●○○○○➤
Fruits	○○○○○➤
Carbohydrates	●○○○○○○○
Protein & Dairy	◐○○○○○○
Fats	○○○○○

1. In Dutch oven or soup kettle, sauté celery, onion, and garlic in oil until tender.
2. Add water, tomatoes, lentils, barley, bouillon, oregano, rosemary, and pepper.
3. Bring to a boil. Reduce heat, cover, and simmer 40 minutes, or until lentils and barley are almost tender.
4. Add carrots. Cover and simmer 15 minutes, or until carrots, lentils, and barley are tender.
5. If you wish, sprinkle each serving with 1 rounded Tbsp. cheese.

Per Serving

Calories 156, Kilojoules 653, Protein 6 g,
Carbohydrates 27 g, Total Fat 3 g, Saturated Fat 0.5 g,
Monounsaturated Fat 2 g, Polyunsaturated Fat 0.5 g,
Cholesterol 0 mg, Sodium 236 mg, Fiber 9 g

Lentil, Spinach, and Rice Soup

Jean Harris Robinson
Cinnaminson, NJ

Makes 10 servings

Prep. Time: 15 minutes
Cooking Time: 1¾ hours

1 large onion, diced
2 carrots, diced
1 celery rib, diced
3 Tbsp. extra-virgin olive oil
1 cup uncooked lentils
6 cups low-fat low-sodium
   chicken, *or* vegetable, stock
4 cups water
1 cup canned diced tomatoes, no salt
   added, undrained
¼ cup uncooked brown rice
1 bag (about 8 cups) fresh spinach,
   washed, dried and chopped (with large
   stems removed)

Pyramid Servings	
Vegetables	●●○○○➤
Fruits	○○○○○➤
Carbohydrates	○○○○○○○○
Protein & Dairy	◐○○○○○○
Fats	●○○○○

1. In large stockpot over medium heat, sauté onion, carrots, and celery in oil for 10 minutes.
2. Add lentils and sauté another 5 minutes. Stir often.
3. Add stock and water. Cover and simmer 45 minutes. Stir occasionally.
4. Add tomatoes and brown rice.
5. Cover and simmer another 40 minutes.
6. Stir in chopped fresh spinach.
7. Cover and cook 5 minutes more.

Per Serving

Calories 156, Kilojoules 653, Protein 8 g,
Carbohydrates 19 g, Total Fat 5 g, Saturated Fat 1 g,
Monounsaturated Fat 3 g, Polyunsaturated Fat 1 g,
Cholesterol 0 mg, Sodium 129 mg, Fiber 8 g

Tomato and Barley Soup

Lizzie Ann Yoder
Hartville, OH

Makes 6 servings

Prep. Time: 20–30 minutes
Cooking Time: 1–1½ hours

½ cup uncooked medium
  barley
1 cup chopped onion
2 ribs celery, including tops,
  cut up
3 cups chopped fresh
  tomatoes
2 Tbsp. fresh basil, *or* ½ tsp. dried basil
6 cups low-sodium, fat-free chicken, *or*
  vegetable, stock
1–2 cups sliced fresh mushrooms, *optional*,
  not included in analyses

1. In large stockpot combine all ingredients.
2. Bring to a boil and simmer, covered, 1 to
1½ hours, or until barley is tender.
3. If you wish, stir in mushrooms 30
minutes before end of cooking time.

Pyramid Servings

Vegetables	●○○○○▶
Fruits	○○○○○▶
Carbohydrates	●○○○○○○○
Protein & Dairy	○○○○○○○
Fats	○○○○○

Per Serving

Calories 108, Kilojoules 452, Protein 7 g,
Carbohydrates 18 g, Total Fat 1 g, Saturated Fat 0.6 g,
Monounsaturated Fat 0.2 g, Polyunsaturated Fat 0.2 g,
Cholesterol 5 mg, Sodium 158 mg, Fiber 4 g

Indian Tomato Rice Soup

Valerie Drobel
Carlisle, PA

Makes 6 servings

Prep. Time: 15 minutes
Cooking Time: 45–50 minutes

1 Tbsp. olive oil
2 cups chopped onion
3 cloves garlic, minced
1 tsp. cumin
1 tsp. coriander
⅓ cup raw basmati rice,
  rinsed
4 cups low-fat, low-sodium chicken stock
2 cups chopped fresh tomatoes
2 Tbsp. chopped cilantro

1. In large stockpot, sauté onion and garlic
10 minutes, or until onion is translucent.
2. Add seasonings and sauté 3 minutes.
3. Add rice. Stir to coat grains.
4. Add stock. Cover and bring to a boil.
5. Reduce heat and cook until rice is tender,
approximately 25 minutes.
6. Stir in tomatoes and heat through, about
5 minutes.
7. Add cilantro and serve.

Pyramid Servings

Vegetables	●○○○○▶
Fruits	○○○○○▶
Carbohydrates	◐○○○○○○○
Protein & Dairy	○○○○○○○
Fats	●○○○○

Per Serving

Calories 104, Kilojoules 435, Protein 4 g,
Carbohydrates 15 g, Total Fat 3 g, Saturated Fat 1 g,
Monounsaturated Fat 2 g, Polyunsaturated Fat *trace*,
Cholesterol 3 mg, Sodium 99 mg, Fiber 2 g

Wild Rice Mushroom Soup

Kelly Amos
Pittsboro, NC

Makes 4 servings

Prep. Time: 15–20 minutes
Cooking Time: 35 minutes

Pyramid Servings

Vegetables	●○○○○➤
Fruits	○○○○○➤
Carbohydrates	●○○○○○○○
Protein & Dairy	○○○○○○○
Fats	●○○○○

1 Tbsp. olive oil
half a white onion, chopped
¼ cup chopped celery
¼ cup chopped carrots
1½ cups sliced fresh white
    mushrooms
½ cup white wine, *or* ½ cup low-sodium,
    fat-free chicken broth
2½ cups low-sodium, fat-free chicken
    broth
1 cup fat-free half-and-half
2 Tbsp. flour
¼ tsp. dried thyme
black pepper
1 cup cooked wild rice

1. Put olive oil in stockpot and heat. Carefully add chopped onion, celery, and carrots. Cook until tender.

2. Add mushrooms, white wine, and chicken broth.

3. Cover and heat through.

4. In a bowl, blend half-and-half, flour, thyme, and pepper. Then stir in cooked wild rice.

5. Pour rice mixture into hot stockpot with vegetables.

6. Cook over medium heat. Stir continually until thickened and bubbly.

Per Serving

Calories 170, Kilojoules 711, Protein 7 g,
Carbohydrates 20 g, Total Fat 5 g, Saturated Fat 1 g,
Monounsaturated Fat 3 g, Polyunsaturated Fat 1 g,
Cholesterol 6 mg, Sodium 190 mg, Fiber 1.5 g

Creamy Potato Chowder

Sylvia Beiler
Lowville, NY

Makes 4 servings

Prep. Time: 5 minutes
Cooking Time: 30–35 minutes

Pyramid Servings

Vegetables	●○○○○➤
Fruits	○○○○○➤
Carbohydrates	●○○○○○○○
Protein & Dairy	◐○○○○○○
Fats	○○○○○

1 tsp. olive oil
½ cup chopped onion
½ cup chopped celery
2 garlic cloves
1 carrot, diced
2 cups cubed unpeeled
    potatoes
2 Tbsp. flour
2 cups skim milk
1½ cup reduced sodium, low-fat chicken,
    or vegetable, broth
1 cup frozen corn, thawed
pepper to taste

1. Heat oil in large saucepan over medium heat. Add onion, celery, and garlic. Sauté 2 minutes.

2. Add carrot and potatoes. Sauté 3 minutes.

3. Sprinkle flour over carrot and potatoes. Cook 1 minute, stirring continually.

4. Add remaining ingredients and bring to a boil.

5. Lower heat, cover, and simmer 20–25 minutes, or until carrot and potatoes are soft.

6. To thicken soup, mash vegetables somewhat before serving.

Per Serving

Calories 181, Kilojoules 757, Protein 9 g,
Carbohydrates 32 g, Total Fat 2 g, Saturated Fat 0.5 g,
Monounsaturated Fat 1 g, Polyunsaturated Fat 0.5 g,
Cholesterol 4 mg, Sodium 131 mg, Fiber 4 g

Potato Cheese Soup

Dorothy VanDeest
Memphis, TN

Makes 6 servings

Prep. Time: 15 minutes
Cooking Time: 30 minutes

3 medium (about 1 lb.)
  potatoes, peeled and
  quartered
1 small onion, finely minced
1 cup water
½ tsp. salt
3 cups fat-free milk
2 Tbsp. tub-style margarine, non-
  hydrogenated
2 Tbsp. flour
2 Tbsp. fresh parsley, minced
⅛ tsp. white pepper
¾ cup (3 ozs.) shredded low-fat cheddar
  cheese

1. Bring potatoes, onion, water, and salt to a boil in a saucepan.
2. Reduce heat. Cover and simmer until potatoes are tender. Do not drain.
3. Mash slightly. Stir in milk.
4. In a small bowl, blend margarine, flour, parsley, and pepper together. Stir into potato mixture.
5. Cook and stir over medium heat until mixture becomes bubbly and thickened.
6. Remove from heat. Add cheese, stirring until almost melted.

Pyramid Servings	
Vegetables	○○○○○➤
Fruits	○○○○○➤
Carbohydrates	●○○○○○○○
Protein & Dairy	●○○○○○○
Fats	○○○○○

Per Serving

Calories 185, Kilojoules 774, Protein 10g,
Carbohydrates 24g, Total Fat 5g, Saturated Fat 1.5g,
Monounsaturated Fat 1.2g, Polyunsaturated Fat 2.3g,
Cholesterol 6mg, Sodium 405mg, Fiber 1.5g

Dietitian's tip: Making stock at home is the surefire way to avoid the high sodium content of most canned broth. Browning the vegetables before simmering them imparts color and flavor to the finished stock. Since vegetables yield their flavors quickly, in little more than half an hour you can have a pot full of flavorful stock to use in other recipes.

A Tip —

In order to prevent peeled potatoes from discoloring, drop them into a cup of cold water with ½ teaspoon cream of tartar dissolved in it. Drain the potatoes when you're ready to use them.

Spinach and Potato Soup

Jane S. Lippincott
Wynnewood, PA

Makes 9 servings

Prep. Time: 30 minutes
Cooking Time: 45–50 minutes

Pyramid Servings

Vegetables
●○○○○➤

Fruits
○○○○○➤

Carbohydrates
●○○○○○○○○

Protein & Dairy
○○○○○○○

Fats
●○○○○

2 ribs celery, chopped
1 medium onion, chopped
1 clove garlic, minced
6 cups chopped fresh spinach
2 Tbsp. olive oil
4 potatoes, unpeeled and
    sliced ¼" thick
32 ozs. low-fat, low-sodium chicken, *or*
    vegetable, stock, *or* less, depending
    upon how thick you like your soup
1 tsp. mustard seeds
1 Tbsp. white wine vinegar
pepper to taste
chopped chives for garnish

1. Chop celery, onion, garlic, and spinach first so they're ready. Set aside, keeping vegetables separate from each other.
2. In large stockpot heat olive oil on low or medium. Add onions. Cook until soft, about 10 minutes.
3. Add garlic and cook just until slightly softened.
4. Add celery, sliced potatoes, stock, and mustard seeds. Cover and simmer 25–30 minutes, or until potatoes are soft.
5. Use a potato masher to mash the mixture up a bit.
6. Add chopped spinach and vinegar. Simmer uncovered for 10 minutes more.
7. Serve with pepper and chives sprinkled on top of individual servings.

Per Serving

Calories 145, Kilojoules 607, Protein 7 g,
Carbohydrates 21 g, Total Fat 4 g, Saturated Fat 1 g,
Monounsaturated Fat 2.5 g, Polyunsaturated Fat 0.5 g,
Cholesterol 0 mg, Sodium 137 mg, Fiber 4.5 g

Tip: Try Swiss chard, collards, or kale instead of spinach. If using one of those greens, add in Step 4.

Cheese and Corn Chowder

Mary Ann Bowman, East Earl, PA

Makes 6 servings

Prep. Time: 15–20 minutes
Cooking Time: 25–30 minutes

Pyramid Servings

Vegetables
◐○○○○➤

Fruits
○○○○○➤

Carbohydrates
◐○○○○○○○○

Protein & Dairy
◐○○○○○○○

Fats
○○○○○

½ cup water
2 cups unpeeled diced potatoes
1 cup diced carrots
1 cup chopped celery
½ tsp. salt
¼ tsp. pepper
2 cups cream-style corn
1½ cups skim milk
⅔ cup grated low-fat cheddar cheese

1. Combine first six ingredients in saucepan. Bring to a boil.
2. Turn heat down. Cover and simmer 10 minutes.
3. Add creamed corn. Cover and simmer 5 more minutes.
4. Add milk and cheese. Stir until cheese melts and chowder is heated through. Do not boil.

Per Serving

Calories 91, Kilojoules 381, Protein 7 g,
Carbohydrates 14 g, Total Fat 1 g, Saturated Fat 0.6 g,
Monounsaturated Fat 0.3 g, Polyunsaturated Fat 0.1 g,
Cholesterol 4 mg, Sodium 397 mg, Fiber 1.6 g

Tip: If you have only whole-kernel corn, chop it lightly in blender.

Sweet Potato, Corn, and Kale Soup

Ellie Oberholtzer
Smoketown, PA

Makes 8 servings

Prep. Time: 15 minutes
Cooking Time: 35–40 minutes

2 lbs. sweet potatoes
4 cups reduced-sodium, low-fat chicken, *or* vegetable, broth
4 cups water
4 cups frozen corn, no salt added
½ lb. chopped kale
pepper as desired
sprinkle of paprika

Pyramid Servings	
Vegetables	●○○○○➤
Fruits	○○○○○➤
Carbohydrates	●●●○○○○○
Protein & Dairy	○○○○○○○
Fats	○○○○○

1. Peel and dice sweet potatoes.
2. Add to broth and water in large stockpot.
3. Cover. Bring to boil. Reduce heat and simmer until potatoes are soft but still holding their shape, about 15 minutes.
4. Stir in frozen corn. Continue to simmer 10–15 minutes, or until corn becomes tender.
5. Add kale. Simmer 5 minutes more.
6. Season individual servings with pepper if you wish, and paprika.

Per Serving

Calories 228, Kilojoules 954, Protein 7g,
Carbohydrates 46g, Total Fat 1.8g, Saturated Fat 0.4g,
Monounsaturated Fat 0.6g, Polyunsaturated Fat 0.8g,
Cholesterol 0mg, Sodium 456mg, Fiber 6g

Roasted Red Peppers, Vegetables, and Sweet Potato Soup

Melanie Mohler, Ephrata, PA

Makes 6 servings

Prep. Time: 40 minutes
Cooking Time: 1 hour and 40 minutes

2 Tbsp. extra-virgin olive oil
1 medium onion, diced
2 red bell sweet peppers, halved and seeded
2 medium sweet potatoes, peeled and cubed (about 2 cups)
3–4 cloves garlic, minced
15-oz. can pinto beans, rinsed and drained
15-oz. can diced tomatoes with herbs, no salt added, undrained
4 cups low-sodium, fat-free chicken broth
croutons and grated cheese for garnish, *optional*, not included in analyses

Pyramid Servings	
Vegetables	●●○○○➤
Fruits	○○○○○➤
Carbohydrates	◐○○○○○○○
Protein & Dairy	◐○○○○○○
Fats	●○○○○

1. In large stockpot, heat oil and brown onions.
2. Meanwhile, roast peppers in toaster oven at 450°, or broil. Lay cut side down on baking tray. Roast until skin is blackened, about 15–20 minutes.
3. Put roasted peppers in paper bag for 15 minutes until cool. Peel off skin. Chop peppers.
4. Add peppers, sweet potatoes, garlic, beans, tomatoes, and broth to pot. Bring to a boil.
5. Reduce heat, cover, and simmer 90 minutes.
6. Puree soup carefully and in small batches in blender until smooth, or leave partially chunky.
7. If you wish, garnish individual servings with croutons and/or grated cheese.

Per Serving

Calories 180, Kilojoules 753, Protein 7g,
Carbohydrates 27g, Total Fat 5g, Saturated Fat 1g,
Monounsaturated Fat 3g, Polyunsaturated Fat 1g,
Cholesterol 4mg, Sodium 340mg, Fiber 6g

Flavorful Tomato Soup

Shari Ladd, Hudson, MI

Makes 4 servings

Prep. Time: 10 minutes
Cooking Time: 20 minutes

Pyramid Servings	
Vegetables ●●●○○➤	
Fruits ○○○○○➤	
Carbohydrates ●○○○○○○○	
Protein & Dairy ●○○○○○○	
Fats ○○○○○	

2 Tbsp. chopped onions
1 Tbsp. extra-virgin olive oil
3 Tbsp. flour
2 tsp. sugar
½ tsp. pepper
¼ tsp. dried basil
½ tsp. dried oregano
¼ tsp. dried thyme
1 quart stewed tomatoes, no salt added, undrained
2 cups skim milk

1. Sauté onions in oil in stockpot.
2. Stir in flour and seasonings.
3. Stir in stewed tomatoes, stirring constantly. Bring to a boil and boil 1 minute.
4. Add 2 cups milk. If soup is too thick, add a little water. Stir well.
5. Simmer 10 minutes but do not boil.

Per Serving

Calories 174, Kilojoules 728, Protein 7 g,
Carbohydrates 30 g, Total Fat 3 g, Saturated Fat 0.5 g,
Monounsaturated Fat 2 g, Polyunsaturated Fat 0.5 g,
Cholesterol 2 mg, Sodium 152 mg, Fiber 4 g

Dietitian's tip: You may substitute about 5 cups chopped fresh tomatoes in place of stewed. When fresh tomatoes are at their peak, their intense flavor makes this soup a treat. Serve this soup with grilled vegetables for a light summer lunch or supper.

Creamy Asparagus Soup

Mary Riha
Antigo, WI

Makes 4 servings

Prep. Time: 15 minutes
Cooking Time: 35–40 minutes

Pyramid Servings	
Vegetables ●●○○○➤	
Fruits ○○○○○➤	
Carbohydrates ●○○○○○○○	
Protein & Dairy ○○○○○○○	
Fats ●○○○○	

2 Tbsp. sesame seeds
1 tsp. olive oil
medium onion, chopped
2 medium potatoes, cubed
1 lb. asparagus
4 cups low-fat, low-sodium chicken, *or* vegetable, stock, *divided*

1. In a good-sized stockpot, sauté sesame seeds in olive oil until brown.
2. Add onion and potatoes. Cook, stirring, until potatoes begin to brown and stick to the pot.
3. Break asparagus into pieces and add to potato mixture, along with 2 cups chicken stock.
4. Bring to a boil. Cover, reduce heat, and simmer until potatoes are done, about 10–15 minutes.
5. Remove stockpot from stove. Blend soup mixture carefully and in batches until smooth.
6. Stir in remaining 2 cups chicken stock. Cover and heat through.

Per Serving

Calories 174, Kilojoules 728, Protein 10 g,
Carbohydrates 23 g, Total Fat 5 g, Saturated Fat 1 g,
Monounsaturated Fat 2 g, Polyunsaturated Fat 2 g,
Cholesterol 5 mg, Sodium 163 mg, Fiber 4 g

Low-Fat Broccoli Soup

Carolyn Snader
Ephrata, PA
Joyce Nolt
Richland, PA

Makes 4 servings

Prep. Time: 15–20 minutes
Cooking Time: 12 minutes

1 lb. (about 5 cups) chopped
  fresh, *or* frozen, broccoli
½ cup chopped onion
14½-oz. can low-sodium,
  fat-free chicken, *or*
  vegetable, broth
2 Tbsp. cornstarch
12-oz. can evaporated skim milk
½ cup low-fat cheddar cheese, grated

Pyramid Servings		
Vegetables ●●○○○▸		
Fruits ○○○○○▸		
Carbohydrates ○○○○○○○○		
Protein & Dairy ●○○○○○○○		
Fats ○○○○○		

1. In a good-sized stockpot, cook broccoli and onion in chicken broth 5–10 minutes.
2. Carefully puree half of mixture in blender.
3. Stir back into remaining broccoli in stockpot.
4. Place cornstarch in jar with tight-fitting lid. Pour in a little milk. Cover and shake until smooth.
5. Pour rest of milk into jar. Cover and shake until smooth. Stir into soup.
6. Cover and simmer 2 minutes.
7. Top each individual serving with 2 Tbsp. grated cheese.

Per Serving

Calories 165, Kilojoules 690, Protein 15 g,
Carbohydrates 22 g, Total Fat 2 g, Saturated Fat 1 g,
Monounsaturated Fat 0.4 g, Polyunsaturated Fat 0.6 g,
Cholesterol 8 mg, Sodium 285 mg, Fiber 3 g

Curried Carrot Bisque

Kathy Stoltzfus
Leola, PA

Makes 6 servings

Prep. Time: 20 minutes
Cooking Time: 30 minutes

8 medium carrots, peeled and
  chopped
1 onion, chopped
1 tart apple, peeled and
  chopped
1 tsp. curry powder
1 garlic clove, crushed
¼ tsp. ground coriander
¼ tsp. salt
⅛ tsp. allspice
3 cups low-fat, low-sodium chicken, *or*
  vegetable, broth
1 cup skim milk
chopped fresh cilantro leaves

Pyramid Servings		
Vegetables ●○○○○▸		
Fruits ○○○○○▸		
Carbohydrates ○○○○○○○○		
Protein & Dairy ○○○○○○○○		
Fats ○○○○○		

1. In heavy stockpot, combine carrots, onion, apple, curry powder, garlic, coriander, salt, allspice, and broth.
2. Cover and cook until carrots are very tender, approximately 20 minutes.
3. Carefully puree, half at a time, in blender or food processor fitted with a metal blade.
4. Return pureed soup to stockpot. Gradually stir in milk.
5. Heat until heated through.
6. Sprinkle cilantro on top of individual servings.

Per Serving

Calories 81, Kilojoules 339, Protein 4 g,
Carbohydrates 15 g, Total Fat 0.6 g, Saturated Fat 0.2 g,
Monounsaturated Fat 0.1 g, Polyunsaturated Fat 0.3 g,
Cholesterol 3 mg, Sodium 242 mg, Fiber 3 g

Tip: You may substitute soy milk or rice milk for skim milk.

Garden Vegetable Soup with Pasta

Jan McDowell
New Holland, PA

Makes 6 servings

Prep. Time: 20 minutes
Cooking Time: 30 minutes

Pyramid Servings		
Vegetables	●○○○○➤	
Fruits	○○○○○➤	
Carbohydrates	●○○○○○○	
Protein & Dairy	○○○○○○○	
Fats	●○○○○	

1 Tbsp. olive oil
1 chopped onion
1 tsp. chopped garlic
1 small zucchini, chopped
½ lb. fresh mushrooms, sliced
  or chopped
1 bell sweet pepper, chopped
24-oz. can tomatoes, no salt added,
  undrained
1 Tbsp. fresh basil
2 cups water
3 reduced-sodium vegetable bouillon
  cubes
2 cups whole-grain rotini, cooked
dash of hot sauce, *optional*

1. Heat olive oil in 4-quart saucepan.
2. Sauté onion and garlic in oil until tender.
3. Add zucchini, mushrooms, bell pepper, tomatoes, basil, water, and bouillon.
4. Bring to a boil. Cover and simmer 10 minutes.
5. Meanwhile, cook rotini and drain. Add to soup.
6. Cover and heat through.
7. Pass hot sauce to be added to individual servings, if desired.

Per Serving		
Calories 123, Kilojoules 515, Protein 4 g,		
Carbohydrates 20 g, Total Fat 3 g, Saturated Fat 0.5 g,		
Monounsaturated Fat 1.5 g, Polyunsaturated Fat 1 g,		
Cholesterol *trace*, Sodium 61 mg, Fiber 5 g		

Veggie Minestrone

Dorothy VanDeest
Memphis, TN

Makes 8 servings

Prep. Time: 15 minutes
Cooking Time: 25–30 minutes
Standing Time: 5–10 minutes

Pyramid Servings		
Vegetables	●○○○○➤	
Fruits	○○○○○➤	
Carbohydrates	●○○○○○○○	
Protein & Dairy	●○○○○○○	
Fats	○○○○○	

1 large onion, chopped
1 garlic clove, minced
4 cups fat-free low-sodium
  chicken, *or* vegetable, broth
16-oz. can kidney beans,
  rinsed and drained
½ cup elbow macaroni, uncooked
14½-oz. can diced tomatoes, undrained,
  no salt added
2 medium carrots, sliced thin
¼ tsp. dried oregano
10-oz. pkg. frozen chopped spinach,
  thawed
½ cup grated Parmesan cheese

1. Lightly spray inside bottom of stockpot. Sauté onion and garlic until tender.
2. Add broth, beans, macaroni, tomatoes, carrots, and oregano.
3. Cover and cook until vegetables and macaroni are tender, about 20 minutes.
4. Stir in spinach. Bring to a boil.
5. Remove pan from heat. Let stand, covered, 5–10 minutes before serving.
6. Sprinkle 1 Tbsp. grated Parmesan on each individual bowl of this comfort soup.

Per Serving		
Calories 139, Kilojoules 582, Protein 9 g,		
Carbohydrates 21 g, Total Fat 2 g, Saturated Fat 0.5 g,		
Monounsaturated Fat 1.1 g, Polyunsaturated Fat 0.4 g,		
Cholesterol 7 mg, Sodium 374 mg, Fiber 6 g		

Easy Cream of Vegetable Soup

Norma Grieser
Sebring, FL

Makes 6 cups

Prep. Time: 20 minutes
Cooking Time: 20 minutes

¼ cup chopped celery
¼ cup chopped onion
1 Tbsp. canola oil
3 Tbsp. flour
½ tsp. salt
pepper to taste
1 bay leaf, *or* herb of your choice
3 cups skim milk
2 cups fresh *or* frozen vegetables of
 your choice, cut up or sliced (spinach,
 asparagus, broccoli, cauliflower, peas,
 carrots, tomatoes, mushrooms); *if using
 canned vegetables,* use ones without
 added salt

Pyramid Servings

Vegetables
●●○○○▶

Fruits
○○○○○▶

Carbohydrates
○○○○○○○○

Protein & Dairy
◑○○○○○○

Fats
○○○○○

1. In large stockpot, sauté celery and onion in oil.

2. Over low heat, stir in flour, salt, pepper, and herbs.

3. Add milk, stirring constantly. Cook over medium heat until hot and bubbly.

4. Meanwhile, chop or slice 2 cups vegetables.

5. Steam or microwave them until crisp-tender.

6. Stir vegetables into thickened creamy sauce and heat through.

Per Serving

Calories 110, Kilojoules 460, Protein 6 g,
Carbohydrates 15 g, Total Fat 3 g, Saturated Fat 0.5 g,
Monounsaturated Fat 1.5 g, Polyunsaturated Fat 1 g,
Cholesterol 3 mg, Sodium 271 mg, Fiber 1 g

Tips:

1. If you want cream of chicken soup, add reduced-sodium chicken bouillon. (One tsp. or 1 cube reduced-sodium chicken bouillon adds about 100 milligrams of sodium to each serving.)

2. This recipe can be used as soup itself, or you can use it in any recipe calling for cream soup.

A Tip —

Add a Tablespoon or two of milk when cooking cauliflower; the cauliflower will remain attractively white.

Vegetarian Chili

Lois Hess
Lancaster, PA

Makes 8 servings

Prep. Time: 30 minutes
Cooking Time: 30 minutes

Pyramid Servings	
Vegetables	●○○○○►
Fruits	○○○○○►
Carbohydrates	◑○○○○○○○
Protein & Dairy	●○○○○○○
Fats	◑○○○○

1 cup tomato juice, no salt added
½ cup raw bulgur
1 Tbsp. olive, canola, *or* saffron, oil for sauté
4 cloves garlic
1½ cups chopped onion
1 cup chopped celery
1 cup chopped carrots
1 cup chopped tomatoes
1 tsp. cumin
1 tsp. dried basil
1–1½ tsp. chili powder, depending upon your taste preferences
1 cup chopped sweet bell green peppers
2 16-oz. cans red kidney beans, rinsed and drained
juice of half a lemon
3 Tbsp. tomato paste, no salt added
dash cayenne pepper, *or* ¼ tsp. coarsely ground black pepper
chopped fresh parsley for garnish

1. Heat tomato juice to a boil. Pour over bulgur in a bowl. Cover and let stand 15 minutes.
2. Meanwhile, sauté garlic and onion in oil in large stockpot.
3. Add celery, carrots, tomatoes, and spices.
4. When vegetables are almost tender, add peppers. Cook until tender.
5. Stir in all remaining ingredients. Cover and heat gently.
6. Top individual servings with parsley.

Per Serving

Calories 174, Kilojoules 728, Protein 8 g,
Carbohydrates 31 g, Total Fat 2.5 g, Saturated Fat 0.5 g,
Monounsaturated Fat 1.5 g, Polyunsaturated Fat 0.5 g,
Cholesterol 0 mg, Sodium 489 mg, Fiber 8 g

Dietitian's tip: To add more variety in flavor, color, and texture to chili, add several different beans, including kidney, garbanzo, or black beans, or add more chopped vegetables, such as carrots and celery. If you add these vegetables, increase the amount of liquid to accommodate the added ingredients.

Steamy Vegetarian Chili

Lavina Hochstedler, Grand Blanc, MI

Makes 12 servings

Prep. Time: 20 minutes
Cooking Time: 50–60 minutes

Pyramid Servings	
Vegetables	●●○○○►
Fruits	○○○○○►
Carbohydrates	◑○○○○○○○
Protein & Dairy	●○○○○○○
Fats	●○○○○

1 large onion, chopped
1 large green sweet bell pepper
1 large red sweet bell pepper
3 medium carrots, thinly sliced
6 garlic cloves, minced
2 Tbsp. olive oil
28-oz. can crushed tomatoes, no salt added, undrained
14½-oz. can kidney beans, rinsed and drained
16-oz. can hominy, rinsed and drained
15-oz. can pinto beans, rinsed and drained
15-oz. can garbanzos (chickpeas), rinsed and drained
2 cups water
8 ozs. tomato paste, no salt added
3 Tbsp. chili powder
2 Tbsp. Worcestershire sauce
1 Tbsp. ground cumin

2 tsp. dried thyme
2 tsp. dried parsley flakes
½ tsp. pepper

1. In Dutch oven or soup kettle, sauté onions, peppers, carrots, and garlic in oil for 15 minutes, or until vegetables are tender.
2. Stir in remaining ingredients. Bring to a boil.
3. Reduce heat. Cover and simmer 30–40 minutes, or until heated through.

Per Serving

Calories 223, Kilojoules 933, Protein 9 g,
Carbohydrates 38 g, Total Fat 4 g, Saturated Fat 0.7 g,
Monounsaturated Fat 2 g, Polyunsaturated Fat 1.3 g,
Cholesterol 0 mg, Sodium 384 mg, Fiber 11 g

Tips:
1. If you don't care for hominy, omit it. Or replace it with a 16-oz. can of black beans, rinsed and drained.
2. If the recipe is too large, skip the hominy and garbanzo beans, or cut the recipe ingredients in half.

Roasted Vegetable Gazpacho
JB Miller, Indianapolis, IN

Makes 6 servings

Prep. Time: 30 minutes
Baking Time: 20–25 minutes
Chilling Time: 4 hours

2 red bell sweet peppers, left whole
2 yellow bell sweet peppers, left whole
2 large red onions, quartered
2 Tbsp. extra-virgin olive oil
pepper to taste
1-lb. (about 4 cups) medium zucchini, cut in ½"-thick slices

Pyramid Servings

Vegetables
●●●○○►

Fruits
○○○○○►

Carbohydrates
○○○○○○○○

Protein & Dairy
○○○○○○○

Fats
●○○○○

2 lbs. (about 7 medium) vine-ripened tomatoes, cored, quartered, and seeds removed
3 cloves garlic
2 Tbsp. chopped fresh basil
1 Tbsp. chopped fresh oregano
1 cup cold water
2 Tbsp. lime juice, *or* more to taste

1. Preheat oven to 375°.
2. Place peppers and onions in large mixing bowl. Toss with olive oil and black pepper.
3. Spoon peppers and onions into large shallow baking dishes or onto cookie sheets with sides. *Allow seasoned olive oil to remain in mixing bowl.* Place peppers and onions in oven.
4. Meanwhile, stir zucchini and tomatoes into large mixing bowl with remaining seasoned olive oil.
5. After peppers and onions have roasted 10–12 minutes, add zucchini and tomatoes to baking dishes.
6. Roast 10–12 minutes, or until peppers are soft and vegetables have browned along the edges and wrinkled. Total roasting time will be 20–25 minutes.
7. Remove baking dishes from oven. Lift out peppers and place in bowl. Cover with plastic wrap. Let cool 10 minutes. Then peel and seed peppers over a bowl, saving the juices.
8. Coarsely chop all vegetables.
9. Place chopped vegetables in food processor together with garlic, basil, oregano, and 1 cup cold water.
10. Blend at high speed until smooth. Strain through a fine mesh sieve.
11. Place mixture in covered container. Refrigerate 4 hours before serving.
12. Adjust seasoning with pepper to taste.
13. Mix in lime juice just before serving.

Per Serving

Calories 127, Kilojoules 531, Protein 4 g,
Carbohydrates 18 g, Total Fat 5 g, Saturated Fat 0.7 g,
Monounsaturated Fat 3.3 g, Polyunsaturated Fat 1 g,
Cholesterol 0 mg, Sodium 21 mg, Fiber 5 g

Tip: Be sure gazpacho is chilled thoroughly before serving. It's best served in a chilled bowl or glass.

Zesty Pumpkin Soup

Miriam Christophel
Goshen, IN

Makes 6 servings

Prep. Time: 15 minutes
Cooking Time: 25–30 minutes

Pyramid Servings	
Vegetables ●○○○○➤	
Fruits ○○○○○➤	
Carbohydrates ◐○○○○○○○	
Protein & Dairy ○○○○○○○	
Fats ●○○○○	

2 Tbsp. olive oil
1 cup chopped onions
1 garlic clove, crushed
1 tsp. curry powder
½ tsp. salt
⅛–¼ tsp. ground coriander
⅛ tsp. crushed red pepper
3 cups fat-free low-sodium chicken, *or* vegetable, broth
1¾ cups solid-pack pumpkin
1 cup fat-free half-and-half
chopped chives as garnish, *optional*

1. In large pan, sauté onion and garlic in olive oil.
2. Add curry, salt, coriander, and red pepper. Cook one minute.
3. Add broth and boil gently, uncovered, 15–20 minutes.
4. Stir in pumpkin and half-and-half. Cook 5 minutes.
5. Pour into blender. Cover and carefully blend until creamy.
6. Top individual servings with chives if you wish.

Per Serving

Calories 113, Kilojoules 473 Protein 4 g,	
Carbohydrates 13 g, Total Fat 5 g, Saturated Fat 1 g,	
Monounsaturated Fat 3.5 g, Polyunsaturated Fat 0.5 g,	
Cholesterol 4 mg, Sodium 326 mg, Fiber 3 g	

Tip: You can substitute butternut squash for the pumpkin with little change in flavor.

Apple Butternut Squash Soup

Ann Bender
New Hope, VA

Makes 6 servings

Prep. Time: 30 minutes
Cooking Time: 30 minutes

Pyramid Servings	
Vegetables ○○○○○➤	
Fruits ◐○○○○➤	
Carbohydrates ●○○○○○○○	
Protein & Dairy ○○○○○○○	
Fats ○○○○○	

3 cups butternut, *or* acorn, squash, peeled, seeded, and cubed
1 large apple, peeled and sliced
1 Tbsp. tub-style margarine, non-hydrogenated
half a small onion (1½ Tbsp.) chopped
1 clove garlic
2 Tbsp. flour
¼ tsp. dried thyme
¼ tsp. salt, *or* North Woods seasoning
⅛ tsp. pepper
10½-oz. can low-fat low-sodium chicken, *or* vegetable, broth
2 Tbsp. fat-free sour cream

1. Steam squash and apple in steamer or microwave until very tender.
2. In large saucepan, sauté onion and garlic in margarine until onion is clear.
3. Stir flour and seasonings into saucepan.
4. Add broth. Heat, stirring continually until smooth and slightly thickened.
5. Pour broth and cooked vegetables into blender. Cover and blend carefully until smooth.
6. Serve immediately. Top each individual serving with 1 tsp. sour cream.

Per Serving

Calories 81, Kilojoules 339, Protein 2 g,	
Carbohydrates 14 g, Total Fat 2 g, Saturated Fat 0.5 g,	
Monounsaturated Fat 0.5 g, Polyunsaturated Fat 1 g,	
Cholesterol 1.5 mg, Sodium 164 mg, Fiber 2 g	

Turkey Sausage and Cabbage Soup

Bonita Stutzman
Harrisonburg, VA

Makes 8 servings

Prep. Time: 20 minutes
Cooking Time: 1 hour, or more

1½ cups chopped onions
2 cloves garlic, finely chopped
¾ lb. turkey sausage, chopped in small pieces
6 cups green cabbage, shredded
3 lbs. canned tomatoes, no salt added, undrained
1½ quarts water
1 Tbsp. dried basil
2 tsp. dried oregano
¼ tsp. black pepper

Pyramid Servings	
Vegetables	●●●○○▸
Fruits	○○○○○▸
Carbohydrates	○○○○○○○○
Protein & Dairy	◐○○○○○○
Fats	○○○○○

1. Spray inside bottom of stockpot lightly with cooking spray. Sauté onions and garlic until tender.
2. Add chopped sausage. Cook until lightly browned.
3. Stir in remaining ingredients.
4. Cover. Simmer until cabbage is very tender.

Per Serving

Calories 129, Kilojoules 540, Protein 9 g,
Carbohydrates 15 g, Total Fat 4 g, Saturated Fat 1 g,
Monounsaturated Fat 2 g, Polyunsaturated Fat 1 g,
Cholesterol 28 mg, Sodium 486 mg, Fiber 4.5 g

Sausage, Beans and Rice Soup

Sharon Easter
Yuba City, CA

Makes 5 servings

Prep. Time: 5–10 minutes
Cooking Time: 25–30 minutes

½ lb. turkey sausage (see recipe on page 190)
3 16-oz. cans low-sodium, fat-free chicken, *or* vegetable, broth
28-oz. can diced tomatoes, no salt added, undrained
¼ tsp. pepper
½ tsp. dried oregano
½ cup uncooked brown rice
15-oz. can cannellini beans, rinsed and drained

Pyramid Servings	
Vegetables	●○○○○▸
Fruits	○○○○○▸
Carbohydrates	◐○○○○○○○
Protein & Dairy	●◐○○○○○
Fats	○○○○○

1. Brown sausage in Dutch oven over medium-high heat, about 5 minutes. Drain off drippings.
2. Stir in broth, tomatoes, and seasonings. Bring to a boil.
3. Stir in rice and beans. Cover and simmer 15–20 minutes, or until rice is tender.

Per Serving

Calories 220, Kilojoules 920, Protein 19 g,
Carbohydrates 33 g, Total Fat 1.5 g, Saturated Fat 0.5 g,
Monounsaturated Fat 0.5 g, Polyunsaturated Fat 0.5 g,
Cholesterol 20 mg, Sodium 483 mg, Fiber 7 g

Dietitian's tip: White beans get their name from their light color. You can use any variety in this recipe, including marrow beans, Great Northern beans, or navy beans. White beans are a good source of many nutrients, including iron, folate, magnesium, phosphorus, and potassium.

Turkey Vegetable Soup

Elva Bare
Lancaster, PA

Makes 12 servings

Prep. Time: 30–40 minutes
Cooking Time: 35–40 minutes

1 lb. lean ground turkey breast
2 tsp. no-salt Italian seasoning
¼ tsp. paprika
¼ tsp. pepper
2 Tbsp. olive oil, *divided*
½ cup chopped celery
1 cup onion, chopped
2 14-oz. cans low-sodium fat-free chicken broth
1 cup cabbage, chopped
1 cup carrots, chopped
1 cup cut fresh green beans
15-oz. can cannellini beans, rinsed and drained
15-oz. can black beans, rinsed and drained
14½-oz. can Italian diced tomatoes, undrained, no salt added
½ cup cooked elbow macaroni
1 envelope George Washington Golden seasoning, *optional*, not included in analyses
¼ cup mozzarella cheese, shredded

Pyramid Servings

Vegetables
●●○○○➤

Fruits
○○○○○➤

Carbohydrates
○○○○○○○○

Protein & Dairy
●○○○○○○○

Fats
○○○○○

1. In large non-stick stockpot, sauté first 4 ingredients in 1 Tbsp. oil until turkey is no longer pink.
2. Sauté celery and onion in stockpot until almost tender.
3. Add broth, cabbage, carrots, and green beans. Cook 15–20 minutes.
4. Add cannellini and black beans, tomatoes, cooked macaroni, and seasoning if you wish. Cover and heat through.
5. Add water if soup becomes too thick.
6. Sprinkle each individual serving with 1 teaspoon cheese.

Per Serving

Calories 167, Kilojoules 699, Protein 15 g, Carbohydrates 18 g, Total Fat 4 g, Saturated Fat 1 g, Monounsaturated Fat 2 g, Polyunsaturated Fat 1 g, Cholesterol 17 mg, Sodium 164 mg, Fiber 5 g

Tuscany Peasant Soup

Alice Valine
Elma, NY

Makes 8 servings

Prep. Time: 20 minutes
Cooking Time: 25 minutes

½ lb. bulk turkey sausage
  (see recipe on page 190)
1 onion, chopped
2–3 cloves garlic, minced
2 15-oz. cans cannellini
  beans, *or* great northern
  beans, rinsed and drained
2 14½-oz. cans diced tomatoes, no salt
  added, undrained
2 14-oz. cans low-fat, low-sodium chicken
  broth
2 tsp. no-salt Italian seasoning
3 medium zucchini, sliced
4 cups fresh spinach leaves, chopped, *or*
  baby spinach, unchopped
shredded Parmesan, *or* Romano, cheese,
  optional, not included in analyses

Pyramid Servings		
Vegetables ●●○○○➤		
Fruits ○○○○○➤		
Carbohydrates ○○○○○○○○		
Protein & Dairy ●○○○○○○		
Fats ○○○○○		

1. In Dutch oven or stockpot, cook sausage over medium heat until no longer pink. Drain off drippings.
2. Add onions and garlic. Sauté until tender.
3. Stir in beans, tomatoes, broth, seasoning, and zucchini. Cook uncovered 10 minutes.
4. Add spinach and heat until just wilted.
5. Serve with cheese, if you wish.

Per Serving

Calories 198, Kilojoules 828, Protein 17 g,
Carbohydrates 31 g, Total Fat 1 g, Saturated Fat 0.5 g,
Monounsaturated Fat 0.3 g, Polyunsaturated Fat 0.2 g,
Cholesterol 11 mg, Sodium 132 mg, Fiber 8 g

Dietitian's tip: Cannellini beans are white kidney beans. They're an excellent source of folate and a good source of iron and fiber. Their high-quality protein makes them a great stand-in for meat.

Turkey Chili

Julette Rush
Harrisonburg, VA

Makes 5 servings

Prep. Time: 15 minutes
Cooking Time: 30 minutes

½ lb. ground turkey breast
1 cup chopped onions
½ cup chopped green bell
  sweet pepper
½ cup chopped red bell sweet
  pepper
14½-oz. can diced tomatoes, no salt added,
  undrained
15-oz. can solid-pack pumpkin
15½-oz. can pinto beans, rinsed and
  drained
½ cup water
2 tsp. chili powder
½ tsp. garlic powder
¼ tsp. black pepper
¾ tsp. ground cumin
14½-oz. can low-sodium, fat-free chicken
  broth
1 cup low-fat shredded cheddar cheese

Pyramid Servings		
Vegetables ●●●○○➤		
Fruits ○○○○○➤		
Carbohydrates ○○○○○○○○		
Protein & Dairy ●○○○○○○		
Fats ○○○○○		

1. In large stockpot, sauté turkey, onions, and bell peppers until turkey is browned and vegetables are softened.
2. Mix in tomatoes, pumpkin, beans, water, seasonings, and broth. Reduce heat to low.
3. Cover and simmer 20 minutes. Stir occasionally.
4. Top individual servings with cheese.

Per Serving

Calories 232, Kilojoules 971, Protein 24 g,
Carbohydrates 28 g, Total Fat 3 g, Saturated Fat 1.6 g,
Monounsaturated Fat 0.8 g, Polyunsaturated Fat 0.6 g,
Cholesterol 25 mg, Sodium 375 mg, Fiber 9 g

Turkey Chili Con Carne

Jackie Stefl
E. Bethany, NY

Makes 10 servings

Prep. Time: 15 minutes
Cooking Time: 2 hours and 10 minutes

Pyramid Servings

Vegetables
●○○○○➤

Fruits
○○○○○➤

Carbohydrates
●○○○○○○○○

Protein & Dairy
●○○○○○○

Fats
○○○○○

1 medium onion
1 medium green bell sweet pepper
1½ lbs. extra-lean ground turkey breast
1 Tbsp. extra-virgin olive oil
15½-oz. can kidney beans, rinsed and drained
15¼-oz. can black beans, rinsed and drained
15¼-oz. can corn, no salt added, drained
28-oz. can crushed tomatoes, no salt added, undrained
1 Tbsp. chili powder
1 tsp. cinnamon
1 tsp. ground cumin
2 low-sodium beef bouillon cubes
2 cups water
1½ cups grated low-fat cheddar cheese, *optional*, not included in analyses
¾ cup low-fat sour cream, *optional*, not included in analyses

1. Chop onion and green pepper. Place in large stockpot, along with ground turkey and olive oil.
2. Sauté until meat is no longer pink and vegetables are tender.
3. Stir kidney and black beans and corn into stockpot.
4. Stir tomatoes, seasonings, bouillon cubes, and water into pot.
5. Cover. Simmer 2 hours. Stir occasionally.
6. Garnish individual servings, if you wish, with 1 rounded Tbsp. low-fat cheese and sour cream.

Per Serving

Calories 201, Kilojoules 841, Protein 21 g,
Carbohydrates 23 g, Total Fat 3 g, Saturated Fat 0.6 g,
Monounsaturated Fat 2 g, Polyunsaturated Fat 0.4 g,
Cholesterol 27 mg, Sodium 298 mg, Fiber 7 g

Tip: For spicier chili, add more chili powder to taste.

Dietitian's tip: To add more variety in flavor, color and texture to chili, add several different beans, including kidney, garbanzo or black beans, or add more chopped vegetables, such as carrots and celery. If you add these vegetables, increase the amount of liquid to accommodate the added ingredients.

Turkey Rice Soup

Janeen L. Zimmerman, Denver, PA

Makes 10 servings

Prep. Time: 20 minutes
Cooking Time: 40 minutes

Pyramid Servings

Vegetables
●●○○○➤

Fruits
○○○○○➤

Carbohydrates
●●○○○○○○

Protein & Dairy
◐○○○○○○

Fats
○○○○○

4 celery ribs, sliced thin
1 onion, chopped
2 Tbsp. olive oil
4 carrots, shredded
⅓ cup whole wheat pastry flour
½ tsp. pepper
2 cups skim milk
4 cups raw wild rice, cooked according to package directions
2⅔ cups raw brown rice, cooked according to package directions
3 cups cooked turkey
3 Tbsp. low-sodium chicken bouillon granules
8 cups water
2 cups low-fat grated cheese, *optional*, not included in analyses

1. In a large stockpot, sauté celery and onion in olive oil.

2. Add carrots. Cook and stir 1–2 minutes.

3. Remove cooked vegetables from pot. Set aside.

4. Combine flour, pepper, and milk in stockpot. Bring to almost boiling, stirring frequently until thickened. Do not scorch or curdle milk.

5. Meanwhile, cook 2 kinds of rice according to package directions.

6. Add both kinds of cooked rice, cooked turkey, bouillon granules, celery mixture, water, and cheese if you wish, to thickened creamy base in stockpot.

7. Cover. Heat thoroughly and serve.

Per Serving

Calories 223, Kilojoules 933, Protein 12 g,
Carbohydrates 35 g, Total Fat 4 g, Saturated Fat 0.6 g,
Monounsaturated Fat 2.4 g, Polyunsaturated Fat 1 g,
Cholesterol 15 mg, Sodium 95 mg, Fiber 4 g

Dietitian's tip: Use the turkey leftovers from a holiday meal or family gathering to make a hearty turkey soup. To limit the sodium content, this recipe uses low-sodium chicken broth or granules.

Lentil Barley Stew with Chicken

Ilene Bontrager
Arlington, KS

Makes 4 servings

Prep. Time: 15 minutes
Cooking Time: 1–2 hours

⅓ cup uncooked lentils
⅓ cup uncooked green split peas
⅓ cup uncooked pearl barley
1 carrot, cut in fine dice
half an onion, chopped
1 small rib celery, sliced thin
¼ tsp. pepper
1 quart low-sodium, fat-free chicken, *or* beef, broth
1 cup chicken, cooked and diced

Pyramid Servings	
Vegetables	●○○○○➤
Fruits	○○○○○➤
Carbohydrates	●○○○○○○○
Protein & Dairy	●◐○○○○○
Fats	○○○○○

1. Rinse lentils, peas, and barley.

2. Place in 4–6 quart stockpot. Add all remaining ingredients, except chicken.

3. Simmer, covered, 1–2 hours, or until lentils, peas, and barley are soft.

4. Stir in chicken. Cover and heat through.

Per Serving

Calories 247, Kilojoules 1033, Protein 24 g,
Carbohydrates 33 g, Total Fat 2 g, Saturated Fat 1 g,
Monounsaturated Fat 0.5 g, Polyunsaturated Fat 0.5 g,
Cholesterol 35 mg, Sodium 185 mg, Fiber 11 g

Chicken Barley Soup

Ida H. Goering
Dayton, VA

Makes 6 servings

Prep. Time: 20 minutes
Cooking Time: 1 hour

Pyramid Servings	
Vegetables	●●○○○➤
Fruits	○○○○○➤
Carbohydrates	●○○○○○○○
Protein & Dairy	○○○○○○○
Fats	○○○○○

6 cups low-sodium, fat-free
   chicken broth
1½ cups diced carrots
1 cup diced celery
½ cup chopped onion
¾ cup uncooked barley
2–3 cups (about 6 ozs.) cooked and cut-up
   chicken
14½-oz. can diced tomatoes, no salt added,
   undrained
½ tsp. black pepper
1 bay leaf
2 Tbsp. chopped fresh parsley, *or* 2 tsp.
   dried parsley

1. Combine all ingredients except parsley in large kettle.
2. Cover and bring to boil.
3. Simmer, covered, for one hour. Stir occasionally.
4. Just before serving, remove bay leaf. Stir in parsley.

Per Serving

Calories 173, Kilojoules 724, Protein 14 g,
Carbohydrates 26 g, Total Fat 1.5 g, Saturated Fat 0.7 g,
Monounsaturated Fat 0.3 g, Polyunsaturated Fat 0.5 g,
Cholesterol 21 mg, Sodium 239 mg, Fiber 7 g

Chicken Noodle Soup

Mary Martins
Fairbank, IA

Makes 12 servings

Prep. Time: 1 hour
Cooking Time: 3–3¼ hours

Pyramid Servings	
Vegetables	●●○○○➤
Fruits	○○○○○➤
Carbohydrates	●○○○○○○○
Protein & Dairy	●○○○○○○
Fats	○○○○○

4-lb. stewing chicken, skin
   removed and cut up
2 quarts water
2 14½-oz. cans low-fat low-
   sodium chicken broth
5 celery ribs, coarsely
   chopped, *divided*
3 medium carrots, sliced, *divided*
2 medium onions, quartered, *divided*
⅔ cup coarsely chopped green bell sweet
   pepper, *divided*
½ tsp. pepper
1 bay leaf
2 tsp. salt
8 ozs. uncooked whole wheat pasta

1. In large stockpot, combine chicken, water, broth, half the celery, half the carrots, half the onions, half the green pepper, ½ teaspoon pepper, and bay leaf. Bring to a boil.
2. Reduce heat. Cover and simmer 2½ hours, or until chicken is tender.
3. Meanwhile, chop remaining onion. Set aside.
4. Remove chicken from broth. When cool enough to handle, remove meat from bones and cut into bite-size pieces. Discard bones and skin. Set chicken aside. (This will equal about 3 lbs. cooked meat.)
5. Strain broth and skim fat.
6. Return broth to kettle. Add salt, chopped onion and remaining celery, carrots, and green pepper.
7. Bring to a boil. Reduce heat. Cover and simmer 10–12 minutes, or until vegetables are crisp-tender.

8. Add noodles and chicken.

9. Cover and simmer 12–15 minutes, or until pasta is tender.

Per Serving

Calories 229, Kilojoules 958, Protein 28 g,
Carbohydrates 19 g, Total Fat 4 g, Saturated Fat 1 g,
Monounsaturated Fat 2 g, Polyunsaturated Fat 1 g,
Cholesterol 80 mg, Sodium 152 mg, Fiber 3 g

Chicken and Chili Stew

Susan Kasting, Jenks, OK

Makes 4 servings

Prep. Time: 20 minutes
Cooking Time: 30 minutes

Pyramid Servings

Vegetables
●●○○○➤
Fruits
○○○○○➤
Carbohydrates
●○○○○○○○
Protein & Dairy
●◐○○○○○
Fats
○○○○○

14½-oz. can low-sodium, fat-free chicken broth, *divided*
1 lb. boneless, skinless chicken breasts, cut into bite-size pieces
4 cloves garlic, minced
1–2 jalapeño chili peppers, seeded and diced
1 Tbsp. cornstarch
1 medium red bell sweet pepper, diced
1 medium carrot, sliced
15-oz. can corn, drained, no salt added
1 tsp. cumin
2 Tbsp. chopped cilantro

1. In good-sized stockpot, heat ¾ cup broth to boiling.

2. Add chicken to broth. Cook about 5 minutes, or until no longer pink.

3. Add garlic and chili peppers. Cook 2 minutes.

4. In a bowl, stir cornstarch into remaining broth.

5. When smooth, add to chicken/chili mix. Cook, stirring, until thickened.

6. Stir in remaining ingredients.

7. Cover. Let simmer 20 minutes, stirring occasionally.

Per Serving

Calories 231, Kilojoules 967, Protein 30 g,
Carbohydrates 23 g, Total Fat 2 g, Saturated Fat 0.4 g,
Monounsaturated Fat 1 g, Polyunsaturated Fat 0.6 g,
Cholesterol 67 mg, Sodium 147 mg, Fiber 2 g

Southwest Vegetable Soup

Joyce G. Zuercher
Hesston, KS

Makes 10 servings

Prep. Time: 30 minutes
Cooking Time: 45 minutes

1 Tbsp. canola oil
1 cup diced celery
¾ cup chopped onion
1 clove garlic, finely chopped
¼ cup chopped bell pepper
4 cups diced canned
   tomatoes, no salt added, undrained
2 cups tomato sauce, no salt added
2 cups low-fat low-sodium chicken broth
2 cups diced carrots
2 cups green beans
½ cup frozen green peas
¾ cup corn
15-oz. can black beans, rinsed and
   drained
hot peppers, dried and crushed or
   chopped, according to your taste
   preferences
1 tsp. chili seasoning
½ tsp. cumin
3 cups chopped, cooked chicken
pepper to taste

   1. In large stockpot, cook celery, onion, garlic, and bell pepper in oil until transparent.
   2. Add all other ingredients. Cover and simmer together at least 30 minutes, or until vegetables are done to your liking.
   3. Adjust seasonings to your taste.

Pyramid Servings

Vegetables	●○○○○➤
Fruits	○○○○○➤
Carbohydrates	●○○○○○○○
Protein & Dairy	●○○○○○○
Fats	○○○○○

Per Serving

Calories 210, Kilojoules 879, Protein 19 g,
Carbohydrates 26 g, Total Fat 3 g, Saturated Fat 0.5 g,
Monounsaturated Fat 1.5 g, Polyunsaturated Fat 1 g,
Cholesterol 37 mg, Sodium 283 mg, Fiber 7 g

Tip: Use fresh vegetables for this recipe if at all possible. But if you can't, choose canned or frozen veggies without added salt.

Dietitian's tip: Scaling a recipe—changing the number of servings—isn't as simple as it sounds. Some recipes, such as casseroles, soups, and stews, usually lend themselves to simply increasing or decreasing the main ingredients (adjust seasonings to taste). Other recipes don"t. For example, baked goods may not turn out well if doubled or tripled. If you're increasing a recipe and lack time to experiment, make several individual batches. This way you end up with the amount you need based on the original recipe.

A Tip —

   Don't grind or shake salt, pepper, spices, or dried herbs over steaming cooking pots. The steam will cause mildew in the containers. If you do shake the seasonings over a steaming pot, leave the containers' lids off for about 10 minutes before closing them.

Spicy Chicken Soup with Edamame

JB Miller
Indianapolis, IN

Makes 8 servings

Prep. Time: 20 minutes
Cooking Time: 40 minutes

Pyramid Servings		
Vegetables	●○○○○➤	
Fruits	○○○○○➤	
Carbohydrates	○○○○○○○○	
Protein & Dairy	●●○○○○○○	
Fats	○○○○○	

1½ lbs. boneless, skinless, chicken breasts, cubed
1 bunch (about 6) green onions, thinly sliced
1 red bell sweet pepper, chopped
1 yellow bell sweet pepper, chopped
2 jalapeño peppers, seeded and finely chopped
4 cloves garlic
½ tsp. ground ginger
½ tsp. dried sage
½ tsp. ground pepper
4 cups fat-free, low-sodium chicken broth
3 cups fresh, *or* frozen, edamame (shelled soybeans)

1. Place large skillet that has been lightly sprayed with cooking spray over medium heat. Add chicken and sauté just until no longer pink. Remove chicken from pan.

2. Sauté onions, peppers, including jalapeños, and garlic in same skillet.

3. Place chicken and sautéed vegetables in stockpot. Add seasonings. Mix thoroughly.

4. Add chicken broth. Cover and simmer 20 minutes.

5. Add edamame. Simmer 5 more minutes.

Per Serving

Calories 173, Kilojoules 724, Protein 27 g,
Carbohydrates 8 g, Total Fat 4 g, Saturated Fat 1 g,
Monounsaturated Fat 2 g, Polyunsaturated Fat 1 g,
Cholesterol 52 mg, Sodium 131 mg, Fiber 3 g

Spicy African Chicken Peanut Soup

Rhoda Atzeff
Lancaster, PA

Makes 8 servings

Prep. Time: 15 minutes
Cooking Time: 40 minutes

Pyramid Servings		
Vegetables	●○○○○➤	
Fruits	○○○○○➤	
Carbohydrates	○○○○○○○○	
Protein & Dairy	◑○○○○○○	
Fats	●○○○○	

1 tsp. sesame oil
1 cup onions, chopped
1 large green bell sweet pepper, seeded and finely chopped
2 cloves garlic, minced *or* pressed
4 cups low-sodium, fat-free chicken broth
16-oz. can crushed tomatoes, no salt added, undrained
½ tsp. red pepper flakes
1 Tbsp. curry powder
⅛ tsp. black pepper
1 cup diced cooked chicken
¼ cup uncooked brown rice
¼ cup smooth peanut butter

1. In large stockpot, heat sesame oil over medium heat. Sauté onions, green peppers, and garlic until onions begin to brown.

2. Stir in broth, tomatoes, red pepper flakes, curry powder, pepper, chicken, and rice.

3. Simmer uncovered over low heat for 30 minutes, or until rice is tender.

4. Whisk in peanut butter until soup is completely smooth. Heat through.

Per Serving

Calories 145, Kilojoules 607, Protein 11 g,
Carbohydrates 14 g, Total Fat 5 g, Saturated Fat 1.3 g,
Monounsaturated Fat 2.7 g, Polyunsaturated Fat 1 g,
Cholesterol 17 mg, Sodium 144 mg, Fiber 2 g

Egg Drop Chicken Soup

Kathryn Yoder
Minot, ND

Makes 6 servings

Prep. Time: 10 minutes
Cooking Time: 12–15 minutes

Pyramid Servings	
Vegetables	○○○○○➤
Fruits	○○○○○➤
Carbohydrates	○○○○○○○○
Protein & Dairy	◑○○○○○○
Fats	○○○○○

4½ cups water
4 low-sodium chicken
    bouillon cubes
4 ozs. cooked chicken,
    shredded
½ cup carrot, finely shredded
1 tsp. finely chopped fresh parsley, *or* ½
    tsp. dried parsley
1 tsp. low-sodium soy sauce
2 egg whites, lightly beaten
4 tsp. scallions, sliced

1. In large saucepan, dissolve bouillon cubes in water over medium heat.
2. Add shredded chicken, carrot, parsley, and soy sauce.
3. Bring to a boil, stirring occasionally. Continue boiling, 4–5 minutes.
4. Slowly dribble lightly beaten egg whites into boiling soup, stirring constantly until the egg has cooked.
5. Serve with scallions as garnish.

Per Serving

Calories 45, Kilojoules 188, Protein 7 g,
Carbohydrates 2 g, Total Fat 1 g, Saturated Fat 0.2 g,
Monounsaturated Fat 0.5 g, Polyunsaturated Fat 0.3 g,
Cholesterol 16 mg, Sodium 480 mg, Fiber *trace*

Minestrone

Elva Bare
Lancaster, PA

Makes 14 servings

Prep. Time: 30 minutes
Cooking Time: 40–60 minutes

Pyramid Servings	
Vegetables	●○○○○➤
Fruits	○○○○○➤
Carbohydrates	◑○○○○○○○
Protein & Dairy	●○○○○○○
Fats	○○○○○

1 lb. 95%-lean ground beef
½ cup chopped onion
1 clove garlic, cut fine
1 celery rib, chopped
2 14-oz. cans reduced-sodium
    fat-free chicken broth
2 14-oz. cans reduced-sodium fat-free beef
    broth
14-oz. can diced tomatoes, undrained, no
    salt added
14-oz. can Italian tomatoes, undrained, no
    salt added
1½ cups sliced zucchini
16-oz. can kidney beans, rinsed and
    drained
16-oz. can black beans, rinsed and
    drained
1½ cups fresh, *or* frozen, corn
1½ cups shredded cabbage
1–2 tsp. no-salt Italian seasoning
½ cup uncooked whole wheat elbow
    macaroni

1. In large stockpot, sauté beef, onion, garlic, and celery until beef is no longer pink.
2. Stir in broths, tomatoes, zucchini, beans, corn, cabbage, and seasoning.
3. Cover. Bring to a boil.
4. Add macaroni. Stir and reduce heat.
5. Cover and simmer 20 minutes, or until macaroni is soft.

Per Serving

Calories 168, Kilojoules 703, Protein 15 g,
Carbohydrates 23 g, Total Fat 2 g, Saturated Fat 1 g,
Monounsaturated Fat 0.7 g, Polyunsaturated Fat 0.3 g,
Cholesterol 21 mg, Sodium 262 mg, Fiber 6 g

Note: I made a double portion of this soup in the spring and froze two 2-quart containers. Then, a few weeks ago, I served it to our daughters, granddaughters, and great-granddaughters on a cold day. Most weeks they come one day for lunch. I like to serve the minestrone with either a Caesar salad or a baby spinach salad garnished with fruits, nuts, and cheese.

Quick and Hearty Vegetable Soup

Berenice M. Wagner
Dodge City, KS
Sherri Grindle
Goshen, IN

Makes 8 servings

Prep. Time: 10 minutes
Cooking Time: 35–40 minutes

Pyramid Servings

Vegetables
●●○○○➤

Fruits
○○○○○➤

Carbohydrates
◐○○○○○○○

Protein & Dairy
◐○○○○○○

Fats
○○○○○

½ lb. 95%-lean ground beef
½ cup chopped onion
1 clove garlic, minced
5 cups water
14½-oz. can diced tomatoes, undrained, no salt added
¾ cup uncooked quick-cooking barley
2 low-salt beef bouillon cubes
½ cup sliced carrots
½ tsp. crushed dried basil
1 bay leaf
9-oz. pkg. frozen mixed vegetables

1. In 4-quart saucepan, brown meat. Drain off drippings.
2. Add onion and garlic. Cook until onion is tender.
3. Stir in remaining ingredients, except frozen vegetables.

4. Cover and bring to a boil. Reduce heat. Simmer, covered, 10 minutes, stirring occasionally.
5. Add frozen vegetables. Cook 10 minutes longer. Add more water if soup becomes too thick.

Per Serving

Calories 139, Kilojoules 582, Protein 10 g,
Carbohydrates 21 g, Total Fat 2 g, Saturated Fat 1.2 g,
Monounsaturated Fat 0.6 g, Polyunsaturated Fat 0.2 g,
Cholesterol 17 mg, Sodium 218 mg, Fiber 5 g

Dietitian's tip: To increase the amount of nutrients in your diet—including vitamins, minerals, and fiber—try adding three times as many vegetables as meat on pizzas or in casseroles, soups, and stews. Better yet, go meatless!

Beef Mushroom Barley Soup

Becky Frey
Lebanon, PA

Makes 8 servings

Prep. Time: 20 minutes
Cooking Time: 2¼ hours

Pyramid Servings	
Vegetables	●○○○○►
Fruits	○○○○○►
Carbohydrates	❶○○○○○○○
Protein & Dairy	●○○○○○○
Fats	○○○○○

1 lb. boneless beef chuck,
  cubed
½ Tbsp. olive oil
2 cups chopped onion
½ cup sliced celery
1 cup sliced carrots
1 lb. fresh mushrooms, sliced
2 cloves garlic, crushed
½ tsp. dried thyme, *optional*
8 cups low-fat, low-sodium beef broth, *or*
  2 14½-oz. cans
½ cup uncooked pearl barley
½ tsp. freshly ground pepper
3 Tbsp. chopped fresh parsley, *or* 1 Tbsp.
  dried parsley

1. In large saucepan brown beef on all sides
in oil. Remove beef and set aside.

2. Add onion, celery, and carrots to oil in
saucepan. Sauté over medium heat about 5
minutes.

3. Add mushrooms, garlic, and thyme. Cook
and stir about 2 minutes.

4. Add meat and all remaining ingredients,
except the parsley, to saucepan. Bring to a boil.

5. Cover. Reduce heat and simmer about 2
hours, or until beef and barley are tender. If stew
becomes too thick, add more water or broth.

6. Add parsley and serve piping hot.

Per Serving	
Calories 175, Kilojoules 732, Protein 16g,	
Carbohydrates 17g, Total Fat 5g, Saturated Fat 1.5g,	
Monounsaturated Fat 2.5g, Polyunsaturated Fat 1g,	
Cholesterol 32mg, Sodium 232mg, Fiber 4g	

Stuffed Sweet Pepper Soup

Moreen Weaver
Bath, NY

Makes 10 servings

Prep. Time: 20 minutes
Cooking Time: 1¼ hours

Pyramid Servings	
Vegetables	●●○○○►
Fruits	○○○○○►
Carbohydrates	●○○○○○○○
Protein & Dairy	●○○○○○○
Fats	○○○○○

1 lb. 95%-lean ground beef
2 quarts low-sodium tomato
  juice
3 medium red, *or* green, bell
  sweet peppers, diced
1½ cups chili sauce, no salt
  added
1 cup uncooked brown rice
2 celery ribs, diced
1 large onion, diced
3 low-sodium chicken bouillon cubes
2 garlic cloves, minced

1. In large kettle over medium heat, cook
beef until no longer pink. Drain off drippings.

2. Add remaining ingredients. Bring to a boil.

3. Reduce heat. Simmer, uncovered, for 1
hour, or until rice is tender.

Per Serving	
Calories 228, Kilojoules 954, Protein 14g,	
Carbohydrates 36g, Total Fat 3g, Saturated Fat 1g,	
Monounsaturated Fat 1.5g, Polyunsaturated Fat 0.5g,	
Cholesterol 28mg, Sodium 182mg, Fiber 5g	

Beef and Black Bean Chili

Eileen B. Jarvis
St. Augustine, FL

Makes 8 servings

Prep. Time: 15 minutes
Cooking Time: 15–20 meetings

1 lb. 95%-lean ground beef
2 15-oz. cans no-salt-added
   black beans, rinsed and
   drained, *divided*
½ cup water
1 cup medium, *or* hot,
   chunky salsa
2 8-oz. cans no-salt-added tomato sauce
1 Tbsp. chili powder
low-fat sour cream, *optional*, not included
   in analyses
reduced-fat cheddar cheese, grated,
   optional, not included in analyses

Pyramid Servings

| Vegetables |
| ●○○○○► |
| Fruits |
| ○○○○○► |
| Carbohydrates |
| ○○○○○○○○ |
| Protein & Dairy |
| ●●○○○○○○ |
| Fats |
| ○○○○○ |

1. Brown meat in large saucepan over medium-high heat. Drain off drippings.

2. While meat cooks, drain, rinse, and mash 1 can black beans.

3. Add mashed beans, second can of rinsed and drained beans, water, salsa, tomato sauce, and seasoning into saucepan. Stir well.

4. Cover. Cook over medium heat 10 minutes. Stir occasionally.

5. If you wish, top individual servings with sour cream and/or reduced-fat cheese.

Per Serving

Calories 250, Kilojoules 1046, Protein 22 g,
Carbohydrates 32 g, Total Fat 4 g, Saturated Fat 1.5 g,
Monounsaturated Fat 1.5 g, Polyunsaturated Fat 1 g,
Cholesterol 35 mg, Sodium 302 mg, Fiber 11 g

Dietitian's tip: For convenience, canned black beans instead of the dried variety are used in this recipe. Although canned beans typically contain more sodium than home-cooked beans, you can rinse and drain them before use to help lessen the amount of sodium by about 40 percent.

A Tip —

Buy sturdy kitchen tools. Buy ones that fit well into your hands. Take care of them and they will last a very long time.

Hearty Tomato Beef Soup

Beverly High
Bradford, PA

Makes 6 servings

Prep. Time: 20 minutes
Cooking Time: 35–40 minutes

Pyramid Servings	
Vegetables	●●○○○➤
Fruits	○○○○○➤
Carbohydrates	○○○○○○○○
Protein & Dairy	●○○○○○○○
Fats	○○○○○

½ lb. 95%-lean ground beef
½ cup chopped onion
2 cups tomato juice, no salt
    added
1 cup sliced carrots
½ cup chopped green, *or* red,
    bell sweet peppers
1 cup diced potatoes
⅛ tsp. black pepper
4 cups skim milk
⅓ cup flour

1. Brown meat and onion in large skillet or kettle. Drain off meat drippings.
2. Stir tomato juice, vegetables, and pepper into pan with meat and onions.
3. Cover and simmer until vegetables are tender, approximately 20–25 minutes.
4. Combine flour and milk in a bowl. Stir until smooth.
5. Stir milk mixture into soup. Continue stirring frequently until soup is hot and thickened. Do not allow to boil.

Per Serving

Calories 177, Kilojoules 741, Protein 16 g,
Carbohydrates 24 g, Total Fat 2 g, Saturated Fat 1 g,
Monounsaturated Fat 0.8 g, Polyunsaturated Fat 0.2 g,
Cholesterol 27 mg, Sodium 118 mg, Fiber 2 g

Tip: For more texture, substitute one 14½-oz. can diced tomatoes, undrained and with no salt added, for the tomato juice.

Dot's Senate Bean Soup

Dorothea Ladd
Ballston Lake, NY

Makes 8 servings

Prep. Time: 20–30 minutes
Cooking Time: 25 minutes

Pyramid Servings	
Vegetables	●○○○○➤
Fruits	○○○○○➤
Carbohydrates	○○○○○○○○
Protein & Dairy	●○○○○○○○
Fats	●○○○○

2 large carrots, sliced
2 ribs celery, sliced
2 cloves garlic, minced
1 large onion, diced
2 Tbsp. olive oil
3 15-oz. cans low-fat low-
    sodium chicken broth
2 15-oz. cans cannellini beans, *or* great
    northern beans, rinsed and drained
1 Tbsp. dried parsley
1 pinch of sage
1½ cups diced lean ham

1. Prepare vegetables first. Slice carrots and celery, mince garlic, dice onion.
2. Put olive oil in 6-quart kettle with heavy bottom. Sauté vegetables about 5 minutes.
3. Add chicken broth, beans, parsley, sage, and ham.
4. Cover. Simmer 20 minutes. Stir occasionally.

Per Serving

Calories 207, Kilojoules 866, Protein 15 g,
Carbohydrates 26 g, Total Fat 5 g, Saturated Fat 1 g,
Monounsaturated Fat 3 g, Polyunsaturated Fat 1 g,
Cholesterol 15 mg, Sodium 300 mg, Fiber 6 g

Ham and Bean Soup

Susie Nisley
Millersburg, OH

Makes 10 servings

Prep. Time: 20 minutes
Soaking Time: 2 hours
Cooking Time: 1–1½ hours

Pyramid Servings	
Vegetables	●●○○○▶
Fruits	○○○○○▶
Carbohydrates	○○○○○○○
Protein & Dairy	●◐○○○○○
Fats	○○○○○

1 lb. dry navy beans
1 lb. extra-lean ham, diced
1 green bell sweet pepper,
　diced
1 small onion, chopped
half a carrot, diced
1 medium potato, unpeeled and diced
1 cup tomato juice, no salt added
2 tsp. garlic powder
½ tsp. cumin
½ tsp. black pepper
1 tsp. Mrs. Dash™, *or* other salt-free
　seasoning
1 bunch fresh cilantro, chopped

1. Cover beans with water in large stockpot. Soak 2 hours.
2. Drain beans. Cover beans with fresh water again in stockpot.
3. Add ham. Cover and cook 30 minutes.
4. Stir in remaining ingredients, except cilantro.
5. Cover. Cook another 30 minutes, or until vegetables are cooked to your liking.
6. Stir in chopped fresh cilantro just before serving.

Per Serving

Calories 231, Kilojoules 967, Protein 19 g,
Carbohydrates 35 g, Total Fat 2 g, Saturated Fat 0.4 g,
Monounsaturated Fat 0.6 g, Polyunsaturated Fat 1 g,
Cholesterol 20 mg, Sodium 490 mg, Fiber 12 g

Green Bean Soup

Carla Keslowsky
Hillsboro, KS

Makes 4 servings

Prep. Time: 20 minutes
Cooking Time: 1–1½ hours

Pyramid Servings	
Vegetables	●●●○○▶
Fruits	○○○○○▶
Carbohydrates	●○○○○○○
Protein & Dairy	◐○○○○○○
Fats	○○○○○

1 ham hock
1½ cups water
ham broth and water to
　equal 6 cups
2 potatoes, peeled and cubed
½ cup onions, chopped
1 sprig fresh dill weed, *or* ½ tsp. dried dill
16-oz. pkg. frozen, no salt added, green
　beans, or 1 lb. fresh beans
½ tsp. black pepper
½ cup fat-free milk

1. In large stockpot, cook hock over medium heat in about 1½ cups water. Meat is finished cooking when it pulls away from bone.
2. Pour broth into tall glass or cylinder. Fat can be skimmed off as broth cools. Or place in refrigerator until broth is congealed. Remove fat, which rises to the top.
3. Debone and cut up meat. Set aside.
4. Return broth, with fat removed, to stockpot. Add potatoes, onions, dill weed, beans, and pepper to broth mixture.
5. Cook, covered, until potatoes and beans are tender.
6. Add milk and ham. Heat through and serve.

Per Serving

Calories 203, Kilojoules 849, Protein 11 g,
Carbohydrates 29 g, Total Fat 5 g, Saturated Fat 1.5 g,
Monounsaturated Fat 2.5 g, Polyunsaturated Fat 1 g,
Cholesterol 24 mg, Sodium 77 mg, Fiber 5 g

Sweet Potato Chowder

Deborah Heatwole
Waynesboro, GA

Makes 6 servings

Prep. Time: 15 minutes
Cooking Time: 25–30 minutes

1 celery rib, chopped
½ cup cooked, finely
  chopped, lean ham
2 Tbsp. olive oil
2 14½-oz. cans low-fat low-
  sodium chicken broth
3 medium potatoes, peeled and cubed
2 large sweet potatoes, peeled and cubed
2 Tbsp. dried minced onion
½ tsp. garlic powder
½ tsp. dried oregano
½ tsp. dried parsley
¼ tsp. black pepper
¼ tsp. crushed red pepper flakes
¼ cup flour
2 cups skim milk

1. In large stockpot, sauté celery and ham in oil.
2. Stir in broth. Add white and sweet potatoes and seasonings.
3. Bring almost to a boil. Reduce heat, cover, and simmer for 12 minutes, or until potatoes are tender.
4. Combine flour and milk in a bowl until smooth. Stir into soup.
5. Bring to a boil. Cook, stirring continually, for 2 minutes, or until thickened and bubbly. Be careful not to scorch or curdle milk.

Pyramid Servings

Vegetables
○○○○○➤

Fruits
○○○○○➤

Carbohydrates
●○○○○○○○

Protein & Dairy
●○○○○○○

Fats
●○○○○

Per Serving

Calories 223, Kilojoules 933, Protein 10 g,
Carbohydrates 33 g, Total Fat 5 g, Saturated Fat 1 g,
Monounsaturated Fat 3.5 g, Polyunsaturated Fat 0.5 g,
Cholesterol 10 mg, Sodium 344 mg, Fiber 4 g

Napa Cabbage and Pork Soup

Shirley Unternahrer
Wayland, IA

Makes 8 servings

Prep. Time: 10 minutes
Cooking Time: 10 minutes
Standing Time: 15 minutes

1½ quarts water
½ lb. lean ground pork* (not
  sausage)
2 Tbsp. fish sauce (found in
  Asian foods section)
½ tsp. sugar
1 head (about 8 cups) Napa cabbage, *or*
  bok choy, cleaned and chopped into 1"
  strips
6 green onions, chopped

1. Bring water to boil in large stockpot.
2. Pinch off pieces of pork, about the size of a quarter, form into balls, and drop into boiling water.
3. Boil 5 minutes. Skim foam off top. (Foam will come to surface as meat cooks.) Throw away foam. (This process also removes fat.)
4. Stir fish sauce and sugar into boiling broth. You can use more or less fish sauce, depending upon your taste preferences.
5. Add cabbage, or bok choy, and green onions.
6. Cover stockpot. Turn off burner. Let stand 15 minutes.
7. Serve over brown rice (not included in analyses).

Pyramid Servings

Vegetables
●○○○○➤

Fruits
○○○○○➤

Carbohydrates
○○○○○○○○

Protein & Dairy
◐○○○○○○

Fats
○○○○○

Per Serving

Calories 80, Kilojoules 335, Protein 7 g,
Carbohydrates 2 g, Total Fat 5 g, Saturated Fat 2 g,
Monounsaturated Fat 2 g, Polyunsaturated Fat 1 g,
Cholesterol 18 mg, Sodium 419 mg, Fiber 1 g

* **Nutrition Note:** *Ask your butcher to grind pork loin for you. The meat is very lean. It should be ground to about the consistency of hamburger.*

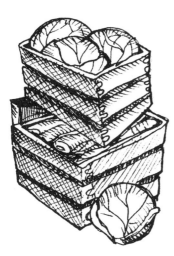

Maryland Crab Soup
Jan Rankin
Millersville, PA

Makes 8 servings

Prep. Time: 15–20 minutes
Cooking Time: 1 hour and
*   15 minutes*

Pyramid Servings

Vegetables ●○○○○➤
Fruits ○○○○○➤
Carbohydrates ●○○○○○○○
Protein & Dairy ◑○○○○○○
Fats ○○○○○

3 ribs celery, diced
2 carrots, diced
2 cups chopped onions
2 cups diced potatoes
4 cups fat-free low-sodium
   beef broth
20-oz. can tomatoes, undrained, no salt
   added
1 tsp. dried thyme
1 tsp. pepper
1 lb. lump crabmeat
4 Tbsp. whole wheat pastry flour
½ cup cold water

1. In large saucepan, combine celery, carrots, onions, potatoes, beef broth, tomatoes, thyme, and pepper. Cover and cook over low heat 1 hour. Stir occasionally.
2. Stir in crabmeat.
3. Mix flour and water in jar with tight-fitting lid. Shake until smooth.
4. Stir into soup, stirring constantly. Cook over low heat 5 minutes, or until thickened and bubbly.

Per Serving

Calories 134, Kilojoules 561, Protein 13 g,
Carbohydrates 18 g, Total Fat 1 g, Saturated Fat 0.3 g,
Monounsaturated Fat 0.3 g, Polyunsaturated Fat 0.4 g,
Cholesterol 34 mg, Sodium 417 mg, Fiber 3 g

A Tip —

Get all your ingredients together before starting a recipe. Place them on the left side of your work area. Move them to the right side as you finish with them.

Salmon Chowder

Millie Martin
Mount Joy, PA
Betty K. Drescher
Quakertown, PA

Makes 6 servings

Prep. Time: 15–20 minutes
Cooking Time: 35 minutes

Pyramid Servings	
Vegetables	●○○○○➤
Fruits	○○○○○➤
Carbohydrates	●○○○○○○○
Protein & Dairy	●○○○○○○
Fats	●○○○○

3 diced potatoes
2 Tbsp. minced onion
2 Tbsp. diced celery
1 lb. can salmon, no salt added
½ cup corn
1 tsp. sage
1 tsp. dried basil
pepper to taste
1 quart skim milk
2 Tbsp. chopped fresh parsley
lemon zest, *optional*, **not included in analyses**

1. In stockpot, cook potatoes, onions, and celery in small amount of water until tender.
2. Empty salmon into bowl. Remove bones and skin from salmon. Pull fish apart into pieces.
3. Add salmon, corn, seasonings, and milk to vegetables in stockpot.
4. Cover. Heat slowly until very hot.
5. Top with chopped parsley, and lemon zest if you wish.

Per Serving

Calories 248, Kilojoules 1038, Protein 23 g, Carbohydrates 28 g, Total Fat 5 g, Saturated Fat 1.2 g, Monounsaturated Fat 2 g, Polyunsaturated Fat 1.8 g, Cholesterol 45 mg, Sodium 135 mg, Fiber 3 g

Clam and Tortellini Soup

Mary Seielstad
Sparks, NV

Makes 8 servings

Prep. Time: 10 minutes
Cooking Time: 20–25 minutes

Pyramid Servings	
Vegetables	●○○○○➤
Fruits	○○○○○➤
Carbohydrates	●○○○○○○○
Protein & Dairy	●○○○○○○
Fats	○○○○○

1 tsp. olive oil
1 tsp. minced garlic
1 rib celery, sliced
1 medium carrot, sliced thin
28-oz. can diced Italian-style tomatoes, no salt added, undrained
14-oz. can reduced sodium chicken broth
9-oz. pkg. cheese tortellini
10-oz. can baby whole clams, undrained
1½ tsp. dried basil
dash of black pepper

1. In stockpot, sauté oil, garlic, celery, and carrot until tender-crisp.
2. Add tomatoes, broth, and tortellini to stockpot.
3. Cover and bring to a boil. Reduce heat and simmer, partially covered, until tortellini is cooked, about 7–9 minutes.
4. Stir in undrained clams and basil. Cook 1 minute.
5. Top individual servings with pepper.

Per Serving

Calories 202, Kilojoules 845, Protein 16 g, Carbohydrates 26 g, Total Fat 4 g, Saturated Fat 2 g, Monounsaturated Fat 1 g, Polyunsaturated Fat 1 g, Cholesterol 39 mg, Sodium 353 mg, Fiber 2 g

Note: Soup may be garnished with a little shredded Parmesan cheese, if you wish (not included in analyses).

Breakfasts and Brunches

Berry Breakfast Parfait

Susan Tjon
Austin, TX

Makes 4 servings

Prep. Time: 15 minutes

2 cups fat-free vanilla yogurt,
    sweetened with low-calorie
    sweetener
¼ tsp. ground cinnamon
1 cup sliced strawberries
½ cup blueberries
½ cup raspberries
1 cup low-fat granola

Pyramid Servings

Vegetables
○○○○○➤

Fruits
●●○○○➤

Carbohydrates
◑○○○○○○○

Protein & Dairy
◑○○○○○○

Fats
○○○○○

1. Combine yogurt and cinnamon in small bowl.

2. Combine fruit in medium bowl.

3. For each parfait, layer ¼ cup fruit mixture, then 2 Tbsp. granola, followed by ¼ cup yogurt mixture in parfait glass (or whatever container you choose).

4. Repeat layers once more and top with a sprinkling of granola.

Per Serving

Calories 192, Kilojoules 803, Protein 7 g,
Carbohydrates 37 g, Total Fat 2.5 g, Saturated Fat 0.5 g,
Monounsaturated Fat 1.5 g, Polyunsaturated Fat 0.5 g,
Cholesterol 2 mg, Sodium 137 mg, Fiber 4 g

Tip: Use fresh fruit for these parfaits whenever you can.

Shirred Jumbo Eggs

Willard Roth
Elkhart, IN

Makes 4 servings

Prep. Time: 15 minutes
Baking Time: 10–15 minutes

Pyramid Servings	
Vegetables	○○○○○➤
Fruits	○○○○○➤
Carbohydrates	○○○○○○○○
Protein & Dairy	●○○○○○○
Fats	○○○○○

1 small onion, chopped
1 garlic clove, minced
water
4 jumbo eggs
freshly ground pepper
4 Tbsp. skim milk
4 Tbsp. fresh Parmesan, *or* Asiago cheese, grated

1. In a small skillet, sauté onion and garlic in a bit of water. Drain. Divide vegetables among four glass or stoneware baking cups.

2. Break an egg atop onion in each cup. Season with freshly ground pepper.

3. Add 1 tablespoon milk to each cup.

4. Top each with 1 tablespoon freshly grated cheese.

5. Place cups on baking sheet. Place in preheated 350° oven for 10–15 minutes (the longer the time in the oven, the harder the egg).

Per Serving

Calories 115, Kilojoules 481, Protein 9 g,
Carbohydrates 6 g, Total Fat 5 g, Saturated Fat 1.5 g,
Monounsaturated Fat 2.5 g, Polyunsaturated Fat 1 g,
Cholesterol 216 mg, Sodium 148 mg, Fiber 0.5 g

Note: "Shirred" means to bake an egg without its shell.

Dietitian's tip: According to the American Heart Association, people may consume three to four egg yolks a week and stay within cholesterol recommendations. This allows for occasional "sunny-side up" breakfasts. In recipes, in place of one whole egg you can substitute two egg whites or the specified amount of cholesterol-free egg substitute.

Huevos en Rabo de Mestiza

Marlene Fonken, Upland, CA

Makes 1 serving

Prep Time: 3 minutes
Cooking Time: 5–7 minutes

Pyramid Servings	
Vegetables	●●○○○➤
Fruits	○○○○○➤
Carbohydrates	○○○○○○○○
Protein & Dairy	●○○○○○○
Fats	●○○○○

1 cup Tomato/Chili Poaching Sauce (see recipe on page 254)
1 egg
1 oz. low-fat Jack, *or* cheddar, cheese, shredded

1. Heat sauce in a small saucepan.
2. Break egg in middle of heated sauce.
3. Top with cheese.
4. Cover and cook approximately 3–5 minutes, or until egg is set and cheese is melted.

Per Serving

Calories 190, Kilojoules 795, Protein 15 g,
Carbohydrates 10 g, Total Fat 10 g, Saturated Fat 3 g,
Monounsaturated Fat 5 g, Polyunsaturated Fat 2 g,
Cholesterol 210 mg, Sodium 393 mg, Fiber 3 g

Turkey Sausage

Becky Frey, Lebanon, PA

Makes 6 servings

Prep. Time: 10 minutes
Broiling Time: 10–15 minutes

Pyramid Servings	
Vegetables	○○○○○➤
Fruits	○○○○○➤
Carbohydrates	○○○○○○○○
Protein & Dairy	●○○○○○○
Fats	○○○○○

¾ lb. extra-lean skinless turkey, ground
¼ tsp. pepper
¼ tsp. dried basil
¼ tsp. dried sage

¼ tsp. dried oregano
1 egg white
⅛ tsp. allspice
⅛ tsp. nutmeg
⅛ tsp. garlic powder
⅛ tsp. chili powder
⅛ tsp. Tabasco sauce, *optional*
2 Tbsp. water

1. Mix all ingredients together in a large bowl.
2. Shape into 6 patties. Place on baking sheet.
3. Broil 2–3" from heat 5–7 minutes.
4. Flip burgers over. Broil 5–7 more minutes.

Per Serving

Calories 64, Kilojoules 268, Protein 14 g,
Carbohydrates *trace*, Total Fat 1 g, Saturated Fat 0.2 g,
Monounsaturated Fat 0.7 g, Polyunsaturated Fat 0.1 g,
Cholesterol 22 mg, Sodium 50 mg, Fiber *trace*

Tips:

1. This turkey sausage can be shaped into meatballs and used with spaghetti or another favorite sauce.

2. I often brown this sausage and use it in any casserole in which I want a sausage flavor, but without the extra fat or salt of commercially made sausage.

Spinach Mushroom Frittata

JB Miller, Indianapolis, IN

Makes 6 servings

Prep. Time: 20 minutes
Cooking/Baking Time: 25–30 minutes

3 cloves garlic, minced
1 cup onion, chopped
1 tsp. olive oil
½ lb. fresh mushrooms, sliced
½ tsp. dried thyme

Pyramid Servings

Vegetables	●○○○○▶
Fruits	○○○○○▶
Carbohydrates	○○○○○○○
Protein & Dairy	●○○○○○○
Fats	○○○○○

10-oz. bag fresh spinach
egg substitute equivalent to 10 eggs
1 tsp. dried dill, *or* 1 Tbsp. fresh dill
¼ tsp. black pepper
¼ cup feta cheese

1. Preheat oven to 350°.
2. In a large 10" or 12" non-stick skillet, sauté garlic and onions in 1 teaspoon olive oil for about 5 minutes.
3. Add mushrooms and thyme. Cook an additional 5 minutes. Remove skillet from stove.
4. Place spinach in a separate saucepan. Add 1 Tbsp. water. Cover and cook until just wilted.
5. Drain spinach and let cool in a colander.
6. Squeeze out any liquid. Chop leaves.
7. In a good-sized bowl, beat together egg substitute, dill, and pepper.
8. Stir in spinach, mushroom mixture, and feta cheese.
9. Clean non-stick skillet. Spray liberally with vegetable spray. Return skillet to stove over medium heat.
10. When skillet is hot, pour in egg mixture. Place in oven, uncovered.
11. Check frittata in 10 minutes. Check every 5 minutes thereafter until center of frittata is slightly firm. Do not over-cook.
12. When frittata is done, place a large serving platter over skillet. Flip skillet over so frittata falls onto the plate.
13. Cut into six servings and serve.

Per Serving

Calories 117, Kilojoules 490, Protein 12 g,
Carbohydrates 9 g, Total Fat 3 g, Saturated Fat 1 g,
Monounsaturated Fat 1.3 g, Polyunsaturated Fat 0.7 g,
Cholesterol 5 mg, Sodium 300 mg, Fiber 3 g

Tips:

1. If the pan is not prepared properly with vegetable spray, the frittata will stick to the bottom.

2. Flipping the frittata onto the serving plate is best done with two people!

Dietitian's tip: *This breakfast bake uses egg substitutes instead of whole eggs, which cuts the amount of fat, calories, and cholesterol.*

European Breakfast Muesli

Willard Roth
Elkhart, IN

Makes 5 servings; approximately
⅔ cup/serving

Prep. Time: 10 minutes
Chilling Time: 2–8 hours

1 cup whole grain quick oats,
    uncooked
6 ozs. fat-free vanilla yogurt,
    sweetened with low-calorie
    sweetener
1 cup skim milk
¼ cup honey
⅓ cup ground flaxseed
½ cup dried cherries, *or* dried cranberries
1 cup fresh, *or* frozen, blueberries
5 tsp. sliced almonds

Pyramid Servings	
Vegetables	ooooo▸
Fruits	●●oooo▸
Carbohydrates	●ooooooo
Protein & Dairy	ooooooo
Fats	●oooo
Sweets	●

1. Combine all ingredients except blueberries and almonds in bowl. Stir well.
2. Cover and refrigerate at least two hours (overnight is preferable).
3. Serve as is, first dividing blueberries among the 5 servings. Then top each serving with 1 tsp. sliced almonds.

Per Serving

Calories 293, Kilojoules 1226, Protein 8 g,
Carbohydrates 55 g, Total Fat 5 g, Saturated Fat 0.5 g,
Monounsaturated Fat 1.5 g, Polyunsaturated Fat 3 g,
Cholesterol 1 mg, Sodium 51 mg, Fiber 7 g

Tip: Leftover portion may be refrigerated for several days.

A Tip —
Try out a recipe you've never had before. It is fun to see the family react to it.

Swiss Oatmeal

Jean Shoner
York, PA

Makes 4 servings

Prep. Time: 10 minutes
Standing Time: 5–10 minutes

1 cup rolled oats, uncooked
8 ozs. non-fat plain yogurt
¼ cup skim milk
2 tsp. sugar
1 small Granny Smith apple,
    unpeeled and chopped into
    bite-sized pieces
1 small banana, sliced into bite-sized
    pieces
2 Tbsp. raisins
2 Tbsp. dried currants
2 Tbsp. dried cherries

Pyramid Servings	
Vegetables	ooooo▸
Fruits	●●oooo▸
Carbohydrates	●ooooooo
Protein & Dairy	ooooooo
Fats	ooooo

1. Mix oats, yogurt, milk, and sugar in a good-sized bowl. Allow to stand 5–10 minutes.
2. Stir in all the fruit and enjoy.

Per Serving

Calories 212, Kilojoules 887, Protein 7 g,
Carbohydrates 42 g, Total Fat 2 g, Saturated Fat 0.3 g,
Monounsaturated Fat 0.5 g, Polyunsaturated Fat 1.2 g,
Cholesterol 1.5 mg, Sodium 58 mg, Fiber 4 g

Tip: Change the varieties of fresh fruit to suit the season.

Baked Oatmeal

Lovina Baer
Conrath, WI
Edwina Stoltzfus
Narvon, PA

Makes 8 servings

Prep. Time: 10 minutes
Baking Time: 30 minutes

1 Tbsp. canola oil
½ cup unsweetened
    applesauce
⅓ cup brown sugar
egg substitute equivalent to
    2 eggs, *or* 4 egg whites
3 cups uncooked rolled oats
2 tsp. baking powder
1 tsp. cinnamon
1 cup skim milk

Pyramid Servings	
Vegetables	○○○○○➤
Fruits	●○○○○➤
Carbohydrates	●○○○○○○○
Protein & Dairy	○○○○○○○
Fats	●○○○○
Sweets	◑

1. In a good-sized bowl, stir together oil, applesauce, sugar, and eggs.
2. Add dry ingredients and milk. Mix well.
3. Spray 9 × 13 baking pan generously with nonstick cooking spray. Spoon oatmeal mixture into pan.
4. Bake uncovered at 350° for 30 minutes.

Per Serving

Calories 204, Kilojoules 854, Protein 8g,
Carbohydrates 34g, Total Fat 4g, Saturated Fat 0.7g,
Monounsaturated Fat 1.9g, Polyunsaturated Fat 1.4g,
Cholesterol 0.5mg, Sodium 105mg, Fiber 4g

Tip: You can mixed this in the evening and refrigerate it overnight. Just pop it in the oven first thing when you get up.

Breakfast Barley

Deborah Heatwole
Waynesboro, GA

Makes 6 servings

Prep. Time: 5–10 minutes
Cooking Time: 30 minutes
Standing Time: 5–10 minutes

1½ cups uncooked pearl
    barley
3 cups water
1 tsp. canola oil
⅓ cup chopped walnuts, *or*
    pecans
½ cup raisins
½ tsp. salt
brown sugar, *optional*, not included in
    analyses
skim milk, *optional*, not included in
    analyses

Pyramid Servings	
Vegetables	○○○○○➤
Fruits	●○○○○➤
Carbohydrates	●●○○○○○○
Protein & Dairy	○○○○○○○
Fats	●○○○○

1. Toast barley in dry heavy saucepan over medium heat about 5 minutes. Stir continually.
2. Carefully pour in 3 cups water, being careful not to steam yourself.
3. Reduce heat to a bare simmer. Cover and cook 20 minutes.
4. Meanwhile, lightly toast nuts in oil in another skillet or saucepan. Stir continually.
5. When barley finishes cooking, mix nuts, raisins, and salt into it, stirring well.
6. Cover and cook 5 minutes more.
7. Remove lid. Cover pan with a folded towel and then put lid back on.
8. Remove from heat. Let stand 5–10 minutes.
9. Serve with brown sugar and milk if you wish.

Per Serving

Calories 257, Kilojoules 1075, Protein 5g,
Carbohydrates 49g, Total Fat 5g, Saturated Fat 0.4g,
Monounsaturated Fat 1.5g, Polyunsaturated Fat 3.1g,
Cholesterol 0mg, Sodium 200mg, Fiber 9g

Berry-Topped Wheat Germ Pancakes

Anne Nolt
Thompsontown, PA

Makes 6 servings

Prep. Time: 10 minutes
Cooking Time: 15–20 minutes

1 cup whole wheat pastry
    flour
½ cup wheat germ
1 Tbsp. sugar
2 tsp. baking powder
¼ tsp. baking soda
¾ cup orange juice
¾ cup fat-free plain yogurt
2 Tbsp. canola oil
egg substitute equivalent to 1 large egg, *or*
    2 egg whites
2 cups blueberries

Pyramid Servings

Vegetables
○○○○○➤

Fruits
●○○○○➤

Carbohydrates
●●○○○○○○

Protein & Dairy
○○○○○○○

Fats
○○○○○

Sweets
◑

1. In medium bowl, combine dry ingredients. Mix well.
2. In small bowl, combine orange juice, yogurt, oil, and egg. Blend well.
3. Add liquid ingredients to dry ingredients.
4. Add 2 cups blueberries.
5. Stir everything together gently, just until dry ingredients are moistened.
6. Pour batter by ¼ cupfuls onto hot, lightly greased griddle or into large skillet.
7. Turn when bubbles form on top.
8. Cook until second side is golden brown.
9. Serve with Blueberry Sauce.

Blueberry Sauce

¼ cup sugar
2 Tbsp. cornstarch
1 cup water
4 cups blueberries

1. In medium saucepan combine sugar and cornstarch. Gradually stir in water.
2. Add blueberries.
3. Bring to a boil over medium heat.
4. Boil 2 minutes, stirring constantly.
5. Remove from heat. Serve with pancakes.

Per Serving

Calories 300, Kilojoules 1255, Protein 8 g,
Carbohydrates 58 g, Total Fat 5 g, Saturated Fat 0.5 g,
Monounsaturated Fat 3 g, Polyunsaturated Fat 1.5 g,
Cholesterol 0 mg, Sodium 175 mg, Fiber 7 g

Pumpkin and Ginger Pancakes

Christie Detamore-Hunsberger
Harrisonburg, VA

Makes 12 pancakes, 2 pancakes per
    serving

Prep. Time: 10 minutes
Cooking Time: 15–20 minutes

1 cup whole wheat pastry flour
1 tsp. baking powder
½ tsp. baking soda
½ tsp. cinnamon
½ tsp. ground ginger
½ tsp. nutmeg
¾ cup pumpkin
¾ cup skim milk
½ cup plain non-fat yogurt
2 Tbsp. oil
1 large egg, beaten

Pyramid Servings

Vegetables
○○○○○➤

Fruits
○○○○○➤

Carbohydrates
●●○○○○○○

Protein & Dairy
○○○○○○○

Fats
○○○○○

1. In a mixing bowl, combine 6 dry ingredients.
2. Stir in 5 wet ingredients.
3. When well combined, drop by ¼ cupfuls onto griddle or into skillet.
4. Cook until bubbles form on top.
5. Flip. Cook until second side is golden brown.

Per Serving

Calories 146, Kilojoules 611, Protein 6 g,
Carbohydrates 20 g, Total Fat 5 g, Saturated Fat 0.5 g,
Monounsaturated Fat 3 g, Polyunsaturated Fat 1.5 g,
Cholesterol 1 mg, Sodium 195 mg, Fiber 4 g

Tip: These pancakes turn into a party if you serve them with ginger butter (please note that the butter ingredients are not included in the recipe's nutritional analyses): ¼ cup (half a stick) softened butter, 1 tsp. candied or fresh ginger, 1 lb. powdered sugar. Stir together in a large bowl until smooth. (Add more ground ginger to the pancake batter itself for a more intense taste.)

Multigrain Pancakes

Deborah Heatwole, Waynesboro, GA

Makes 6 servings

Prep. Time: 5–10 minutes
Cooking Time: 10–15 minutes

1 cup whole wheat pastry flour
½ cup all-purpose flour
¼ cup cornmeal
¼ cup buckwheat flour
2 tsp. baking powder
¼ tsp. baking soda
egg substitute equivalent to 2 eggs, *or* 4 egg
    whites
1 Tbsp. canola oil
2 cups skim milk

Pyramid Servings

Vegetables ○○○○○➤
Fruits ○○○○○➤
Carbohydrates ●●○○○○○○
Protein & Dairy ○○○○○○○
Fats ●○○○○

1. In a good-sized bowl, mix together dry ingredients thoroughly.

2. Add egg substitute or whites, oil, and milk. Stir well to combine.

3. Cook by ¼ cupfuls on a non-stick or cast iron skillet sprayed with non-stick cooking spray.

4. When bubbles begin to form on pancakes, flip and brown other side.

5. Serve with maple syrup, honey, or your choice of toppings (not included in analyses).

Per Serving

Calories 195, Kilojoules 816, Protein 9 g,
Carbohydrates 34 g, Total Fat 3 g, Saturated Fat 0.2 g,
Monounsaturated Fat 1.5 g, Polyunsaturated Fat 1.3 g,
Cholesterol 1.6 mg, Sodium 200 mg, Fiber 3 g

Oatmeal Waffles

Deborah Heatwole, Waynesboro, GA

Makes 6 servings

Prep. Time: 5–10 minutes
Cooking Time: 3–5 minutes

1 cup whole wheat pastry flour
⅔ cup uncooked rolled, *or*
    quick, oats
⅓ cup cornmeal
2 tsp. baking powder
¼ tsp. baking soda
2 cups skim milk
1 Tbsp. canola oil
egg substitute equivalent to 2 eggs, *or* 4 egg
    whites, beaten

Pyramid Servings

Vegetables ○○○○○➤
Fruits ○○○○○➤
Carbohydrates ●●○○○○○○
Protein & Dairy ○○○○○○○
Fats ●○○○○

1. Combine dry ingredients in mixing bowl.

2. Stir in milk, oil, and beaten egg substitute or whites.

3. When batter is well blended, cook in waffle iron according to appliance instructions.

4. If you wish, serve with maple syrup, honey, or blueberry preserves (not included in analyses).

Per Serving

Calories 192, Kilojoules 803, Protein 9 g,
Carbohydrates 33 g, Total Fat 3 g, Saturated Fat 0.3 g,
Monounsaturated Fat 1.7 g, Polyunsaturated Fat 1 g,
Cholesterol 1.6 mg, Sodium 200 mg, Fiber 3 g

Baked Blueberry French Toast

Carol Eberly, Harrisonburg, VA

Makes 9 servings

Prep. Time: 15 minutes
Chilling Time: 8 hours, or overnight
Cooking Time: 20 minutes

Pyramid Servings	
Vegetables ○○○○○▸	
Fruits ❶○○○○▸	
Carbohydrates ●○○○○○○○	
Protein & Dairy ❶○○○○○○	
Fats ○○○○○	

12" long French, *or*
  sourdough, baguette
4 egg whites
1 cup fat-free soy milk
¼ tsp. nutmeg
1 tsp. vanilla
4 Tbsp. brown sugar, *divided*
¾ cup blueberries, coarsely chopped
1 Tbsp. canola oil
¼ cup chopped pecans, toasted, *optional*
  (not included in analyses)

1. Spray 9" square baking dish with cooking spray.
2. Cut 10 1"-thick slices from baguette. Arrange in baking dish.
3. In a large bowl, whisk egg whites until frothy.
4. Then whisk in milk, nutmeg, vanilla, and 2 tablespoons brown sugar.
5. Pour evenly over bread, turning slices to coat evenly.
6. Cover pan. Chill at least 8 hours or overnight, until liquid is absorbed by bread.
7. Preheat oven to 400°.
8. Drop blueberries evenly over bread.
9. In a small bowl, stir together 2 tablespoons brown sugar and oil, and pecans if you wish. Spoon evenly over bread.
10. Bake, uncovered, about 20 minutes, until liquid from blueberries is bubbling. Serve with pure maple syrup (not included in analyses) if you wish.

Per Serving	
Calories 146, Kilojoules 611, Protein 5 g,	
Carbohydrates 25 g, Total Fat 3 g, Saturated Fat 0.5 g,	
Monounsaturated Fat 1.5 g, Polyunsaturated Fat 1 g,	
Cholesterol 0 mg, Sodium 259 mg, Fiber 1	

Wholesome Granola

Natalia Showalter, Mt. Solon, VA

Makes about 8 cups; ¼ cup per serving

Prep. Time: 10 minutes
Cooking Time: 45 minutes

Pyramid Servings	
Vegetables ○○○○○▸	
Fruits ○○○○○▸	
Carbohydrates ●○○○○○○○	
Protein & Dairy ○○○○○○○	
Fats ●○○○○	

4 cups uncooked rolled oats
⅔ cup oat bran
⅓ cup wheat germ
½ cup puffed whole wheat
  cereal
½ cup raw sunflower seeds
1 cup chopped pecans, *or* almonds
¼ cup flaxseed
⅓ cup brown sugar
½ tsp. cinnamon
½ cup honey, warmed
¼ cup canola oil
dried blueberries, *optional**
dried cranberries, *optional**
raisins, *optional**

1. Combine dry ingredients in large bowl.
2. In a separate bowl, stir together warm honey and oil.
3. Pour honey and oil over dry mixture. Stir until coated.
4. Spread on lightly greased baking sheet.
5. Bake, uncovered, at 275° for 45 minutes, stirring every 12 minutes.
6. Remove from oven and allow to cool. The granola will likely stick to pan as it cooks. Just use a turner to loosen from pan.
7. If you wish, stir dried fruit into granola.
8. Store in containers with tightly-fitting lids to keep fresh. Place in freezer if you anticipate not eating it all in a week or two.

Per Serving	
Calories 122, Kilojoules 510, Protein 3 g,	
Carbohydrates 17 g, Total Fat 5 g, Saturated Fat 0.6 g,	
Monounsaturated Fat 2.4 g, Polyunsaturated Fat 2 g,	
Cholesterol 0 mg, Sodium 1.5 mg, Fiber 2 g	

* Note: Optional ingredients are not included in the nutrient analyses.

Tip: If you wish to leave the nuts raw, add them to the granola after it has cooled.

Blueberry and Oatmeal Breakfast Cake

Jean Butzer
Batavia, NY

Peanut Butter Granola

Yvonne Kauffman Boettger, Harrisonburg, VA

Makes 16 cups; ¼ cup per serving

Prep. Time: 15 minutes
Cooking Time: 37–38 minutes

Pyramid Servings	
Vegetables	○○○○○▸
Fruits	○○○○○▸
Carbohydrates	●○○○○○○○
Protein & Dairy	○○○○○○○
Fats	●○○○○
Sweets	◐

1 cup honey
½ cup canola, *or* olive, oil
1 cup natural peanut butter, no salt added
½ tsp. salt
1 Tbsp. cinnamon
1 cup water
12 cups uncooked rolled oats
1 cup chopped pecans
1 cup cornmeal
1 cup ground flaxseed
1 cup wheat germ

1. Combine first 6 ingredients in microwave-safe bowl. Microwave on high 2–3 minutes.
2. Stir until peanut butter is melted.
3. Combine remaining ingredients in a large mixing bowl.
4. Add liquids and mix well.
5. Divide between two greased 9 × 13 baking pans.
6. Bake, uncovered, at 325° for 20 minutes.
7. Stir and bake, uncovered, another 15 minutes.
8. When completely cool, break up granola and store in containers with tight-fitting lids. Store in fridge or freezer.

Per Serving	
Calories 151, Kilojoules 632, Protein 4 g,	
Carbohydrates 22 g, Total Fat 5 g, Saturated Fat 1 g,	
Monounsaturated Fat 2.5 g, Polyunsaturated Fat 1.5 g,	
Cholesterol 0 mg, Sodium 20 mg, Fiber 3 g	

Makes 8 servings

Prep. Time: 15 minutes
Baking Time: 25 minutes

Pyramid Servings	
Vegetables	○○○○○▸
Fruits	●○○○○▸
Carbohydrates	●◐○○○○○○
Protein & Dairy	○○○○○○○
Fats	●○○○○

1½ cups whole wheat pastry flour
¾ cup uncooked rolled oats
⅓ cup sugar
2 tsp. baking powder
¼ tsp. cinnamon, *optional*
¾ cup skim milk
2 Tbsp. canola oil
2 Tbsp. mashed banana, *or* unsweetened applesauce
egg substitute equivalent to 1 egg, *or* 2 egg whites
1 cup blueberries, fresh *or* frozen

1. Preheat oven to 400°. Spray 8" round baking pan with cooking spray.
2. Combine flour, oats, sugar, baking powder, and cinnamon if you wish, in medium-sized mixing bowl.
3. In 2-cup measure, mix milk, oil, mashed banana or applesauce, and egg.
4. Add wet ingredients to flour mixture. Stir until just moistened.
5. Gently fold in blueberries.
6. Spoon into baking pan.
7. Bake, uncovered, 20–25 minutes, or until tester inserted in center of cake comes out clean.

Per Serving	
Calories 211, Kilojoules 883, Protein 9 g,	
Carbohydrates 33 g, Total Fat 5 g, Saturated Fat 0.5 g,	
Monounsaturated Fat 2.5 g, Polyunsaturated Fat 2 g,	
Cholesterol 1 mg, Sodium 125 mg, Fiber 4 g	

Banana-Oat Breakfast Cookies

Mary Ann Lefever
Lancaster, PA

Makes 12 cookies; 1 cookie/serving

Prep. Time: 15 minutes
Baking Time: 14–16 minutes, per baking sheet

1 large banana, mashed
  (about ½ cup)
½ cup chunky natural
  (unsalted and unsweetened)
  peanut butter, *or* regular
  chunky peanut butter
½ cup honey
1 tsp. vanilla
1 cup uncooked rolled oats
½ cup whole wheat pastry flour
¼ cup nonfat dry milk powder
2 tsp. ground cinnamon
¼ tsp. baking soda
1 cup dried cranberries, *or* raisins

Pyramid Servings

Vegetables	○○○○○➤
Fruits	●○○○○➤
Carbohydrates	●○○○○○○○
Protein & Dairy	○○○○○○○
Fats	●○○○○
Sweets	◐

1. Preheat oven to 350°. Lightly coat two baking sheets with non-stick cooking spray. Set aside.

2. In large bowl, stir together banana, peanut butter, honey, and vanilla.

3. In a small bowl, combine oats, flour, milk powder, cinnamon, and baking soda.

4. Stir oat mixture into banana mixture until combined.

5. Stir in dried cranberries.

6. Using a ¼-cup measure, drop dough into mounds 3" apart on prepared baking sheets.

7. With a thick spatula dipped in water, flatten and spread each dough mound into a 2¾"-round, about ½" thick.

8. Bake, one sheet at a time, 14–16 minutes, or until cookies are lightly browned.

9. Transfer cookies to wire racks to cool completely.

10. Store in airtight container or re-sealable plastic bag for up to three days, or freeze for up to two months. Thaw before serving.

Per Serving

Calories 203, Kilojoules 849, Protein 5 g,
Carbohydrates 35 g, Total Fat 5 g, Saturated Fat 1 g,
Monounsaturated Fat 2.5 g, Polyunsaturated Fat 1.5 g,
Cholesterol 0.3 mg, Sodium 92 mg, Fiber 3 g

Dietitian's tip: Scaling a recipe—changing the number of servings—isn't as simple as it sounds. Some recipes, such as casseroles, soups, and stews, usually lend themselves to simply increasing or decreasing the main ingredients (adjust seasonings to taste). Other recipes don't. For example, baked goods may not turn out well if doubled or tripled. If you're increasing a recipe and lack time to experiment, make several individual batches. This way you end up with the amount you need based on the original recipe.

A Tip —

  I always keep 1-cup measuring cups in my flour canister. That way I can reach in and measure what I need from that one cup.

Breads

Apple Cranberry Muffins
Judy Buller, Bluffton, OH

Makes 12 servings

Prep. Time: 20 minutes
Baking Time: 15 minutes

1⅓ cups whole wheat pastry flour
⅓ cup brown sugar
2 tsp. baking powder
½ tsp. baking soda
½ tsp. cinnamon
⅛ tsp. nutmeg
pinch of cloves
egg substitute equivalent to 2 eggs, *or* 4 egg whites
¼ cup canola oil
1 cup fat-free sour cream
1 large Granny Smith apple, peeled and shredded
½ cup fresh, *or* frozen, cranberries cut in half
½ cup chopped walnuts, *optional*, not included in analyses

Pyramid Servings

Vegetables	○○○○○▷
Fruits	○○○○○▷
Carbohydrates	●○○○○○○○
Protein & Dairy	○○○○○○○
Fats	●○○○○

1. Heat oven to 400°. Spray nonstick canola spray on bottom of 12 muffin cups.
2. In large bowl, whisk together flour, sugar, baking powder, baking soda, cinnamon, nutmeg, and cloves.
3. In medium bowl, whisk together egg substitute, oil, and sour cream until blended.
4. Stir apples and cranberries, and walnuts if you wish, into wet ingredients. Mix well.
5. Add wet mixture to dry mixture, stirring just until blended.
6. Divide batter among muffin cups.
7. Bake 15 minutes, or until toothpick inserted in centers of muffins comes out clean.
8. Cool 5–10 minutes before serving.

Per Serving
Calories 126, Kilojoules 527, Protein 3 g,
Carbohydrates 19 g, Total Fat 4.5 g, Saturated Fat 0.4 g,
Monounsaturated Fat 3 g, Polyunsaturated Fat 1.1 g,
Cholesterol 2 mg, Sodium 143 mg, Fiber 2 g

Apple Raisin Bran Muffins

Virginia Graybill
Hershey, PA

Makes 18 muffins

Prep. Time: 15 minutes
Standing time: 10 minutes
Baking Time: 18 minutes

1½ cups dry raisin bran
    cereal
¾ cup skim milk
¼ cup corn oil
egg substitute equivalent to
    2 eggs, beaten
1 tsp. vanilla
½ cup honey
1½ cups chopped unpeeled apples
⅓ cup chopped walnuts
2½ cups whole wheat flour
2½ tsp. baking powder
½ tsp. baking soda
1 tsp. cinnamon

Pyramid Servings

Vegetables	○○○○○➤
Fruits	◑○○○○➤
Carbohydrates	●○○○○○○○
Protein & Dairy	○○○○○○○
Fats	●○○○○

1. In a large bowl, combine dry cereal, milk, oil, egg substitute, vanilla, and honey. Let stand 10 minutes.
2. Stir in apples and nuts.
3. In a separate bowl, combine flour, baking powder, baking soda, and cinnamon.
4. Add dry ingredients to first mixture. Stir just until moistened.
5. Divide batter evenly among 18 lightly greased muffin cups.
6. Bake at 350° for approximately 18 minutes, or until tester inserted in centers of muffins comes out clean.

Per Serving

Calories 158, Kilojoules 661, Protein 4g,
Carbohydrates 25g, Total Fat 5g, Saturated Fat 1g,
Monounsaturated Fat 2g, Polyunsaturated Fat 2g,
Cholesterol *trace*, Sodium 115mg, Fiber 3g

Dietitian's tip: You can reduce salt by one-half in many recipes for baked goods that don't require yeast—or even eliminate it. For foods that require yeast, don't reduce the amount of salt, which is necessary for leavening. Without salt, the foods may become dense and flat. For most main dishes, salads, soups, and other foods, however, you can reduce the salt by one-half or omit it completely.

Orange Bran Flax Muffins

Alice Rush
Quakertown, PA

Makes 24 servings

Prep. Time: 15–20 minutes
Baking Time: 18–20 minutes

1½ cups dry oat bran
1 cup all-purpose flour
¾ cup ground flaxseed
1 cup wheat bran
1 Tbsp. baking powder
½ tsp. salt
2 oranges, peeled and sectioned to remove
    membranes and seeds
1 cup brown sugar
1 cup low-fat buttermilk
⅓ cup canola oil
egg substitute equivalent to 2 eggs, *or* 4 egg
    whites
1 tsp. baking soda
1½ cups raisins

Pyramid Servings

Vegetables	○○○○○➤
Fruits	◑○○○○➤
Carbohydrates	●○○○○○○○
Protein & Dairy	○○○○○○○
Fats	◑○○○○

1. Preheat oven to 375°. Line two 12-cup muffin pans with paper liners, or coat cups lightly with cooking spray.
2. In a large bowl, combine oat bran, flour, flaxseed, wheat bran, baking powder, and salt. Set aside.

3. In blender or food processor, combine orange sections, brown sugar, buttermilk, oil, egg substitute, and baking soda. Blend well.

4. Pour orange mixture into dry ingredients. Mix until well blended.

5. Stir in raisins.

6. Divide batter evenly among muffin cups.

7. Bake 18–20 minutes, or until toothpick inserted in centers comes out clean.

8. Cool in pans 5 minutes and then remove muffins to cooling rack.

Per Serving

Calories 142, Kilojoules 594, Protein 4 g,
Carbohydrates 22 g, Total Fat 5 g, Saturated Fat 0.5 g,
Monounsaturated Fat 2.5 g, Polyunsaturated Fat 2 g,
Cholesterol 0.5 mg, Sodium 155 mg, Fiber 3.5 g

2. Stir in flour, baking soda, and salt.

3. In a separate bowl, mash bananas with egg whites, honey, and applesauce.

4. Add banana mixture to cereal mixture, stirring until just moistened.

5. Fold in raisins or cranberries.

6. Spoon batter into 12 muffin pans sprayed lightly with cooking spray.

7. Bake at 375° for 20 minutes, or until tester inserted in centers of muffins comes out clean.

8. Cool muffins in pan on wire rack for 3 minutes. Remove from pan.

Per Serving

Calories 120, Kilojoules 502, Protein 3 g,
Carbohydrates 27 g, Total Fat *trace*, Saturated Fat *trace*,
Monounsaturated Fat *trace*, Polyunsaturated Fat *trace*,
Cholesterol *trace*, Sodium 193 mg, Fiber 2 g

Tip: Over-ripe bananas can be peeled and frozen in a plastic container until you're ready to use them.

Banana Raisin Muffins

Jean Butzer
Batavia, NY

Makes 12 servings

Prep. Time: 10 minutes
Standing Time: 10 minutes
Baking Time: 20 minutes

1 cup dry bran cereal of your
   choice
¼ cup skim milk
1 cup all-purpose white flour
1 tsp. baking soda
¼ tsp. salt
2 very ripe bananas
3 egg whites
¼ cup honey
¼ cup unsweetened applesauce
¾ cup raisins, *or* dried cranberries

Pyramid Servings

Vegetables
○○○○○➤

Fruits
●○○○○➤

Carbohydrates
●○○○○○○○

Protein & Dairy
○○○○○○○

Fats
○○○○○

1. In a large mixing bowl, combine cereal with milk. Let stand 10 minutes to soften.

A Tip —

Measure carefully especially when baking. When you have mastered the basics don't be afraid to create.

Lemon Blueberry Muffins

Sally Holzem
Schofield, WI

Makes 18 servings

Prep. Time: 15 minutes
Baking Time: 26 minutes

Pyramid Servings

Vegetables
○○○○○➤

Fruits
❶○○○○➤

Carbohydrates
●○○○○○○○

Protein & Dairy
○○○○○○○

Fats
●○○○○

2½ cups all-purpose flour
¼ cup sugar
2 tsp. baking powder
½ tsp. baking soda
¼ tsp. salt
1½ cups low-fat buttermilk
⅓ cup olive oil
1 Tbsp. grated lemon rind
1 tsp. vanilla extract
egg substitute equivalent to 1 egg, *or* 2 egg
    whites, beaten
1½ cups frozen, unsweetened blueberries,
    thawed
2 Tbsp. sugar
1 Tbsp. lemon juice

1. Combine first 5 ingredients in a large bowl. Make a well in center of mixture.
2. In a separate bowl, combine buttermilk, oil, lemon rind, vanilla, and egg.
3. Add wet ingredients to well in flour mixture, stirring just until dry ingredients are moistened.
4. Fold in blueberries.
5. Spoon batter into muffin pans coated lightly with cooking spray, or lined with paper baking cups, filling ¾ full.
6. Bake muffins at 375° for 20 minutes, or until tester inserted in centers of muffins comes out clean.
7. In a small bowl, combine 2 Tbsp. sugar and lemon juice.
8. Brush hot muffins with lemon-sugar mixture.
9. Bake an additional 6 minutes, or until golden brown.

Per Serving

Calories 133, Kilojoules 556, Protein 3 g,
Carbohydrates 20 g, Total Fat 4 g, Saturated Fat 0.8 g,
Monounsaturated Fat 3 g, Polyunsaturated Fat 0.2 g,
Cholesterol 1 mg, Sodium 122 mg, Fiber 1 g

Good Go-Alongs: Theses are great served with Spiced Fruit Salad (page 111) for a late morning brunch.

Dietitian's tip: The colorful outermost layer of the lemon, called the zest, is full of essential oils that contribute lively flavor and aroma to this recipe. Remove the zest by grating it with the fine rasps of a hand-held grater to form fine particles.

Pineapple Carrot Muffins

Christie Detamore-Hunsberger
Harrisonburg, VA

Makes 12 servings

Prep. Time: 15 minutes
Baking Time: 15 minutes

Pyramid Servings

Vegetables
○○○○○➤

Fruits
●○○○○➤

Carbohydrates
●○○○○○○○

Protein & Dairy
○○○○○○○

Fats
○○○○○

1 cup fine, *or* coarse, dry
    oat bran
1 cup unbleached flour
2 tsp. baking powder
½ tsp. baking soda
1 tsp. cinnamon
1 cup low-fat buttermilk
⅓ cup honey
2 Tbsp. unsweetened applesauce
8-oz. can crushed pineapple, packed in
    water, drained
1 medium carrot, shredded
½ cup raisins

1. Mix first 5 dry ingredients together in a large bowl.

2. In a separate bowl, mix remaining ingredients.

3. Mix fruit mixture into dry ingredients until just combined.

4. Fill non-stick muffin tins ⅔ full.

5. Bake at 375° for 15 minutes, or until toothpick inserted in centers of muffins comes out clean.

Per Serving

Calories 129, Kilojoules 540, Protein 4 g, Carbohydrates 27 g, Total Fat 1 g, Saturated Fat 0.3 g, Monounsaturated Fat 0.4 g, Polyunsaturated Fat 0.3 g, Cholesterol 2 mg, Sodium 141 mg, Fiber 2 g

Whole Wheat Pumpkin Muffins

Sylvia Beiler, Lowville, NY

Makes 24 servings

Prep. Time: 15–20 minutes
Baking Time: 15 minutes

1 cup sugar
⅓ cup canola oil
egg substitute equivalent to 3 eggs, *or* 6 egg whites
1½ cups pumpkin
½ cup water
3 cups whole wheat pastry flour
1½ tsp. baking powder
1 tsp. baking soda
¾ tsp. ground cloves
1 tsp. ground cinnamon
1 tsp. ground nutmeg
1 cup raisins
½ cup chopped walnuts

Pyramid Servings

Vegetables
○○○○○➤

Fruits
○○○○○➤

Carbohydrates
●○○○○○○○

Protein & Dairy
○○○○○○○○

Fats
●○○○○

1. Preheat oven to 400°.

2. In a large mixer bowl combine sugar, oil, egg substitute, pumpkin, and water.

3. In a separate bowl, mix together flour, baking powder, soda, and spices.

4. Add dry ingredients to first mixture. Blend with electric mixer.

5. Stir in raisins and walnuts by hand.

6. Spoon mixture into 24 lightly greased muffin cups.

7. Bake 15 minutes, or until tester inserted in centers of muffins comes out clean.

Per Serving

Calories 145, Kilojoules 607, Protein 4 g, Carbohydrates 24 g, Total Fat 4 g, Saturated Fat 0.3 g, Monounsaturated Fat 2.2 g, Polyunsaturated Fat 1.5 g, Cholesterol 0 mg, Sodium 84 mg, Fiber 2.5 g

Tips:
1. Use half white flour if all whole wheat is too heavy for you.
2. These muffins freeze well for future use.

Dietitian's tip: All walnuts are high in phosphorus, zinc, copper, iron, potassium, and vitamin E and low in saturated fat. But English walnuts have twice as many omega-3 fatty acids as black walnuts do.

Raspberry Chocolate Scones

Vonnie Oyer, Hubbard, OR

Makes 12 servings

Prep. Time: 15 minutes
Baking Time: 10–12 minutes

Pyramid Servings	
Vegetables	○○○○○▸
Fruits	○○○○○▸
Carbohydrates	●○○○○○○○
Protein & Dairy	○○○○○○○○
Fats	●○○○○
Sweets	◐

1 cup whole wheat pastry
  flour
1 cup all-purpose flour
1 Tbsp. baking powder
¼ tsp. baking soda
⅓ cup trans-fat-free buttery
  spread
½ cup fresh, *or* frozen,
  raspberries
¼ cup miniature chocolate chips
1 cup, plus 2 Tbsp., plain non-fat yogurt
2 Tbsp. honey
½ tsp. sugar
¼ tsp. cinnamon

1. Mix flours, baking powder, and baking soda in a large mixing bowl.
2. Cut in buttery spread until crumbly.
3. Add berries and chocolate chips. Mix gently.
4. Mix yogurt and honey together in a small bowl.
5. Add yogurt mixture to flour mixture, mixing until just blended.
6. Place ball of dough on countertop. Knead one or two times.
7. Roll into a ½"-thick circle. Cut into 12 wedges. Place on lightly greased baking sheet.
8. Mix sugar and cinnamon together in small bowl.
9. Sprinkle over top of scones.
10. Bake at 400° for 10–12 minutes.

Per Serving

Calories 152, Kilojoules 636, Protein 4 g,
Carbohydrates 23 g, Total Fat 5 g, Saturated Fat 1.5 g,
Monounsaturated Fat 2.5 g, Polyunsaturated Fat 1 g,
Cholesterol *trace*, Sodium 165 mg, Fiber 2 g

Zucchini Bread with Cranberries

Renita Denlinger
Denver, PA

Makes 8 servings

Prep. Time: 20 minutes
Baking Time: 12–19 minutes

Pyramid Servings	
Vegetables	○○○○○▸
Fruits	◐○○○○▸
Carbohydrates	●○○○○○○○
Protein & Dairy	○○○○○○○○
Fats	●○○○○

½ cup sugar
½ cup shredded zucchini
⅓ cup skim milk
1 Tbsp. corn oil
egg substitute equivalent to 1
  egg, *or* 2 egg whites
1 cup whole wheat flour
2 tsp. baking powder
½ tsp. cinnamon
½ tsp. ground cloves
½ cup dried cranberries

1. Preheat oven to 400°.
2. In a large bowl, combine sugar, zucchini, milk, oil, and egg substitute. Mix well.
3. In a separate bowl, combine dry ingredients.
4. Add dry ingredients to zucchini mixture.
5. Fold in dried cranberries.
6. Spoon into bread pan that has been generously sprayed with non-stick cooking spray.
7. Bake at 400° for 12–19 minutes, or until tester inserted in center comes out clean.

Per Serving

Calories 148, Kilojoules 619, Protein 3 g,
Carbohydrates 30 g, Total Fat 2 g, Saturated Fat 0.4 g,
Monounsaturated Fat 0.6 g, Polyunsaturated Fat 1 g,
Cholesterol *trace*, Sodium 80 mg, Fiber 2 g

Dietitian's tip: Zucchini — a popular type of summer squash — has a mild flavor and cucumber-like appearance. Summer squash contains lutein, a phytochemical thought to protect vision. Shredded zucchini creates moist breads and cakes and is an ideal addition to soups, sauces, and casseroles.

Carrot 'n Spice Quick Bread

Sally Holzem
Schofield, WI

Makes 1 loaf; ½" slice per serving

Prep. Time: 20 minutes
Baking Time: 45 minutes

Pyramid Servings

Vegetables
○○○○○➤

Fruits
◐○○○○➤

Carbohydrates
◐○○○○○○○

Protein & Dairy
○○○○○○○

Fats
●○○○○

½ cup sifted all-purpose flour
1 cup whole wheat flour
2 tsp. baking powder
½ tsp. baking soda
½ tsp. ground cinnamon
¼ tsp. ground ginger
⅓ cup trans-fat-free buttery blend,
   softened to room temperature
¼ cup, plus 2 Tbsp., firmly packed brown
   sugar
⅓ cup skim milk
2 Tbsp. unsweetened orange juice
egg substitute equivalent to 1 egg, *or* 2 egg
   whites, beaten
1 tsp. vanilla extract
1 tsp. grated orange rind
1½ cups shredded carrots
2 Tbsp. golden raisins
1 Tbsp. finely chopped walnuts

1. Combine first 6 ingredients in a small
bowl. Set aside.

2. Using a mixer, or stirring vigorously by
hand, cream buttery blend in a good-sized
mixing bowl.

3. Gradually add sugar, beating well.

4. Beat in milk, orange juice, egg, vanilla,
and orange rind.

5. Stir in carrots, raisins, and walnuts.

6. Add reserved dry ingredients. Mix well.

7. Spoon batter into 2½ × 4½ × 8½ loaf pan
coated with cooking spray.

8. Bake at 375° for 45 minutes, or until
wooden pick inserted in center comes out clean.

9. Cool in pan 10 minutes. Remove from pan
and let cool completely on wire rack.

Per Serving

Calories 103, Kilojoules 431, Protein 2 g,
Carbohydrates 15 g, Total Fat 4 g, Saturated Fat 0.6 g,
Monounsaturated Fat 2 g, Polyunsaturated Fat 1.4 g,
Cholesterol *trace*, Sodium 129 mg, Fiber 1 g

Tip: *Slicing fruit breads is always easier after
chilling the loaf in the refrigerator overnight.*

Good Go-Alongs: *This bread is great with a
hearty beef soup such as Beef Mushroom Barley
Soup (page 182) for fall, or with a cup of tea for a
scrumptious morning snack.*

A Tip —

Read the whole recipe before beginning
to cook.

Sour Cream Corn Bread

Edwina Stoltzfus
Narvon, PA

Makes 9 servings

Prep. Time: 15 minutes
Baking Time: 15–20 minutes

egg substitute equivalent to 1
    egg, *or* 2 egg whites, beaten
¼ cup skim milk
2 Tbsp. canola oil
1 cup fat-free sour cream
¾ cup cornmeal
½ cup whole wheat flour
½ cup flour
¼ cup sugar
2 tsp. baking powder
½ tsp. baking soda

Pyramid Servings
Vegetables ooooo➤
Fruits ooooo➤
Carbohydrates ●●oooooo
Protein & Dairy ooooooo
Fats ●oooo

1. Place egg substitute in good-sized mixing bowl and beat.

2. Add milk, oil, and sour cream and combine well.

3. In a separate bowl, combine all dry ingredients.

4. Add dry ingredients to wet ones. Mix together just until moistened.

5. Spoon into 8" square baking pan, sprayed lightly with non-stick cooking spray.

6. Bake at 375° 15–20 minutes, or until tester inserted in center comes out clean.

Per Serving

Calories 170, Kilojoules 711, Protein 4 g,
Carbohydrates 26 g, Total Fat 5 g, Saturated Fat 2 g,
Monounsaturated Fat 2 g, Polyunsaturated Fat 1 g,
Cholesterol 8 mg, Sodium 185 mg, Fiber 2 g

Dietitian's tip: Stone-ground cornmeal—dried corn that has been ground into a grain—includes the nutritious bran and hull, making it a good source of nutrients, including fiber, vitamin C, and potassium.

Loaded Bread

Judi Robb
Manhattan, KS

Makes 1 loaf, ½"-thick slice per serving

Prep. Time: 20 minutes
Rising Time: 2½–3¼ hours
Baking Time: 40 minutes

3 Tbsp. oil
1 Tbsp. yeast
⅓ cup fructose*
1⅓ cups hot water
1⅔ cups whole wheat flour
2 cups unbleached flour
1 tsp. salt
2 Tbsp. ground flaxseed
⅓ cup cranberries
2 Tbsp. finely chopped pecans
2 Tbsp. finely chopped cashews
2 Tbsp. finely chopped almonds
2 Tbsp. finely chopped pumpkin seeds
2 Tbsp. finely chopped sunflower seeds

Pyramid Servings
Vegetables ooooo➤
Fruits ooooo➤
Carbohydrates ●●oooooo
Protein & Dairy ooooooo
Fats ●oooo

1. In a large bowl, mix together oil, yeast, fructose, and hot water. Let stand 10 minutes.

2. In a separate bowl, mix together remaining ingredients.

3. Add dry ingredients to yeast mixture. Mix well.

4. On a lightly floured surface, knead dough 5–8 minutes, or until smooth and elastic, adding more flour if needed.

5. Cover and set in a warm place. Let rise until double (1–1½ hours).

6. Punch down. Form into a loaf and place in a 2½ × 4½ × 8½ loaf pan that has been generously sprayed with non-stick cooking spray. Or make about 17 small rolls.

7. Cover and set in a warm place. Let rise until almost double in size.

8. Bake at 350° for 40 minutes, or until bread is golden brown and springs back when poked gently.

Per Serving

Calories 155, Kilojoules 649, Protein 4 g,
Carbohydrates 24 g, Total Fat 5 g, Saturated Fat 0.5 g,
Monounsaturated Fat 3 g, Polyunsaturated Fat 1.5 g,
Cholesterol *trace*, Sodium 139 mg, Fiber 3 g

* Note: The fructose in this recipe is crystalline fructose, available in many grocery stores and found with baking ingredients. It is made from fructose-enriched corn syrup that has been allowed to crystallize or dry.

Dietitian's tip: Scaling a recipe—changing the number of servings—isn't as simple as it sounds. Some recipes, such as casseroles, soups, and stews, usually lend themselves to simply increasing or decreasing the main ingredients (adjust seasonings to taste). Other recipes don't. For example, baked goods may not turn out well if doubled or tripled. If you're increasing a recipe and lack time to experiment, make several individual batches. This way you end up with the amount you need based on the original recipe.

A Tip —

Do not put your good knife in the dishwasher.

14-Grain Bread

Esther Hartzler, Carlsbad, NM

Makes 3 loaves, ½"-thick slice per serving

Prep. Time: 45 minutes
Rising Time: 2½– 3 hours
Baking Time: 35–40 minutes

Pyramid Servings

Vegetables
○○○○○➤
Fruits
○○○○○➤
Carbohydrates
●○○○○○○○○
Protein & Dairy
○○○○○○○
Fats
○○○○○

1 cup dry 9-grain cereal
½ cup unsalted sunflower seeds
2½ Tbsp. sesame seeds
2½ Tbsp. amaranth
1½ Tbsp. yeast
2 cups whole wheat flour, plus
3 cups warm water
2½ Tbsp. dry millet
2½ Tbsp. flaxseed
⅓ cup canola oil
⅓ cup honey
1 Tbsp. sea salt
¼ cup wheat gluten

1. Place all ingredients in bowl of a strong and sturdy mixer, with a mixer bowl at least 4½ quarts in size. Mix 10 minutes.
2. If needed, add more whole wheat flour until mixture cleans side of bowl.
3. Knead 12 minutes on low speed.
4. Form into 3 loaves. Place each in a 2½ × 4½ × 8½ loaf pan that has been generously sprayed with non-stick cooking spray.
5. Cover pans and place in warm spot. Let rise until double, about 2½–3 hours.
6. Bake at 350° 35–40 minutes.

Per Serving

Calories 58, Kilojoules 243, Protein 2 g,
Carbohydrates 8 g, Total Fat 2 g, Saturated Fat 0.2 g,
Monounsaturated Fat 1 g, Polyunsaturated Fat 0.8 g,
Cholesterol *trace*, Sodium 139 mg, Fiber 1 g

Tip: I like to measure the grains and combine them in a zip-loc bag, and then freeze them in advance of baking. Keep the whole wheat flour separate, however.

Wholesome Harvest Bread

Kathryn Good
Dayton, VA

*Makes 3 loaves, 17 slices/loaf, each
sliced ½" thick*

Prep. Time: 20–30 minutes
Rising Time: 4–5 hours
Baking Time: 30–35 minutes

½ cup cornmeal
½ cup honey
⅓ cup (5⅓ Tbsp.) butter, *or*
 olive oil
1 Tbsp. salt
2 cups boiling water
2 pkgs. yeast
½ cup warm water
1 tsp. sugar
egg substitute equivalent to 2 eggs, *or* 4 egg
 whites
1 cup rye flour
2 cups whole wheat flour
3 Tbsp. poppy seeds
1 cup sunflower seed kernels
4 cups unbleached bread flour

1. In a small bowl, combine cornmeal, honey, butter or olive oil, salt, and boiling water. Let stand until mixture cools to lukewarm.

2. Meanwhile, in a large mixing bowl combine yeast, warm water, and sugar. Stir until yeast and sugar dissolve.

3. Beat eggs into yeast mixture.

4. When cornmeal mixture is lukewarm, mix into yeast mixture.

5. Stir in rye flour, wheat flour, and seeds.

6. On a lightly floured surface, knead in bread flour until dough is smooth and elastic.

7. Return dough to bowl. Cover and place in a warm spot. Let rise until double, about 2½–3 hours.

8. Form into 3 loaves. Place each in a 2½ × 4½ × 8½ loaf pan that has been generously sprayed with cooking spray.

Pyramid Servings

Vegetables
○○○○○➤

Fruits
○○○○○➤

Carbohydrates
●◐○○○○○○

Protein & Dairy
○○○○○○○

Fats
○○○○○

9. Cover pans and place in a warm spot.

10. Let rise until almost double in size, about 1½–2 hours.

11. Bake at 350° for approximately 30 minutes, or until tops are golden.

Per Serving

Calories 101, Kilojoules 423, Protein 3 g,
Carbohydrates 17 g, Total Fat 3 g, Saturated Fat 0.5 g,
Monounsaturated Fat 1.5 g, Polyunsaturated Fat 1 g,
Cholesterol 0 mg, Sodium 142 mg, Fiber 1.5 g

The Best Honey Whole Wheat Bread

Pamela Metzler
Gilman, WI

*Makes 4 loaves of bread, 17 slices/loaf,
 each ½" thick*

Prep. Time: 20–30 minutes
Rising Time: 3–4 hours
Baking Time: 25 minutes

1 cup dry rolled oats
3 cups water
3 cups whole wheat flour
¾ cup soy flour
¾ cup ground flaxseed, *or* flaxseed meal
3 Tbsp. flaxseed
3 Tbsp. sesame seeds
3 Tbsp. poppy seeds
4½ Tbsp. yeast
1 Tbsp. sea salt
1 cup unsweetened applesauce
½ cup honey
¼ cup olive oil
about 5 cups unbleached white flour

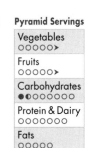

Pyramid Servings

Vegetables
○○○○○➤

Fruits
○○○○○➤

Carbohydrates
●◐○○○○○○

Protein & Dairy
○○○○○○○

Fats
○○○○○

1. In microwave-safe bowl, microwave oatmeal mixed with water to about 120–130°.

2. In mixer bowl of a heavy stand mixer with dough hook, combine whole wheat flour, soy flour, ground flaxseed or meal, seeds, yeast, and salt. Stir to mix.

3. Add applesauce, honey, and oil. Mix by hand.

4. Add hot water with oatmeal. Mix by hand.

5. When blended, start mixing with dough hook of mixer and continue for about 3 minutes.

6. Slowly add white flour until dough comes away from sides of bowl and becomes smooth and elastic.

7. Cover dough in bowl and place in a warm spot. Let rise until about double in size, about 1½–2 hours.

8. Punch dough down. Turn onto countertop. Divide evenly into 4 pieces.

9. Shape into 4 loaves. Place in 2½ × 4½ × 8½ loaf pans that have been generously sprayed with non-stick cooking spray.

10. Cover and place in a warm spot. Allow to rise until nearly double in size, about 1½–2 hours.

11. Bake at 350° for 25 minutes, or until tops of loaves are golden.

12. Remove from pans and cool on rack.

Per Serving

Calories 91, Kilojoules 381, Protein 3 g,
Carbohydrates 16 g, Total Fat 2 g, Saturated Fat 0.4 g,
Monounsaturated Fat 1 g, Polyunsaturated Fat 0.6 g,
Cholesterol 0 mg, Sodium 104 mg, Fiber 2 g

Tip: This is not a fast, easy recipe, but if you like to make a nutritious bread, this is for you. Making good bread takes practice, so keep trying. Be sure to knead it long enough. Like most baked goods, this bread is great right out of the oven.

Spelt Tortillas
Shari Ladd, Hudson, MI

Makes 10 servings

Prep. Time: 5–7 minutes
Chilling Time: 4–24 hours
Warming Time: 1–2 hours
Cooking Time: 40 seconds

Pyramid Servings

Vegetables ○○○○○➤
Fruits ○○○○○➤
Carbohydrates ●○○○○○○○○
Protein & Dairy ○○○○○○○
Fats ●○○○○

2 cups spelt flour
½ tsp. sea salt
3 Tbsp. canola oil
½ cup water

1. Mix all ingredients together in bowl.

2. Place dough on lightly floured countertop. Knead until smooth.

3. Return dough to bowl. Cover. Refrigerate 4–24 hours.

4. When ready to use, bring dough to room temperature.

5. Divide into 10 pieces. Roll each very thin on dry surface. (No need to use more flour.)

6. Heat skillet, preferably cast iron, until hot. Reduce to medium-high heat.

7. Place tortilla in hot skillet. Fry until bubbly, about 20 seconds.

8. Flip and fry other side, again about 20 seconds.

Per Serving

Calories 114, Kilojoules 477, Protein 2 g,
Carbohydrates 15 g, Total Fat 5 g, Saturated Fat 0.5 g,
Monounsaturated Fat 2.5 g, Polyunsaturated Fat 2 g,
Cholesterol 0 mg, Sodium 116 mg, Fiber 2.5 g

Tip: You can use whole wheat flour instead of spelt flour if you wish.

Dietitian's tip: Serve these tortillas with salsa. Salsa is very low in calories but can be high in sodium. If you're watching your sodium intake, use low-sodium salsa or garnish instead with pico de gallo — a relish made with chopped tomatoes, jalapeños, red onions, cilantro and green onions. See recipes for Fresh Salsa, Fresh Chunky Cherry Tomato Salsa, and Summer Salsa in this book.

Quick Pizza Dough

Becky Frey
Lebanon, PA

*Makes 2 10" pizza crusts (6 slices/
pizza; 1 slice/serving)*

Prep. Time: 10 minutes
Rising Time: 5 minutes
Baking Time: 20 minutes

1 Tbsp. yeast
1 cup warm water
1 Tbsp. sugar
½ tsp. salt
2 Tbsp. canola oil
1¼ cups all-purpose flour
1¼ cups whole wheat flour

Pyramid Servings		
Vegetables		
○○○○○➤		
Fruits		
○○○○○➤		
Carbohydrates		
●❶○○○○○○		
Protein & Dairy		
○○○○○○○		
Fats		
○○○○○		

1. In a good-sized bowl, dissolve yeast in
water.
2. Stir in sugar, salt, and oil.
3. Add enough of each flour to make a fairly
stiff dough.
4. Cover bowl and set in warm place. Let
dough rise 5 minutes.
5. Turn dough onto countertop. Knead until
smooth and elastic, using whatever you need
of remaining flour.
6. Spray 2 10" pizza pans with non-stick
cooking spray. Press dough onto pans, stretch-
ing as needed.
7. Spread with your favorite low-calorie
toppings.
8. Bake at 400–425° for about 20 minutes,
or until lightly browned.

Per Serving

Calories 112, Kilojoules 469, Protein 3 g,
Carbohydrates 20 g, Total Fat 2 g, Saturated Fat 0.2 g,
Monounsaturated Fat 1.7 g, Polyunsaturated Fat 0.1 g,
Cholesterol 0 mg, Sodium 99 mg, Fiber 2 g

Tip: We like to top our pizzas with caramelized
onions and sweet bell pepper. Slice 2 large onions
and chop a large red or green pepper. Put a
tablespoon or less olive oil in a large non-stick
skillet. Stir in onion and pepper. Cook on low
heat, covered, for 45–60 minutes. Stir occasionally. When onions are golden and as tender as you
like them, remove from heat and season with a bit
of balsamic vinegar. Spread over pizza crust.

Dietitian's tip: For a crispier pizza, bake on a
pizza stone — a heavy, round plate that simulates
the brick bottoms of some commercial pizza
ovens. For best results, put the pizza stone on the
lowest oven shelf.

Desserts

Tasty Tofu Brownie Snacks

Mary Ann Lefever
Lancaster, PA

Makes 9 servings

Prep. Time: 10–15 minutes
Baking Time: 22 minutes
Cooling Time: 15 minutes

1⅓ cups whole wheat pastry
   flour
½ tsp. baking soda
½ tsp. cinnamon
⅓ cup European-processed
   cocoa powder, unsweetened
¼ cup unsweetened applesauce
1 tsp. canola oil
½ cup honey
1 pkg. Mori-Nu Silken Lite Firm Tofu,
   drained
1 tsp. vanilla extract
2 Tbsp. chopped walnuts, *optional*, not
   included in analyses

Pyramid Servings

Vegetables	○○○○○▸
Fruits	○○○○○▸
Carbohydrates	●○○○○○○○
Protein & Dairy	◑○○○○○○
Fats	○○○○○

1. Preheat oven to 350°.
2. Cut piece of waxed paper to fit in bottom of 8 × 8 baking pan. With paper removed, spray bottom and sides of pan with non-stick cooking spray. Place waxed paper on top of greased pan bottom and spray top of waxed paper.
3. In food processor fitted with metal chopping blade, process all dry ingredients (excluding walnuts). Empty into small bowl and set aside.
4. Place all wet ingredients in food processor and process until smooth, scraping bowl sides occasionally.
5. Add dry mixture all at once to wet ingredients in food-processor bowl.
6. Pulse to blend until dry ingredients are just moistened.
7. Scrape mixture into prepared pan. Sprinkle with nuts if you wish.
8. Bake for 22 minutes, or until brownies pull away from sides.
9. Let cool 15 minutes before cutting into squares.

Per Serving
Calories 138, Kilojoules 577, Protein 5 g,
Carbohydrates 28 g, Total Fat 1 g, Saturated Fat 0.3 g,
Monounsaturated Fat 0.4 g, Polyunsaturated Fat 0.3 g,
Cholesterol 0 mg, Sodium 104 mg, Fiber 3 g

Chocolate Chip Meringue Drops

Bonnie Whaling
Clearfield, PA

Makes 40 cookies, 3 cookies/serving

Prep. Time: 15–20 minutes
Baking Time: 1 hour
Standing Time: 2 hours

Pyramid Servings	
Vegetables	○○○○○➤
Fruits	○○○○○➤
Carbohydrates	○○○○○○○
Protein & Dairy	○○○○○○○
Fats	○○○○○
Sweets	●

2 large egg whites
½ cup sugar
1 tsp vanilla extract
3 Tbsp. cocoa powder, unsweetened
½ cup semi-sweet mini chocolate chips

1. Preheat oven to 250°.
2. Line 2 baking sheets with parchment paper or aluminum foil. Set aside.
3. In large mixer bowl, beat egg whites until they hold stiff peaks.
4. Beat in sugar one tablespoon at a time.
5. Then beat in vanilla.
6. Reduce speed to low and beat in cocoa powder.
7. With a spatula, fold in chocolate chips.
8. Drop batter by rounded teaspoonfuls onto baking sheets, spacing cookies 1" apart.
9. Bake 1 hour.
10. Turn off oven and let cookies remain in oven 2 hours longer.
11. Remove from baking sheets and store in airtight container.

Per Serving
Calories 66, Kilojoules 276, Protein 1 g,
Carbohydrates 12 g, Total Fat 2 g, Saturated Fat 0.5 g,
Monounsaturated Fat 1 g, Polyunsaturated Fat 0.5 g,
Cholesterol 0 mg, Sodium 9 mg, Fiber *trace*

Tip: *Don't make these on a humid day. The mixture will be sticky and hard to handle.*

Fruit-Filled Chocolate Meringues

Gwendolyn Chapman
Gwinn, MI

Makes 6 servings

Prep. Time: 15–20 minutes
Baking Time: 45 minutes
Cooling Time: 1 hour

Pyramid Servings	
Vegetables	○○○○○➤
Fruits	●○○○○➤
Carbohydrates	○○○○○○○
Protein & Dairy	○○○○○○○
Fats	○○○○○
Sweets	●

2 egg whites at room temperature
¼ tsp. cream of tartar
½ tsp. vanilla extract
½ cup sugar
2 Tbsp. dry cocoa powder, unsweetened
3 cups assorted berries and fruit
2 tsp. powdered sugar

1. Preheat oven to 275°.
2. Line cookie sheet with parchment paper.
3. In mixer bowl, beat egg whites with cream of tartar and vanilla until soft peaks form.
4. Beat in sugar 1 Tbsp. at a time until stiff peaks form.
5. Sprinkle cocoa powder over top and fold in gently by hand.
6. Drop by ¼-cup portions onto parchment paper, spacing cookies 1" apart. Indent each with back of spoon.
7. Bake 45 minutes, or until dry to touch.
8. Remove meringues from oven and cool.
9. Fill center of each cooled meringue with fruit. Sprinkle with powdered sugar. Serve immediately.

Per Serving
Calories 110, Kilojoules 460, Protein 2 g,
Carbohydrates 25 g, Total Fat 0.4 g, Saturated Fat 0.1 g,
Monounsaturated Fat 0.1 g, Polyunsaturated Fat 0.2 g,
Cholesterol *trace*, Sodium 22 mg, Fiber 4 g

Tip: *If fresh berries aren't available, use thawed frozen raspberries.*

Sugarplum Drops

Mary E. Wheatley

Mashpee, MA

*Makes 2½ dozen cookies;
1 cookie/serving*

Prep. Time: 30 minutes
Chilling Time: 1 hour

½ cup raisins
½ cup (about 10) dried
  apricots
½ cup chopped dates
¾ cup dried cranberries
¾ cup pecans
1 cup blanched almonds
¼ cup orange juice without pulp
½ cup granulated sugar (raw sugar looks
  very nice)

Pyramid Servings	
Vegetables	○○○○○►
Fruits	●○○○○►
Carbohydrates	○○○○○○○○
Protein & Dairy	○○○○○○○
Fats	●○○○○

1. Combine dried fruits and nuts in food processor. Pulse until mixture is coarse. Don't over-process!
2. Add orange juice and pulse again just until mixture sticks together.
3. Shape mixture into 1" balls.
4. Roll each ball in sugar.
5. Place on a baking sheet (or other good-sized flat surface) in a single layer and refrigerate.
6. When thoroughly chilled, move to serving bowl or covered storage container.

Per Serving
Calories 92, Kilojoules 385, Protein 1 g,
Carbohydrates 13 g, Total Fat 4 g, Saturated Fat 0.3 g,
Monounsaturated Fat 2.7 g, Polyunsaturated Fat 1 g,
Cholesterol 0 mg, Sodium 2 mg, Fiber 1.5 g

Honey Milk Balls

Kathy Hertzler

Lancaster, PA

Makes 12 servings; 2 balls/serving

Prep. Time: 15 minutes
Chilling Time: 15 minutes

½ cup honey
1 cup natural peanut butter
  (if you wish, make your
  own by grinding peanuts)
2 cups instant non-fat dry
  milk powder

Pyramid Servings	
Vegetables	○○○○○►
Fruits	○○○○○►
Carbohydrates	○○○○○○○○
Protein & Dairy	●○○○○○○
Fats	○○○○○
Sweets	◑

1. Mix honey and peanut butter in medium bowl. Stir until well mixed.
2. Add dry milk, stirring until well combined. You may need to use your fingers.
3. Chill about 15 minutes in fridge.
4. Roll into balls the size of small walnuts.
5. Place in airtight container and keep chilled in refrigerator until ready to serve.

Per Serving
Calories 153, Kilojoules 640, Protein 7 g,
Carbohydrates 19 g, Total Fat 5 g, Saturated Fat 1 g,
Monounsaturated Fat 3 g, Polyunsaturated Fat 1 g,
Cholesterol 2 mg, Sodium 103 mg, Fiber 0.6 g

Apple-Walnut Cookies

Rhonda Burgoon
Collingswood, NJ

Makes 36 cookies; 2 cookies/serving

Prep. Time: 20 minutes
Baking Time: 10–12 minutes

1 cup dry rolled oats
½ cup walnuts, chopped
1 cup whole wheat pastry
   flour
½ tsp. baking soda
¼ tsp. baking powder
¼ tsp. salt
½ tsp. ground cinnamon
¼ tsp. ground ginger
2 egg whites
1 Granny Smith apple peeled, cored, and
   grated
¼ cup unsweetened applesauce
½ cup light brown sugar, packed
2 Tbsp. canola oil
½ tsp. vanilla extract
½ cup raisins

Pyramid Servings

Vegetables	ⵔⵔⵔⵔⵔ➤
Fruits	ⵔⵔⵔⵔⵔ➤
Carbohydrates	ⵔⵔⵔⵔⵔⵔⵔⵔ
Protein & Dairy	ⵔⵔⵔⵔⵔⵔⵔ
Fats	ⵔⵔⵔⵔⵔ
Sweets	◐

1. Heat oven to 375°. Spray 2 baking sheets with non-stick cooking spray.

2. Place oats and nuts on separate unsprayed baking sheets. Toast in oven until golden, about 8 minutes. Set aside.

3. Meanwhile, combine flour, baking soda, baking powder, salt, cinnamon, and ginger in a medium bowl.

4. In a large bowl, combine egg whites, grated apple, applesauce, brown sugar, oil, and vanilla.

5. Stir in combined dry ingredients until well blended.

6. Stir in raisins, oats, and nuts.

7. Drop dough onto prepared baking sheets by tablespoonfuls placed 2" apart.

8. Bake 10–12 minutes, or until cookies are lightly browned.

9. Cool on wire racks for 3 minutes. Cool completely before serving.

Per Serving
Calories 119, Kilojoules 498, Protein 3 g,
Carbohydrates 18 g, Total Fat 4 g, Saturated Fat 0.3 g,
Monounsaturated Fat 1.7 g, Polyunsaturated Fat 2 g,
Cholesterol 0 mg, Sodium 81 mg, Fiber 2 g

Tip: Store in an airtight container for up to 2 days.

Dietitian's tip: With most recipes, you can reduce the amount of fat, sugar and sodium without losing the flavor. By cutting fat and sugar, you also cut calories. Typically you can reduce the amount of sugar by one-third to one-half. When you use less sugar, add spices such as cinnamon, cloves, allspice and nutmeg or flavorings such as vanilla extract or almond flavoring to enhance the sweetness of the food.

A Tip —

A small ice cream scoop works well for making uniformly-sized cookies.

Low-Fat Rhubarb Bars
Kathy Rodkey, Halifax, PA

Makes 20 bars; 1 bar/serving

Prep. Time: 20 minutes
Baking Time: 45 minutes

1 cup flour
½ cup dry All-Bran cereal
1 cup uncooked rolled oats
1 tsp. baking soda
¼ tsp. salt
¾ cup lightly packed brown
   sugar
2 egg whites
½ cup low-fat sour cream
1 tsp. vanilla
2 cups cut-up rhubarb

Topping:
⅓ cup lightly packed brown sugar
½ cup chopped nuts
1 tsp. cinnamon
2 Tbsp. canola oil

Pyramid Servings	
Vegetables	○○○○○➤
Fruits	◑○○○○➤
Carbohydrates	◑○○○○○○○
Protein & Dairy	○○○○○○○
Fats	●○○○○

1. Mix all ingredients together in order as listed, except topping ingredients, in a good-sized bowl.
2. Spread into 9 × 13 baking pan, generously greased with non-stick cooking spray.
3. Mix topping ingredients in a small bowl.
4. Sprinkle over bars.
5. Bake at 350° for 45 minutes.

Per Serving
Calories 108, Kilojoules 452, Protein 3 g,
Carbohydrates 16 g, Total Fat 3.5 g, Saturated Fat 0.2 g,
Monounsaturated Fat 1.5 g, Polyunsaturated Fat 1.8 g,
Cholesterol *trace*, Sodium 113 mg, Fiber 2 g

Multi-Fruit Crisp
Heidi Roggie
Big Lake, AK

Makes 8 servings

Prep. Time: 20–30 minutes
Baking Time: 30 minutes

1½ cups of 4 fruits, fresh *or*
   frozen (a total of 6 cups)—
   blackberries, raspberries,
   blueberries, apples,
   peaches, rhubarb, or others
1¼ cups water
¼ cup sugar
2 Tbsp. cornstarch
¼ cup whole wheat pastry flour
½ cup dry rolled oats
3 Tbsp. canola oil
⅓ cup brown sugar
⅓ cup chopped walnuts, *optional*, not
   included in analyses

Pyramid Servings	
Vegetables	○○○○○➤
Fruits	●○○○○➤
Carbohydrates	●○○○○○○○
Protein & Dairy	○○○○○○○
Fats	●○○○○

1. Mix fruit together gently in a large bowl.
2. Spoon into 9 × 13 baking pan, generously greased with non-stick cooking spray.
3. In a saucepan cook water, sugar, and cornstarch together over medium heat, stirring constantly until thickened.
4. Pour mixture over fruit.
5. In the fruit mixing bowl, combine flour, oats, oil, and brown sugar, and nuts if you wish, until crumbly.
6. Sprinkle evenly over fruit.
7. Bake, uncovered, at 375° for 30 minutes, or until fruit bubbles and is soft.

Per Serving
Calories 174, Kilojoules 728, Protein 2 g,
Carbohydrates 30 g, Total Fat 5 g, Saturated Fat 0.5 g,
Monounsaturated Fat 2.5 g, Polyunsaturated Fat 2 g,
Cholesterol 0 mg, Sodium 4 mg, Fiber 3 g

Peach-Rhubarb Crisp

Dorothy VanDeest
Memphis, TN

Makes 6 servings

Prep. Time: 15 minutes
Baking Time: 35–40 minutes

5 cups peeled, sliced
    fresh peaches, *or* frozen
    unsweetened peach slices
1 cup fresh, *or* frozen, sliced
    rhubarb
⅓ cup sugar
2 tsp. lemon juice
¼ tsp. apple-pie spice, *or*
    ground cinnamon
½ cup uncooked rolled oats
⅓ cup packed brown sugar
¼ cup whole wheat pastry flour
¼ tsp. ground cinnamon
¼ cup trans-fat-free buttery spread
2 Tbsp. broken walnuts, *or* pecans

Pyramid Servings	
Vegetables	○○○○○➤
Fruits	●○○○○➤
Carbohydrates	◑○○○○○○○
Protein & Dairy	○○○○○○○
Fats	●●○○○
Sweets	●

   1. For filling, thaw fruit, if frozen. Do not drain.
   2. In large bowl, combine fruit, ⅓ cup sugar, lemon juice, and apple pie spice. Transfer to a 2-quart square baking dish, generously greased with non-stick baking spray.
   3. To make topping, combine oats, brown sugar, flour, and cinnamon in a medium bowl.
   4. With pastry blender, cut in buttery spread until mixture resembles coarse crumbs.
   5. Stir in nuts.
   6. Sprinkle over filling in baking dish.
   7. Bake at 375° for 35–40 minutes, or until fruit is tender, filling is bubbling around edges, and topping is golden.

Per Serving

Calories 266, Kilojoules 1113, Protein 3 g,	
Carbohydrates 40 g, Total Fat 10 g, Saturated Fat 2 g,	
Monounsaturated Fat 3 g, Polyunsaturated Fat 5 g,	
Cholesterol 0 mg, Sodium 106 mg, Fiber 4 g	

Dietitian's tip: Freestone peaches have pits you can easily remove, while clingstone peaches have flesh that clings to the pit. To easily pit and slice peaches for baking, choose freestone peaches, such as Elegant Lady or O'Henry.

Baked Apples

Jean Butzer, Batavia, NY

Makes 4 servings

Prep. Time: 10 minutes
Baking Time: 30–40 minutes

4 medium-sized tart apples,
    cored, but left whole and
    unpeeled
4 tsp. no-sugar-added
    strawberry fruit spread
½ tsp. ground cinnamon
1½ cups orange juice

Pyramid Servings	
Vegetables	○○○○○➤
Fruits	●○○○○➤
Carbohydrates	○○○○○○○○
Protein & Dairy	○○○○○○○
Fats	○○○○○
Sweets	●

   1. Place apples in foil-lined 8 × 8 baking pan, generously greased with non-stick cooking spray.
   2. Spoon 1 teaspoon jam into center of each apple.
   3. Sprinkle each apple with cinnamon.
   4. Pour orange juice into pan around apples.
   5. Bake, uncovered, at 400° 30–40 minutes, or until apples are tender. Serve immediately.

Per Serving

Calories 127, Kilojoules 531, Protein 1 g,	
Carbohydrates 31 g, Total Fat *trace*, Saturated Fat *trace*,	
Monounsaturated Fat *trace*, Polyunsaturated Fat *trace*,	
Cholesterol 0 mg, Sodium 2 mg, Fiber 3 g	

Tips:
   1. I like to use reduced-sugar cranberry juice in place of the orange juice.
   2. Instead of strawberry, you can use other fruit spreads.

Apple Dessert
Elaine Good
Lititz, PA

Makes 10 servings

Prep. Time: 20 minutes
Baking Time: 45 minutes

¼ cup trans-fat-free buttery
   spread
¾ cup brown sugar
¾ cup whole wheat pastry
   flour
1 tsp. cinnamon
2 Tbsp. shredded coconut, *optional*,
   not included in analyses
2 Tbsp. chopped nuts, *optional*,
   not included in analyses
8 cups sliced apples

Pyramid Servings
Vegetables ○○○○○▸
Fruits ❶○○○○▸
Carbohydrates ❶○○○○○○○
Protein & Dairy ○○○○○○○
Fats ❶○○○○

1. Heat oven to 350°.
2. Place buttery spread in 10" pie plate.
Place in oven to melt.
3. In a separate bowl, combine sugar, flour,
and cinnamon, and coconut and nuts if you
wish.
4. Stir dry ingredients into melted spread
until crumbs form.
5. Remove about half of crumbs. Set aside.
6. Spread remaining crumbs evenly over
bottom of pie plate.
7. Add apple slices to pie plate, mounding up
as needed to fill pan.
8. Carefully top with reserved crumbs.
9. Bake 45 minutes. Serve warm with milk
if you wish (not included in analyses).

Per Serving

Calories 114, Kilojoules 477, Protein 1 g,
Carbohydrates 17 g, Total Fat 5 g, Saturated Fat 1 g,
Monounsaturated Fat 1 g, Polyunsaturated Fat 3 g,
Cholesterol 0 mg, Sodium 62 mg, Fiber 3 g

Low-Fat and Still Good Fruit Cobbler
Michelle Showalter
Bridgewater, VA

Makes 6 servings

Prep. Time: 15 minutes
Baking Time: 30 minutes

3 cups total mixture of fresh,
   or frozen, blackberries,
   cherries, peaches
1 cup whole wheat pastry
   flour
½ cup sugar
½ tsp. baking powder
½ cup skim milk
½ cup non-fat plain yogurt

Pyramid Servings
Vegetables ○○○○○▸
Fruits ❶○○○○▸
Carbohydrates ❶○○○○○○○
Protein & Dairy ○○○○○○○
Fats ○○○○○

1. Lightly spray a 9 × 9 baking pan with
non-stick cooking spray. Put fruit in bottom of
pan.
2. Mix remaining ingredients in bowl.
3. Spread over fruit.
4. Bake at 350° for 30 minutes, or until
toothpick inserted in center comes out clean.
5. Enjoy with cold skim milk (not included
in analyses).

Per Serving

Calories 122, Kilojoules 510, Protein 5 g,
Carbohydrates 25 g, Total Fat *trace*, Saturated Fat *trace*,
Monounsaturated Fat *trace*, Polyunsaturated Fat *trace*,
Cholesterol 1 mg, Sodium 60 mg, Fiber 5 g

Fresh Fruit Dessert

Natalia Showalter
Mt. Solon, VA

Makes 12 servings

Prep. Time: 20–25 minutes
Cooking Time: 5–10 minutes
Cooling Time: 30 minutes

Pyramid Servings

Vegetables
○○○○○➤
Fruits
●○○○○➤
Carbohydrates
○○○○○○○○
Protein & Dairy
○○○○○○○
Fats
○○○○○

Dressing:
1 Tbsp. sugar
1½ Tbsp. fruit pectin (for
    example, Sure Jell™)
6-oz. can unsweetened
    pineapple juice
½ tsp. vanilla extract, *optional*

10 cups total of any of the following fresh
    fruits, alone or mixed:
apples
pineapple
red and white grapes
kiwi
strawberries
blueberries
peaches
raspberries
pears

1. To make dressing, combine sugar and fruit pectin in small saucepan.
2. Add pineapple juice, stirring until smooth.
3. Cook and stir over medium heat until thickened.
4. Remove from heat and add vanilla if you wish. Allow dressing to cool.
5. Wash and cut fruit into bite-size pieces.
6. Place any combination of fruit you want into large mixing bowl until you have 10 cups of chopped or sliced fruit. *If you're using fresh berries, add to salad just before serving.*
7. Pour cooled sauce over fruit. Toss gently to coat.

8. Refrigerate until ready to serve. Stir in fresh berries, if you're including them, just before serving.

Per Serving

Calories 66, Kilojoules 276, Protein 1 g,
Carbohydrates 16 g, Total Fat *trace*, Saturated Fat *trace*,
Monounsaturated Fat *trace*, Polyunsaturated Fat *trace*,
Cholesterol 0 mg, Sodium *trace*, Fiber 2 g

Tip: This salad can be made up to 6 hours before serving. Although the leftovers get juicier, the salad is delicious the next day.

Dietitian's tip: Pineapple contains an enzyme called "bromelain" that breaks down protein in milk, meat, and gelatin. This makes fresh pineapple perfect for marinating meats but makes salads containing sour cream or cottage cheese watery. Canned or cooked pineapple can be used, however, because it's been heated and the enzyme is destroyed.

A Tip —

    If you can read a recipe and follow directions you can cook.

Golden Fruit Compote
Willard Roth
Elkhart, IN

Makes 6 servings

Prep. Time: 5 minutes
Cooking Time: 10–15 minutes

Pyramid Servings

Vegetables
○○○○○➤

Fruits
●●○○○➤

Carbohydrates
○○○○○○○○

Protein & Dairy
○○○○○○○

Fats
○○○○○

15-oz. can juice-packed
    apricot halves, undrained
15-oz. can juice-packed
    pineapple chunks,
    undrained
¼ cup golden raisins
1 Tbsp. fresh lemon juice
2 sticks cinnamon, *or* ¼ tsp. ground
    cinnamon
4 whole cloves
2 unpeeled yellow apples, cored and sliced

1. Combine ingredients, except apples, in medium saucepan.
2. Bring to a boil. Reduce heat, cover, and simmer 5 minutes.
3. Stir in apples. Cook about 3 minutes, or until apples are heated but not soft.
4. Remove cloves. Serve warm.

Per Serving

Calories 117, Kilojoules 490, Protein 1 g,
Carbohydrates 29 g, Total Fat *trace*, Saturated Fat *trace*,
Monounsaturated Fat *trace*, Polyunsaturated Fat *trace*,
Cholesterol 0 mg, Sodium 10 mg, Fiber 3 g

Dietitian's tip: Simple and natural is nutritious and delicious!

Dried Fruit Compote
Lois Mae E. Kuh
Penfield, NY

Makes 8 servings

Prep. Time: 5 minutes
Standing Time: 8 hours, or
    overnight
Cooking Time: 5 minutes

Pyramid Servings

Vegetables
○○○○○➤

Fruits
●●●○○➤

Carbohydrates
○○○○○○○○

Protein & Dairy
○○○○○○○

Fats
○○○○○

6 ozs. canned apple juice
    concentrate
1 lb. assorted dried fruit
    (plums, peaches, apricots,
    apples)
2–3 whole cloves
½ Tbsp. lemon juice

1. In a large saucepan, bring apple juice concentrate to a boil.
2. Stir in dried fruit and cloves.
3. Let stand overnight.
4. Remove cloves. Add lemon juice.
5. Serve at room temperature or chilled.

Per Serving

Calories 184, Kilojoules 770, Protein 2 g,
Carbohydrates 45 g, Total Fat *trace*, Saturated Fat *trace*,
Monounsaturated Fat *trace*, Polyunsaturated Fat *trace*,
Cholesterol 0 mg, Sodium 21 mg, Fiber 5 g

Frozen Fruit Dessert

Carol Eberly
Harrisonburg, VA

Makes 8 servings

Prep. Time: 10 minutes
Freezing Time: 8 hours, or
*   overnight*
Thawing Time: 1–2 hours

Pyramid Servings	
Vegetables ○○○○○➤	
Fruits ●●○○○➤	
Carbohydrates ○○○○○○○	
Protein & Dairy ○○○○○○○	
Fats ○○○○○	

6-oz. can frozen orange juice,
    dissolved in 1 cup hot
    water
2 Tbsp. lemon juice
15-oz. can crushed unsweetened pineapple
    with juice
4 bananas, sliced

1. Mix all ingredients together in order listed in a large bowl.

2. Put in serving bowl. Cover and freeze.

3. When ready to serve, remove from freezer, let it thaw until slushy, and serve.

4. Freeze what's left for next time.

Per Serving

Calories 127, Kilojoules 531, Protein 1 g,
Carbohydrates 31 g, Total Fat *trace*, Saturated Fat *trace*,
Monounsaturated Fat *trace*, Polyunsaturated Fat *trace*,
Cholesterol 0 mg, Sodium 2 mg, Fiber 2 g

Berry Nougat Crunch

Anita King
Bellefontaine, OH

Makes 8 servings

Prep. Time: 10 minutes
Optional Thawing Time: 20
*   minutes*

Pyramid Servings	
Vegetables ○○○○○➤	
Fruits ●○○○○➤	
Carbohydrates ○○○○○○○	
Protein & Dairy ○○○○○○○	
Fats ●●○○○	
Sweets ●	

5 cups berries, fresh or frozen
¾ cup chopped almonds
½ cup raisins
¼ cup almond butter, softened
2 Tbsp. maple syrup, *or* honey
lemon juice, *optional*, not
    included in analyses

1. Spoon your choice of fresh or frozen berries into a large mixing bowl: blueberries, raspberries, blackberry frozen mix, or frozen sweet cherries are all good. You may use them in combination, or use just one berry.

2. Fold in nuts and raisins.

3. In a small mixing bowl, stir almond butter and maple syrup together until well blended. Add 2 Tbsp. or so of lemon juice if you like for some zing.

4. Stir gently into fruit and nuts.

5. If you're using frozen fruit, allow to thaw for about 20 minutes before serving so fruit remains partially frozen. Serve in dessert glasses.

Per Serving

Calories 214, Kilojoules 895, Protein 5 g,
Carbohydrates 27 g, Total Fat 10 g, Saturated Fat 1 g,
Monounsaturated Fat 6 g, Polyunsaturated Fat 3 g,
Cholesterol 0 mg, Sodium 38 mg, Fiber 4 g

Red, White, and Blue Parfait

Becky Gehman
Bergton, VA

Makes 4 servings

Prep. Time: 15 minutes

Creamy Filling:
1 cup low-fat vanilla yogurt,
  sweetened with low-calorie
  sweetener
¼ cup fat-free cream cheese
  (Neufchatel), softened
1 tsp. honey

1 pint fresh strawberries, sliced, *divided*
1½ cups fresh blueberries, *divided*

1. Make Creamy Filling by placing yogurt, cream cheese, and honey into bowl. Beat until fluffy.

2. Assemble parfaits by placing ⅓ cup strawberries in each of 6 parfait glasses.

3. Top each with 3 Tbsp. Creamy Filling.

4. Top that with ¼ cup blueberries in each glass.

5. Garnish each by dividing remaining topping.

6. Chill until ready to serve.

Pyramid Servings

Vegetables	○○○○○▸
Fruits	●○○○○▸
Carbohydrates	○○○○○○○○
Protein & Dairy	◑○○○○○○
Fats	○○○○○

Per Serving

Calories 100, Kilojoules 418, Protein 5 g,
Carbohydrates 20 g, Total Fat 1 g, Saturated Fat 0.4 g,
Monounsaturated Fat 0.2 g, Polyunsaturated Fat 0.4 g,
Cholesterol 2 mg, Sodium 116 mg, Fiber 3 g

Ambrosia Parfaits

Irene Klaeger
Inverness, FL

Makes 4 servings

Prep. Time: 15 minutes

16-oz. carton low-fat vanilla
  yogurt, sweetened with
  low-calorie sweetener,
  divided
¼ cup no-sugar-added
  crushed pineapple in juice,
  drained
1 banana, peeled and cut into ¼" slices
11-oz. can mandarin oranges in light
  syrup, drained
1 Tbsp. flaked coconut, toasted
4 fresh strawberries, sliced

1. Spoon yogurt onto several layers of heavy duty paper towels and spread to ½" thickness. Cover with additional paper towels. Let stand 5 minutes.

2. Scrape yogurt into bowl using a rubber spatula.

3. Stir in drained pineapple.

4. Spoon 2 Tbsp. yogurt mixture into each of 4 parfait glasses.

5. Top evenly with banana slices and orange slices.

6. Dollop remaining yogurt over orange slices.

7. Sprinkle evenly with coconut.

8. Top each with sliced strawberries.

Pyramid Servings

Vegetables	○○○○○▸
Fruits	●●○○○▸
Carbohydrates	○○○○○○○○
Protein & Dairy	◑○○○○○○
Fats	○○○○○

Per Serving

Calories 177, Kilojoules 741, Protein 6 g,
Carbohydrates 34 g, Total Fat 2 g, Saturated Fat 1.6 g,
Monounsaturated Fat 0.3 g, Polyunsaturated Fat 0.1 g,
Cholesterol 7 mg, Sodium 77 mg, Fiber 2 g

Festive Holiday Trifle

Willard Roth
Elkhart, IN

Makes 14 servings

Prep. Time: 20 minutes
Cooking Time: 12–15 minutes
Chilling Time: 30 minutes

Pyramid Servings

Vegetables	○○○○○►
Fruits	●○○○○►
Carbohydrates	○○○○○○○○
Protein & Dairy	◐○○○○○○
Fats	○○○○○
Sweets	●

Whipped Topping:
**1 cup low-fat vanilla yogurt,
sweetened with low-calorie
sweetener**
**¼ cup fat-free cream cheese
(Neufchatel), softened**
1 tsp. honey

Blancmange:
½ cup sugar
5 Tbsp. cornstarch
⅛ tsp. salt, *optional*
2½ cups lite vanilla soymilk
1 Tbsp. vanilla (preferably clear)

10½-oz. angel food loaf cake, cubed
2 ozs. liqueur (e.g., amaretto)
1 lb. fresh, *or frozen*, strawberries, sliced
2 kiwis, peeled and sliced

1. To make Whipped Topping, place yogurt, cream cheese, and honey into bowl. Beat until fluffy.

2. Refrigerate Topping while assembling rest of recipe.

3. To make Blancmange, combine sugar with cornstarch, and salt if you wish, in 2-quart saucepan.

4. In microwave-safe bowl, microwave soymilk 2–3 minutes, or until steaming hot but not boiling.

5. Add heated soymilk gradually to sugar and cornstarch in saucepan, over low heat. Stir constantly.

6. When milk thickens, reduce heat to low, and continue to cook and stir at least 8 more minutes.

7. Remove from heat. Add vanilla.

8. Chill Blancmange at least 30 minutes. Whisk before layering into Trifle.

9. To assemble Trifle, layer into glass bowl: half the angel food cake cubes; a sprinkling of half the liqueur; half the strawberries; half the batch of Blancmange; half the Whipped Topping.

10. Repeat layers a second time.

11. Arrange kiwis symmetrically on top of final layer of Topping.

Per Serving

Calories 181, Kilojoules 757, Protein 4 g,
Carbohydrates 35 g, Total Fat 2.5 g, Saturated Fat 1.5 g,
Monounsaturated Fat 0.5 g, Polyunsaturated Fat 0.5 g,
Cholesterol 7 mg, Sodium 200 mg, Fiber 2 g

A Tip —

Clean up your kitchen as you go. Don't wait until there is a mountain of dishes to do.

Strawberry Fluff

Shari Ladd
Hudson, MI

Makes 6 servings

Prep. Time: 15 minutes
Chilling Time: 2–3 hours

.3-oz. pkg. sugar-free
  strawberry gelatin

Creamy Filling:
1 cup low-fat vanilla yogurt,
  sweetened with low-calorie
  sweetener
¼ cup fat-free cream cheese (Neufchatel),
  softened
1 tsp. honey

¼ whole angel food cake, cut into cubes
3 cups sliced fresh strawberries

1. Prepare gelatin according to package
directions. Refrigerate 1 hour in a good-sized
bowl.
2. Meanwhile, make Creamy Filling by
placing yogurt, cream cheese, and honey into
bowl. Beat until fluffy.
3. To assemble Fluff, scatter pieces of cake
evenly in 8" pan.
4. Layer berries evenly over cake.
5. After gelatin has been refrigerated for 1
hour, whip Creamy Filling into gelatin.
6. Spoon over berries.
7. Cover and chill until set, about another
hour or so.

Pyramid Servings

Vegetables	○○○○○➤
Fruits	❶○○○○➤
Carbohydrates	❶○○○○○○○
Protein & Dairy	❶○○○○○○○
Fats	○○○○○

Per Serving

Calories 136, Kilojoules 569, Protein 5 g,
Carbohydrates 19 g, Total Fat 4.5 g, Saturated Fat 3 g,
Monounsaturated Fat 1 g, Polyunsaturated Fat 0.5 g,
Cholesterol 14 mg, Sodium 200 mg, Fiber 2 g

Sour Cream Apple Kuchen

Sharon Easter
Yuba City, CA

Makes 8 servings

Prep. Time: 15 minutes
Baking Time: 30–35 minutes

1½ cups flour
½ cup sugar
2 tsp. baking powder
¼ tsp. salt
½ tsp. cinnamon
1 cup chopped unpeeled
  apple
egg substitute equivalent to
  1 egg, *or* 2 egg whites, beaten
½ cup skim milk
2 Tbsp. oil
½ cup fat-free sour cream
¼ cup chopped nuts

1. In a large mixing bowl, sift flour with
sugar, baking powder, salt, and cinnamon.
2. Stir apples into flour mixture.
3. In a separate bowl, blend together egg
substitute, milk, and oil.
4. Stir wet ingredients into flour mixture
until well blended.
5. Turn batter into greased 9" round cake
pan or deep-dish pie pan.
6. Spoon sour cream over top in spiral
pattern, leaving center uncovered.
7. Top with nuts.
8. Bake at 400° for 30–35 minutes, or until
tester inserted in center comes out clean.
9. Serve warm or cold.

Pyramid Servings

Vegetables	○○○○○➤
Fruits	●○○○○➤
Carbohydrates	●○○○○○○○
Protein & Dairy	○○○○○○○
Fats	●○○○○
Sweets	◑

Per Serving

Calories 199, Kilojoules 833, Protein 6 g,
Carbohydrates 33 g, Total Fat 5 g, Saturated Fat 0.5 g,
Monounsaturated Fat 3 g, Polyunsaturated Fat 1.5 g,
Cholesterol 2 mg, Sodium 200 mg, Fiber 3 g

Honey-Sweetened Spice Cake

Doyle Rounds
Bridgewater, VA

Makes 12 servings

Prep. Time: 15 minutes
Cooling Time: 20–30 minutes
Baking Time: 25 minutes

1 cup raisins
1 cup water
1⅓ cups unsweetened
   applesauce
2 eggs, beaten
2 Tbsp. honey
⅓ cup vegetable oil
1 tsp. baking soda
2 cups whole wheat pastry flour
1½ tsp. ground cinnamon
½ tsp. ground nutmeg
1 tsp. vanilla extract

Pyramid Servings		
Vegetables ○○○○○➤		
Fruits ●○○○○➤		
Carbohydrates ●○○○○○○○		
Protein & Dairy ○○○○○○○		
Fats ●○○○○		

  1. In a saucepan, cook raisins in water until water evaporates.
  2. Pour into mixing bowl and let cool.
  3. When raisins are cool, stir in applesauce, eggs, honey, and oil. Mix well.
  4. Blend in baking soda and flour.
  5. Stir in cinnamon, nutmeg, and vanilla, blending well.
  6. Pour into greased 8 × 8 baking pan.
  7. Bake at 350° for 25 minutes, or until tester inserted in center of cake comes out clean.

Per Serving

Calories 172, Kilojoules 720, Protein 4g,
Carbohydrates 29g, Total Fat 5g, Saturated Fat 0.5g,
Monounsaturated Fat 3.5g, Polyunsaturated Fat 1g,
Cholesterol 0mg, Sodium 126mg, Fiber 3g

Date and Nut Cake

Gladys Longacre
Susquehanna, PA

Makes 12 servings

Prep. Time: 15–20 minutes
Cooking/Baking Time: 35–40 minutes

8 ozs. dates, chopped
1 cup cold water
½ cup sugar
½ cup unsweetened
   applesauce
2 Tbsp. canola oil
1 egg, separated
pinch of salt
1 tsp. baking soda
1½ cups whole wheat pastry flour
⅓ cup chopped walnuts
1 tsp. vanilla

Pyramid Servings		
Vegetables ○○○○○➤		
Fruits ●○○○○➤		
Carbohydrates ●○○○○○○○		
Protein & Dairy ○○○○○○○		
Fats ●○○○○		

  1. Put chopped dates in saucepan with cold water. Cover and bring to a boil.
  2. Remove from heat. Let stand while preparing rest of ingredients.
  3. In a good-sized mixing bowl, cream sugar, applesauce, and canola oil.
  4. Stir in egg yoke (reserve white) and pinch of salt.
  5. Stir baking soda into dates.
  6. Stir flour and date mixture into creamed sugar mixture.
  7. Stir in walnuts and vanilla, blending well.
  8. In a clean bowl, beat egg white until stiff.
  9. Fold into batter.
  10. Lightly grease 7 × 12 baking pan with non-stick cooking spray. Spoon batter into pan.
  11. Bake at 350° for 25–30 minutes, or until tester inserted in center of cake comes out clean.

Per Serving

Calories 181, Kilojoules 757, Protein 4 g,
Carbohydrates 33 g, Total Fat 5 g, Saturated Fat 1 g,
Monounsaturated Fat 2 g, Polyunsaturated Fat 2 g,
Cholesterol 18 mg, Sodium 112 mg, Fiber 3 g

7. Spoon batter into baking pan, being careful not to disturb crumbs on bottom of pan.

8. Top batter with reserved ⅞ cup crumbs.

9. Bake at 325° 30 minutes, or until tester inserted in center of cake comes out clean.

Per Serving

Calories 246, Kilojoules 1029, Protein 5 g,
Carbohydrates 41 g, Total Fat 7 g, Saturated Fat 1 g,
Monounsaturated Fat 4 g, Polyunsaturated Fat 2 g,
Cholesterol 0.5 mg, Sodium 180 mg, Fiber 3 g

Tips:

1. An 8 × 8 baking pan will also work for this recipe.

2. Serve warm from the oven, or warm cake up later when ready to serve.

3. Before mixing in soda and spices, check to make sure that you have 1¾ cups crumbs in the mixing bowl, and that you haven't taken out too much for topping or for the bottom of the pan.

Ginger Crumb Cake

Mary Kathryn Yoder
Harrisonville, MO

Makes 9 servings

Prep. Time: 20 minutes
Baking Time: 30 minutes

Pyramid Servings

Vegetables
○○○○○►

Fruits
○○○○○►

Carbohydrates
●●○○○○○○

Protein & Dairy
○○○○○○○

Fats
●○○○○

Sweets
●

2 cups whole wheat flour
⅓ cup trans-fat-free buttery
    spread
1 cup raw sugar
¼ tsp. baking soda
1 tsp. baking powder
½ tsp. nutmeg
½ tsp. ground ginger
½ tsp. cinnamon
egg substitute equivalent to 1 egg, *or* 2 egg
    whites
½ cup low-fat buttermilk

1. In a good-sized bowl, mix flour and buttery spread with a pastry cutter until crumbs the size of peas form.

2. Add sugar. Mix with your hands to blend thoroughly.

3. Measure out ⅞ cup crumbs. Set aside for topping.

4. Measure out another ⅞ cup crumbs. Spread in bottom of greased 9 × 9 baking pan.

5. To the remaining 1¾ cups crumbs in mixing bowl, add baking soda and spices.

6. When thoroughly blended, beat in egg substitute and buttermilk.

A Tip —

Cooking with someone else is always more fun than cooking solo.

Wacky Chocolate Cake

Margaret Wenger Johnson
Keezletown, VA

Makes 20 servings

Prep. Time: 15 minutes
Baking Time: 30 minutes

3 cups whole wheat pastry
 flour
1 cup sugar
3 Tbsp. unsweetened cocoa
 powder
½ tsp. salt
2¼ tsp. soda
1 Tbsp. vanilla
2 Tbsp. vinegar
½ cup canola oil
2 cups boiling water

Pyramid Servings	
Vegetables	○○○○○▸
Fruits	○○○○○▸
Carbohydrates	◐○○○○○○○
Protein & Dairy	○○○○○○○
Fats	●○○○○
Sweets	●

1. In a good-sized mixing bowl, sift together flour, sugar, cocoa powder, salt, and soda.

2. Make 3 holes in dry ingredients. Pour vanilla, vinegar, and oil into those holes.

3. Add boiling water. Beat two minutes by hand, or with a mixer. (This will make a thin batter.)

4. Pour batter into greased 9 × 13 baking pan, or 3 greased 8" round baking pans for a layer cake.

5. Bake at 350° for 30 minutes, or until tester inserted in center of cake comes out clean.

Per Serving

Calories 145, Kilojoules 607, Protein 2 g,
Carbohydrates 23 g, Total Fat 5 g, Saturated Fat 0.5 g,
Monounsaturated Fat 3.5 g, Polyunsaturated Fat 1 g,
Cholesterol 0 mg, Sodium 200 mg, Fiber 2 g

Cheesecake

Sharon Shank
Bridgewater, VA

Makes 8 servings

Prep. Time: 15 minutes
Cooling Time: 2–3 hours

2 Tbsp. cold water
1 envelope unflavored gelatin
2 Tbsp. lemon juice
½ cup skim milk, heated
 almost to boiling
egg substitute equivalent to 1
 egg, *or* 2 egg whites
¼ cup sugar
1 tsp. vanilla
2 cups low-fat cottage cheese
lemon zest, *optional*

Pyramid Servings	
Vegetables	○○○○○▸
Fruits	○○○○○▸
Carbohydrates	○○○○○○○○
Protein & Dairy	◐○○○○○○
Fats	○○○○○
Sweets	◐

1. Combine water, gelatin, and lemon juice in blender container. Process on low speed 1–2 minutes to soften gelatin.

2. Add hot milk, processing until gelatin is dissolved.

3. Add egg substitute, sugar, vanilla, and cheese to blender container. Process on high speed until smooth.

4. Pour into 9" pie plate or round flat dish.

5. Refrigerate 2–3 hours.

6. If you wish, top with grated lemon zest just before serving.

Per Serving

Calories 80, Kilojoules 335, Protein 9 g,
Carbohydrates 10 g, Total Fat *trace*, Saturated Fat *trace*,
Monounsaturated Fat *trace*, Polyunsaturated Fat *trace*,
Cholesterol 3 mg, Sodium 200 mg, Fiber *trace*

Dietitian's tip: *The colorful outermost layer of the lemon, called the "zest," is full of essential oils that contribute lively flavor and aroma to this recipe. Remove the zest by grating it with the fine rasps of a hand-held grater to form fine particles.*

Strawberry Shortcake Cups

Joanna Harrison
Lafayette, CO

Makes 8 servings

Prep. Time: 20 minutes
Baking Time: 12 minutes
Cooling Time: 7 minutes

1 quart (4 cups) fresh
   strawberries
3 Tbsp. agave nectar,* or
   honey, *divided*
1½ cups whole wheat pastry
   flour
1 tsp. baking powder
⅛ tsp. salt
¼ cup trans-fat-free buttery spread
egg substitute equivalent to 1 egg, *or* 2 egg
   whites
½ cup skim milk

Pyramid Servings

Vegetables
○○○○○➤

Fruits
●○○○○➤

Carbohydrates
●○○○○○○○

Protein & Dairy
○○○○○○○

Fats
●○○○○

1. Mash or slice strawberries in a bowl. Stir in 2 Tbsp. agave nectar. Set aside.

2. In a good-sized mixing bowl, combine flour, baking powder, salt, and 1 Tbsp. agave nectar.

3. Cut buttery spread into dry ingredients with pastry cutter or 2 knives until crumbly.

4. In a small bowl, beat egg substitute and milk together.

5. Stir wet ingredients into flour mixture just until moistened.

6. Fill eight greased muffin cups ⅔ full of batter.

7. Bake at 425° for 12 minutes, or until golden.

8. Allow cakes to cool in baking tins 7 minutes. Then remove from muffin cups to cool on wire rack.

9. Just before serving, split shortcakes in half horizontally. Spoon berries over cake halves.

Per Serving

Calories 173, Kilojoules 724, Protein 5 g,
Carbohydrates 26 g, Total Fat 6 g, Saturated Fat 1.5 g,
Monounsaturated Fat 1 g, Polyunsaturated Fat 3.5 g,
Cholesterol *trace*, Sodium 183 mg, Fiber 4 g

* **Note:** *Agave nectar is a sweet, honey-like syrup made from the succulent cactus-like agave plant. You may substitute honey if you don't have agave nectar.*

A Tip —

   When a recipes calls for a quantity of oil, I substitute ½ applesauce and ½ oil. This makes things moist and healthier.

Morning Glory Cupcakes
Barb Harvey
Quarryville, PA

Makes 20 servings

Prep. Time: 15 minutes
Baking Time: 18–22 minutes
Cooling Time: 5 minutes

Pyramid Servings
Vegetables
OOOOO➤
Fruits
●OOOO➤
Carbohydrates
●OOOOOOO
Protein & Dairy
OOOOOOO
Fats
●●OOO

2 cups whole wheat flour
1 cup sugar
2 tsp. baking soda
2 tsp. ground cinnamon
2 cups shredded carrots
⅓ cup chopped dried apricots
⅓ cup sunflower kernels
⅓ cup flaked coconut
⅓ cup semi-sweet chocolate chips
2 medium-sized ripe bananas, mashed
egg substitute equivalent to 3 eggs
½ cup vegetable oil
2 tsp. vanilla extract

1. In large mixing bowl, combine flour, sugar, baking soda, and cinnamon.
2. Add carrots, apricots, sunflower kernels, coconut, and chocolate chips.
3. Stir in mashed bananas.
4. In separate bowl, beat eggs, oil, and vanilla together.
5. Stir wet ingredients into carrot mixture just until moistened.
6. Fill 20 greased or paper-lined cupcake cups ⅔ full.
7. Bake at 375° 18–22 minutes, until tester inserted into centers of cupcakes comes out clean.
8. Cool 5 minutes. Remove from pans to wire racks.

Per Serving

Calories 193, Kilojoules 808, Protein 4 g,
Carbohydrates 28 g, Total Fat 8 g, Saturated Fat 2 g,
Monounsaturated Fat 2 g, Polyunsaturated Fat 4 g,
Cholesterol *trace*, Sodium 158 mg, Fiber 3 g

Pumpkin Cupcakes
Katrina Smith
Sheldon, WI

Makes 24 servings

Prep. Time: 20 minutes
Baking Time: 15 minutes

Pyramid Servings
Vegetables
OOOOO➤
Fruits
◐OOOO➤
Carbohydrates
◐OOOOOOO
Protein & Dairy
OOOOOOO
Fats
●OOOO
Sweets
◐

egg substitute equivalent to 4 eggs
½ cup canola oil
¾ cup honey
2 cups pumpkin
3 cups whole wheat flour
2 tsp. cinnamon
3 tsp. baking powder
2 tsp. baking soda
¼ tsp. salt
1 tsp. ground ginger
1 cup raisins, *optional*, not included in analyses

1. In a large mixing bowl, beat egg substitute, oil, and honey together until frothy.
2. Stir in pumpkin.
3. In a separate bowl, combine dry ingredients, including raisins if you wish.
4. Slowly blend dry ingredients into wet ingredients.
5. Fill 24 individual cupcake papers ½–⅔ full.
6. Bake at 350° 15 minutes, or until toothpick inserted in centers of cupcakes comes out clean.

Per Serving

Calories 141, Kilojoules 590, Protein 3 g,
Carbohydrates 21 g, Total Fat 5 g, Saturated Fat 0.5 g,
Monounsaturated Fat 1.5 g, Polyunsaturated Fat 3 g,
Cholesterol *trace*, Sodium 180 mg, Fiber 2.5 g

Tasty Apple Pie

Norma Saltzman, Shickley, NE
Charlotte Shaffer, East Earl, PA

Makes 8 servings

Prep. Time: 30 minutes
Standing Time: 15 minutes
Baking Time: 55 minutes

Pyramid Servings

| Vegetables |
| ○○○○○➤ |
| Fruits |
| ●○○○○➤ |
| Carbohydrates |
| ●○○○○○○○ |
| Protein & Dairy |
| ○○○○○○○ |
| Fats |
| ●●○○○ |

Pie Crust:
1 cup dry rolled oats
¼ cup whole wheat pastry flour
¼ cup ground almonds
2 Tbsp. brown sugar, packed
3 Tbsp. canola oil
1 Tbsp. water

1. To prepare Crust, mix dry ingredients together in good-sized mixing bowl.
2. In a separate bowl, mix oil and water together with a whisk.
3. Add oil-water mixture to dry ingredients. Mix until dough holds together. Add a bit more water if needed.
4. Press dough into 9" pie plate.
5. Set aside until Filling is prepared.

Filling:
6 cups (about 4 large) sliced and peeled tart apples
⅓ cup frozen apple juice concentrate
2 Tbsp. quick-cooking tapioca
1 tsp. cinnamon

1. In a large bowl, combine all ingredients except nuts.
2. Let stand 15 minutes.
3. Stir and then spoon into prepared pie crust.
4. Bake at 425° 15 minutes.
5. Reduce heat to 350° and bake 40 minutes, or until apples are tender.

Per Serving

Calories 215, Kilojoules 900, Protein 3 g,
Carbohydrates 31 g, Total Fat 9 g, Saturated Fat 1 g,
Monounsaturated Fat 5 g, Polyunsaturated Fat 3 g,
Cholesterol 0 mg, Sodium 16 mg, Fiber 4 g

Mocha Chiffon Pie

Ann Bender
New Hope, VA

Makes 8 servings

Prep. Time: 15 minutes
Cooking Time: 5 minutes
Cooling Time: 2–3 hours

Pyramid Servings

| Vegetables |
| ○○○○○➤ |
| Fruits |
| ○○○○○➤ |
| Carbohydrates |
| ○○○○○○○○ |
| Protein & Dairy |
| ◐○○○○○○ |
| Fats |
| ○○○○○ |
| Sweets |
| ● |

1 Tbsp. plain gelatin
¼ cup cold water
½ cup sugar
2 Tbsp. cocoa powder, unsweetened
1 tsp. dry instant coffee
⅛ tsp. salt
1½ cups evaporated skim milk
8 Tbsp. light frozen whipped topping, thawed

1. In a small bowl, dissolve gelatin in cold water.
2. Mix sugar, cocoa powder, dry coffee, and salt in saucepan.
3. Stir milk into saucepan. Heat to boiling, stirring frequently.
4. Add gelatin mixture and stir until dissolved.
5. Cool in fridge until mixture is slightly congealed.
6. Pour into 9" pie pan.
7. Cool in fridge until completely set.
8. Serve each pie wedge topped with 1 Tbsp. whipped topping.

Per Serving

Calories 111, Kilojoules 464, Protein 7 g,
Carbohydrates 19 g, Total Fat 1 g, Saturated Fat 0.5 g,
Monounsaturated Fat 0.3 g, Polyunsaturated Fat 0.2 g,
Cholesterol 2 mg, Sodium 100 mg, Fiber *trace*

Pumpkin Mousse Pie

Nadine L. Martinitz
Salina, KS

Makes 8 servings

Prep. Time: 20 minutes
Cooking Time: 1 minute
Chilling Time: 1–2 hours

Pyramid Servings	
Vegetables	○○○○○➤
Fruits	◗○○○○➤
Carbohydrates	●○○○○○○○
Protein & Dairy	○○○○○○○
Fats	●○○○○
Sweets	◗

15-oz. can pumpkin
¼ cup sugar
1¼ tsp. pumpkin pie spice
½ tsp. vanilla extract
¼ cup water
1 envelope unflavored gelatin
2½ cups fat-free frozen
whipped topping, thawed, *divided*
6-oz. reduced-fat graham cracker crust
pumpkin pie spice for garnish, *optional*

1. Combine pumpkin, sugar, 1¼ tsp. pumpkin pie spice, and vanilla in large bowl. Beat with whisk until blended. Set aside.
2. Place water in small saucepan. Sprinkle gelatin over top. Let stand until gelatin softens, about 1 minute.
3. Place saucepan over low heat and cook, stirring continually, until gelatin completely dissolves, about 1 minute.
4. Gradually pour dissolved gelatin mixture into pumpkin mixture, beating with whisk until blended.
5. Gently fold 2 cups thawed whipped topping into pumpkin mixture.
6. Spread filling in graham cracker crust. Refrigerate until firm.
7. Fill pastry bag with remaining whipped topping. Decoratively pipe over filling. Or simply drop dollops of remaining topping over pie.
8. Garnish with a few sprinkles of pumpkin pie spice.

Per Serving

Calories 188, Kilojoules 787, Protein 4 g, Carbohydrates 30 g, Total Fat 5 g, Saturated Fat 1 g, Monounsaturated Fat 2.5 g, Polyunsaturated Fat 1.5 g, Cholesterol 0 mg, Sodium 96 mg, Fiber 1 g

Sweet-Potato Banana Custard

Monica Hochstedler Carlson
Harrisonburg, VA

Makes 6 servings

Prep. Time: 20 minutes
Baking Time: 40–45 minutes

Pyramid Servings	
Vegetables	○○○○○➤
Fruits	◗○○○○➤
Carbohydrates	◗○○○○○○○
Protein & Dairy	◗○○○○○○
Fats	○○○○○

1 cup peeled sweet potato,
cooked and mashed
½ cup (about 2) small
bananas, mashed
1 cup evaporated skim milk
2 Tbsp. brown sugar, packed
⅓ cup egg substitute, beaten
¼ tsp. salt, *optional,* **not included in**
analyses
¼ cup raisins
1 Tbsp. sugar
1 tsp. ground cinnamon

1. In medium bowl, stir together mashed sweet potato and banana.
2. Add milk, blending well.
3. Add brown sugar and egg substitute, and salt if you wish, mixing thoroughly.
4. Spray 1-quart baking dish with non-stick cooking spray. Transfer sweet potato mixture to baking dish.
5. In a small bowl, combine raisins, sugar, and cinnamon. Sprinkle over top of sweet-potato mixture.
6. Bake in preheated 325° oven 40–45 minutes, or until knife inserted near center comes out clean.

Per Serving

Calories 113, Kilojoules 473, Protein 5 g,	
Carbohydrates 23 g, Total Fat *trace*, Saturated Fat *trace*,	
Monounsaturated Fat *trace*, Polyunsaturated Fat *trace*,	
Cholesterol 0 mg, Sodium 185 mg, Fiber 1 g	

Tip: This recipe is a wonderful, light fall or winter dessert when sweet potatoes are available. It's an alternative to a pumpkin or sweet potato pie.

Banana Mousse
Lois Hess
Lancaster, PA

Makes 4 servings

Prep. Time: 15 minutes
Chilling Time: 2 hours

Pyramid Servings

Vegetables
○○○○○➤
Fruits
●○○○○➤
Carbohydrates
○○○○○○○○
Protein & Dairy
◑○○○○○○
Fats
○○○○○

3 Tbsp. skim milk
1 medium banana, cut in quarters
4 tsp. sugar
1 tsp. vanilla extract
1 cup plain low-fat yogurt
1 banana cut into 8 slices

1. Place milk, medium banana cut in quarters, sugar, and vanilla into blender. Process for 15 seconds at high speed until smooth.
2. Pour mixture into small bowl. Fold in yogurt.
3. Chill two hours.
4. Spoon into four dessert dishes.
5. Garnish each dish of mousse with two banana slices just before serving.

Per Serving

Calories 108, Kilojoules 452, Protein 4 g,	
Carbohydrates 21 g, Total Fat 1 g, Saturated Fat 0.25 g,	
Monounsaturated Fat 0.5 g, Polyunsaturated Fat 0.25 g,	
Cholesterol 3 mg, Sodium 48 mg, Fiber 1.5 g	

Orange Panna Cotta
Marilyn Mowry
Irving, TX

Makes 4 servings

Prep. Time: 10 minutes
Cooking Time: 10 minutes
Chilling Time: 8 hours, or overnight

Pyramid Servings

Vegetables
○○○○○➤
Fruits
○○○○○➤
Carbohydrates
○○○○○○○○
Protein & Dairy
●○○○○○○
Fats
○○○○○
Sweets
●

2 cups evaporated skim milk
1 envelope unflavored gelatin
¼ cup sugar
1 tsp. vanilla extract
1 tsp. orange extract
1 tsp. grated orange peel
pinch of salt
½ cup fat-free vanilla yogurt, sweetened with low-calorie sweetener
ground cinnamon

1. Combine milk and gelatin in nonstick pan. Let stand until gelatin softens, about 5 minutes.
2. Cook over low heat, stirring constantly, until gelatin dissolves completely, about 5 minutes.
3. Whisk in sugar, both extracts, orange peel, and salt. Bring to a simmer, stirring frequently.
4. Divide evenly among 4 small ramekins or custard cups.
5. Cool slightly. Then cover and refrigerate overnight.
6. To serve, top each with 2 Tbsp. fat-free vanilla yogurt and a sprinkle of cinnamon.

Per Serving

Calories 185, Kilojoules 774, Protein 12 g,	
Carbohydrates 31 g, Total Fat 1 g, Saturated Fat 0.2 g,	
Monounsaturated Fat 0.7 g, Polyunsaturated Fat 0.1 g,	
Cholesterol 7 mg, Sodium 168 mg, Fiber *trace*	

Chocolate Goodness

Patricia Howard
Green Valley, AZ

Makes 4 servings

Prep. Time: 10 minutes
Chilling Time: 1 hour

1¾ cups cold skim milk
1 pkg. (2.1-oz.) sugar-free
  chocolate pudding
¼ cup sour cream
½ tsp. almond extract
2 Tbsp. chopped nuts

Pyramid Servings	
Vegetables	○○○○○➤
Fruits	○○○○○➤
Carbohydrates	○○○○○○○○
Protein & Dairy	◑○○○○○○○
Fats	◑○○○○

1. Combine milk, dry pudding, sour cream, and extract in a chilled bowl.
2. Using a wire whisk, stir until thickened.
3. Divide into 4 small serving bowls.
4. Cover and refrigerate for an hour.
5. Top with nuts just before serving.

Per Serving

Calories 70, Kilojoules 293, Protein 2 g,
Carbohydrates 7 g, Total Fat 4 g, Saturated Fat 1.6 g,
Monounsaturated Fat 1.5 g, Polyunsaturated Fat 0.9 g,
Cholesterol 5 mg, Sodium 200 mg, Fiber 0.5 g

Grape Juice Tapioca

Margaret Wenger Johnson
Keezletown, VA

Makes 6 servings

Prep. Time: 3 minutes
Cooking Time: 7–20 minutes
Chilling Time: 4 hours

4 cups purple grape juice, no
  sugar added
¼ cup sugar, *optional*, not
  included in analyses
⅔ cup dry regular, *or* minute,
  tapioca
2 Tbsp. lemon juice

Pyramid Servings	
Vegetables	○○○○○➤
Fruits	●○○○○➤
Carbohydrates	●○○○○○○○
Protein & Dairy	○○○○○○○○
Fats	○○○○○

1. Pour grape juice into 2-quart saucepan. Stir in sugar if you wish. Cover and heat until simmering.
2. Stir in tapioca and cook until clear. (If using regular tapioca, stir frequently to prevent sticking on bottom of pan).
3. Stir in lemon juice. Remove from heat.
4. Cool until room temperature.
5. Refrigerate until well chilled.

Per Serving

Calories 146, Kilojoules 611, Protein *trace*,
Carbohydrates 35 g, Total Fat *trace*, Saturated Fat *trace*,
Monounsaturated Fat *trace*, Polyunsaturated Fat *trace*,
Cholesterol 0 mg, Sodium 3.5 mg, Fiber *trace*

Rice Pudding

Betty Moore
Plano, IL

Makes 6 servings

Prep. Time: 15 minutes
Baking Time: 30–40 minutes
Standing Time: 15–20 minutes

1 egg
3 egg whites
12-oz. can fat-free evaporated
    milk
⅓ cup brown sugar
1 tsp. vanilla
1 cup cooked brown rice
½ cup raisins
⅛ tsp. nutmeg, *optional*

Pyramid Servings	
Vegetables	○○○○○➤
Fruits	◑○○○○➤
Carbohydrates	◑○○○○○○○
Protein & Dairy	●○○○○○○
Fats	○○○○○

1. Spray a 1½-quart baking dish with non-stick spray.

2. In medium bowl, combine egg, egg whites, milk, sugar, and vanilla. Mix well.

3. Stir in rice and raisins, and nutmeg if you wish.

4. Pour into prepared dish.

5. Cover and bake at 350° for 30–40 minutes. Remove from oven.

6. Stir. Cover. Let stand until liquid is absorbed.

7. Serve immediately, or warm gently before serving.

Per Serving

Calories 172, Kilojoules 720, Protein 6 g,
Carbohydrates 30 g, Total Fat 1 g, Saturated Fat 0.3 g,
Monounsaturated Fat 0.5 g, Polyunsaturated Fat 0.2 g,
Cholesterol 35 mg, Sodium 62 mg, Fiber 1 g

Frozen Dream Pops

Janelle Reitz
Lancaster, PA

Makes 8 servings; 1 pop/serving

Prep. Time: 10 minutes
Freezing Time: 6 hours

6-oz. can unsweetened orange
    juice concentrate, thawed
    slightly
2 cups low-fat plain yogurt
1 tsp. vanilla

Pyramid Servings	
Vegetables	○○○○○➤
Fruits	◑○○○○➤
Carbohydrates	○○○○○○○○
Protein & Dairy	◑○○○○○○
Fats	○○○○○

1. Mix fruit juice concentrate and yogurt together in a bowl.

2. Pour into 8 popsicle molds. (You can also use 3-oz. paper cups. Cover each with foil. Insert plastic spoons or wooden sticks through the foil.)

3. Freeze until solid.

Per Serving

Calories 74, Kilojoules 310, Protein 4 g,
Carbohydrates 12 g, Total Fat 1 g, Saturated Fat 0.6 g,
Monounsaturated Fat 0.2 g, Polyunsaturated Fat 0.2 g,
Cholesterol 4 mg, Sodium 43 mg, Fiber *trace*

A Tip —

Always have ingredients for simple recipes on hand.

Strawberry-Apple Pops

Vonda Ebersole
Mt. Pleasant Mills, PA

Makes 10 servings; 1 pop/serving

Prep. Time: 10 minutes
Chilling Time: 4 or more hours

Pyramid Servings

Vegetables	○○○○○➤
Fruits	◐○○○○➤
Carbohydrates	○○○○○○○○
Protein & Dairy	○○○○○○○
Fats	○○○○○

2 cups whole unsweetened
   strawberries
1 cup unsweetened
   applesauce
1 Tbsp. corn syrup

1. Crush strawberries in blender.
2. Add applesauce and corn syrup.
3. Blend until smooth.
4. Pour mixture evenly into 10 popsicle molds, or 10 3-oz. paper cups.
5. Place in freezer. If using paper cups, 1 hour after placing in freezer, insert wooden sticks into center of each popsicle. Place back in freezer until frozen.

Per Serving

Calories 32, Kilojoules 134, Protein *trace*,
Carbohydrates 8 g, Total Fat *trace*, Saturated Fat *trace*,
Monounsaturated Fat *trace*, Polyunsaturated Fat *trace*,
Cholesterol 0 mg, Sodium 2 mg, Fiber 1.5 g

Tip: You can use fresh or frozen strawberries.

Banana Orange Pops

Kathy Keener Shantz
Lancaster, PA

Makes 12 servings; 1 pop/serving

Prep. Time: 10 minutes
Freezing Time: 3–4 hours

Pyramid Servings

Vegetables	○○○○○➤
Fruits	◐○○○○➤
Carbohydrates	○○○○○○○○
Protein & Dairy	◐○○○○○○
Fats	○○○○○

2 ripe bananas
6 ozs. (¾ cup) orange juice
   concentrate, slightly
   thawed
12 ozs. silken soft tofu

1. Combine all ingredients in food processor or blender. Blend until smooth.
2. Pour into 12 popsicle molds, or 12 3-oz. paper cups.
3. Place in freezer. If using paper cups, remove after 1 hour and insert a wooden stick in center of each cup. Return to freezer.
4. Freeze until solid.

Per Serving

Calories 55, Kilojoules 230, Protein 2 g,
Carbohydrates 10 g, Total Fat *trace*, Saturated Fat *trace*,
Monounsaturated Fat *trace*, Polyunsaturated Fat *trace*,
Cholesterol 0 mg, Sodium 2 mg, Fiber 0.5 g

Tip: Peel ripe bananas and freeze for later use.

Beverages

Blueberry-Pomegranate Smoothie

Dena Tompkins
Huntersville, NC

Makes 2 servings

Prep. Time: 10 minutes

1 cup skim milk
1 cup fresh *or* frozen
   blueberries
seeds from 1 small-medium
   pomegranate
1 Tbsp. lemon juice
1 Tbsp. honey
6–8 ice cubes (if using frozen berries omit
   ice cubes)

1. Combine all ingredients except ice cubes in blender. Blend well.

2. Gradually add ice cubes (unless using frozen berries). Continue blending until smooth enough to draw up with straw.

Pyramid Servings

Vegetables
○○○○○➤

Fruits
●●○○○➤

Carbohydrates
○○○○○○○○

Protein & Dairy
◑○○○○○○○

Fats
○○○○○

Per Serving

Calories 169, Kilojoules 707, Protein 5 g,
Carbohydrates 38 g, Total Fat 0.4 g, Saturated Fat 0.2 g,
Monounsaturated Fat 0.1 g, Polyunsaturated Fat 0.1 g,
Cholesterol 2.4 mg, Sodium 58 mg, Fiber 2 g

Berry-Citrus Smoothie

SuAnne Burkholder
Millersburg, OH

Makes 2 servings

Prep. Time: 10 minutes

2 navel oranges, peeled and
pith removed, cut into
chunks
1 cup frozen raspberries
1 cup frozen blueberries

Puree ingredients in blender
until smooth. Serve immediately.

Pyramid Servings
Vegetables ○○○○○➤
Fruits ●●○○○➤
Carbohydrates ○○○○○○○○
Protein & Dairy ○○○○○○○
Fats ○○○○○

Per Serving

Calories 136, Kilojoules 569, Protein 2 g,
Carbohydrates 31 g, Total Fat 0.6 g, Saturated Fat 0.1 g,
Monounsaturated Fat 0.2 g, Polyunsaturated Fat 0.3 g,
Cholesterol 0 mg, Sodium *trace*, Fiber 8 g

Four Fruit Yogurt Smoothie

Janet Oberholtzer
Ephrata, PA

Makes 4 servings

Prep. Time: 10 minutes

1 cup frozen unsweetened
strawberries
1 cup frozen unsweetened
peaches
¾ cup frozen unsweetened
blueberries
1 large ripe banana
1 cup fat-free peach, *or* strawberry, yogurt,
sweetened with low-calorie sweetener
1 cup skim milk

1. Combine all ingredients in blender or
food processor.
2. Process until smooth, stopping to scrape
sides and push ingredients down into blender
as needed.
3. Pour into serving glasses.

Pyramid Servings
Vegetables ○○○○○➤
Fruits ●○○○○➤
Carbohydrates ○○○○○○○○
Protein & Dairy ◑○○○○○○
Fats ○○○○○

Per Serving

Calories 119, Kilojoules 498, Protein 5 g,
Carbohydrates 24 g, Total Fat 0.5 g, Saturated Fat 0.2 g,
Monounsaturated Fat 0.1 g, Polyunsaturated Fat 0.2 g,
Cholesterol 2 mg, Sodium 60 mg, Fiber 3 g

Wake-Me-Up Smoothie
Carol Collins
Holly Springs, NC

Makes 2 servings

Prep. Time: 5–10 minutes

¾ cups fresh pineapple
   chunks, *or* unsweetened
   canned pineapple chunks,
   drained
1½ cups halved strawberries
1 cup apple juice
6-oz. container fat-free
   vanilla yogurt, sweetened with low-
   calorie sweetener
1 small, *or* half a large, banana

1. Put all ingredients into blender. Blend
until smooth.
2. Pour into two large glasses.

Pyramid Servings

Vegetables	○○○○○➤
Fruits	●●○○○➤
Carbohydrates	○○○○○○○○
Protein & Dairy	◐○○○○○○
Fats	○○○○○

Per Serving

Calories 188, Kilojoules 787, Protein 5 g,
Carbohydrates 41 g, Total Fat 0.7 g, Saturated Fat 0.25 g,
Monounsaturated Fat 0.15 g, Polyunsaturated Fat 0.3 g,
Cholesterol 1.7 mg, Sodium 56 mg, Fiber 4 g

Peach Milk Shake
Alice Whitman
Lancaster, PA

Makes 4 servings

Prep. Time: 10–15 minutes

2 cups frozen peaches
2 cups skim milk
2 Tbsp. honey

1. Place peaches, milk, and
honey in blender.
2. Blend until thoroughly
mixed.
3. Pour into glasses to serve.

Pyramid Servings

Vegetables	○○○○○➤
Fruits	◐○○○○➤
Carbohydrates	○○○○○○○○
Protein & Dairy	◐○○○○○○
Fats	○○○○○

Per Serving

Calories 98, Kilojoules 410, Protein 5 g,
Carbohydrates 20 g, Total Fat *trace*, Saturated Fat *trace*,
Monounsaturated Fat *trace*, Polyunsaturated Fat *trace*,
Cholesterol 2.4 mg, Sodium 52 mg, Fiber 1 g

*Tip: During peach season, I purchase fresh
peaches, peel them, and freeze them on baking
sheets. Then I bag them in 2-cup packages so my
children can easily grab a bag and make a healthy
fruit drink instead of having a soda.*

Peaches and Cream Power Shake

Virginia Graybill
Hershey, PA

Makes 2 servings

Prep. Time: 20 minutes
Chilling Time: 1 hour

¼ cup boiling water
1 peach-flavored tea bag
1¼ cups diced fresh peaches
¾ cup low-fat plain yogurt
2 Tbsp. honey
1 Tbsp. soy protein powder, *optional*, not included in analyses
½ Tbsp. ground flaxseed
1 cup ice cubes

Pyramid Servings	
Vegetables	○○○○○▸
Fruits	●○○○○▸
Carbohydrates	○○○○○○○○
Protein & Dairy	◐○○○○○○
Fats	○○○○○
Sweets	◐

1. Pour boiling water over tea bag in teapot or small saucepan to make tea concentrate.

2. Let stand a few minutes to steep. Remove bag.

3. Chill liquid for an hour in the fridge.

4. Combine chilled tea concentrate with remaining ingredients in blender.

5. Whirl until smooth.

Per Serving

Calories 162, Kilojoules 678, Protein 6 g, Carbohydrates 33 g, Total Fat 1 g, Saturated Fat 0.1 g, Monounsaturated Fat 0.3 g, Polyunsaturated Fat 0.6 g, Cholesterol 2 mg, Sodium 74 mg, Fiber 2 g

Tip: Make several batches of tea concentrate ahead of time and keep on hand in the refrigerator.

V5 Juice/5-Vegetable Juice

Anita King
Bellefontaine, OH

Makes 8 servings

Prep. Time: 30 minutes
Cooking Time: 45 minutes
Cooling Time: 3 hours

5 lbs. ripe tomatoes, chopped
½ cup water
¼ cup chopped green bell sweet pepper
¼ cup chopped carrot
¼ cup chopped celery
¼ cup lemon juice
2 Tbsp. chopped onion
½ tsp. salt
1–1½ small Serrano pepper, *optional*, not included in analyses

Pyramid Servings	
Vegetables	●●○○○▸
Fruits	○○○○○▸
Carbohydrates	○○○○○○○○
Protein & Dairy	○○○○○○○
Fats	○○○○○

1. Combine all ingredients in large soup pot.

2. Bring to a boil. Reduce heat, cover, and simmer 30 minutes.

3. Allow to cool to room temperature.

4. Press through food mill or Victorio strainer.

5. Refrigerate until chilled.

6. Shake or stir before serving.

Per Serving

Calories 57, Kilojoules 238, Protein 3 g, Carbohydrates 11 g, Total Fat 0.5 g, Saturated Fat 0.1 g, Monounsaturated Fat 0.15 g, Polyunsaturated Fat 0.25 g, Cholesterol 0 mg, Sodium 165 mg, Fiber 4 g

Appetizers and Snacks

Hummus from Scratch

Melanie Thrower
McPherson, KS

*Makes 24 servings; about 2 Tbsp./
serving*

Prep. Time: 10 minutes
*Soaking Time: 8 hours, or
overnight*
Cooking Time: 1½ hours

Pyramid Servings

| Vegetables |
| ○○○○○▶ |
| Fruits |
| ○○○○○▶ |
| Carbohydrates |
| ○○○○○○○ |
| Protein & Dairy |
| ●○○○○○○○ |
| Fats |
| ◑○○○○ |

**16-oz. bag dried chickpeas
(garbanzo beans)**
⅔ cup lemon juice
3 cloves garlic
**⅔ cup peanut butter, *or* tahini (sesame
seed paste)**
½ cup chopped cilantro
2–3 Tbsp. ground cumin
1 Tbsp. olive oil

1. Place chickpeas in large stockpot. Cover
with water. Let stand overnight.
2. In the morning, discard soaking water.
3. Cover with fresh water.

4. Cover and cook 1–1½ hours over low-
medium heat, or until tender.
5. Drain off any liquid. Pour beans into food
processor.
6. Add all other ingredients, except olive oil,
to processor.
7. Blend until smooth. Add additional lemon
juice and cumin to suit your taste.
8. Place hummus in serving dish. Drizzle
with olive oil.
9. Serve as a dip with cut-up fresh vegetables, baked chips, or pita bread. Or use as a
spread on a sandwich with vegetables.

Per Serving

Calories 133, Kilojoules 556, Protein 6 g,
Carbohydrates 16 g, Total Fat 5 g, Saturated Fat 0.7 g,
Monounsaturated Fat 2.3 g, Polyunsaturated Fat 2 g,
Cholesterol 0 mg, Sodium 39 mg, Fiber 6 g

*Tip: You can freeze the hummus and use it up to
a week later.*

239

Quick Hummus

Kathy Keener Shantz
Lancaster, PA
Katrina Rose
Woodbridge, VA

Makes 16 servings; 2 Tbsp./serving

Prep. Time: 10 minutes

1 clove garlic, crushed
15-oz. can garbanzo beans,
    rinsed and drained
2 Tbsp. lemon juice
2 Tbsp. olive oil
⅛ tsp. cumin
⅛ tsp. salt
⅓ cup tahini (sesame seed paste)

Pyramid Servings

Vegetables	⃝⃝⃝⃝⃝▸
Fruits	⃝⃝⃝⃝⃝▸
Carbohydrates	⃝⃝⃝⃝⃝⃝⃝⃝
Protein & Dairy	◑⃝⃝⃝⃝⃝⃝
Fats	◑⃝⃝⃝⃝

1. Put all ingredients in food processor or
blender, adding 2 Tbsp. water or so, if needed.
Blend to make a smooth consistency.
2. Serve with whole wheat pita bread or use
as a dip for vegetables.

Per Serving

Calories 76, Kilojoules 318, Protein 2 g,
Carbohydrates 7 g, Total Fat 4.6 g, Saturated Fat 0.6 g,
Monounsaturated Fat 2.5 g, Polyunsaturated Fat 1.5 g,
Cholesterol 0 mg, Sodium 99 mg, Fiber 1.5 g

*Tip: If oil has separated in tahini, stir before
measuring.*

*Variation: Add 6-oz. container roasted red
peppers, rinsed and drained, to Step 1.*
—**Katrina Rose**, Woodbridge, VA

Black Bean Hummus

Melanie Mohler
Ephrata, PA

Makes about 2½ cups; ¼ cup/serving

Prep. Time: 10 minutes

15-oz. cans black beans,
    rinsed and drained
1 Tbsp. tahini (sesame seed
    paste)
2 Tbsp. olive oil
1 lime, juiced
1 tsp. ground cumin
pepper to taste
2 garlic cloves, sliced, *optional*

Pyramid Servings

Vegetables	⃝⃝⃝⃝⃝▸
Fruits	⃝⃝⃝⃝⃝▸
Carbohydrates	⃝⃝⃝⃝⃝⃝⃝⃝
Protein & Dairy	◑⃝⃝⃝⃝⃝⃝
Fats	⃝⃝⃝⃝⃝

1. In food processor or blender, combine all
ingredients and process until smooth.
2. Serve with tortilla chips, raw vegetable
sticks, or breads.

Per Serving

Calories 58, Kilojoules 243, Protein 2 g,
Carbohydrates 5 g, Total Fat 3.5 g, Saturated Fat 0.5 g,
Monounsaturated Fat 2.5 g, Polyunsaturated Fat 0.5 g,
Cholesterol 0 mg, Sodium 80 mg, Fiber 2 g

*Dietitian's tip: For convenience, canned black
beans instead of the dried variety are used in this
recipe. Although canned beans typically contain
more sodium than home-cooked beans, you can
rinse and drain them before use to help lessen the
amount of sodium by about 40 percent.*

A Tip —

Don't be afraid to try new or unusual
ingredients.

Black-Olive Sweet-Potato Hummus

Naomi Brubaker, Lewisburg, PA

Makes 6 servings

Prep. Time: 10 minutes
Baking Time: 1 hour
Cooling Time: 30 minutes

Pyramid Servings

Vegetables
○○○○○➤

Fruits
○○○○○➤

Carbohydrates
○○○○○○○○

Protein & Dairy
●○○○○○○

Fats
●○○○○

1 small (about 6-oz.) sweet
  potato
15-oz. can garbanzo beans,
  drained and rinsed
1 Tbsp. extra-virgin olive oil
½ cup chopped kalamata olives
2 medium cloves garlic, chopped
¼ tsp. crushed red pepper flakes
1–2 Tbsp. water, depending on consistency
  you prefer
⅓ cup fresh basil leaves
pepper to taste
¼ cup minced sun-dried tomatoes for
  garnish

1. Wrap sweet potato in foil and bake at
400° for 1 hour or until soft.
2. Remove potato from oven, unwrap, and
let cool. Scoop out insides of sweet potato and
place in food processor. Add garbanzo beans,
olive oil, olives, garlic, red pepper flakes, and
water. Pulse until soft and smooth. Add ⅓ cup
basil leaves and pulse 10 seconds.
3. Season with pepper and transfer to
serving bowl.
4. Garnish with sun-dried tomatoes.

Per Serving

Calories 153, Kilojoules 640, Protein 4 g,
Carbohydrates 23 g, Total Fat 5 g, Saturated Fat 0.6 g,
Monounsaturated Fat 2.4 g, Polyunsaturated Fat 2 g,
Cholesterol 0 mg, Sodium 300 mg, Fiber 5 g

*Tip: Serve with broccoli florets, baby carrots, and
pepper strips for dipping, or, spread on a whole
wheat or whole grain tortilla, top with sprouts,
and roll up for a healthy wrap.*

White Bean Skordalia (Dip)

Kathy Hertzler
Lancaster, PA

*Makes 16 servings; approximately
  ¼ cup/serving*

Prep. Time: 45 minutes
*Standing/Chilling Time:
  30 minutes – 8 hours*

Pyramid Servings

Vegetables
○○○○○➤

Fruits
○○○○○➤

Carbohydrates
○○○○○○○○

Protein & Dairy
◑○○○○○○

Fats
○○○○○

2 cups cubed day-old French
  bread, crusts removed
19-oz. can cannellini beans,
  rinsed and drained
3 cloves garlic, coarsely chopped
½ tsp. ground black pepper
1 Tbsp. fresh lemon juice
2 Tbsp. olive oil
½ cup water
crushed black pepper
lemon slices

1. Place bread cubes in food processor fitted
with metal blade. Process into coarse crumbs.
2. Add beans, garlic, pepper, and lemon
juice. Blend until almost smooth.
3. With machine running, pour in olive oil
and ½ cup water. Blend to incorporate.
4. Transfer to serving bowl. Let stand at
least 30 minutes to allow flavors to blend, or
cover and refrigerate overnight.
5. Garnish with crushed black pepper and
lemon slices. Serve with fresh raw vegetables.

Per Serving

Calories 54, Kilojoules 226, Protein 2 g,
Carbohydrates 8 g, Total Fat 2 g, Saturated Fat 0.2 g,
Monounsaturated Fat 1.3 g, Polyunsaturated Fat 0.5 g,
Cholesterol 0 mg, Sodium 118 mg, Fiber 2 g

Refried Bean Dip

Betty Moore
Plano, IL

Makes 16 servings; approximately ¼ cup/serving

Prep. Time: 10 minutes

16-oz. can fat-free refried beans
4-oz. can diced green chili peppers, undrained
2 cups (8 ozs.) shredded fat-free cheddar cheese
1½ tsp. chili powder
¼ tsp. ground cumin
hot sauce, *optional*

Pyramid Servings	
Vegetables	○○○○○▸
Fruits	○○○○○▸
Carbohydrates	○○○○○○○○
Protein & Dairy	◐○○○○○○○
Fats	○○○○○

1. Combine beans, peppers (with liquid), cheese, chili powder, cumin, and 2 drops hot pepper sauce. Mix well. Add more or less hot pepper sauce depending on your taste.
2. Cover and refrigerate until ready to serve.
3. Serve with fresh vegetables or fat-free tortilla chips.

Per Serving

Calories 50, Kilojoules 209, Protein 5 g,
Carbohydrates 5 g, Total Fat 1 g, Saturated Fat 0.5 g,
Monounsaturated Fat 0.3 g, Polyunsaturated Fat 0.2 g,
Cholesterol 3 mg, Sodium 200 mg, Fiber 2 g

Dietitian's tip: Beans are a good way to add fiber to your diet, especially soluble fiber. Generally, ½ cup of cooked beans provides 4 to 6 grams of fiber. The soluble fiber can help lower blood cholesterol. Beans are also high in protein, complex carbohydrates and iron.

Guacamole

Joyce Shackelford
Green Bay, WI

Makes 5 cups; ½ cup/serving

Prep. Time: 15 minutes

3 avocados, peeled
¼ cup onion minced
¾ tsp. garlic powder
½ tsp. chili powder
2 Tbsp. lemon juice
1 large ripe tomato, chopped

Pyramid Servings	
Vegetables	●○○○○▸
Fruits	○○○○○▸
Carbohydrates	○○○○○○○○
Protein & Dairy	○○○○○○○○
Fats	●○○○○

1. Cut avocados in half and remove seed. With spoon scoop out insides and put in medium bowl. Add onion, garlic and chili powders, and lemon juice.
2. With a masher, squash avocados until creamy.
3. Chop tomato and fold in, mixing everything together well.
4. Serve as a dip, sandwich filling, or garnish.

Per Serving

Calories 73, Kilojoules 305, Protein 1 g,
Carbohydrates 5 g, Total Fat 5 g, Saturated Fat 0.5 g,
Monounsaturated Fat 4 g, Polyunsaturated Fat 0.5 g,
Cholesterol 0 mg, Sodium 5 mg, Fiber 3 g

Salmon Dip for Vegetables

Dede Peterson
Rapid City, SD

Makes 6 servings
Prep. Time: 20 minutes

15-oz. can salmon, no salt added, flaked and drained
½ cup light sour cream
¼ cup diced celery
2 Tbsp. green onion, chopped
2 Tbsp. sweet bell pepper, diced
1 Tbsp. lemon juice
2 tsp. fresh dill, chopped

Pyramid Servings

| Vegetables |
| ○○○○○➤ |
| Fruits |
| ○○○○○➤ |
| Carbohydrates |
| ○○○○○○○○ |
| Protein & Dairy |
| ●○○○○○○ |
| Fats |
| ○○○○○ |

1. Mix all ingredients.
2. Cover and chill until ready to serve.
3. Serve with assorted raw vegetables such as bell peppers, zucchini, carrots, cucumbers, cauliflower, jicama, broccoli, radishes, etc.

Per Serving

Calories 124, Kilojoules 519, Protein 15 g,
Carbohydrates 5 g, Total Fat 5 g, Saturated Fat 2 g,
Monounsaturated Fat 2 g, Polyunsaturated Fat 1 g,
Cholesterol 45 mg, Sodium 70 mg, Fiber *trace*

Fat-Free Strawberry Yogurt Dip

Katrina Eberly
Stevens, PA

Makes 14 servings; approximately ¼ cup/serving
Prep. Time: 15 minutes

1½ cups fresh, *or* frozen, whole strawberries
8 ozs. fat-free strawberry yogurt, sweetened with low-calorie sweetener
1 cup fat-free whipped topping
assorted fruit, *or* angel food cake

Pyramid Servings

| Vegetables |
| ○○○○○➤ |
| Fruits |
| ○○○○○➤ |
| Carbohydrates |
| ○○○○○○○○ |
| Protein & Dairy |
| ○○○○○○○ |
| Fats |
| ○○○○○ |
| Sweets |
| ◐ |

1. In a bowl, mash berries.
2. Add yogurt and mix well.
3. Fold in whipped topping.
4. Serve with fruit or cake.

Per Serving

Calories 32, Kilojoules 134, Protein 1 g,
Carbohydrates 7 g, Total Fat 0.2 g, Saturated Fat 0.1 g,
Monounsaturated Fat 0.07 g, Polyunsaturated Fat 0.03 g,
Cholesterol 1 mg, Sodium 13 mg, Fiber 0.3 g

Tip: Any fruit works well with this recipe — peaches, raspberries, blueberries.

Fresh Salsa

Barbara Kuhns, Millersburg, OH

Makes 3 cups; ½ cup/serving

Prep. Time: 20 minutes

3 tomatoes
½ cup green sweet bell peppers
¼ cup onions, chopped
1 tsp. garlic powder
1 tsp. cumin
¼ tsp. ground red pepper
2 tsp. vinegar
1 tsp. olive oil
2 tsp. lemon juice

Pyramid Servings

Vegetables
●○○○○►

Fruits
○○○○○►

Carbohydrates
○○○○○○○○

Protein & Dairy
○○○○○○○

Fats
○○○○○

1. Chop vegetables.
2. Add remaining ingredients and mix well.
3. Serve.

Per Serving

Calories 26, Kilojoules 109, Protein 1 g,
Carbohydrates 4 g, Total Fat 1 g, Saturated Fat 0.1 g,
Monounsaturated Fat 0.6 g, Polyunsaturated Fat 0.3 g,
Cholesterol 0 mg, Sodium 5 mg, Fiber 1 g

Fresh Chunky Cherry Tomato Salsa

JB Miller, Indianapolis, IN

Makes 8 servings; ⅓ cup/serving

Prep. Time: 15 minutes
Marinating Time: 2 hours

½ cucumber, seeded and cut
  into small dice
2 cups cherry tomatoes,
  quartered
1 garlic clove, finely chopped

Pyramid Servings

Vegetables
●○○○○►

Fruits
○○○○○►

Carbohydrates
○○○○○○○○

Protein & Dairy
○○○○○○○

Fats
●○○○○

1 lemon
2 Tbsp. chili oil
¼ tsp. dried pepper flakes
2 Tbsp. fresh dill
pepper to taste

1. Prepare cucumber and tomatoes in mixing bowl. Add finely chopped garlic.
2. Grate lemon rind finely and add to tomatoes along with juice of lemon.
3. Add chili oil, pepper flakes, and dill. Stir and let marinate at room temperature for at least 2 hours.
4. Serve with whole wheat crackers or baked tortilla chips.

Per Serving

Calories 40, Kilojoules 167, Protein *trace*,
Carbohydrates 3 g, Total Fat 3 g, Saturated Fat 0.4 g,
Monounsaturated Fat 1.6 g, Polyunsaturated Fat 1 g,
Cholesterol 0 mg, Sodium 2 mg, Fiber 0.5 g

Black Bean Salsa

Barbara Tenney
Delta, PA

Makes 7½ cups; ⅓ cup/serving

Prep. Time: 15 minutes

2 15-oz. cans black beans,
  rinsed and drained
16-oz. can whole-kernel corn,
  rinsed and drained
4 Roma/plum tomatoes,
  seeded and chopped
1 large avocado, peeled and
  chopped
½ cup red onion, finely chopped
¼ cup chopped fresh cilantro, according to
  your taste preference
3 Tbsp. lime juice
1 Tbsp. olive oil

Pyramid Servings

Vegetables
○○○○○►

Fruits
○○○○○►

Carbohydrates
○○○○○○○○

Protein & Dairy
●○○○○○○○

Fats
○○○○○

1 Tbsp. red wine vinegar
½ tsp. freshly ground pepper

1. Combine all ingredients in large bowl.
2. Cover and chill. Serve with baked tortilla chips.

Per Serving

Calories 56, Kilojoules 234, Protein 2 g,
Carbohydrates 9 g, Total Fat 1.7 g, Saturated Fat 0.2 g,
Monounsaturated Fat 1 g, Polyunsaturated Fat 0.5 g,
Cholesterol 0 mg, Sodium 77 mg, Fiber 3 g

Fruit Salsa
Maryann Markano
Wilmington, DE

Makes 4 servings; ⅓ cup/serving

Prep. Time: 15 minutes
Marinating Time: 20 minutes

¾ cup chopped strawberries
⅓ cup chopped blueberries
2 Tbsp. chopped green bell
   sweet pepper
2 Tbsp. chopped carrot
1 Tbsp. chopped onion
2 tsp. cider vinegar
1 tsp. minced jalapeño pepper*

Pyramid Servings

Vegetables
○○○○○➤
Fruits
○○○○○➤
Carbohydrates
○○○○○○○○
Protein & Dairy
○○○○○○○
Fats
○○○○○

1. Combine all ingredients in small bowl.
2. Let stand 20 minutes to allow flavors to blend.

Per Serving

Calories 19, Kilojoules 79, Protein *trace*,
Carbohydrates 5 g, Total Fat *trace*, Saturated Fat *trace*,
Monounsaturated Fat *trace*, Polyunsaturated Fat *trace*,
Cholesterol 0 mg, Sodium 3 mg, Fiber 1 g

* Note: Wear gloves and wash hands after chopping jalapeño.

Fresh Tomato Crostini
Marilyn Mowry
Irving, TX

Makes 4 servings

Prep. Time: 20 minutes
Marinating Time: 30 minutes

4 plum tomatoes, chopped
¼ cup minced fresh basil
2 tsp. olive oil
1 clove garlic, minced
freshly ground pepper
¼ lb. crusty Italian peasant
   bread, cut into 4 slices and toasted

Pyramid Servings

Vegetables
●○○○○➤
Fruits
○○○○○➤
Carbohydrates
●○○○○○○○
Protein & Dairy
○○○○○○○
Fats
●○○○○

1. Combine tomatoes, basil, oil, garlic, and pepper in good-sized bowl.
2. Cover and let stand 30 minutes.
3. Divide tomato mixture with any juices among the toast. Serve at room temperature.

Per Serving

Calories 120, Kilojoules 502, Protein 4 g,
Carbohydrates 19 g, Total Fat 3.5 g, Saturated Fat 0.5 g,
Monounsaturated Fat 2 g, Polyunsaturated Fat 1 g,
Cholesterol 0 mg, Sodium 172 mg, Fiber 2 g

Mini Eggplant Pizzas

Maryann Markano
Wilmington, DE

Makes 4 servings

Prep. Time: 20 minutes
Cooking/Baking Time: 11–13 minutes

Pyramid Servings	
Vegetables ●○○○○➤	
Fruits ○○○○○➤	
Carbohydrates ○○○○○○○○	
Protein & Dairy ○●○○○○○○	
Fats ●○○○○	

1 eggplant, 3" diameter
½ tsp. dried oregano
¼ tsp. dried basil
½ tsp. garlic powder
1 Tbsp. olive oil
⅛ tsp. black pepper
1 large ripe tomato, cut into 4 slices
¼ cup low-sodium, low-fat pizza sauce
½ cup shredded reduced-fat mozzarella cheese

1. Preheat oven to 425°.
2. Peel eggplant and cut into 4 ½"-thick slices.
3. Combine spices and set aside.
4. Brush both sides of eggplant with oil and season with pepper.
5. Arrange on baking sheet and bake until browned, about 8 minutes. Turn once during baking to brown both sides.
6. Place a tomato slice on each eggplant slice and sprinkle with spice mixture. Drizzle each slice with 1 Tbsp. pizza sauce.
7. Top with cheese and bake until cheese melts, about 3–5 minutes. Serve hot.

Per Serving

Calories 128, Kilojoules 536, Protein 6 g,	
Carbohydrates 13 g, Total Fat 5 g, Saturated Fat 1.5 g,	
Monounsaturated Fat 3 g, Polyunsaturated Fat 0.5 g,	
Cholesterol 5 mg, Sodium 133 mg, Fiber 5 g	

Tip: Since the eggplant is usually large enough to make more than 4 slices, I double the other ingredients and make 8 "pizzas."

Quesadillas

Betty Moore
Plano, IL

Makes 16 servings; 2 pieces/serving

Prep. Time: 15 minutes
Baking Time: 13–18 minutes

Pyramid Servings	
Vegetables ○○○○○➤	
Fruits ○○○○○➤	
Carbohydrates ●○○○○○○○	
Protein & Dairy ○●○○○○○○	
Fats ○○○○○	

4-oz. can diced green chili peppers, drained
half a small onion, diced
¼ tsp. ground cumin
8 10" fat-free flour tortillas
2 cups (8 ozs.) shredded reduced-fat Monterey Jack cheese

1. In bowl combine peppers, onion, and cumin.
2. Sprinkle each tortilla with cheese using ¼ cup cheese on each.
3. Divide pepper mixture between tortillas, spreading it over cheese.
4. Roll up each tortilla and put in greased 9 × 13 baking pan. Cover pan with foil. Bake at 350° for 10–15 minutes, or until cheese melts.
5. Remove foil. Turn oven to broil.
6. Broil 4" from heat for 1½ minutes per side, or until lightly browned.
7. Cut each tortilla into 4 pieces.
8. Serve with your favorite salsa for dipping.

Per Serving

Calories 103, Kilojoules 431, Protein 6 g,	
Carbohydrates 16 g, Total Fat 3 g, Saturated Fat 1.5 g,	
Monounsaturated Fat 0.5 g, Polyunsaturated Fat 1 g,	
Cholesterol 10 mg, Sodium 200 mg, Fiber 6 g	

Dietitian's tip: The traditional unleavened bread wrappers of Mexico, tortillas are a versatile way to add grains to your day. Tortillas divide into two basic categories: corn and wheat. Wheat tortillas, made from white flour, are often labeled "flour tortillas." Whole-wheat tortillas are made from whole-grain flour.

Spicy Tofu Burritos

Esther Nafziger

Bluffton, OH

Makes 8 servings; 2 pieces/serving

Prep. Time: 10–15 minutes
Cooking/Baking Time: 10–15
  minutes

Pyramid Servings

| Vegetables |
| ●○○○○➤ |
| Fruits |
| ○○○○○➤ |
| Carbohydrates |
| ◐○○○○○○○ |
| Protein & Dairy |
| ◐○○○○○○ |
| Fats |
| ○○○○○ |

4 7–8" fat-free flour tortillas
1 Tbsp. olive oil
½ cup chopped onion
1½ tsp. ground cumin
½ tsp. turmeric
12 ozs. (about 2 cups) firm light tofu,
  crumbled
1 cup chopped red bell sweet pepper
1½ Tbsp. minced, seeded jalapeño chili
1 clove minced garlic
½ cup (2 ozs.) grated low-fat, reduced-
  sodium mozzarella cheese
1 cup thinly sliced Romaine lettuce
6 Tbsp. chopped fresh cilantro
1 lime cut into 4 wedges

1. Preheat oven to 350°. Wrap tortillas in foil. Place in oven until heated through, about 15 minutes.

2. Meanwhile, heat oil in large nonstick skillet over medium-high heat. Add onion and sauté until golden, about 5 minutes.

3. Add cumin and turmeric; stir 30 seconds.

4. Add tofu, red bell pepper, jalapeño, and garlic and sauté until heated through, about 3 minutes.

5. Add cheese and stir until melted, about 1 minute.

6. Spoon tofu mixture down center of each tortilla, dividing tofu equally. Top with lettuce and cilantro. Squeeze juice from lime wedges over top.

7. Wrap tortilla around filling. Insert 4 toothpicks into each burrito and cut into 4 pieces. Serve.

Per Serving

| Calories 127, Kilojoules 531, Protein 7 g, |
| Carbohydrates 19 g, Total Fat 4 g, Saturated Fat 0.8 g, |
| Monounsaturated Fat 1.7 g, Polyunsaturated Fat 1.5 g, |
| Cholesterol 3 mg, Sodium 197 mg, Fiber 8 g |

Avocado Egg Salad

Melanie Mohler

Ephrata, PA

Makes 4 servings

Prep. Time: 10 minutes

Pyramid Servings

| Vegetables |
| ○○○○○➤ |
| Fruits |
| ○○○○○➤ |
| Carbohydrates |
| ○○○○○○○○ |
| Protein & Dairy |
| ◐○○○○○○ |
| Fats |
| ●○○○○ |

4 eggs, hard-cooked and
  chopped (reserve 2 yolks
  for another use)
1 large avocado, chopped
pepper to taste
2 Tbsp. lemon juice
⅛ tsp. garlic powder, *optional*

1. In a serving bowl, combine eggs and avocado.

2. Sprinkle with pepper, lemon juice, and garlic powder. Stir gently.

3. Use as topping for crackers or as sandwich filling. Eat immediately or store in fridge.

Per Serving

| Calories 101, Kilojoules 423, Protein 5 g, |
| Carbohydrates 4 g, Total Fat 7 g, Saturated Fat 1.5 g, |
| Monounsaturated Fat 4.5 g, Polyunsaturated Fat 1 g, |
| Cholesterol 104 mg, Sodium 61 mg, Fiber 2.5 g |

Salmon-Stuffed Eggs

Ruth C. Hancock
Earlsboro, OK

Makes 12 servings

Prep. Time: 15 minutes

12 eggs, hard-boiled and shelled
6-oz. can salmon, no salt added, drained and flaked
½ cup light mayonnaise
1 Tbsp. finely chopped fresh dill weed
⅛ tsp. black pepper

Pyramid Servings	
Vegetables	○○○○○▶
Fruits	○○○○○▶
Carbohydrates	○○○○○○○○
Protein & Dairy	◑○○○○○○
Fats	○○○○○

1. Cut eggs in half lengthwise and remove yolks to medium bowl. Set aside egg whites. Reserve half of the yolks for another use.
2. Add salmon, mayonnaise, dill, and pepper to yolks. Mix until well combined.
3. Spoon or pipe salmon mixture back into egg whites.
4. Serve, or cover and chill until ready to serve.

Per Serving

Calories 70, Kilojoules 293, Protein 8 g,	
Carbohydrates 2 g, Total Fat 3 g, Saturated Fat 1 g,	
Monounsaturated Fat 1.2 g, Polyunsaturated Fat 0.8 g,	
Cholesterol 112 mg, Sodium 150 mg, Fiber *trace*	

Tips:
1. You can fill a plastic storage bag with the filling. Snip corner of bag, and then pipe filling into egg whites.
2. Garnish with paprika and sprig of fresh dill.

Mushrooms in Red Wine

Donna Lantgen
Arvada, CO

Makes 6 servings

Prep. Time: 5 minutes
Cooking Time: 15–30 minutes

1 lb. fresh mushrooms, cleaned
4 cloves garlic, chopped
¼ cup onion, chopped
1 Tbsp. olive oil
1 cup red wine

Pyramid Servings	
Vegetables	●○○○○▶
Fruits	○○○○○▶
Carbohydrates	○○○○○○○○
Protein & Dairy	○○○○○○○
Fats	◑○○○○
Sweets	◑

   Put all ingredients in skillet. Heat over low heat 15–30 minutes.

Per Serving

Calories 75, Kilojoules 314, Protein 2 g,	
Carbohydrates 5 g, Total Fat 2.5 g, Saturated Fat 0.3 g,	
Monounsaturated Fat 1.7 g, Polyunsaturated Fat 0.5 g,	
Cholesterol 0 mg, Sodium 6 mg, Fiber 1 g	

Dietitian's tip: When cleaning mushrooms, don't immerse them in water because they'll soak up the water like a sponge. Instead, wipe the mushrooms clean with a damp cloth or sturdy paper towel.

Cinnamon Tortilla Chips with Fruit Salsa

Esther Becker
Gordonville, PA

Makes 10 servings; 8 pieces/serving

Prep. Time: 15 minutes
Baking Time: 10 minutes
Chilling Time: 2–3 hours

Tortilla Crisps:
8 whole wheat tortillas
1 Tbsp. sugar
½ Tbsp. cinnamon
cooking spray

Fruit Salsa:
Fresh fruit – apples, oranges, kiwi, strawberries, grapes, etc. to equal approximately 3 cups diced
2 Tbsp. sugar-free jam of your choice
1 Tbsp. honey
2 Tbsp. orange juice

1. Preheat oven to 350°.
2. Cut tortillas into 10 wedges. Spread on cookie sheets. Spray with cooking spray.
3. Combine sugar and cinnamon. Sprinkle over tortilla wedges.
4. Bake 10–12 minutes, or until crisp.
5. Cut fruit into ¼" to ½" dice. Gently mix cut-up fruit together.
6. In a separate bowl, mix jam, honey, and orange juice.
7. Gently mix with fruit.
8. Cover and refrigerate for 2–3 hours.
9. Serve as a dip or topping for Tortilla Chips.

Pyramid Servings	
Vegetables	○○○○○▸
Fruits	●○○○○▸
Carbohydrates	●○○○○○○○
Protein & Dairy	○○○○○○○
Fats	○○○○○
Sweets	◑

Per Serving
Calories 129, Kilojoules 540, Protein 2 g,
Carbohydrates 23 g, Total Fat 3 g, Saturated Fat 1 g,
Monounsaturated Fat 1.5 g, Polyunsaturated Fat 0.5 g,
Cholesterol 0 mg, Sodium 90 mg, Fiber 3 g

Zippy Tortilla Chips

Marguerite Baumgartner
Versailles, MO

Makes 4 servings; 2 tortillas/serving or 12 pieces

Prep. Time: 20 minutes
Baking Time: 9–10 minutes

1 tsp. brown sugar
½ tsp. garlic powder
½ tsp. onion powder
½ tsp. ground cumin
½ tsp. paprika
¼ tsp. cayenne pepper
8 6" corn tortillas
olive oil cooking spray

1. Combine first 6 ingredients in small bowl.
2. Stack tortillas (4 at a time) and cut into 6 wedges.
3. Arrange in single layer on baking sheet coated with nonstick cooking spray.
4. Spray wedges lightly and sprinkle with seasoning mixture.
5. Bake at 375° for 9–10 minutes, or until lightly browned.
6. Cool for 5 minutes before serving.

Pyramid Servings	
Vegetables	○○○○○▸
Fruits	○○○○○▸
Carbohydrates	●◑○○○○○○
Protein & Dairy	○○○○○○○
Fats	○○○○○

Per Serving
Calories 118, Kilojoules 494, Protein 3 g,
Carbohydrates 23 g, Total Fat 1.5 g, Saturated Fat 0.2 g,
Monounsaturated Fat 0.3 g, Polyunsaturated Fat 1 g,
Cholesterol 0 mg, Sodium 24 mg, Fiber 3.5 g

Munchie Mix

Dena Tompkins
Huntersville, NC

Makes 6½ cups; ¼ cup/serving

Prep. Time: 10 minutes

1 cup roasted unsalted soy
   nuts
1½ cups shelled walnuts,
   whole or halved
1 cup roasted, unsalted
   sunflower kernels
1 cup multigrain pretzel
   sticks, broken in half
½ cup banana chips
½ cup dried blueberries
½ cup dried cherries

Pyramid Servings	
Vegetables	○○○○○▸
Fruits	●○○○○▸
Carbohydrates	●○○○○○○○
Protein & Dairy	○○○○○○○
Fats	●○○○○

Mix all ingredients in large mixing bowl
and serve.

Per Serving

Calories 136, Kilojoules 569, Protein 4 g,
Carbohydrates 12 g, Total Fat 8 g, Saturated Fat 1.5 g,
Monounsaturated Fat 1.5 g, Polyunsaturated Fat 5 g,
Cholesterol 0 mg, Sodium 48 mg, Fiber 3 g

Tips:

*1. You can substitute pumpernickel sticks for
the multigrain sticks to change the flavor.*

*2. You can make this ahead of time and then
divide it into plastic individual snack-bag servings.
These will be ready to grab and go. Prepared
servings discourage overeating.*

Dietitian's tip: *Use banana chips that have not
been fried. This will cut the calories in this snack
by one-third and you save 1 fat Pyramid Serving.*

Pizza-Flavored Popcorn

Cindy Stauffer
Stevens, PA

Makes about 12 cups; 2 cups/serving

Prep. Time: 15 minutes

2 Tbsp. grated reduced-fat
   Parmesan cheese
1 tsp. garlic powder
1 tsp. Italian herb seasoning
1 tsp. paprika
dash pepper
3 quarts air-popped popcorn
3 Tbsp. canola oil

Pyramid Servings	
Vegetables	○○○○○▸
Fruits	○○○○○▸
Carbohydrates	●○○○○○○○
Protein & Dairy	○○○○○○○
Fats	●○○○○

1. Blend first 5 ingredients well in food
processor.

2. In a large bowl, toss popcorn with oil.

3. Sprinkle with seasoning and toss to mix.

Per Serving

Calories 109, Kilojoules 456, Protein 2 g,
Carbohydrates 13 g, Total Fat 5 g, Saturated Fat 0.5 g,
Monounsaturated Fat 3 g, Polyunsaturated Fat 1.5 g,
Cholesterol 1 mg, Sodium 30 mg, Fiber 2.5 g

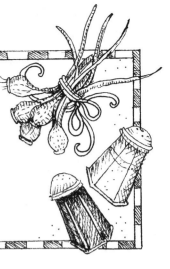

Sauces, Seasonings, and Dressings

Pear Honey
Alta Metzler
Willow Street, PA

Makes 7½–8 cups; 3 Tbsp./serving

Prep. Time: 1 hour
Cooking Time: 30–45 minutes

17–18 medium-large fresh
  pears
20-oz. can unsweetened
  crushed pineapple in
  natural juice
1½ cups sugar

1. Peel and core pears. Grind
in food chopper. Place in large kettle. Add
pineapple and mix sugar in gradually.

2. Cook until thickened, about 30–45
minutes, stirring frequently to prevent
burning.

3. Pour into jars and seal or freeze.

Pyramid Servings	
Vegetables	ooooo➤
Fruits	ooooo➤
Carbohydrates	oooooooo
Protein & Dairy	ooooooo
Fats	ooooo
Sweets	◑

Per Serving
Calories 70, Kilojoules 293, Protein *trace*,
Carbohydrates 17 g, Total Fat *trace*, Saturated Fat *trace*,
Monounsaturated Fat *trace*, Polyunsaturated Fat *trace*,
Cholesterol 0 mg, Sodium 1 mg, Fiber 2 g

Variation: Add 3 Tbsp. lemon juice after honey
is cooked and thickened.
    —**Shirley Sears**, Tiskilwa, IL

Blueberry Apple Butter

Willard Roth
Elkhart, IN

Makes 1⅓ cups; 2 teaspoons/serving

Prep. Time: 15 minutes
Cooking Time: 15 minutes

Pyramid Servings	
Vegetables ○○○○○►	
Fruits ○○○○○►	
Carbohydrates ○○○○○○○○	
Protein & Dairy ○○○○○○○	
Fats ○○○○○	

1 lb. cooking apples, cored
  and quartered
½ cup fresh, *or* frozen,
  blueberries
2 Tbsp. apple juice
½ tsp. ground cinnamon
1 Tbsp. butter, softened
1 Tbsp. fresh lemon juice

1. Toss apples, blueberries, and apple juice
in large saucepan.
2. Cook over high heat until fruit is soft,
12–15 minutes.
3. Cool.
4. Blend in processor or blender until
smooth.
5. Add butter and lemon juice halfway
through.
6. Use as spread for breads and muffins.
Store in refrigerator up to two weeks.

Per Serving

Calories 12, Kilojoules 50, Protein 0 g,
Carbohydrates 3 g, Total Fat *trace*, Saturated Fat *trace*,
Monounsaturated Fat *trace*, Polyunsaturated Fat *trace*,
Cholesterol 1 mg, Sodium 2 mg, Fiber *trace*

Blueberry Sauce

Esther J. Yoder
Hartville, OH

Makes 6–7 servings

Prep. Time: 5–6 minutes
Cooking Time: 6–7 minutes

Pyramid Servings	
Vegetables ○○○○○►	
Fruits ●○○○○►	
Carbohydrates ○○○○○○○○	
Protein & Dairy ○○○○○○○	
Fats ○○○○○	

3 Tbsp. sugar
2 Tbsp. cornstarch
¼ cup water
1½ cups fresh, *or* frozen,
  blueberries, *divided*
1 Tbsp. lemon juice

1. In saucepan combine sugar and
cornstarch. Stir in water to make smooth
paste.
2. Add blueberries. Bring to a boil. Stir
while simmering for about 5 minutes.
3. Chill before serving over low-fat ice
cream or cake (not included in analyses).

Per Serving

Calories 51, Kilojoules 213, Protein *trace*,
Carbohydrates 13 g, Total Fat *trace*, Saturated Fat *trace*,
Monounsaturated Fat *trace*, Polyunsaturated Fat *trace*,
Cholesterol *trace*, Sodium *trace*, Fiber 1 g

Herb and Mustard Dressing
Susan Tjon
Austin, TX

Makes ¾ cup; 2 tablespoons/serving

Prep. Time: 10 minutes

¼ cup water
3 Tbsp. balsamic, *or* cider, vinegar
1½ Tbsp. Dijon, *or* deli-style, mustard
1½ Tbsp. extra-virgin olive oil
1 tsp. dried basil leaves
1 tsp. dried thyme leaves
1 tsp. dried rosemary
1 small clove garlic, minced

Pyramid Servings

Vegetables
○○○○○➤

Fruits
○○○○○➤

Carbohydrates
○○○○○○○○

Protein & Dairy
○○○○○○○

Fats
●○○○○

1. In small jar with tight-fitting lid, combine all ingredients. Shake well.
2. Refrigerate until ready to use.
3. Shake before serving.

Per Serving

Calories 41, Kilojoules 172, Protein *trace*,
Carbohydrates 2 g, Total Fat 3 g, Saturated Fat 0.4 g,
Monounsaturated Fat 2.4 g, Polyunsaturated Fat 0.2 g,
Cholesterol 0 mg, Sodium 92 mg, Fiber *trace*

Herb Salad Dressing
Renita Denlinger
Denver, PA

Makes ⅔ cup; 2 tablespoons/serving

Prep. Time: 10 minutes or less

2 Tbsp. powdered fruit pectin (Sure-Jell™)
½ tsp. (or more to taste) dried herb (choose one: basil, thyme, tarragon, savory, or dill weed)
4 tsp. sugar
¼ tsp. ground mustard
¼ tsp. pepper
½ cup water
4 tsp. vinegar
2 garlic cloves, minced

Pyramid Servings

Vegetables
○○○○○➤

Fruits
○○○○○➤

Carbohydrates
○○○○○○○○

Protein & Dairy
○○○○○○○

Fats
○○○○○

1. In a small bowl or jar with tight-fitting lid, combine first 5 ingredients.
2. Stir in water, vinegar, and garlic. Chill.
3. Serve over greens and vegetables of your choice.

Per Serving

Calories 4, Kilojoules 16, Protein *trace*,
Carbohydrates *trace*, Total Fat 0 g, Saturated Fat 0 g,
Monounsaturated Fat 0 g, Polyunsaturated Fat 0 g,
Cholesterol 0 mg, Sodium 140 mg, Fiber *trace*

Tomato/Chili Poaching Sauce

Marlene Fonken
Upland, CA

Makes about 6 cups sauce; about 1 cup/serving

***Prep. Time:** 5 minutes*
***Cooking Time:** 15 minutes*

Pyramid Servings	
Vegetables	●●○○○▸
Fruits	○○○○○▸
Carbohydrates	○○○○○○○○
Protein & Dairy	○○○○○○○
Fats	◐○○○○

1 Tbsp., plus 1 tsp., olive oil
1 cup onion, thinly sliced
3 cups canned chopped
    tomatoes, no salt added,
    undrained
4-oz. can diced green chilies, undrained
1 cup low-fat, low-sodium chicken broth
⅛ tsp. pepper
1 tsp. Mexican seasoning, no salt added

1. In saucepan, sauté onion in oil until tender.
2. Add tomatoes and green chilies to pan. Cook 5 minutes.
3. Add remaining ingredients. Cook at least 5 minutes more, or until hot.

Per Serving

Calories 70, Kilojoules 293, Protein 1 g,
Carbohydrates 10 g, Total Fat 3 g, Saturated Fat 0.5 g,
Monounsaturated Fat 2 g, Polyunsaturated Fat 0.5 g,
Cholesterol 1 mg, Sodium 150 mg, Fiber 3 g

Tip: Poach chicken or seafood in this sauce. Or make yourself a grand brunch or supper dish—Huevos en Rabo de Mestiza (see recipe on page 190)!

Marinade for Grilling

Samuel and Sadie Mae Stoltzfus
Bird-In-Hand, PA

Makes ¾ cup

***Prep. Time:** 2–3 minutes*

Pyramid Servings	
Vegetables	○○○○○▸
Fruits	○○○○○▸
Carbohydrates	○○○○○○○○
Protein & Dairy	○○○○○○○
Fats	◐○○○○

¼ cup low-sodium soy sauce
⅓ cup water
2 Tbsp. olive oil
1 tsp. lemon juice
1 clove garlic, minced
2 Tbsp. brown sugar
½ tsp. black pepper
1 tsp. vinegar

1. Mix ingredients together in a small bowl.
2. Use as marinade for turkey fillets, turkey cutlets, boneless skinless chicken breasts, or beef steaks.

Per Serving

Calories 30, Kilojoules 126, Protein *trace,*
Carbohydrates 3 g, Total Fat 2 g, Saturated Fat 0.1 g,
Monounsaturated Fat 1.6 g, Polyunsaturated Fat 0.3 g,
Cholesterol 0 mg, Sodium 176 mg, Fiber *trace*

Dietitian's tip: Marinades are seasoned liquids used to add flavor and make food tender. Because most marinades contain an acidic ingredient (juice, vinegar, wine), it's important not to marinate foods too long. The acid can break down the food and make it mushy. Most vegetables and fish require shorter amounts of time to marinate—30 minutes to an hour—whereas large cuts of meat can be marinated up to 8 hours.

Salt Substitute Herb Mixtures

Ann Bender
New Hope, VA

Makes about ¼ cup of each mixture

Prep. Time: 5 minutes

#1:
1 Tbsp. onion powder
1 Tbsp. paprika
1 Tbsp. parsley
1 tsp. garlic powder
1 tsp. dried basil

#2:
2½ tsp. dried marjoram
2½ tsp. dried savory
2 tsp. dried thyme
2 tsp. rosemary
1½ tsp. dried sage

1. Mix each mixture together in separate small bowls.
2. Transfer each mixture to a separate herb shaker.
3. Remember, use an herb shaker instead of a salt shaker. These are both good on meats and vegetables.

Pyramid Servings

Vegetables	○○○○○➤
Fruits	○○○○○➤
Carbohydrates	○○○○○○○○
Protein & Dairy	○○○○○○○
Fats	○○○○○

Per Serving

Calories 0, Kilojoules 0, Protein 0g,
Carbohydrates 0g, Total Fat 0g, Saturated Fat 0g,
Monounsaturated Fat 0g, Polyunsaturated Fat 0g,
Cholesterol 0mg, Sodium 0mg, Fiber 0g

A Tip —

Substitute whole wheat flour for some of the white flour in bread, rolls, cookies and cakes.

Salt Substitute #3

Mary Ann Lefever
Lancaster, PA

Makes about ¼ cup

Prep. Time: 5 minutes

1 Tbsp. garlic powder
1 tsp. dried basil
1 tsp. black pepper
1 tsp. mace
1 tsp. dried marjoram
1 tsp. onion powder
1 tsp. sage
1 tsp. savory
1 tsp. dried thyme
1 tsp. dried parsley
½ tsp. cayenne pepper

1. Mix all seasonings together.
2. Transfer to an herb shaker.

Pyramid Servings

Vegetables	○○○○○➤
Fruits	○○○○○➤
Carbohydrates	○○○○○○○○
Protein & Dairy	○○○○○○○
Fats	○○○○○

Per Serving

Calories 0, Kilojoules 0, Protein 0g,
Carbohydrates 0g, Total Fat 0g, Saturated Fat 0g,
Monounsaturated Fat 0g, Polyunsaturated Fat 0g,
Cholesterol 0mg, Sodium *trace*, Fiber 0g

Three Hints

1 If you'd like to cook more at home—without being in a frenzy—go off by yourself with your cookbook some evening and make a week of menus. Then make a grocery list from that. Shop from your grocery list.

2 Thaw frozen food in a bowl in the fridge (not on the counter-top). If you forget to stick the food in the fridge, put it in a microwave-safe bowl and defrost it in the microwave just before you're ready to use it.

3 Let roasted meat, as well as pasta dishes with cheese, rest for 10–20 minutes before slicing or dishing. That will allow the juices to re-distribute themselves throughout the cooked food. You'll have juicier meat, and a better presentation of your pasta dish.

Equivalent Measurements

dash = little less than ⅛ tsp.

3 teaspoons = 1 Tablespoon

2 Tablespoons = 1 oz.

4 Tablespoons = ¼ cup

5 Tablespoons plus 1 tsp. = ⅓ cup

8 Tablespoons = ½ cup

12 Tablespoons = ¾ cup

16 Tablespoons = 1 cup

1 cup = 8 ozs. liquid

2 cups = 1 pint

4 cups = 1 quart

4 quarts = 1 gallon

1 stick butter = ¼ lb.

1 stick butter = ½ cup

1 stick butter = 8 Tbsp.

Beans, 1 lb. dried = 2–2½ cups (depending upon the size of the beans)

Bell peppers, 1 large = 1 cup chopped

Cheese, hard (for example, cheddar, Swiss, Monterey Jack, mozzarella), 1 lb. grated = 4 cups

Cheese, cottage, 1 lb. = 2 cups

Chocolate chips, 6-oz. pkg. = 1 scant cup

Crackers (butter, saltines, snack), 20 single crackers = 1 cup crumbs

Herbs, 1 Tbsp. fresh = 1 tsp. dried

Lemon, 1 medium-sized = 2–3 Tbsp. juice

Lemon, 1 medium-sized = 2–3 tsp. grated rind

Mustard, 1 Tbsp. prepared = 1 tsp. dry or ground mustard

Oatmeal, 1 lb. dry = about 5 cups dry

Onion, 1 medium-sized = ½ cup chopped

Pasta

Macaronis, penne, and other small or tubular shapes, 1 lb. dry = 4 cups uncooked

Noodles, 1 lb. dry = 6 cups uncooked

Spaghetti, linguine, fettucine, 1 lb. dry = 4 cups uncooked

Potatoes, white, 1 lb. = 3 medium-sized potatoes = 2 cups mashed

Potatoes, sweet, 1 lb. = 3 medium-sized potatoes = 2 cups mashed

Rice, 1 lb. dry = 2 cups uncooked

Sugar, confectioners, 1 lb. = 3½ cups sifted

Whipping cream, 1 cup unwhipped = 2 cups whipped

Whipped topping, 8-oz. container = 3 cups

Yeast, dry, 1 envelope (¼ oz.) = 1 Tbsp.

Kitchen Tools and Equipment You May Have Overlooked

1 Make sure you have a little electric vegetable chopper, the size that will handle 1 cup of ingredients at a time.

2 Don't try to cook without a good paring knife that's sharp (and holds its edge) and fits in your hand.

3 Almost as important—a good chef's knife (we always called it a "butcher" knife) with a wide, sharp blade that's about 8 inches long, good for making strong cuts through meats.

4 You really ought to have a good serrated knife with a long blade, perfect for slicing bread.

5 Invest in at least one broad, flexible, heat-resistant spatula. And also a narrow one.

6 You ought to have a minimum of 2 wooden spoons, each with a 10–12 inch-long handle. They're perfect for stirring without scratching.

7 Get a washable cutting board. You'll still need it, even though you have an electric vegetable chopper (#1 above).

8 A medium-sized whisk takes care of persistent lumps in batters, gravies, and sauces when there aren't supposed to be any.

9 Get yourself a salad spinner.

Index

About Mayo Clinic

Mayo Clinic—one of the world's oldest and largest multispecialty group practices—comprises more than 45,000 physicians, scientists, nurses, and other staff at its Rochester, Minnesota.; Jacksonville, Florida.; and Arizona locations; and its regional community-based health care practices. At Mayo Clinic, patient care, medical education, and medical research work together for the good of the patient. With this depth of medical knowledge, experience, and expertise, Mayo Clinic occupies an unparalleled position as an award-winning health information resource.

About the Author

Phyllis Pellman Good is a *New York Times* bestselling author whose books have sold nearly 10 million copies.

Good is the author of the first book in the *Fix-It and Enjoy-It* series, **Fix-It and Enjoy-It Cookbook: All-Purpose, Welcome-Home Recipes**, for stove-top and oven use. That flagship book, along with **Fix-It and Enjoy-It Diabetic Cookbook: Stove-Top and Oven Recipes–for Everyone** and **Fix-It and Enjoy-It 5-Ingredient Recipes**, are a "cousin" series to the phenomenally successful *Fix-It and Forget-It* cookbooks.

Good authored the national #1 bestselling cookbook **Fix-It and Forget-It Cookbook: Feasting with Your Slow Cooker** (with Dawn J. Ranck), which appeared on *The New York Times* bestseller list, as well as the bestseller lists of *USA Today*, *Publishers Weekly*, and *Book Sense*. And she is the author of **Fix-It and Forget-It Lightly: Healthy, Low-Fat Recipes for Your Slow Cooker**, which has also appeared on *The New York Times* bestseller list. In addition, Good authored **Fix-It and Forget-It 5-Ingredient Favorites:** **Comforting Slow-Cooker Recipes**; **Fix-It and Forget-It Recipes for Entertaining: Slow Cooker Favorites for All the Year Round** (with Ranck); and **Fix-It and Forget-It Diabetic Cookbook** (with the American Diabetes Association), also in the series.

Among Good's other cookbooks are **Fix-It and Forget-It Big Cookbook: 1400 Best Slow Cooker Recipes!**, **The Best of Amish Cooking**, and **The Central Market Cookbook**.

Phyllis Pellman Good is Senior Editor at Good Books. (Good Books has published hundreds of titles by more than 135 different authors.) She received her B.A. and M.A. in English from New York University. She and her husband, Merle, live in Lancaster, Pennsylvania. They are the parents of two young-adult daughters.

For a complete listing of books by Phyllis Pellman Good, as well as excerpts and reviews, visit www.Fix-ItandEnjoy-It.com, or www.GoodBooks.com.

National Bestsellers!

More than 8.9 million copies sold!

⇨ **For stove-top and oven:**

"Little fuss. Lots of flavor. We busy people love that!"
– *Phyllis*

Fix-It and Enjoy-It! Cookbook

Fix-It and Enjoy-It! Diabetic Cookbook

Fix-It and Enjoy-It! 5-Ingredient Recipes

Fix-It and Enjoy-It! Healthy Cookbook

⇨ **For slow cookers:**

    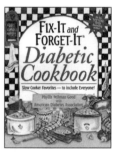

Fix-It and Forget-It 5-Ingredient Favorites

Fix-It and Forget-It Cookbook

Fix-It and Forget-It Lightly

Fix-It and Forget-It Recipes for Entertaining

Fix-It and Forget-It Diabetic Cookbook

Fix-It and Forget-It Big Cookbook

Fix-It and Don't Forget-It A Cook's Journal

Fix-It and Forget-It Box of Recipe Cards

New York Times bestselling author
Phyllis Pellman Good